THE ASH

THE MEDIEVAL AND RENAISSANCE WORLD

CYNTHIA O. HO, SHERYL D. SAWIN, W.M. SPELLMAN, EDITORS

Pegasus Press

The University of North Carolina at Asheville
One University Heights Asheville, North Carolina 28804

Pegasus Press
Asheville, North Carolina

Library of Congress Cataloguing-in-Publications Data

The Asheville reader : the medieval and Renaissance world / edited
by Cynthia O. Ho, Sheryl D. Sawin, W. M. Spellman.
p. cm.
ISBN 1-889818-14-3 (alk. paper)
1. Civilization, Medieval—Sources. 2. Renaissance—Sources.
I. Ho, Cynthia O. (Cynthia Olson), 1947- II. Sawin, Sheryl D. (Sheryl Drobny),
1964- III. Spellman, W.M.
CB351.A595 1999
909.07—dc21 98-50113
CIP

Petrus Plancius *[Cover] World Map from* Itenerario *by Jon Huygen Van Linschoten.*

This book is made to last.
It is printed on acid-free
paper to library specifications.
The typeface is Garamond Book.

Printed in the United States of America.

THE ASHEVILLE READER

THE MEDIEVAL AND RENAISSANCE WORLD

TABLE OF CONTENTS

Acknowledgements

We would like to thank the following people for their contributions to this book:

Peg Downes, for her selections from and introductions to Georgio Vasari's *The Lives of the Most Eminent Painters, Sculptors and Architects*; Benvenuto Cellini's *Autobiography*; Michelangelo's Letter, and the *Malleus Maleficarum*.

Susan McMichaels, for her introduction to *The Testament* of St. Clare of Assisi.

Gordon Wilson, for his introduction to and selection of materials found in the section entitled "The Rise of European Universities," as well as Abelard's *Sic et Non*, John Peckham's Letter to Pope Gregory III and St. Francis's "Canticle of Brother Sun."

R. F. Yeager, for his introduction to and translation of "The Dream of the Rood."

Adrienne Hollifield, for her talented and diligent management of the materials in the book, her careful copyediting, her sensitive and sensible questions, and her astute revision suggestions.

The Pegasus Press staff, for their patience and good cheer as we all worked to make this project successful.

The Humanities Program at The University of North Carolina, Asheville, for its support and encouragement throughout this project.

Cynthia O. Ho
Sheryl D. Sawin
W. M. Spellman

Illustrations

"Mother Church," reprinted from *Hildegard of Bingen*. Used with the permission of Paulist Press.

Title page of *The Wonderful Discovery of the Witchcrafts of Margaret and Phillipa Flower*. This item is reproduced by permission of The Huntington Library, San Marino, California.

Title page of "Hic Mulier: Or the Man-Woman." This item is reproduced by permission of The Huntington Library, San Marino, California.

Title page of "Haec Vir: Or the Womanish-Man." This item is reproduced by permission of The Huntington Library, San Marino, California.

Petrus Plancius reproduced by permission of The Huntington Library, San Marino, California

General Introduction

Welcome to Humanities 214. The Asheville Reader has been designed with the goal of presenting students with a wide variety of primary source documents composed by women and men during the medieval and early modern periods of history. The majority of the readings focus on the Western experience, but a significant number come from other important global traditions. Each of the readings addresses one or more of the main themes of investigation opened in Humanities 214, themes of continuing interest across the Humanities sequence and of significance to all of us at the start of the twenty-first century.

Each reading is preceded by a brief introduction, where we have attempted to provide the reader with essential background and with a set of questions organized around the Program's main themes. Our reflections on self, on others, on nature, and on god[s] have long been at the core of the human journey, irrespective of geographic, cultural, religious, and political differences. The readings included in this volume challenge each of us to negotiate these perennial issues and problems in a critical and creative manner. Our study of the medieval and early modern periods will provide historical context for our current efforts at understanding in a global community where interdependence is becoming the norm rather than the exception. The women and men of the medieval and early modern world offer thoughtful—and often provocative—views on matters of profound concern to every generation. Perhaps something of their world view, their vision of the human condition, is with us even today. We hope that you find the excursion worthwhile.

Note to the Reader

The selections in this book are reprinted with much of the original spelling, punctuation, and phrasing of the time periods in which they were written. The editors have emended the writings of King James, the speeches of Queen Elizabeth I, the writings on the suspected witchcraft of Margaret and Phillipa Flower, and the dialogues of "Hic Mulier" and "Haec Vir" to make them more in keeping with modern usage.

Deletions of material by the editors of this book are indicated by this symbol ❖❖❖ Materials deleted from the reprinted source are indicated by ellipses.

Early Christian Culture

ST. BENEDICT OF NURSIA

ca. 480–543 C.E.

Monastic institutions played a pivotal role in the culture of Europe's early Middle Ages. Monks were instrumental in the conversion of pagan peoples to Christianity, and monastic communities gradually developed as centers of teaching and learning. The earliest forms of monastic life emerged in the lands of the eastern Mediterranean and in Egypt, where devout believers abandoned their fellows for the solitary—and ascetic—life of the hermit. Many of these recluses sought to separate themselves from a Church which had become increasingly associated with the Roman state.

As an alternative to the hermitic model, St. Pachomius (ca. 290–346 C.E.) founded an ordered community of monks in Egypt. This "cenobitic" monasticism combined manual labor with prayer throughout the day, and it was this model which would become the norm in the West. Around 520 Benedict, who was born in Italy four years after the deposition of the last Western Roman emperor, and who had for three years lived as a hermit near the town of Subiaco, established a monastic community at the hilltop site of Monte Cassino, located between Rome and Naples. Benedict's *Rule* for monks was actually a compilation of many rules which emphasized moderation and communal stability, and this directive text shaped monastic life in the West for centuries. Pope Gregory the Great (589–604 C.E.), himself the author of an influential work on church governance called the *Book of Pastoral Care*, thought that Benedict's *Rule* was "remarkable for its discernment and clarity of language." Poverty, chastity, and unquestioning obedience to one's abbot were at the heart of the Benedictine pattern. Each day combined an unvarying routine of manual labor and corporate prayer, with additional time reserved for private meditation and study.

Benedictine monasticism in general, and the *Rule* in particular, directly address some of the key themes in Humanities 214: the proper relationship between self and society, between the individual and the larger community, between subordinate and superior. During Benedict's lifetime, Italy was occupied by Germanic invaders and then devastated by the armies of the Eastern Emperor Justinian. Soon after his death the Lombards overran much of the peninsula and attacked the monastery at Monte Cassino. Within this difficult context, marked by the collapse of Roman authority in the West, did it make sense for a man like Benedict to stress the priority of the group before the individual? Do personal material desires have any place in a godly community of medieval Christians? What sorts of personal characteristics does Benedict endorse? Does the *Rule* have an application in a modern society where individual rights, freedoms, property, and "choice" are at the core of our cultural assumptions?

from *The Rule*

PROLOGUE

Hearken, my son, to the precepts of the master and incline the ear of thy heart; freely accept and faithfully fulfil the instructions of a loving father, that by the labour of obedience thou mayest return to him from whom thou hast strayed by the sloth of disobedience. To thee are my words now addressed, whosoever thou mayest be that renouncing thine own will to fight for the true King, Christ, dost take up the strong and glorious weapons of obedience.

And first of all, whatever good work thou undertakest, ask him with most instant prayer to perfect it, so that he who has deigned to count us among his sons may never be provoked by our evil conduct. For we must always so serve him with the gifts which he has given us, that he may never as an angry father disinherit his children, nor yet as a dread lord be driven by our sins to cast into everlasting punishment the wicked servants who would not follow him to glory.

Up with us then at last, for the Scripture arouseth us, saying: "Now is the hour for us to rise from sleep." Let us open our eyes to the divine light, and let us hear with attentive ears the warning that the divine voice crieth daily to us: "Today if ye will hear his voice, harden not your hearts." And again: "He that hath ears to hear, let him hear what the Spirit saith to the churches." And what doth he say? "Come, ye children, hearken unto me: I will teach you the fear of the Lord. Run while ye have the light of life, lest the darkness of death overtake you."

And the Lord, seeking his workman among the multitudes to whom he thus crieth, saith again: "What man is he that desireth life and would fain see good days?" And if hearing him thou answer, "I am he," God saith to thee: "If thou wilt have true and everlasting life, keep thy tongue from evil and thy lips that they speak no guile. Turn away from evil and do good: seek after peace and pursue it." And when you have done these things, my eyes will be upon you and my ears open unto your prayers. And before you call upon me, I shall say to you, "Lo, here I am." What can be sweeter to us, dearest brethren, than this voice of our Lord inviting us? Behold in his loving mercy the Lord showeth us the way of life.

Let us, therefore, gird our loins with faith and the performance of good works, and following the guidance of the Gospel walk in his paths, so that we may merit to see him who has called us unto his kingdom. And, if we wish to dwell in the tabernacle of his kingdom, except we run thither with good deeds we shall not arrive. But let us ask the Lord with the prophet: "Lord, who shall dwell in thy tabernacle, or who shall rest upon thy holy hill?" Then, brethren, let us hear the Lord answering and showing us the way to that tabernacle and saying: "He that walketh without blemish and doth that which is right; he that speaketh truth in his heart, who hath used no deceit in his tongue, nor done evil to his neighbour, nor believed ill of his neighbour." He that taketh the evil spirit that tempteth him, and casteth him and his temptation from the sight of his heart, and bringeth him to naught; who graspeth his evil suggestions as they arise and dasheth them to pieces on the rock that is Christ. Such men as these, fearing the Lord, are not puffed up on account of their good works, but judging that they can do no good of themselves and that all cometh from God, they magnify the Lord's work in them, using the word of the prophet: "Not unto us, O Lord, not unto us, but unto thy name give the glory." So the apostle Paul imputed nothing of his preaching to himself, but said: "By he grace of God I am what I am." And again he saith: "He that glorieth, let him glory in the Lord."

Wherefore the Lord also saith in the Gospel: "He that heareth these my words and doth them, shall be likened to a wise man that built his house upon a rock. The floods came and the winds blew, and they beat upon that house, and it fell not, for it was founded upon a rock." Having given us these instructions, the Lord daily expects us to make our life correspond with his holy admonitions. And the days of our life are lengthened and a respite allowed us for this very reason, that we may amend our evil ways. For the Apostle saith: "Knowest thou not that the patience of God inviteth thee to repentance?" For the merciful Lord saith: "I will not the death of a sinner, but that he should be converted and live."

So, brethren, we have asked the Lord about the dwellers in his tabernacle and have heard what is the duty of him who would dwell therein; it remains for us to fulfil this duty. Therefore our hearts and bodies must be made ready to fight under the holy obedience of his commands; and let us ask God that he be pleased, where our nature is powerless, to give us the help of his grace. And if we would escape the pains of hell and reach eternal life, then must we—while there is still time, while we are in this body and can fulfill all these things by the light of this life—hasten to do now what may profit us for eternity.

Therefore must we establish a school of the Lord's service; in founding which we hope to ordain nothing that is harsh or burdensome. But if, for good reason, for the amendment of evil habit or the preservation of charity, there be some strictness of discipline, do not be at once dismayed and run away from the way of salvation, of which the entrance must needs be narrow. But, as we progress in our monastic life and in faith, our hearts shall be enlarged, and we shall run with unspeakable sweetness of love in the way of God's commandments; so that, never abandoning his rule but persevering in his teaching in the monastery until death, we shall share by patience in the sufferings of Christ, that we may deserve to be partakers also of his kingdom. Amen.

❖❖❖

WHAT KIND OF MAN THE ABBOT SHOULD BE

An abbot who is worthy to rule a monastery should always remember what he is called and realize in his actions the name of a superior. For he is believed to be the representative of Christ in the monastery, and for that reason is called by a name of his, according to the words of the Apostle: "Ye have received the spirit of the adoption of sons, whereby we cry Abba, Father." Therefore the abbot ought not to teach, or ordain, or command anything which is against the law of the Lord; on the contrary, his commands and teaching should be infused into the minds of his disciples like the leaven of divine justice. Let the abbot remember always that at the dread Judgement of God there will be an examination of both these matters, of his teaching and of the obedience of his disciples. And let the abbot realize that the shepherd will have to answer for any lack of profit which the Father of the family may discover in his sheep. On the other hand, if the shepherd have spent all diligence on an unruly and disobedient flock and devoted his care to the amending of its vicious ways, then he will be acquitted at the Judgement and may say to the Lord with the prophet: "I have not hid thy justice within my heart: I have declared thy truth and thy salvation; but they have despised and rejected me." And so at the last, for these sheep disobedient to his care, let death itself bring its penalty.

Therefore, when anyone has received the name of abbot, he ought to rule his disciples with a twofold teaching, displaying all goodness and holiness by deeds and by words, but by deeds rather than by words. To intelligent disciples let him expound the Lord's commandments in words; but to those of harder hearts and ruder minds let him show forth the divine precepts by his example. And whatever he has taught his disciples to be contrary to God's law, let him show by his example that it is not to be done, lest while preaching to others he should himself become a castaway, and lest God should some day say to him in his sin: "Why dost thou repeat my commandments by rote, and boast of my covenant with thee? For thou hast hated to amend thy life and hast cast my words behind thee." And again: "Thou sawest the speck of dust in thy brother's eye and didst not see the beam in thy own."

Let him not make any distinction of persons in the monastery. Let him not love one more than another, unless he find him better in good works and obedience. Let not a free-born monk be put before one that was a slave, unless there be some other reasonable ground for it. But if the abbot, for just reason, think fit so to do, let him fix anyone's order as he will; otherwise let them keep their due places; because, whether slaves or freemen, we are all one in Christ, and have to serve alike in the army of the same Lord. "For there is no respect of persons with God." In this regard only are we distinguished in his sight, if we be found better than others in good works and humility. Therefore let the abbot show an equal love to all, and let the same discipline be imposed on all in accordance with their deserts.

For the abbot in his teaching ought always to observe the rule of the apostle, wherein he says: "Reprove, persuade, rebuke." He must adapt himself to circumstances, now using severity and now persuasion, displaying the rigour of a master or the loving kindness of a father. That is to say, that he must sternly rebuke the undisciplined and restless; but the obedient, meek, and patient, these he should exhort to advance in virtue. As for the negligent and rebellious, we warn him to reprimand and punish them. And let him not shut his eyes to the faults of offenders; but as soon as they begin to appear, let him, as he can, cut them out by the roots, mindful of the fate of Heli, the priest of Silo. Those of gentle disposition and good understanding should be punished for the first and second time, by verbal admonition; but bold, hard, proud, and disobedient characters should be checked at the very beginning of their ill doing by the rod and corporal punishment, according to the text:

"The fool is not corrected with words"; and again: "Beat thy son with the rod and thou shalt deliver his soul from death."

The abbot should always remember what he is and what he is called, and should know that to whom more is committed, from him more is required. Let him realize also how difficult and arduous a task he has undertaken, of ruling souls and adapting himself to many dispositions. One he must humour, another rebuke, another persuade, according to each one's disposition and understanding, and thus adapt and accommodate himself to all in such a way, that he may not only suffer no loss in the sheep committed to him, but may even rejoice in the increase of a good flock.

Above all let him not have greater solicitude for fleeting, earthly, and perishable things, and so overlook or undervalue the salvation of the souls committed to him; but let him always remember that he has undertaken the government of souls and will have to give an account of them. And if he be tempted to complain of lack of means, let him remember the words: "Seek ye first the kingdom of God and his approval, and all these things shall be yours without the asking." And again: "Those that fear him never go wanting." And let him know that he who has undertaken the government of souls, must prepare himself to render an account of them. And whatever number of brethren he knows he has under his care, let him regard it as certain that he will have to give the Lord an account of all these souls on the Day of Judgement, and certainly of his own soul also. And thus, fearing always the examination which the shepherd will have to face for the sheep entrusted to him, and anxious regarding the account which will have to be given for others, he is made solicitous for his own sake also; and while by his admonitions helping others to amend, he himself is cleansed of his faults.

OF CALLING THE BRETHREN TO COUNCIL

As often as any important business has to be done in the monastery, let the abbot call together the whole community and himself set forth the matter. And, having heard the advice of the brethren, let him take council with himself and then do what he shall judge to be most expedient. Now the reason why we have said that all should be called to council, is that God often reveals what is better to the younger. Let the brethren give their advice with all deference and humility, nor venture to defend their opinions obstinately; but let the decision depend rather on the abbot's judgement, so that when he has decided what is the better course, all may obey. However, just as it is proper for disciples to obey their master, so is it becoming that he on his part should dispose all things with prudence and justice.

In all things, therefore, let all follow the Rule as master, nor let anyone rashly depart from it. Let no one in the monastery follow the will of his own heart; nor let anyone presume to contend impudently with his abbot, or to contend with him at all when outside the monastery. Should he presume to do so, let him undergo the discipline of the Rule. The abbot himself, however, should do all things in the fear of God and observance of the Rule, knowing that he will certainly have to render an account of all his judgements to God, the most just Judge. But if the business to be done in the interests of the monastery be of lesser importance, let him use the advice of the seniors only. It is written: "Do all things with counsel, and thy deeds shall not bring thee repentance."

❖❖❖

OF OBEDIENCE

The first degree of humility is obedience without delay. This becometh those who hold nothing dearer to them than Christ. Because of the holy service which they have professed, the fear of hell, and the glory of life everlasting, as soon as anything has been ordered by the superior, they receive it as a divine command and cannot suffer any delay in executing it. Of these doth the Lord say: "He hath listened to me and hath obeyed me." And again he saith to teachers: "He who listens to you, listens to me."

Such as these, therefore, immediately abandoning their own affairs and forsaking their own will, dropping the work they were engaged on and leaving it unfinished, with swift obedience follow up with their deeds the voice of him who commands them. And almost in the same moment of time that the master's order is issued, is the disciple's work completed, in the swiftness of the fear of the Lord; the two things being rapidly accomplished together by those who are impelled by the desire of attaining life everlasting. Therefore they choose the narrow way, according to the Lord's words: "Narrow is the way which leadeth unto life"; so that not living by their own will, and obeying their own desires and passions, but walking by another's judgement and orders, they dwell in monasteries, and desire to have an abbot over them. Assuredly such as these imitate that saying of the Lord wherein he saith: "I came not to do my own will, but the will of him who sent me."

But this obedience itself will then be acceptable to God and pleasing to men, if what is commanded be not done timorously, or tardily, or tepidly, nor with murmuring or the raising of objections. For the obedience which is given to superiors is given to God, since he himself said: "He who listens to you, listens to me." And disciples should give their obedience with a good will, because "God loveth a cheerful giver." For if the disciple obey with an ill will, and murmur not only in words but even in his heart, then even though he fulfil the command, his work will not be acceptable to God, who sees that his heart is murmuring. For work such as this he will gain no reward; nay, rather, he will incur the punishment due to murmurers, unless he amend and make reparation.

OF SILENCE

Let us do as saith the prophet, "I said, I will take heed unto my ways, that I offend not with my tongue. I have set a guard to my mouth. I was dumb and was humbled, and kept silence even from good words." Here the prophet teaches us that if we should at times, for the love of silence, refrain from good talk, we should with more reason still, for fear of sin's punishment, eschew all evil talk. Therefore, on account of the great value of silence, let leave to speak be seldom granted to observant disciples, even though it be for good, holy, and edifying conversations; for it is written: "In much speaking thou shalt not escape sin," and elsewhere: "Death and life are in the power of the tongue." For it becometh the master to speak and to teach; but it befits the disciple to be silent and to listen.

And therefore, if there be anything to be asked from the superior, let it be sought with all humility and respectful submission. But as for buffoonery and talk that is vain and stirs laughter, we condemn such things everywhere with a perpetual ban, and forbid the disciple to open his mouth for such conversation.

Of Humility

Holy Scripture crieth out to us, brethren, saying: "Everyone that exalteth himself shall be humbled, and he that humbleth himself shall be exalted." When it so speaks, it teaches us that all exaltation is a kind of pride; which the prophet shows that he shunned in the words: "Lord, my heart is not exalted nor mine eyes lifted up; neither have I dwelt on high things, nor on marvels that are beyond my reach." And why? "If I was not humbly minded but exalted my soul with pride; as a child that is weaned from his mother, so wilt thou requite my soul."

Wherefore, brethren, if we wish to attain to the summit of humility and desire to arrive speedily at that heavenly exaltation to which we ascend by the humility of the present life, then must we set up a ladder of our ascending actions like unto that which Jacob saw in his vision, whereon angels appeared to him, descending and ascending. By that descent and ascent we must surely understand nothing else than this, that we descend by self-exaltation and ascend by humility. And the ladder erected is our life in this world, which for the humble of heart is raised up by the Lord unto heaven. Now the sides of this ladder are our body and soul, into which sides our divine vocation has fitted various degrees of humility and discipline which we have to climb.

The first degree of humility, then, is that a man keep the fear of God before his eyes, altogether shunning forgetfulness. Let him ever remember all the commandments of God, and how hell will burn for their sins those that despise him; and let him constantly turn over in his heart the eternal which is prepared for those that fear him. And guarding himself always from sins and vices, whether of thought, word, hand, foot, or self-will, and checking also the desires of the flesh, let him consider that God is always beholding him from heaven, that his actions are everywhere visible to the eye of the Godhead, and are constantly being reported to God by the angels. The prophet teaches us this when he represents God as always present in our thoughts: "God searcheth the heart and the reins;" and again: "The Lord knoweth the thoughts of men;" and again he saith: "Thou hast understood my thoughts from afar"; and: "The thought of man shall praise thee." In order then that he may be careful regarding his wrongful thoughts, let the good brother say constantly in his heart: "Then shall I be spotless before him, if I shall have kept myself from my iniquity."

We are, indeed, forbidden to do our own will by Scripture, which saith to us: "Turn away from thine own will." Moreover, we ask God in prayer that his will be done in us.

And rightly are we taught not to do our own will, since we dread that sentence of Scripture: "There are ways which to men seem right, but the ends thereof lead to the depths of hell"; and since we fear also what is said of the careless: "They are corrupt and have become abominable in their pleasures." And in regard to the desires of the flesh, let us believe that God is always present to us, since the prophet says to the Lord: "All my desire is before thee."

We must be on our guard, then, against evil desires, for death lies close by the gate of delight; whence Scripture gives this command: "Go not after thy lusts." So if "the eyes of the Lord behold the good and the evil," and the Lord is ever "looking down from heaven upon the children of men, to see if there be one soul that reflects and seeks God"; and if our deeds are daily, day and night, reported to the Lord by the angels assigned us: then, brethren, must we constantly beware, as the prophet says in the psalm, lest God some day behold us falling into evil ways and turned unprofitable, and spare us for this present time, because he is merciful and awaits our amendment, but should say to us in the future: "These things didst thou do, and I was silent."

The second degree of humility is that a man love not his own will, nor delight in fulfilling his own desires, but carry out in deed the saying of the Lord: "I came not to do my own will, but the will of him who sent me." It is written also: "Self-will hath its punishment, but necessity winneth a crown."

The third degree of humility is that a man for the love of God subject himself to his superior in all obedience, imitating the Lord, of whom the apostle says: "He was made obedient even unto death."

The fourth degree of humility is that, meeting in this obedience with difficulties and contradictions and even injustice, he should with a quiet mind hold fast to patience, and enduring neither tire nor run away; for the Scripture saith: "He that shall persevere to the end shall be saved"; and again, "Let thy heart take courage, and wait thou for the Lord." And showing how the true disciple ought to endure all things, however contrary, for the Lord, it saith in the person of sufferers: "For thy sake we face death at every moment. We are reckoned no better than sheep marked down for slaughter." Then, confident in their hope of the divine reward, they go on with joy to declare: "But in all these things we overcome, through him that hath loved us." And again in another place the Scripture saith: "Thou, O God, hast put us to the proof: thou hast tested us as men test silver in the fire. Thou hast led us into a snare: thou hast bowed our backs with trouble." And to show that we ought to be under a superior, it goeth on to say: "Thou hast set men over our heads." Moreover, in adversities and injuries they patiently fulfil the Lord's commands: when struck on one cheek they offer the other, when robbed of their tunic they surrender also their cloak, when forced to go a mile they go two, with the apostle Paul they bear with false brethren, and they bless those that curse them.

The fifth degree of humility is that he humbly confess and conceal not from his abbot any evil thoughts that enter his heart, and any secret sins that he has committed. To this does Scripture exhort us, saying: "Make known thy way unto the Lord and hope in him." And again: "Confess to the Lord, for he is good, and his mercy endureth for ever." And further: "I have made known my sin to thee, and my faults I have not concealed. I said: I will be my own accuser and confess my faults to the Lord, and with that thou didst remit the guilt of my sin."

The sixth degree of humility is that a monk be content with the meanest and worst of everything, and esteem himself, in regard to the work that is given him, as a bad and unworthy workman, saying to himself with the prophet: "I am brought to nothing; I am all ignorance; I am become as a dumb beast before thee; yet am ever close to thee."

The seventh degree of humility is that he should not only in his speech declare himself lower and of less account than all others, but should in his own inmost heart believe it, humbling himself and saying with the prophet: "But I am a worm and no man, a byword to all men and the laughing-stock of the people. I have been lifted up only to be humbled and confounded"; and again: "It is good for me that thou hast humbled me, that I may learn thy commandments."

The eighth degree of humility is that a monk do nothing except what is commended by the common rule of the monastery and the example of his superiors.

The ninth degree of humility is that a monk restrain his tongue and keep silence, not speaking until he is questioned. For Scripture showeth that "in much talking thou canst not avoid sin"; and that "the talkative man shall not prosper on the earth."

The tenth degree of humility is that he be not ready and prompt to laughter, for it is written: "The fool lifteth up his voice in laughter."

The eleventh degree of humility is that a monk, when he speaks, do so gently and without laughter, humbly and seriously, in few and sensible words, and without clamour. It is written: "A wise man is known by the fewness of his words."

The twelfth degree of humility is that a monk should not only be humble of heart, but should also in his behaviour always manifest his humility to those who look upon him. That is to say, that whether he is at the Work of God, in the oratory, in the monastery, in the garden, on the road, in the fields, or anywhere else, and whether sitting, walking, or standing, he should always have his head bowed and his eyes downcast, pondering always the guilt of his sins, and considering that he is about to be brought before the dread judgement seat of God. Let him constantly say in his heart what was said with downcast eyes by the publican in the Gospel: "Lord, I a sinner am not worthy to raise mine eyes to heaven"; and again with the prophet: "I am bowed down and humbled on every side."

Then, when all these degrees of humility have been climbed, the monk will presently come to that perfect love of God which casts out all fear; whereby he will begin to observe without labour, as though naturally and by habit, all those precepts which formerly he did not observe without fear: no longer for fear of hell, but for love of Christ and through good habit and delight in virtue. And this will the Lord deign to show forth by the power of his Spirit in his workman now cleansed from vice and from sin.

How the Monks Are to Sleep

Let them sleep each one in a separate bed. Let their beds be assigned to them in accordance with the date of their conversion, subject to the abbot's dispositions. If it be possible, let them all sleep in one place; but if their numbers do not allow of this, let them sleep by tens or twenties, with seniors to supervise them. There shall be a light burning in the dormitory throughout the night. Let them sleep clothed and girt with girdles or cords, but not with their belts, so that they may not have their knives at their sides while they are sleeping, and be cut by them in their sleep. Being clothed they will thus always be ready, and rising at the signal without any delay may hasten to forstall one another to the Work of God; yet this with all gravity and self-restraint. The younger brethren shall not have their beds by themselves, but shall be mixed with the seniors. When they rise for the Work of God, let them gently encourage one another, on account of the excuses to which the sleepy are addicted.

Of Excommunication for Faults

If any brother shall be found contumacious, or disobedient, or proud, or a murmurer, or in any way despising and contravening the holy Rule and the orders of his superiors: let such a one, according to our Lord's commandment, be admonished secretly by his superiors for a first and a second time. If he do not amend, let him be rebuked publicly before all. But if even then he do not correct his life, let him suffer excommunication, provided that he understands the gravity of that penalty. If, however, he be perverse, let him undergo corporal punishment.

What the Measure of Excommunication Should Be

The measure of excommunication and punishment should be proportioned to the gravity of the fault, which shall be determined by the abbot. If a brother be found guilty of a lesser fault, let him be excluded from sharing the common table. And this shall be the rule for one who is thus excluded from the common table: Until he have made satisfaction, he shall not intone psalm or antiphon in the oratory, nor read a lesson; and he shall have his meals alone, after the community meals. If the brethren, for instance, eat at the sixth hour, let him eat at the ninth; if they eat at the ninth hour, let him eat in the evening; until by suitable satisfaction he have obtained pardon.

❖❖❖

Whether Monks Should Have Anything of their Own

This vice especially ought to be utterly rooted out of the monastery. Let no one presume to give or receive anything without the abbot's leave, or to have anything as his own, anything whatever, whether book or tablets or pen or whatever it may be; for monks should not have even their bodies and wills at their own disposal. But let them look to the father of the monastery for all that they require, and let it be unlawful to have anything which the abbot has not given or allowed. And, as the Scripture saith, "let all things be common to all, nor let anyone say that anything is his own" or claim it for himself. But if anyone shall be found to indulge in this most wicked vice, let him be admonished once and a second time; if he do not amend, let him undergo punishment.

❖❖❖

Of the Daily Manual Labour

Idleness is the enemy of the soul. The brethren, therefore, must be occupied at stated hours in manual labour, and again at other hours in sacred reading. To this end we think that the times for each may be determined in the following manner. From Easter until September the 14th, the brethren shall start work in the morning and from the first hour until about the fourth do the tasks that have to be done. From the fourth hour until about the sixth let them apply themselves to reading. After the sixth hour, having left the table, let them rest on their beds in perfect silence; or if anyone wishes to read by himself, let him read so as not to disturb the others. Let None be said early, at the middle of the eighth hour; and let them again do what work has to be done until Vespers. But if the circumstances of the place or their poverty require them to gather the harvest themselves, let them not be discontented; for then are they truly monks when they live by the labour of their hands, like our fathers and the apostles. Yet let all things be done in moderation on account of the faint-hearted.

From September the 14th to the beginning of Lent, let them apply themselves to reading up to the end of the second hour. Let Terce be said at that point, and from then until None let them all work at the tasks appointed to them. As soon as the first signal for None has been given, let them all abandon their work and hold themselves ready for the sounding of the second signal. After the meal let them apply themselves to their reading or to the study of the psalms.

In the days of Lent let them apply themselves to their reading from the morning until the end of the third hour, and from then until the end of the tenth hour let them perform the work that is assigned to them. In these days of Lent let them each receive a book from the library, which they shall read through consecutively; let these books be given out at the beginning of Lent. But one or two senior monks should certainly be deputed to go round the monastery at the times when the brethren are occupied in reading, to see that there be no slothful brother who spends his time in idleness or gossip and neglects the reading, so that he not only does himself harm but also disturbs others. If there be such a one (which God forbid), let him be corrected once and a second time; if he do not amend, let him undergo the punishment of the Rule, so that the rest may be afraid. And the brethren should not associate with one another at unseasonable hours.

On Sundays likewise all shall apply themselves to reading, except those who are assigned to various duties. But if there be anyone so careless and slothful that he will not or cannot study or read, let him be given some work to perform, so that he may not be idle. Sick or delicate brethren should be assigned a task or craft of such a kind that on the one hand they be not idle, and on the other be not overborne by excessive toil or driven away from the monastery. The abbot should have consideration for their weakness.

PROCOPIUS

500 C.E.–?

Sometime around 527 C.E., Procopius of Caesarea became the private secretary to General Belisarius, the most important general of the Roman Emperor Justinian. While we can interpret much about the reign of Justinian from the material culture of the Byzantine Empire such as the Hagia Sophia and the intricate mosaics of San Vitale, and while we know of Justinian's project to codify Roman law, one of our best sources of information on Justinian's reign comes from Procopius's writings.

The following selections come from two of Procopius's three works, *History of the Wars* and *The Secret History*, or *Anecdota*. The first reading gives us a glimpse of Empress Theodora's role in her husband's reign, specifically her impact on Justinian's decisions when dealing with the unruly citizens of Constantinople, who were up in arms over Justinian's tax policy. The second reading, from *The Secret History*, describes the scandalous behavior of those in power and raises some fascinating questions about what "history" tells us.

When reading these two "histories" of Justinian's reign, consider how the treatment of Empress Theodora differs. What can we learn about the nature of power? How does this verbal history compare to the visual history of Justinian? Why is one of Procopius's histories "secret"?

from *History of the Wars*

At this same time an insurrection broke out unexpectedly in Byzantium among the populace, and, contrary to expectation, it proved to be a very serious affair, and ended in great harm to the people and to the senate, as the following account will show. In every city the population has been divided for a long time past into the Blue and the Green factions; but within comparatively recent times it has come about that, for the sake of these names and the seats which the rival factions occupy in watching the games, they spend their money and abandon their bodies to the most cruel tortures, and even do not think it unworthy to die a most shameful death. And they fight against their opponents knowing not for what end they imperil themselves, but knowing well that, even if they overcome their enemy in the fight, the conclusion of the matter for them will be to be carried off straightway to the prison, and finally, after suffering extreme torture, to be destroyed. So there grows up in them against their fellow men a hostility which has no cause, and at no time does it cease or disappear, for it gives place neither to the ties of marriage nor of relationship nor of friendship, and the case is the same even though those who differ with respect to these colours be brothers or any other kin. They care neither for things divine nor human in comparison with conquering in these struggles; and it matters not whether a sacrilege is committed by anyone at all against God, or whether the laws and the constitution are violated by friend or by foe; nay even when they are perhaps ill supplied with the necessities of life, and when their fatherland is in the most pressing need and suffering unjustly, they pay no need if only it is likely to go well with their "faction"; for so they name the bands of partisans. And even women join with them in this unholy strife, and they not only follow the men, but even resist them if opportunity offers, although they neither go to the public exhibitions at all, nor are they impelled by any other cause; so that I, for my part, am unable to call this anything except a disease of the soul. This, then, is pretty well how matters stand among the people of each and every city.

But at this time the officers of the city administration in Byzantium were leading away to death some of the rioters. But the members of the two factions, conspiring together and declaring a truce with each other, seized the prisoners and then straightway entered the prison and released all those who were in confinement there, whether they had been condemned on a charge of stirring up sedition, or for any other unlawful act. And all the attendants in the service of the city government were killed indiscriminately; meanwhile, all of the citizens who were sane-minded were fleeing to the opposite mainland, and fire was applied to the city as if it had fallen under the hand of an enemy. The sanctuary of Sophia and the baths of Zeuxippus, and the portion of the imperial residence from the propylaea as far as the so-called House of Ares were destroyed by fire, and besides these both the great colonnades which extended as far as the market place which bears the name of Constantine, in addition to many houses of wealthy men and a vast amount of treasure. During this time the emperor and his consort with a few members of the senate shut themselves up in the palace and remained quietly there. Now the watchword which the populace passed around to one another was Nika, and the insurrection has been called by this name up to the present time. . . .

Now the emperor and his court were deliberating as to whether it would be better for them if they remained or if they took to flight in the ships. And many opinions were expressed favouring either course. And the Empress Theodora also spoke to the following effect: "As to the belief that a woman ought not to be daring among men or to assert herself boldly among those who are holding back from fear, I consider that the present crisis most certainly does not permit us to discuss whether the matter should be regarded in this or in some other way. For in the case of those whose interests have come into the greatest danger nothing else seems best except to settle the issue immediately before them in the best possible way. My opinion then is that the present time, above all others, is inopportune for flight even though it brings safety. For while it is impossible for a man who has seen the light not also to die, for one who has been an emperor it is unendurable to be a fugitive. May I never be separated from this purple, and may I not live that day on which those who meet me shall not address me as mistress. If, now, it is your wish to save yourself, O Emperor, there is no difficulty. For we have much money, and there is the sea, here the boats. However consider whether it will not come about after you have been saved that you would gladly exchange that safety for death. For as for myself, I approve a certain ancient saying that royalty is a good burial-shroud." When the queen had spoken thus, all were filled with boldness, and, turning their thoughts towards resistance, they began to consider how they might be able to defend themselves if any hostile force should come against them.

from *The Secret History*
First Selection

Procopius of Caesarea has written the history of the wars which Justinian, Emperor of the Romans, waged against the barbarians of the East and of the West, relating separately the events of each one, to the end that the long course of time may not overwhelm deeds of singular importance through lack of a record, and thus abandon them to oblivion and utterly obliterate them. The memory of these events he deemed would be a great thing and most helpful to men of the present time, and to future generations as well, in case time should ever again place men under a similar stress. For men who purpose to enter upon a war or at preparing themselves for any kind of struggle may derive some benefit from a narrative of a similar situation in history, inasmuch as this discloses the final result attained by men of an earlier day in a struggle of the same sort, and foreshadows, at least for those who are most prudent in planning, what outcome present events will probably have. Furthermore he had assurance that he was especially competent to write the history of these events, if for no other reason, because it fell to his lot when appointed adviser to the general Belisarius, to be an eye-witness of practically all the events to be described. It was his conviction that while cleverness is appropriate to rhetoric, and inventiveness to poetry, truth alone is appropriate to history. In accordance with this principle he has not concealed the failures of even his most intimate acquaintances, but has written down with complete accuracy everything which befell those concerned, whether it happened to be done well or ill by them.

It will be evident that no more important or mightier deeds are to be found in history than those which have been enacted in these wars,—provided one wishes to base his judgment on the truth. For in them more remarkable feats have been performed than in any other wars with which we are acquainted; unless, indeed, any reader of this narrative should give the place of honour to antiquity, and consider contemporary achievements unworthy to be counted remarkable.

Foreword: The Purpose of This Book. In recording everything that the Roman people has experienced in successive wars up to the time of writing I have followed this plan—that of arranging all the events described as far as possible in accordance with the actual times and places. But from now on I shall no longer keep to that method: in this volume I shall set down every single thing that has happened anywhere in the Roman Empire. The reason is simple. As long as those responsible for what happened were still alive, it was out of the question to tell the story in the way that it deserved. For it was impossible to avoid detection by swarms of spies, or if caught to escape death in its most agonizing form. Indeed, even in the company of my nearest relations I felt far from safe. Then again, in the case of many events which in my earlier volumes I did venture to relate I dared not reveal the reasons for what happened. So in this part of my work I feel it my duty to reveal both the events hitherto passed over in silence and the reasons for the events already described.

But as I embark on a new understanding of a difficult and extraordinarily baffling character, concerned as it is with Justinian and Theodora and the lives they lived, my teeth chatter and I find myself recoiling as far as possible from the task; for I envisage the probability that what I am now about to write will appear incredible and unconvincing to future generations. And again, when in the long course of time the story seems to belong to a rather distant past, I am afraid that I shall be regarded as a mere teller of fairy tales or listed among the tragic poets. One thing, however, gives me confidence to shoulder my heavy task without flinching: my account has no lack of witnesses to vouch for its truth. For my own contemporaries are witnesses fully acquainted with the incidents described, and will pass on to future ages an incontrovertible conviction that these have been faithfully recorded.

And yet there was something else which, when I was all agog to get to work on this volume, again and again held me back for weeks on end. For I inclined to the view that the happiness of our grandchildren would be endangered by my revelations, since it is the deeds of blackest dye that stand in greatest need of being concealed from future generations, rather than they should come to the ears of monarchs as an example to be imitated. For most men in positions of power invariably, through sheer ignorance, slip readily into imitation of their predecessors' vices, and it is to the misdeeds of earlier rulers that they invariably find it easier and less troublesome to turn. But later on I was encouraged to write the story of these events by this reflexion—it will surely be evident to future monarchs that the penalty of their misdeeds is almost certain to overtake them, just as it fell upon the persons described in this book. Then again, their own conduct and character will in turn be recorded for all time; and that will perhaps make them less ready to transgress. For how could the licentious like of Semiramis or the dementia of Sardanaplaus and Nero have been known to anyone in later days, if contemporary historians had not left these things on record? Apart from this, those who in the future, if so it happens, are similarly ill used by the ruling powers will not find this record altogether useless; for it is always comforting for those in distress to know that they are the only ones on whom these blows have fallen.

That is my justification for first recounting the contemptible conduct of Belisarius, and then revealing the equally contemptible conduct of Justinian and Theodora. . . .

Justinian's Misgovernment. When Justinian ascended the throne it took him a very little while to bring everything into confusion. Things hitherto forbidden by law were one by one brought into public life, while established customs were swept away wholesale, as if he had been invested with the forms of majesty on condition that he would change all things to new forms. Long established offices were abolished, and new ones set up to run the nation's business; the laws of the land and the organization of the army were treated in the same way, not because justice required it or the general interest urged him to it, but merely that everything might have a new look and might be associated with his name. If there was anything which he was not in a position to transform then and there, even so he would at least attach his own name to it.

Of the forcible seizure of property and the murder of his subjects he could never have enough: when he had looted innumerable houses of wealthy people he was constantly on the look-out for others, immediately squandering on one foreign tribe or another, or on crazy building schemes, all that he had amassed by his earlier looting. And when he had without any excuse got rid of thousands and thousands of people, or so it would seem, he promptly devised schemes for doing the same to others more numerous still. . . .

Frequently matters agreed between Senate and Emperor ended by being settled quite differently. The Senate sat merely as a picturesque survival, without any power either to register a decision or to do any good, assembling for the sake of appearance and in fulfillment of an old law, since no member of that assembly was ever permitted to utter one word. The Emperor and his consort for the most part made a show of taking sides in the questions at issue, but victory went to the side upon which they had already agreed. If a man had broken the law and felt that victory was not securely his, he had only to fling more gold to this Emperor in order to obtain the passage of a law going clean contrary to all existing statutes. Then if somebody else should call for the first law, which had now been repealed, His Majesty was perfectly prepared to reenact it and substitute it for the new one. There was nothing that remained permanently in force, but the scales of justice wandered at random all over the place, whichever way the greater mass of gold weighing them down succeeded in pulling them. The home of justice was the market-hall, though it had once been the Palace, and there sale-rooms flaunted themselves in which not only the administration of justice by the making of laws too was sold to the highest bidder. . . .

The Arrogance of the Imperial Pair. Among the innovations which Justinian and Theodora made in the conduct of official business are the following.

In previous reigns, when the Senate came into the Emperor's presence it was customary to pay homage in this way. A man of patrician rank used to salute him on the right breast: the Emperor responded by kissing him on the head, and then dismissed him. Everyone else bent his right knee to the Emperor and then retired. To the Empress, however, homage was never paid. But when they came into the presence of Justinian and Theodora all of them, including those who held patrician rank, had to fall on the floor flat on their faces, stretch out their hands and feet as far as they could, touch with their lips one foot of each of Their Majesties, and then stand up again. For Theodora too insisted on this tribute being paid to her, and even claimed the privilege of receiving the ambassadors of Persia and other foreign countries and of bestowing gifts of money on them, as if she were mistress of the Roman Empire—a thing unprecedented in the whole course of history.

Again, in the past persons engaged in conversation with the Emperor called him "Emperor" and his wife "Empress," and addressed each of their ministers by the title appropriate to the rank he held at the moment; but if anyone were to join in conversation with either of these two and refer to the "Emperor" or "Empress" and not call them "Master" and "Mistress," or attempted to speak of any of the ministers as anything but "slaves," he was regarded as ignorant and impertinent; and as if he had committed a shocking offence and had deliberately insulted the last person who should have been so treated; he was sent packing.

[W]hile in earlier reigns few visited the Palace, and they on rare occasions, from the day that these two ascended the throne officials and people of every sort spent their days in the Palace with hardly a break. The reason was that in the old days the officials were allowed to do what was just and proper in accordance with their individual judgements; this meant that while carrying out their official duties they stayed in their own offices, while the Emperor's subjects, neither seeing nor hearing of any resort to force, naturally troubled him very rarely. These two, however, all the time taking everything into their own hands to the detriment of their subjects, compelled everyone to be in constant attendance exactly like slaves. Almost any day one could see all the law-courts pretty well deserted, and at the Emperor's Court an insolent crowd elbowing and shoving, and all the time displaying the most abject servility. Those who were supposed to be close friends of Their Majesties stood there right through the whole day and invariably for a considerable part of the night, getting no sleep or food at the normal times, were worn out completely: this was all that their supposed good fortune brought them.

When, however, they were released from all their misery, the poor wretches engaged in bitter quarrels as to where the wealth of the Romans had gone to. Some insisted that foreigners had got it all; others that the Emperor kept it locked up in a number of small chambers.

One of these days Justinian, if he is a man, will depart this life: if he is Lord of the Demons, he will lay his life aside.

Then all who chance to be still living will know the truth.

Second Selection

Belisarius had a wife, whom I have had occasion to mention in the previous books; her father and grandfather were charioteers who had given exhibitions of their skill in both Byzantium and Thessalonica, and her mother was one of the prostitutes attached to the theatre. This woman, having in her early years lived a lewd sort of a life and having become dissolute in character, not only having consorted much with the cheap sorcerers who surrounded her parents, but also having thus acquired the knowledge of what she needed to know, later became the wedded wife of Belisarius, after having already been the mother of many children. Straightway, therefore, she decided upon being an adulteress from the very start, but she was very careful to conceal this business, not because she was ashamed of her own practices, nor because she entertained any fear so far as her husband was concerned (for she never experienced the slightest feeling of shame for any action whatsoever and she had gained complete control of her husband by means of many tricks of magic), but because she dreaded the punishment the Empress might inflict. . . .

There was a certain youth from Thrace in the household of Belisarius, Theodosius by name. . . . Now when Belisarius was about to embark on the voyage to Libya, he bathed this youth in the sacred bath, from which he lifted him with his own hands, thus making him the adopted child of himself and his wife, as is customary for Christians to make adoptions, and consequently Antonina loved Theodosius, as she naturally would, as being her son through the sacred word, and with very particular solicitude she kept him near herself. And straightway she fell extraordinarily in love with him in the course of this voyage, and having become insatiate in her passion, she shook off both fear and respect for everything both divine and human and had intercourse with him, at first in secret, but finally even in the presence of servants of both sexes. For being by now possessed by this passion and manifestly smitten with love, she could see no longer any obstacle to the deed. And on one occasion Belisarius caught them in the very act in Carthage, yet he willingly allowed himself to be deceived by his wife. For though he found them both in an underground chamber and was transported with rage, she, without either playing the coward or attempting to conceal the deed, remarked, "I came down here in order to hide with the aid of the boy the most valuable of our booty, so that it may not get to the knowledge of the Emperor." Now she said this as a mere pretext, but he, appearing to be satisfied, dropped the matter, though he could see that the belt which supported the drawers of Theodosius, covering his private parts, had been loosened. For under compulsion of love for the woman, he would have it that the testimony of his own eyes was absolutely untrustworthy.

And I think it not inappropriate to describe the appearance of this man. He was neither tall in stature nor particularly short, but of a medium height, yet not thin but slightly fleshy. His face was round and not uncomely; for his complexion remained ruddy even after two days of fasting. But that I may describe his appearance as a whole in few words, I would say that he resembled Domitian, son of Vespasian, very closely, an Emperor who so impressed the Romans who suffered under him that even after they had chopped his whole body into pieces they felt that they had not satisfied their rage against him. . . .

Such was Justinian in appearance; but his character I could not accurately describe. For this man was both an evil-doer and easily led into evil, the sort of a person whom I call a moral pervert, never of his own accord speaking the truth to those with whom he conversed, but having a deceitful and crafty intent behind every word and action, and at same time exposing himself, an easy prey, to those who wished to deceive him. . . .

This Emperor was insincere, crafty, hypocritical, dissembling his anger, double-dealing, clever, a perfect artist in acting out an opinion which he pretended to hold, and even able to produce tears, not from joy or sorrow, but contriving them for the occasion according to the need of the moment, always playing false, yet not carelessly but adding both his signature and the most terrible oaths to bind his agreements, and that too in dealing with his own subjects. But he departed straightway from his agreements and his oaths, just like the vilest slaves, who, through fear of the tortures hanging over them, are induced to make confession of acts which they had denied on oath. He was a fickle friend, a truceless enemy, an ardent devotee of assassination and of robbery, quarrelsome and an inveterate innovator, easily led astray into wrong, but influenced by no counsel to adopt the right, keen to conceive and to execute base designs, but looking upon even the hearing about good things as distasteful. How could any man be competent to describe adequately the character of Justinian? These faults and many others still greater he manifestly possessed to a degree not in accord with human nature. On the contrary, Nature seemed to have removed all baseness from the rest of mankind and to have concentrated it in the soul of this man. And in addition to his other shortcomings, while he was very easy-going as to lending an ear to slanders, yet he was severe as to inflicting punishment. For he never paused for a thorough investigation before reaching a decision, but straightway upon hearing what the slanderer said, he would make his decision and order it published. And he did not hesitate to write orders that called for the capture of towns and the burning of cities and the enslavement of whole peoples, for no reason whatever. Consequently, if one should care to estimate all misfortunes which have befallen the Romans from the earliest times and then to balance against them those of the present day, it seems to me that he would find a greater slaughter of human beings to have been perpetrated by this man than has come to pass in all the preceding time. And while he had no scruples whatever against the quiet acquisition of other men's money—for he never even made any excuse, putting forward justice as a screen in trespassing upon things which did not belong to him—yet when once these had become his own, he was perfectly ready to shew his contempt for the money, with a prodigality in which there was no trace of calculation, and for no reason at all to fling it away to the barbarians. And, to sum up the whole matter, he neither had any money himself, nor would he allow anyone else in the world to have it, as though he were not a victim of avarice, but simply consumed by envy of those who possessed money. Consequently he lightly banished wealth from the Roman world and became the creator of poverty for all.

The traits, then, of Justinian's character, as far as we are able to state them, were roughly these. And he married a wife concerning whom I shall now relate how she was born and reared and how, after being joined to this man in marriage, she overturned the Roman State to its very foundations. There was in Byzantium a certain Acacius, keeper of the animals used in the circus, an adherent of the Green Faction, a man whom they called Master of the Bears. This man had died a natural death during the reign of Anastasius, leaving three girls, Comito, Theodora and Anastasia, the eldest of whom was not yet seven years of age. And the woman, now reduced to utter distress, entered into marriage with another husband, who, she thought, would later on assist her in both the care of the household and in her first husband's occupation. But the Dancing Master of the Greens, a man named Asterius, was bribed by another man to remove these persons from that office and to make no difficulty about putting in the position the man who had given him the money. For the Dancing Masters had authority to administer such matters as they wished. But when the woman saw the whole populace gathered in the Circus, she put garlands on the heads and in both hands of the three girls and caused them to sit as suppliants. And though the Greens were by no means favourable to receiving the supplication, the Blues conferred this position of honour upon them, since their Master of the Bears also had recently died. And when these children came of age, the mother immediately put them on the stage there—since they were fair to look upon—not all three at the same time, but as each one seemed to her to be ripe for this calling. Now Comito, the first one, had already scored a brilliant success among the harlots of her age: and Theodora, the next in order, clothed in a little sleeved frock suitable to a slave girl, would follow her about, performing various services and in particular always carrying on her shoulders the stool on which her sister was accustomed to sit in the assemblies. Now for a time Theodora, being immature, was quite unable to sleep with a man or to have a woman's kind of intercourse with one, yet she did engage in intercourse of a masculine type of lewdness with the wretches, slaves though they were, who, following their masters to the theatre, incidentally took advantage of the opportunity afforded them to carry on this monstrous business, and she spent much time in the brothel in this unnatural traffic of the body. But as soon as she came of age and was at last mature, she joined the women of the stage and straightway became a courtesan, of the sort whom men of ancient times used to call "infantry." For she was neither a flute-player nor a harpist, nay, she had not even acquired skill in the dance, but she sold her youthful beauty to those who chanced to come along, plying her trade with practically her whole body. Later on she was associated with the actors in all the work of the theatre, and she shared their performances with them, playing up to their buffoonish acts intended to raise a laugh. For she was unusually clever and full of gibes, and she immediately became admired for this sort of thing. For the girl had not a particle of modesty, nor did any man ever see her embarrassed, but she undertook shameless services without the least hesitation, and she was the sort of a person who, for instance, when being flogged or beaten over the head, would crack a joke over it and burst into a loud laugh; and she would undress and exhibit to any who chanced along both her front and her rear naked, parts which rightly should be unseen by men and hidden from them.

And as she wantoned with her lovers, she always kept bantering them, and by toying with new devices in intercourse, she always succeeded in winning the hearts of the licentious to her; for she did not even expect that the approach should be made by the man she was with, but on the contrary she herself, with wanton jests and with clownish posturing with her hips, would tempt all who came along, especially if they were beardless youths. Indeed there was never anyone such a slave to pleasure in all forms; for many a time she would go to a community dinner with ten youths or even more, all of exceptional bodily vigour who had made a business of fornication, and she would lie with all her banquet companions the whole night long, and when they were too exhausted to go on, she would go to their attendants, thirty perhaps in number, and pair off with each one of them; yet even so she could not get enough of this wantonness.

On one occasion she entered the house of one of the notables during the drinking, and they say that in the sight of all the banqueters she mounted to the projecting part of the banqueting couch where their feet lay, and there drew up her clothing in a shameless way, not hesitating to display her licentiousness. And though she made use of three openings, she used to take Nature to task, complaining that it had not pierced her breasts with larger holes so that it might be possible for her to contrive another method of copulation there; And though she was pregnant many times, yet practically always she was able to contrive to bring about an abortion immediately.

And often even in the theatre, before the eyes of the whole people, she stripped off her clothing and moved about naked through their midst, having only a girdle about her private parts and her groins, not, however, that she was ashamed to display these too to the populace, but because no person is permitted to enter there entirely naked, but must have at least a girdle about the groins. Clothed in this manner, she sprawled out and lay on her back on the ground. And some slaves, whose duty this was, sprinkled grains of barley over her private parts, and geese, which happened to have been provided for this very purpose, picked them off with their beaks, one by one, and ate them. And when she got up, she not only did not blush, but even acted as if she took pride in this strange performance. For she was not merely shameless herself, but also a contriver of shameless deeds above all others. . . .

EINHARD

ca.770-840

Born into a noble family from the region of Mainz, Einhard was initially educated at the Benedictine monastery of Fulda, founded by St. Boniface. He continued his studies at Charlemagne's Palace School at Aachen, arriving in 791 while the school was still under the direction of the talented English monk Alcuin of York. Einhard became a diplomat and advisor to the Emperor in the early 790s, and with Charlemagne's death in 814 he served as private secretary to Emperor Louis "the Pious." Subsequently he became tutor to Louis's son and heir-apparent Lothair. In later life Einhard retired from the capital and resided as lay abbot of the monastery in Seligenstadt. He was the author of four works, but is best known for his *Vita Caroli* or the *Life of Charlemagne*, a secular biography composed sometime between 825 and 836. Einhard had access to court annals and official records, but he was writing largely from memory as a retired public servant.

Not surprisingly, Einhard's *Life* presents a very favorable account of the Emperor's 46-year reign. In this brief work, embarrassing details are omitted and positive attributes are accentuated. Indeed in terms of its construction, Einhard's *Life* follows closely the model established by the Roman historian Suetonius in his *Lives of the Caesars*, with Suetonius's life of Augustus being the particular example adopted by Einhard for the story of his friend and master. If nothing else, Einhard's imitative style is a good illustration of the strength of the eighth-century Carolingian "Renaissance" fostered by the Emperor at Aachen.

Charlemagne was clearly a key figure in the political and religious life of eighth-century Western Europe. Combining a unique set of personal characteristics and leadership skills, the Emperor was able to consolidate his vast territorial holdings while advancing Christian missionary efforts. In the *Life*, Einhard is principally concerned with the qualities exhibited by a successful leader. What are these qualities and how are they suited to the political, military and cultural environment of early medieval Europe? What is Einhard's view of the proper relationship between the temporal ruler and the Church, and between ruler and subject? Is Einhard's picture of Charlemagne different from the one presented in *The Song of Roland*? In what respects, if at all, are the leadership qualities outlined by Einhard still valid in the late twentieth century?

from *Life of Charlemagne*

IV.

It would be folly, I think, to write a word concerning Charles' birth and infancy, or even his boyhood, for nothing has ever been written on the subject, and there is no one alive now who can give information of it. Accordingly, I have determined to pass that by as unknown, and to proceed at once to treat of his character, his deeds, and such other facts of his life as are worth telling and setting forth, and shall first give an account of his deeds at home and abroad, then of his character and pursuits, and lastly of his administration and death, omitting nothing worth knowing or necessary to know.

V.

His first undertaking in a military way was the Aquitanian war, begun by his father, but not brought to a close; and because he thought that it could be readily carried through, he took it up while his brother was yet alive, calling upon him to render aid. The campaign once opened, he conducted it with the greatest vigor, notwithstanding his brother withheld the assistance that he had promised and did not desist or shrink from his self-imposed task until, by his patience and firmness he had completely gained his ends. He compelled Hunold, who had attempted to seize Aquitania after Waifar's death, and renew the war then almost concluded, to abandon Aquitania and flee to Gascony. Even here he gave him no rest, but crossed the River Garonne, built the castle of Fronsac, and sent ambassadors to Lupus, Duke of Gascony, to demand the surrender of the fugitive, threatening to take him by force unless he were promptly given up to him. Thereupon Lupus chose the wiser course, and not only gave Hunold up, but submitted himself, with the province which he ruled, to the King.

VI.

After bringing this war to an end and settling matters in Aquitania (his associate authority had meantime departed this life), he was induced, by the prayers and entreaties of Hadrian, Bishop of the city of Rome, to wage war on the Lombards. His father before him had undertaken this task at the request of Pope Stephen, but under great difficulties, for certain leading Franks, of whom he usually took counsel, had so vehemently opposed his design as to declare openly that they would leave the King and go home. Nevertheless, the war against the Lombard King Astolf had been taken up and very quickly concluded. Now, although Charles seems to have had similar, or rather just the same grounds for declaring war that his father had, the war itself differed from the preceding one alike in its difficulties and its issue. Pepin, to be sure, after besieging King Astolf a few days in Pavia, had compelled him to give hostages, to restore to the Romans the cities and castles that he had taken, and to make oath that he would not attempt to seize them again: but Charles did not cease, after declaring war, until he had exhausted King Desiderius by a long siege, and forced him to surrender at discretion; driven his son Adalgis, the last hope of the Lombards, not only from his kingdom, but from all Italy; restored to the Romans all that they had lost; subdued Hruodgaus, Duke of Friuli, who was plotting revolution; reduced all Italy to his power, and set his son Pepin as king over it.

At this point I should describe Charles' difficult passage over the Alps into Italy, and the hardships that the Franks endured in climbing the trackless mountain ridges, the heaven-aspiring cliffs and ragged peaks, if it were not my purpose in this work to record the manner of his life rather than the incidents of the wars that he waged. Suffice it to say that this war ended with the subjection of Italy, the banishment of King Desiderius for life, the expulsion of his son Adalgis from Italy, and the restoration of the conquests of the Lombard kings to Hadrian, the head of the Roman Church.

VII.

At the conclusion of this struggle, the Saxon war, that seems to have been only laid aside for the time, was taken up again. No war ever undertaken by the Frank nation was carried on with such persistence and bitterness, or cost so much labor, because the Saxons, like almost all the tribes of Germany, were a fierce people, given to the worship of devils, and hostile to our religion, and did not consider it dishonorable to transgress and violate all law, human and divine. Then there were peculiar circumstances that tended to cause a breach of peace every day. Except in a few places, where large forests or mountain ridges intervened and made the bounds certain, the line between ourselves and the Saxons passed almost in its whole extent through an open country, so that there was no end to the murders, thefts, and arsons on both sides. In this way the Franks became so embittered that they at last resolved to make reprisals no longer, but to come to open war with the Saxons. Accordingly war was begun against them, and was waged thirty-three successive years with great fury; more, however, to the disadvantage of Saxons than of the Franks. It could doubtless have been brought to an end sooner, had it not been for the faithlessness of the Saxons. It is hard to say how often they were conquered, and, humbly submitting to the King, promised to do what was enjoined upon them, gave without hesitation the required hostages, and received the officers sent them from the King. They were sometimes so much weakened and reduced that they promised to renounce the worship of devils, and to adopt Christianity, but they were no less ready to violate these terms than prompt to accept them, so that it is impossible to tell which came easier to them to do; scarcely a year passed from the beginning of the war without changes on their part. But the King did not suffer his high purpose and steadfastness—firm alike in good and evil fortune—to be wearied by any fickleness on their part, or to be turned from the task that he had undertaken; on the contrary, he never allowed their faithless behavior to go unpunished, but either took the field against them in person, or sent his counts with an army to wreak vengeance and exact righteous satisfaction. At last, after conquering and subduing all who had offered resistance, he took ten thousand of those that lived on the banks of the Elbe, and settled them, with their wives and children, in many different bodies here and there in Gaul and Germany. The war that had lasted so many years was at length ended by their acceding to the terms offered by the King; which were renunciation of their national religious customs and the worship of devils, acceptance of the sacraments of the Christian faith and religion, and union with the Franks to form one people.

VIII.

Charles himself fought but two pitched battles in this war, although it was long protracted (one on Mount Osning, at the place called Detmold, and again on the bank of the river Hase, both in the space of little more than a month. The enemy were so routed and overthrown in these two battles that they never afterwards ventured to take the offensive or to resist the attacks of the King, unless they were protected by a strong position. A great many of the Frank as well as of the Saxon nobility, men occupying the highest posts of honor, perished in this war, which only came to an end after the lapse of thirty-two years. So many and grievous were the wars that were declared against the Franks in the meantime, and skillfully conducted by the King, that one may reasonably quest whether his fortitude or his good fortune is to be more admired. The Saxon war began two years before the Italian war, but although it went on without interruption, business elsewhere was not neglected, nor was there any shrinking from other equally arduous contests. The King, who excelled all the princes of time in wisdom and greatness of soul, did not suffer difficulty to deter him or danger to daunt him from anything that had to be taken up or carried through, for he had trained himself to bear and endure whatever came, without yielding in adversity, or trusting to the deceitful favors of fortune in prosperity.

XVII.

This King, who showed himself so great in extending his empire and subduing foreign nations, and was constantly occupied with plans to that end, undertook also very many works calculated to adorn and benefit his kingdom, and brought several of them to completion. Among these, the most deserving of mention are the basilica of the Holy Mother of God at Aix-la-Chapelle, built in the most admirable manner, and a bridge over the Rhine at Mayence, half a mile long, the breadth of the river at this point. This bridge was destroyed by fire the year before Charles died, but, owing to his death so soon after, could not be repaired, although he had intended to rebuild it in stone. He began two palaces of beautiful workmanship—one near his manor called Ingelheim, not far from Mayence; the other at Nimeguen, on the Waal, the stream that washes the south side of the island of the Batavians. But, above all, sacred edifices were the object of his care throughout his whole kingdom; and whenever he found them falling to ruin from age, he commanded the priests and fathers who had charge of them to repair them, and made sure by commissioners that his instructions were obeyed. He also fitted out a fleet for the war with the Northmen; the vessels required for this purpose were built on the rivers that flow from Gaul and Germany into the Northern Ocean. Moreover, since the Northmen continually overran and laid waste the Gallic and German coasts, he caused watch and ward to be kept in all the harbors, and at the mouths of rivers large enough to admit the entrance of vessels, to prevent the enemy from disembarking; and in the South, in Narbonensis and Septimania, and along the whole coast of Italy as far as Rome, he took the same precautions against the Moors, who had recently begun their piratical practices. Hence, Italy suffered no great harm in his time at the hands of the Moors, nor Gaul and Germany from the Northmen, save that the Moors got possession of the Etruscan town of Civita Veccia by treachery, and sacked it, and the Northmen harried some of the islands in Frisia off the German coast.

XVIII.

Thus did Charles defend and increase as well as beautify his kingdom, as is well known; and here let me express my admiration of his great qualities and his extraordinary constancy alike in good and evil fortune. I will now forthwith proceed to give the details of his private and family life.

After his father's death, while sharing the kingdom with his brother, he bore his unfriendliness and jealousy most patiently, and to the wonder of all, could not be provoked to be angry with him. Later he married a daughter of Desiderius, King of the Lombards, at the instance of his mother; but he repudiated her at the end of a year for some reason unknown and married Hildegard, a woman of high birth, of Suabian origin. He had three sons by her—Charles, Pepin, and Louis—and as many daughters—Hruodrud, Bertha, and Gisela. He had three other daughters besides these—Theoderada, Hiltrud, and Ruodhaid—two by his third wife, Fastrada, a woman of East Frankish (that is to say, of German) origin, and the third by a concubine, whose name for the moment escapes me. At the death of Fastrada, he married Liutgard, an Alemannic woman, who bore him no children. After her death he had three concubines—Gersuinda, a Saxon, by whom he had Adaltrud; Regina who was the mother of Drogo and Hugh; and Ethelind, by whom he had Theodoric. Charles' mother, Berthrada, passed her old age with him in great honor; he entertained the greatest veneration for her; and there was never any disagreement between them except when he divorced the daughter of King Desiderius, whom he had married to please her. She died soon after Hildegard, after living to see three grandsons and as many granddaughters in her son's house, and he buried her with great pomp in the Basilica of St. Denis, where his father lay. He had an only sister, Gisela, who had consecrated herself to a religious life from girlhood, and he cherished as much affection for her as for his mother. She also died a few years before him in the nunnery where she had passed her life.

XIX.

The plan that he adopted for his children's education was, first of all, to have both boys and girls instructed in the liberal arts, to which he also turned his own attention. As soon as their years admitted, in accordance with the custom of the Franks, the boys had to learn horsemanship, and to practice war and the chase, and the girls to familiarize themselves with cloth-making, and to handle distaff and spindle, that they might not grow indolent through idleness, and he fostered in them every virtuous sentiment. He only lost three of all his children before his death, two sons and one daughter, Charles, who was the eldest, Pepin, whom he had made King of Italy, and Hruodrud, his oldest daughter, whom he betrothed to Constantine, Emperor of Greeks. Pepin left one son, named Bernard, and five daughters, Adelaide, Atula, Gunti Berthaid, and Theoderada. The King gave striking proof of his fatherly affection at the time of Pepin's death: he appointed the grandson to succeed Pepin, and had the granddaughters brought up with his own daughters. When his sons and his daughter died, he was not so calm as might have been expected from his remarkably strong mind, for his affections were no less strong, and moved him to tears.

XXII.

Charles was large and strong, and of lofty stature, though not disproportionately tall (his height is well known to have been seven times the length of his foot); the upper part of his head was round, his eyes very large and animated, nose a little long, hair fair, and face laughing and merry. Thus his appearance was always stately and dignified, whether he was standing or sitting; although his neck was thick and somewhat short, and his belly rather prominent; but the symmetry of the rest of his body concealed these defects. His gait was firm, his whole carriage manly, and his voice clear, but not so strong as his size led one to expect. His health was excellent, except during the four years preceding his death, when he was subject to frequent fevers; at the last he even limped a little with one foot. Even in those years he consulted rather his own inclinations than the advice of physicians, who were almost hateful to him, because they wanted him to give up roasts, to which he was accustomed, and to eat boiled meat instead. In accordance with the national custom, he took frequent exercise on horseback and in the chase, accomplishments in which scarcely any people in the world can equal the Franks. He enjoyed the exhalations from natural warm springs, and often practiced swimming, in which he was such an adept that none could surpass him; and hence it was that he built his palace at Aix-la-Chapelle, and lived there constantly during his latter years until his death. He used not only to invite his sons to his bath, but his nobles and friends, and now and then a troop of his retinue or bodyguard, so that a hundred or more persons sometimes bathed with him.

XXV.

Charles had the gift of ready and fluent speech, and could express whatever he had to say with the utmost clearness. He was not satisfied with command of his native language merely, but gave attention to the study of foreign ones, and in particular was such a master of Latin that he could speak it as well as his native tongue; but he could understand Greek better than he could speak it. He was so eloquent, indeed, that he might have passed for a teacher of eloquence. He most zealously cultivated the liberal arts, held those who taught them in great esteem, and conferred great honors upon them. He took lessons in grammar of the deacon Peter of Pisa, at that time an aged man. Another deacon, Albin of Britain, surnamed Alcuin, a man of Saxon extraction, who was the greatest scholar of the day, was his teacher in other branches of learning. The King spent much time and labor with him studying rhetoric, dialectics, and especially astronomy; he learned to reckon, and used to investigate the motions of the heavenly bodies most curiously, with an intelligent scrutiny. He also tried to write, and used to keep tablets and blanks in bed under his pillow, that at leisure hours he might accustom his hand to form the letters; however, as he did not begin his efforts in due season, but late in life, they met with ill success.

XXVI.
He cherished with the greatest fervor and devotion the principles of the Christian religion, which had been instilled into him from infancy. Hence it was that he built the beautiful basilica at Aix-la-Chapelle, which he adorned with gold and silver and lamps, and with rails and doors of solid brass. He had the columns and marbles for this structure brought from Rome and Ravenna, for he could not find such as were suitable elsewhere. He was a constant worshipper at this church as long as his health permitted, going morning and evening, even after nightfall, besides attending mass; and he took care that all the services there conducted should be administered with the utmost possible propriety, very often warning the sextons not to let any improper or unclean thing be brought into the building or remain in it. He provided it with a great number of sacred vessels of gold and silver and with such a quantity of clerical robes that not even the doorkeepers who fill the humblest office in the church were obliged to wear their everyday clothes when in the exercise of their duties. He was at great pains to improve the church reading and psalmody, for he was well skilled in both, although he neither read in public nor sang, except in a low tone and with others.

XXVII.
He was very forward in succoring the poor, and in that gratuitous generosity which the Greeks call alms, so much so that he not only made a point of giving in his own country and his own kingdom, but when he discovered that there were Christians living in poverty in Syria, Egypt, and Africa, at Jerusalem, Alexandria, and Carthage, he had compassion on their wants, and used to send money over the seas to them. The reason that he zealously strove to make friends with the kings beyond seas was that he might get help and relief to the Christians living under the rule. He cherished the Church of St. Peter the Apostle at Rome above all other holy and sacred places, and heaped its treasury with vast wealth of gold, silver, and precious stones. He sent great and countless gifts to the pope and throughout his whole reign the wish that he had nearest at heart was to re-establish the ancient authority of the city of Rome under his care and by his influence, and to defend and protect the Church of St. Peter, and to beautify and enrich it out of his own store above all other churches. Although he held it in such veneration, he only repaired to Rome to pay his vows and make his supplications four times during the whole forty-seven years that he reigned.

XXVIII.
When he made his last journey thither, he had also other ends in view. The Romans had inflicted many injuries upon the Pontiff Leo, tearing out his eyes and cutting out his tongue, so that he had been compelled to call upon the King for help. Charles accordingly went to Rome, to set in order the affairs of the Church, which were in great confusion and passed the whole winter there. It was then that he received the

titles of Emperor and Augustus, to which he at first had such an aversion that he declared that he would not have set foot in the Church the day that they were conferred, although it was a great feast-day, if he could have foreseen the design of the Pope. He bore very patiently with the jealousy which the Roman emperors showed upon his assuming these titles, for they took this step very ill; and by dint of frequent embassies and letters, in which he addressed them as brothers, he made their haughtiness yield to his magnanimity, a quality in which he was unquestionably much their superior.

Germanic Christian Poetry

ca. 975 C.E.

The text of "The Dream of the Rood" ("rood" = "cross" in Old English) translated here is found on folios 104b to 106a of a single manuscript which has rested in the Cathedral Library at Vercelli in Italy since the early Middle Ages. The manuscript was written during the late tenth century, perhaps about 975 C.E., in West Saxon, the dialect of the most important Anglo-Saxon kingdom then remaining in England. No one knows how this manuscript found its way from England to Italy, or how it came to be made part of the Vercelli Cathedral Library; but it seems likely that it was left by an Anglo-Saxon cleric of some importance travelling to Rome. Nor do we know when "The Dream of the Rood" was first composed. One suggested date of origin is 700 C.E., the year the True Cross was reportedly unearthed outside of Jerusalem. Such a date is plausible in light of a variety of evidence pointing to oral circulation of versions of the poem at least two centuries before the Vercelli manuscript was transcribed.

The fact that a book containing this poem should be in Italy at all tells us something important about the poem: how highly it was valued in its time. For this we have two other pieces of evidence as well. Portions of "The Dream of the Rood" appear as inscriptions on the Ruthwell and Brussels Crosses, the former an 18-foot high stone cross carved about 700 C.E., and the latter the reliquary containing what at the time of its making was considered to be the largest extant piece of the True Cross, probably a gift sent to King Alfred the Great of England by Pope Marinus in the ninth century C.E. The presence alone of so many witnesses renders "The Dream of the Rood" remarkable. Most Old English poems have survived, like *Beowulf*, in a single copy. A poem carved in stone and in wood, and carefully copied into a manuscript thought fit to be carried on the long journey from England to Italy was highly prized in its time. "The Dream of the Rood" is thus an important artifact for us, with much to say about the ethos, or world-view, of the Germanic Christians of the early Middle Ages.

In "The Dream of the Rood" we can see coming together a number of literary and cultural elements. Structurally it is a dream-vision of sorts, a poetic type common during the Middle Ages, although in no other poem before or after "The Dream of the Rood" does a cross speak. "The Dream of the Rood" also has strong similarities to certain verse riddles—a form of poetry quite popular in Old English. When the Rood describes Christ as a young man climbing up to take his place fearlessly, even eagerly, the poet of "The Dream of the Rood" uses language most often found in battle poetry, and reminds his audience that Christ's sacrifice was intentional, an act of extraordinary courage of the kind a warrior society could respect. Similarly, the Rood casts its own action—standing steadfast in support of its lord even as they both were surrounded by enemies—in the language of Germanic heroic poetry. Visible here is the code of *comitatus*, the system of loyalty unto death of warrior to his lord first described by the Roman general Tacitus in his *Germania*, which he wrote during the first century C.E. while on campaign against the ancestors of the Anglo-Saxon audience of "The Dream of the Rood."

Some questions to think about: how has the poet contrived to present the crucifixion in ways his audience can understand? Why does the Rood change appearance? What is the use of the Cross being the narrator of its own story? What impact does this have, and why would the poet choose to present events in this way, at this point in European history?

The Dream of the Rood

Listen! In the middle of the night, while all men slept in their beds, I dreamed the most marvelous dream. Let me tell you how it went.

It seemed to me that a miraculous tree was spread before me in the air, wound all round with light—the most refulgent of wooden things, like a beacon! Gold covered it, and beautiful jewels at its corners, the corners of the earth, and there were five more there, where the beams crossed. A universe of beautiful angels beheld it from every side. That was no gallows for a convict: holy spirits were transfixed, gazing on it, and so were people around the world, and the whole of the created cosmos too. The sign of victory was magnificent!

And I, sin-stained, wounded by foul deeds, I saw that the radiant tree, richly covered, draped with bright gold, shone gloriously. Jewels encased the tree of the Almighty. But beneath the gold I could see what terrible torture had once been endured there, for on the right side blood had flowed. I was overwhelmed with sadness; and then awe-stricken, before a marvelous sight. As I watched, the vibrant beacon changed its covering and its colors, back and forth: sometimes it was soaken, drenched and slick with flowing blood; sometimes it was dressed again in sparkling gems. Yet still I lay there a long time, much troubled, gazing upon the Healer's tree—until I heard it talking. Then that best of wooden things spoke these words:

"It was years ago—yet do I recall it—at the edge of the woods I was hacked down, chopped away from my root. Powerful enemies laid hold of me there, transformed me into a spectacle for them to gawk at, forced me to heave up their felons. Men bore me upon their shoulders; on a hill they set me up. A multitude of foes fastened me there.

"Then I saw the Lord of all humanity come toward me quickly, bravely, for he meant to climb up on me. Then I did not dare to bend or break, to contradict the command of the Lord, when I saw the earth's surface quake. I could have felled all the enemies about me, had I fallen; but I stood firm. And that young man, who was almighty God himself, stripped off his clothes—so resolute, unflinching. He mounted the hateful gallows, unbowed beneath the stares of many, since then it was his will to be redemption for mankind. When the man embraced me, I quaked, I shook; nonetheless I dared not topple, collapse onto the face of earth. I had to—and I did—stand fast. Raised aloft a cross, I lifted up the mighty king, Wielder of the heavens. I did not dare to fall. They wounded me through with dark nails: the hurts are here on view upon me, gaping, evil-spreading gashes. But to none of them dared I do harm, though they humiliated both of us together. And after he, that warrior, sent forth his spirit, the blood-flow from his side soaked me.

"On that hill I survived many marvels. I saw the God of hosts sorely tormented. Darkness covered the corpse of the king in clouds; overshaded by clouds, a shadow went forth, spread over its splendor. All creation wept; all cried for the King's dying: Christ was on the Cross.

"But then from far off people came there to the Prince: all this I saw myself. I was fearful, and weak with grief; nevertheless I bent down to those men's hands, gladly obedient. They took hold of God Himself then and bore him away from the terrible torture. Those hardy men left me standing, covered with blood; I was hurt through and through with pointed shafts. They laid him down there, weary in his limbs; they stood at his body's head. There they looked upon Heaven's Lord, as for a while he rested himself, exhausted after mighty battle. Then they made a tomb for him, there in full view of me, who murdered him. Out of the bright stone they carved it, and in it they placed the Lord of Victories. Then at evening they began to sing a dirge for him when they thought it time to return homeward, all weary and worn, time to leave the glorious Prince. But little company remained there with him. We stood by, weeping, a long time after the lament of the brave men ceased. The body grew cold, the beautiful house of life. Then we three were all knocked down to the earth: that was a frightening thing, terrible.[1] For us a deep pit was dug; but the followers of the Lord, friends, found out where I was, and embellished me with gold and with silver.

"Now my dear man, you can see how I have borne the torment inflicted by evil men, such grievous pain. Now it is time for every person everywhere on earth, and all things in glorious creation, to honor me and worship me as a sign. The Son of God suffered upon me for a while; because of that I now rise high, majestic, fearless under heaven, and I have power to bring health to everyone who holds me in reverence. One time I was made the most painful of punishments, wholly loathsome to people—until I opened the way for mortal men, the path of right life. Look here! Above all the trees of the forest, the Lord, the splendid Protector of the heavenly kingdom, Almighty God, exalted me then, in the sight of all, exactly as he honored his mother, Mary herself, above all women.

"Now my dear man, I charge you to spread what you have seen and heard among the people; make it clear by what you say that it is the tree of glory on which God All-Powerful suffered for the many sins of men and the past deeds of Adam. Thereon he tasted death, but yet the Lord rose up once more with his mighty strength, for the good of mankind. Then he went up into the heavens. He will journey again to earth, He himself, the Lord, the Almighty God, and his angels with him, to search out humanity on Judgment Day. He who has the power to judge all will then judge each one, just as each deserves for what he has previously done here in this fleeting life. None can be fearless before the word which the Deemer will utter. In front of all he will ask, where is that man who for the sake of his Lord's name wishes to taste biting death, as he did once himself upon the tree? They will be frightened then, and will not know where to begin to answer Christ. But then none there need fear, who has carried the finest of signs in his heart: for by that Cross every soul on earth desiring to dwell with the Ruler will find a way into the kingdom."

Then and there, with a joyful heart and full devotion I prayed before that tree, alone, lacking other company. Filled with longings, my soul felt like soaring forward on the way. Now the hope of my life is for permission to come near the tree of victory alone, oftener than all others, to honor it fully. I am determined, my mind strong and set, my allegiance firm in the Cross for protection. I have now but few powerful friends on earth. All have departed, passed out of the joys of this world, and gone their way to the King of glory. Now in heaven they are alive with the high Father and dwell in glory—and I hope every day that the time has come when the Lord's Cross, which once I saw here on earth, will fetch me from this ephemeral life and carry me to that place of joy, great happiness in heaven, where the people of the Lord sit at banquet, where happiness has no end; and that that Cross will then put me where forever after I may live in glory and enjoy full happiness among the saints.

May the Lord be my friend, who once suffered here on earth on the gallows-tree for all men's sins. He redeemed us and gave us life, and home in heaven. For those who had suffered burning [in hell], he brought hope, and dignity and happiness.[2] The Son was victorious in that campaign; he was strong and successful, when he came with a huge number, the army of souls, into the kingdom of God, the single Ruler All-powerful; it delighted the angels and all the saints who dwelt there in heavenly glory, when their Ruler, almighty God, returned to his home.

NOTES

[1]Christ was crucified along with two thieves; here the Rood refers to itself and the two crosses of the thieves.

[2]The reference is to the Gospel of Nicodemus, considered part of the Bible in the Middle Ages. Nicodemus describes how, during the three days of entombment, Christ journeyed to hell to liberate the holy souls (e.g. Moses, Isaiah) who could not enter heaven until his crucifixion repaid the debt of Adam's original sin.

Religion and Culture in the High Middle Ages

Hildegard of Bingen

1098-1179

Hildegard of Bingen would be an outstanding person in any age, but her accomplishments are even more remarkable in a period which did not encourage women in the fields of writing, theology, musical composition, medicine, and political counsel. As the "tithe," or tenth child in her family, Hildegard was sent at age eight to Jutta, an anchoress. Anchorites led an ascetic life inside a small room shut off from the world. Because they became essentially dead to the world, anchorites received their last rites from the bishop before their confinement in the anchorage. When Jutta died, Hildegard, who was then 38, was elected head of the convent adjacent to the anchorage. Hildegard had visions from the age of three, but she confided them only to Jutta and the monk Volmar, until 1141 when God commanded her in a vision to write them down. Trying to avoid any hint of impropriety or heresy, and because she wanted her visions to be sanctioned, Hildegard wrote to St. Bernard, seeking his blessings. Then, with subsequent papal encouragement, Hildegard wrote her first visionary work *Scivias* (*Know the Ways of the Lord*). Around 1150 Hildegard moved her growing convent from Disibodenberg, where the nuns lived alongside the monks, to Bingen on the banks of the Rhine. Her remaining years were very productive: she composed music and lyrics; wrote two other major visionary works, *Liber vitae meritorum* (*Book of Life's Merits*) and *Liber divinorum operum* (*Book of Divine Works*); composed works on natural history and medicine; and continued her extensive letter-writing. Because she had very little formal education, and could write very little, if at all, Hildegard employed scribes throughout her long career. Her visions present her theology of microcosm and macrocosm: that humans (the microcosm) are the peak of God's creation and therefore mirror the splendor of all creation (the macrocosm). In addition, her visions reflect positive aspects of the feminine and employ significant contemplation of the natural world in the light of faith (so much so that she has been called an "ecological mystic"). For Hildegard, human love is a powerful force for good in the world. Music is also extremely important to Hildegard because it recaptures the original joy and beauty of paradise.

Most medieval women who lacked access to power, and for those who were able, letter-writing was especially important. Hildegard's letters show her growth in self-confidence and authority from her early requests to her later self-assured instructions addressed to both secular and sacred powers. The selection from *Scivias* is accompanied by an illustration of the vision it describes. For the majority of her important visions, Hildegard not only dictated the text of what happened and its interpretation, but she directed the painting of the illustration as well.

Timothy 2:12 states that "No woman is to teach or have authority over men," and in medieval Europe this rule was rigorously enforced. How then might we explain Hildegard's religious influence? In what ways does Hildegard "know" the truth she is teaching? Contrast her way of knowing with that of Thomas Aquinas. In what ways does she argue that the knowledge of God should influence our own lives and the actions of church and state? Augustinian tradition, which gained popularity in the twelfth and thirteenth centuries, links women to the concept of original sin and human frailty. What, then, do you think is Hildegard's purpose in envisioning the Church as a mother?

Woodcut "Mother Church," reprinted from Hildegard of Bingen.

from *Scivias*

Vision Three

The Church, Bride of Christ and Mother of the Faithful

After this I saw the image of a woman as large as a great city, with a wonderful crown on her head and arms from which a splendor hung like sleeves, shining from Heaven to earth. Her womb was pierced like a net with many openings, with a huge multitude of people running in and out. She had no legs or feet, but stood balanced on her womb in front of the altar that stands before the eyes of God, embracing it with her outstretched hands and gazing sharply with her eyes throughout all of Heaven. I could not make out her attire, except that she was arrayed in great splendor and gleamed with lucid serenity, and on her breast shone a red glow like the dawn; and I heard a round of all kinds of music singing about her, "Like the dawn, greatly sparkling."

And that image spreads out its splendor like a garment, saying, "I must conceive and give birth!" And at once, like lightning, there hastened to her a multitude of angels, making steps and seats within her for people, by whom the image was to be perfected.

Then I saw black children moving in the air near the ground like fishes in water, and they entered the womb of the image through the openings that pierced it. But she groaned, drawing them upward to her head, and they went out by her mouth, while she remained untouched. And behold, that serene light with the figure of a man in it, blazing with a glowing fire, which I had seen in my previous vision, again appeared to me, and stripped the black skin off each of them and threw it away; and it clothed each of them in a pure white garment and opened to them the serene light saying to them one by one:

"Cast off the old injustice, and put on the new sanctity. For the gate of your inheritance is unlocked for you. Consider, therefore, how you have been taught, that you may know your Father Whom you have confessed. I have received you, and you have confessed Me. Now, therefore, behold the two paths, one to the East and the other to the North. If you will diligently contemplate Me with your inner vision, as in faith you have been taught, I will receive you into My kingdom. And if you love Me rightly, I will do whatever you shall wish. But if you despise Me and turn away from Me, looking backward and not seeking to know or understand Me, Who am recalling you by pure penitence though you are filthy with sin, and if you run back to the Devil as to your father, then perdition will take you; for you will be judged according to your works, since when I gave you the good you did not choose to know Me."

But the children who had passed through the womb of the image walked in the splendor that surrounded her. And she, benignly gazing on them, said in a sad voice, "These children of mine will return again to dust. I conceive and bear many who oppress me, their mother, by heretical, schismatic and useless battles, by robberies and murders, by adultery and fornication, and by many such errors. Many of these rise again in true penitence to eternal life, but many fall in false obduracy to eternal death.

And again I heard the voice from Heaven saying to me: "The great edifice of living souls, which is constructed in Heaven from living stones, is adorned with the immense beauty of its children's virtues, encircling them as a great city encircles its immense throngs of people, or as a wide net does a multitude of fishes; and however much the work of the faithful thrives in the Christian name, by so much does it blossom with celestial virtues."

I The building of the Church, who redeems her children by Spirit and water

Wherefore now *you see the image of a woman as large as a great city*; this designates the Bride of My Son, who always bears her children by regeneration in the Spirit and in water, for the strong Warrior founded her on a wide base of virtue, that she might hold and perfect the great crowd of His elect; and no enemy can conquer or storm her. She expels unbelief and expands belief, by which it should be understood that in the mortal world each faithful is an example to his neighbor, and so they do great works of virtue in Heaven. And when the just, one by one, shall come to join the children of light, the good they have worked will appear in them, which cannot be seen here among mortal ashes, concealed as it is by the shadow of trouble.

II The Church in her origin was adorned by apostles and martyrs

She has a wonderful crown on her head; for at her origin, when she raised up by the blood of the Lamb, she was fittingly adorned with apostles and martyrs, and thus betrothed with true betrothal to My Son, since in His blood she faithfully formed herself into a firm edifice of holy souls.

III The Church is adorned by the priesthood and almsgiving

And from her arms a splendor hangs like sleeves, shining from Heaven to earth. This is the work of power done by priests, who with purity of heart and hands and in the strength of good works offer the holiest of sacrifices upon the holy altar in the sacrament of the body and blood of their Savior. And the most glorious of their works is to show mercy, always offering generous help for every grief and distributing alms to the poor with a gentle heart while saying with their whole soul, "This is not my property, but that of Him Who created me." And this work, inspired by God, is before His eyes in Heaven, when by the teaching of the Church it is done among the faithful on earth.

IV On the maternal kindness of the Church

Her womb is pierced like a net with many openings, with a huge multitude of people running in and out; that is, she displays her maternal kindness, which is so clever at capturing faithful souls by diverse goads of virtue, and in which the trusting peoples devoutly lead their lives by the faith of their true belief. But He Who casts the net to capture the fishes is My Son, the Bridegroom of His beloved Church, whom He betrothed to Himself in His blood to repair the fall of lost humanity.

V The Church, not yet perfected, will be brought to perfection near the end

She does not yet have legs or feet, for she has not yet been brought to the full strength of her constancy or the full purity of her fulfillment; for when the son of perdition comes to delude the world she will suffer fiery and bloody anguish in all her members from his cruel wickedness. By this calamity, with bleeding wounds, she will be brought to perfection; then let her run swiftly into the heavenly Jerusalem, where she will sweetly rise anew as a bride in the blood of My Son, entering into life with ardor in the joy of her offspring.

VI How the Church devoutly offers up her children in purity

But she stands balanced on her womb in front of the altar that stands before the eyes of God, embracing it with her outstretched hands; for she is always pregnant and procreating children of hers by the true ablution, and offering them devoutly to God by the purest prayers of the saints and the sweet fragrance of chosen virtues both hidden and manifest; which are plain to the clear understanding of the mind's eye when all stain of falsity and all noises of human praise are removed, as incense is purged of a noxious stench that corrupts its smell. This good work is in God's sight the sweetest sacrifice, at which the Church constantly labors, striving with her whole desire for heavenly things in bringing virtues to fruition, and by increase of such fruit thirtyfold, sixtyfold and a hundredfold building the high tower of the celestial walls.

VII No wickedness of devilish art can obscure the Church

And she gazes sharply with her eyes throughout all of Heaven; for her purpose, which she devoutly keeps to in the heavenly places, can be obscured by no wickedness: no persuasion of devilish art, nor error of a wavering people, nor storms over the various countries in which madmen tear themselves to pieces in the fury of their unbelief.

VIII The human mind cannot fully understand the secrets of the Church

You cannot make out her attire, which is to say that the human intellect, weighed down by fragile weakness, cannot fully understand her secrets; *except that she is arrayed in great splendor and gleams with lucid serenity*, for the True Sun shines everywhere around her by the bright inspiration of the Holy Spirit and her most becoming adornments of virtue.

IX On the virginity of Mary

And on her breast shines a red glow like the dawn; for the virginity of the Most Blessed Virgin when she brought forth the Son of God glows with the most ardent devotion in the hearts of the faithful. *And you hear a sound of all kinds of music singing about her, "Like the dawn, greatly sparkling"*; for, as you are now given to understand, all believers should join with their whole wills in celebrating the virginity of that spotless Virgin in the Church.

X On the expansion of the sacrament of the true Trinity

And that image spreads out its splendor like a garment, saying that she has to conceive and give birth, which means that in the Church the sacrament of the true Trinity will more widely expand, for it is her garment in which to shelter the faithful peoples, through whom she grows by the building up of the living stones, who are washed white in the pure font; thus she herself affirms that it is necessary to salvation that she conceive children in blessing and bring them forth in cleansing, by regeneration in the Spirit and water.

XI The ministry of angels is at hand for each of the faithful

And at once, like lightning, there hasten to her a multitude of angels, making steps and seats within her for people, by whom the image is to be perfected; because for each of the faithful there is at hand a fearsome and desirable ministry of blessed spirits; they are building stairs of faith and seats of sovereign quiet for those faithful souls, in whom that happy mother, the Church, will attain to her full beauty.

XII Those regenerated by the Church their mother in the faith of the Trinity

Then you see black children moving in the air near the ground like fishes in water, and they enter the womb of the image through the openings that pierce it. This signifies the blackness of those foolish people who are not yet washed in the bath of salvation, but love earthly things and run about doing them, building their dwelling on their unsteadiness; they come at last to the mother of holiness, contemplate the dignity of her secrets and receive her blessing, by which they are snatched from the Devil and restored to God. Thus they enter the confines of the churchly order in which the faithful person is blessed by salvation, when he says within himself, "I believe in God," and the rest of the articles of faith.

But she groans, drawing them upward to her head, and they go out by her mouth, while she remains untouched. For this blessed mother sighs inwardly when baptism is celebrated by the sacred anointing of the Holy Spirit, because the person is renewed by the true circumcision of the Spirit and water, and thus offered to the Supreme Beatitude Who is the Head of all, and made a member of Christ, regenerated unto salvation by invocation of the Holy Trinity. But in this that mother suffers no hurt, for she will remain forever in the wholeness of virginity, which is the

Catholic faith; for she arose in the blood of the true Lamb, her intimate Bridegroom, Who was born of the untouched Virgin without any corruption of integrity. So too that Bride will remain untouched, so that no schism can corrupt her.

She will often, however, be bothered by the wicked, but with the help of her Bridegroom she will always most strongly defend herself, like a virgin who is often assailed by the cravings of desire through the Devil's art and the arguments of men, but pours out her prayers to God and is forcibly liberated from their temptations and her virginity preserved. So also the Church resists her wicked corrupters, the heretical errors of Christians, Jews and pagans, who infest her and try to corrupt her virginity, which is the Catholic faith. She resists them strongly, lest she be corrupted, for she was and is and will remain a virgin; the true faith which is her virginity keeps its wholeness against all error, so that her honor as a chaste virgin remains uncorrupted by any touch of lust in the modesty of her body.

And thus the Church is the virginal mother of all Christians, since by the mystery of the Holy Spirit she conceives and bears them, offering them to God so that they are called the children of God. And as the Holy Spirit overshadowed the Blessed Mother, so that she miraculously conceived and painlessly bore the Son of God and yet remained a virgin, so does the Holy Spirit illumine the Church, happy mother of believers, so that without any corruption she conceives and bears children naturally, yet remains a virgin. How is this?

XIII Analogy of the balsam, onyx and diamond

As balsam oozes from a tree, and powerful medicines pour from an onyx vessel in which they are stored, and bright light streams without impediment from a diamond, so the Son of God, unopposed by corruption, was born of the Virgin; and so too the Church, His Bride, brings forth her children without being opposed by error, yet remains a virgin in the integrity of her faith.

Letters

Letter One
Hildegard to Bernard of Clairvaux

Most praiseworthy Father Bernard, through God's power you stand wonderfully in highest honor. You are formidable against the indecent foolishness of this world. Full of lofty zeal and in ardent love for God's Son, you capture men with the banner of the holy cross so that they will wage war in the Christian army against the wrath of the pagans. I beseech you, father, by the living God, hear me in what I ask you.

I am very concerned about this vision which opens before me in spirit as a mystery. I have never seen it with the outer eyes of the flesh. I am wretched and more than wretched in my existence as a woman. And yet, already as a child, I saw great things of wonder which my tongue could never have given expression to, if God's spirit hadn't taught me to believe.

Gentle father, you are so secure, answer me in your goodness, me, your unworthy servant girl, whom from childhood has never, not even for one single hour, lived in security. In your fatherly love and wisdom search in your soul, since you are taught by the Holy Spirit, and from your heart give some comfort to your servant girl.

I know in Latin text the meaning of the interpretation of the psalms, the gospels, and the other books which are shown to me through this vision. It stirs my heart and soul like a burning flame and teaches me the depth of interpretation. And yet this vision doesn't teach me writings in the German language; these I don't know. I can simply read them but have no ability to analyze them. Please answer me: what do you make of all of this? I am a person who received no schooling about external matters. It is only within, in my soul, that I have been trained. And that is why I speak in such doubt. But I take consolation from all that I have heard of your wisdom and fatherly love. I have not talked about this to anyone else, because, as I hear it said, there is so much divisiveness among people. There is just one person with whom I have shared this, a monk [Volmar] whom I have tested and whom I have found reliable in his cloistered way of life. I have revealed all of my secrets to him and he has consoled me with the assurance that they are sublime and awe-inspiring.

I beg you, father, for God's sake, that you comfort me. Then I will be secure. More than two years ago, I saw you in my vision as a person who can look at the sun and not be afraid, a very bold man. And I cried because I blushed at my faintheartedness.

Gentle father, mildest of men, I rest in your soul so that through your word you can show me, if you wish, whether I should say these things openly or guard them in silence. For this vision causes me a lot of concern about the extent to which I should talk about what I have seen and heard. For a time, when I was silent about these things, I was confined to my bed with serious illnesses, so intense that I was unable to sit up. This is why I complain to you in such sadness: I will be so easily crushed by the falling wooden beams in the winepress of my nature, that heavy wood growing from the root which sprang up in Adam through Satan's influence and cast him out into a world where there was no fatherland.

But now I lift myself up and hasten to you. I say to you: you will not be crushed. On the contrary, you constantly straighten the wooden beam and hold it upright; in your soul you are a conqueror. But it's not only yourself that you hold upright; you raise the world up towards its salvation. You are the eagle who gazes at the sun.

I ask you by the radiant clarity of the Divine and by the marvelous Word and by sweet tear-gifted repentance, the Spirit of truth, and by the holy sound which echoes through the whole creation: by him, the Word, from whom the world has come to be. By the majesty of the Divine, who in sweet greening power sent the Word into the womb of the Virgin, from whom he took flesh, as the honey is built up around the honeycomb.

And may this sound, the power of the Divine, strike your heart and elevate your soul, so that you do not grow stiffly indifferent through the words of this woman [Hildegard], since you yourself seek out everything with God or with human beings or with any mystery until you press so far forward through the opening of your soul that you discern all of these things in God. Farewell, live well in your soul and be a strong warrior for God. Amen.

LETTER TEN

Hildegard to King Henry II of England

The Lord speaks to a man who holds high office: gifts and more gifts are special to you. Through reigning, guarding, protecting, and providing you should have your heaven. But a bird black as pitch flies to you out of midnight and says: "You have the possibility of doing whatever you want. So do this and that; open the door to such and such a matter. It doesn't do you any good to pay attention to justice. If you always keep your eye on justice, you will be a slave, not a master." But you should give no hearing to the thief who gives you this counsel. For in the primordial past, after you were fashioned from dust to such a beautiful image and likeness and had received the breath of life, that same thief stripped you of great glory. Look then with fervent zeal at the God who created you. For your heart is full of goodwill to do gladly what is good, except when the filthy habits of humankind rush at you and for a time you become entangled in them. Be resolute and flee those entanglements, beloved son of God, and call out to God! God will gladly stretch out a hand to help you. Now live forever and remain in eternal blessedness.

Marie de France

1200s

We have very little information about Marie de France. In one poem she calls herself Marie, in another she says she is from France, and thus the name and sobriquet have been combined for her by modern readers. In 1066 William II, Duke of Normandy, had invaded England and established the reign of the Norman French kings of England. Some scholars speculate that Marie was part of a branch of the king's family; some suggest that she was a nun, and others argue that she was a secular court lady. She wrote for the French-speaking English court of the Henry II and his queen, Eleanor of Aquitaine.

Marie's most famous works are her twelve *Lais*. In her introduction, Marie explains that she uses tales of the Bretons (the ancient Celts of northwestern France) as her sources. Most of the stories involve a love triangle; some involve adultery, but others do not. Each of the lais illustrates a different moral outlook on love, but taken all together they present a comprehensive investigation of love, human and divine.

In her "Prologue," Marie talks about her position as a woman writer. What comments does she make concerning tradition, authority, language, and genre? What clues can you gather that might answer the mystery, "Who was Marie?" In the lai "Chaitivel" Marie tells a tale of *fin amors* that explores the comparative attitudes of women and men on the game of love. Marie closes with a clever question—who are stories of romance really about? How do the stories of the romance tradition explore different issues than do the *chansons de geste* and epics that came before?

from *The Lais of Marie de France*

Prologue

Whoever has received knowledge
and eloquence in speech from God
should not be silent or secretive
but demonstrate it willingly.
5 When a great good is widely heard of,
then, and only then, does it bloom,
and when that good is praised by many,
it has spread its blossoms.
The custom among the ancients—
10 as Priscian testifies—
was to speak quite obscurely
in the books they wrote,
so that those who were to come after
and study them
15 might gloss the letter
and supply its significance from their own wisdom.
Philosophers knew this,
they understood among themselves
that the more time they spent,
20 the more subtle their minds would become
and the better they would know how to keep themselves
from whatever was to be avoided.
He who would guard himself from vice
should study and understand
25 and begin a weighty work
by which he might keep vice at a distance,
and free himself from great sorrow.
That's why I began to think
about composing some good stories
30 and translating from Latin to Romance;
but that was not to bring me fame:
too many others have done it.
Then I thought of the *lais* I'd heard.
I did not doubt, indeed I knew well,
35 that those who first began them
and sent them forth
composed them in order to preserve
adventures they had heard.
I have heard many told;

40 and I don't want to neglect or forget them.
To put them into word and rhyme
I've often stayed awake.
In your honor, noble King,
who are so brave and courteous,
45 repository of all joys
in whose heart all goodness takes root,
I undertook to assemble these *lais*
to compose and recount them in rhyme.
In my heart I thought and determined,
50 sire, that I would present them to you.
If it pleases you to receive them,
you will give me great joy;
I shall be happy forever.
Do not think me presumptuous
55 if I dare present them to you.
Now hear how they begin.

Chaitivel (The Unfortunate One)

It is my desire to bring to mind
a *lai* that I have heard about.
I shall tell you the adventure,
its name, and the city
5 where it was born.
Men call it *The Unfortunate One*,
but there are many
who call it *The Four Sorrows*.

In Brittany, at Nantes, there lived
10 a lady, respected
for her beauty, her education,
and the very best manners.
There wasn't a knight in that land
who had ever done anything praiseworthy,
15 who, if he saw her but once,
did not love and court her.
She could not love them all,
but she didn't want to refuse them either.
It would be better to seek the love
20 of all the ladies in one land
than to separate a single fool from his rag,
for he wants to strike out at once.
The lady grants her favor

according to her goodwill;
25 however, if she doesn't want to hear someone,
she shouldn't abuse him with words
but honor him, hold him dear,
serve his pleasure and be grateful.
The lady I wish to tell you of
30 was so sought after in love,
for her beauty and her merit,
that men thought about her day and night.

In Brittany there were four barons
whose names I do not know;
35 they were not very old
but they had great beauty,
and they were brave, valiant knights,
generous, courtly, open-handed;
they were widely esteemed,
40 noble men of that land.
These four loved the lady,
and took pains to do good deeds;
to win her and her love
each did his utmost.
45 Each one sought her for himself,
put all his efforts into his suit.
There was not one who didn't think
that he was doing better than the others.
The lady had good sense:
50 she took her time to consider,
to find out and to ask
which of them it would be best to love.
They were all of such great merit
one could not choose the best.
55 She didn't want to lose three in order to have one,
so she was nice to each of them;
she gave them all tokens of love,
she sent them all messages.
None of them knew about the others;
60 but no one was able to leave her;
with his service and his prayers
each thought he was succeeding.
At the assembly of knights,
each one wanted to be first,
65 to do well, if he could,
in order to please the lady.
They all considered her their love,

all carried her token,
a ring, or sleeve, or banner,
70 and each one cried her name.
She loved all four and held them all
until one year, after Easter,
a tournament was called,
before the city of Nantes.
75 To meet the four lovers,
men came from other lands:
French and Normans,
Flemish, Brabants,
Boulognese, Angevins,
80 and near neighbors too.
All were anxious to go.
They had stayed there a long time;
then, on the evening of the tournament,
they exchanged blows furiously.
85 The four lovers armed,
left the city;
their knights followed them,
but the burden fell on those four.
Those outside knew them
90 by their tokens and shields;
they sent knights against them,
two from Flanders and two from Hainault,
ready to strike.
There was no one there who did not want to fight.
95 The four saw them approaching,
they had no desire to flee.
Lance lowered, at full speed,
each one chose his partner.
They struck with such vehemence
100 that the four outsiders fell.
The others did not worry about their horses,
but left them riderless;
they took their stand against the fallen
and their knights came to their aid.
105 With their advent, there was a great melee,
many blows struck with swords.
The lady was in a tower,
she knew which were her knights and which their men;
she saw her lovers helping each other
and did not know which one to praise most.

The tournament began,
ranks grew and swelled.
Several times that day
combat was joined before the gate.
115 Her four lovers fought so well,
that they won honor beyond all the others,
until night began to fall
when they should have separated.
But they kept on, recklessly,
120 far from their people, and they paid for it.
For three of them were killed
and the fourth wounded and hurt:
the tip of the lance shot through his thigh
into his body: it came out the other side.
125 They were pierced straight through
and all four fell.
Those who struck them dead
threw their shields onto the ground;
and grieved for them—
130 they had not meant to kill them.
The noise began and the cries,
such mourning was never heard.
The people from the city came
without a thought for the others.
135 In sorrow for these knights,
two thousand
undid their visors,
drew out their hair and beards;
all felt a common grief.
140 Each one was placed upon his shield
and carried to the city
to the lady he had loved.
As soon as she knew the adventure
she fell, fainting, on the hard ground.
145 When she recovered from her faint,
she mourned for each by name.
"Alas," she said, "what shall I do?
I'll never be happy again.
I loved these four knights
150 and desired each one for himself;
there was great good in all of them;
they loved me more than anything.
For their beauty, their bravery,
their merit, their generosity,
155 I made them fix their love on me;

I didn't want to lose them all by taking one.
I don't know which I should grieve for most;
but I cannot conceal or disguise my grief.
I see one wounded, three are dead;
160 nothing in the world can comfort me.
I shall see that the dead are buried
and if the wounded one can be healed,
I shall willingly undertake it,
and find a good doctor for him."
165 She had him brought to her chambers;
then she had the others prepared
with great love, nobly
and richly fitted out.
She made great offerings and gifts
170 in a very rich abbey
where they were buried.
God have mercy on them!
She sent for wise doctors
and assigned them to the knight
175 who lay wounded in her chamber
until he could be healed.
She went to see him often
and comforted him gently;
but she mourned for the other three
180 and suffered great grief for them.
One summer day, after dinner,
the lady was talking to the knight;
then she remembered her great sorrow,
hid her head and her face,
185 she lost herself in her thoughts.
He looked at her
and saw that she was thinking.
He addressed her in a proper way:
"Lady, you are upset.
190 What are you thinking? Tell me.
Give up your sorrow.
You must find comfort somewhere."
"Friend," she said, "I was thinking,
remembering your companions.
195 Never did a lady of my position,
however beautiful, noble, or wise,
love four such men at once,
only to lose them all in a day
except for you, who were wounded;
200 you were in great danger of dying.

Because I have loved you so,
I want my grief to be remembered:
I shall compose a *lai* about the four of you
and call it *The Four Sorrows!*"
205 When he heard her,
the knight quickly answered:
"Lady, compose the new *lai*
but call it *The Unfortunate One*!
and I'll show you why
210 it should have such a name.
The others have been dead some time;
they spent their lives
in great pain that they suffered
because of their love for you;
215 but I, who escaped alive,
am confused and miserable—
the one I could love most in the world
I see coming and going frequently,
speaking with me morning and evening,
220 but I can have no joy from her,
from kisses or embraces,
nor any other good but talk.
You make me suffer a hundred such ills,
that it would be better for me to die.
225 If the *lai* is to be named for me,
let it be called *The Unfortunate One*.
Whoever calls it *The Four Sorrows*
will be changing its real name."
"By my faith," she said, "I like that.
230 Let's call it *The Unfortunate One*."
So the *lai* was begun
and then perfected and performed.
Of those who traveled about with it,
some called it *The Four Sorrows*;
235 either name is apt,
both suit the subject.
The Unfortunate One is the common name.
Here it ends, there is no more;
I've heard no more and I know no more about it;
240 I shall tell you no more of it.

St. Francis of Assisi

1181-1226

The son of an affluent Italian cloth merchant from the small town of Assisi in Italy, Francis Bernadone founded a religious order that broke from the normal Benedictine pattern of cloistered living and obedience within a specific monastery. Instead of separating themselves from the world, the Franciscan Friars Minor—or "little brothers"—lived, worked and preached in the outside world, especially in the towns and cities. Within one century of its founding between 1206 and 1210, over 1,400 Franciscan houses were established in Latin Christian countries, and the overall impact of the Franciscans on the lay community was greater than that of any other order. A female branch of the Franciscans was organized in 1212 and received papal approval in 1219. Known as the Order of the Sisters of St. Francis, it has also been referred to as the Order of St. Clare or Poor Clares, after its founder Clare of Assisi (1194-1253). In addition, an order of laypersons was organized which attracted married men and women who sought to maintain a special tie with the celibate groups. This lay group, first mentioned in documents around the year 1230, went by the name of the Order of Penitence. The Franciscan order continues as a vital part of the Roman Catholic communion to this day.

Around the age of 25, Francis abandoned his desire to follow his father in business and underwent a conversion process that was based on a deep desire to model himself after the life of Christ and the Apostles. Animated by the words in Matthew 19:21, "If you wish to go the whole way, go, sell your possessions, and give to the poor," and Matthew 16:24, "If anyone wishes to be a follower of mine, he must leave self behind," Francis embraced a literal understanding of the text and gathered around himself a small band of like-minded followers. Pope Innocent III gave his approval to the Franciscan program of working with and preaching to the urban poor, and the work of drawing up a formal rule or set of organizational guidelines was undertaken. The excerpts included here are drawn from a *Rule* prepared by St. Francis around 1223 and approved by the papacy.

Given Francis's background, how do these directives clash with the emerging urban and commercial culture of the High Middle Ages? In what respects might the *Rule* pose a threat to the hierarchical, legalistic, and increasingly opulent culture of the Church in Rome? Considering their lifestyles, why were the Franciscans enormously popular with the laity? In what ways can we distinguish between the Benedictines and the Franciscans? Does the *Rule* of St. Francis have any value for us at the start of the twenty-first century when addressing the question: "How should we live"?

The second selection from St. Francis, the "Canticle of Brother Sun," was composed in the vernacular in 1225. Notice how Francis constructs the relationship between nature and the divine. Contemporary authors such as Lynn White have maintained that Christianity has contributed to the current ecological crisis. These writers suggest that some Christian authors like Thomas Aquinas present a very anthropocentric view of creation. Because humans are rational spiritual beings with a soul that lives beyond the death of the body, they are superior to animals, plants, and minerals, all of which are soulless. These inferior material beings can be used—some might even say abused—in order to serve human purposes. In contrast to this anthropocentric view is the belief of other Christians like Francis of Assisi to whom the sun and moon are important creatures—our brother and sister. Lynn White has even described Francis as the patron saint of ecologists. As you read the "Canticle," consider the significance of Francis's construction of worshipping the divine through nature. In what ways might he be indebted to "pagan" practices? How is his expression of thanks uniquely Christian? What can this text tell us about the medieval world-view?

The Later Rule of the Friars Minor

CHAPTER I

In the name of the Lord? The Life of the Friars Minor begins:

The rule and life of the Friars Minor is this: to observe the holy Gospel of our Lord Jesus Christ by living in obedience, without anything of their own, and in chastity. Brother Francis promises obedience and reverence to the Lord Pope Honorius and his canonically elected successors and to the Roman Church. And let the other brothers be bound to obey Brother Francis and his successors.

CHAPTER II

Those who wish to embrace this life and how they should be received

If there are any who wish to accept this life and come to our brothers, let them send them to the ministers provincial, to whom and to no other is permission granted for receiving brothers. The ministers should diligently examine them concerning the Catholic faith and the sacraments of the Church. And if they believe all these things and are willing to profess them faithfully and observe them steadfastly to the end; and [if] they have no wives, or if they have wives [who] have already taken a vow of continence and are of such an age that suspicion cannot be raised about them, [and who] have already entered a monastery or have given their husbands permission by the authority of the bishop of the diocese, let the ministers speak to them the words of the holy Gospel (cf. Mt 19:21) that they should go and sell all that belongs to them and strive to give it to the poor. If they cannot do this, their good will suffices. And the brothers and their ministers beware not to become solicitous over their temporal affairs, so that they may freely dispose of their goods as the Lord may inspire them. But if they stand in need of counsel the ministers may have permission to send them to some God-fearing persons who may advise them how they should give what they have to the poor. Then they may be given the clothes of probation namely, two tunics without a hood, a cord, short trousers, and a little cape reaching to the cord, unless at some time it seems [proper] to these same ministers before God to make other provisions. When the year of probation is ended, let them be received into obedience, whereby they promise to observe this life and rule always. And in no way shall it be lawful for them to leave this Order, according to the decree of the Lord Pope, since, according to the Gospel: "No one having put his hand to the plow and looking back is fit for the kingdom of God" (Lk 9:62). And those who have already promised obedience may have one tunic with a hood, and, if they wish, another without a hood. And those who are forced by necessity may wear shoes. And let all the brothers wear poor clothes, and let them mend them with pieces of sackcloth or other material, with the blessing of God. I admonish and exhort them not to look down or pass judgment on those people whom they see wearing soft and colorful clothing and enjoying the choicest food and drink; instead, each must criticize and despise himself.

CHAPTER III

The Divine Office and Fasting and
The way the Brothers should go about the world

The clerical [brothers] shall celebrate the Divine Office according to the rite of the holy Roman Church, except for the Psalter, for which reason they may have breviaries. The lay [brothers], however, shall pray twenty-four Our Fathers for Matins, five for Lauds, seven for each of the hours of Prime, Terce, Sext, and None, twelve for Vespers, and seven for Compline. And they shall pray for the dead. And [all the brothers] shall fast from the feast of All Saints until the Nativity of the Lord. May those who fast voluntarily for that holy Lent which begins at Epiphany and continues for forty days, which the Lord consecrated by His own fast (cf. Mt 4:2), be blessed by the Lord; and those who do not wish to keep it shall not be obliged. But they shall fast during that other Lent which lasts until the Resurrection. At other times, however, they are not bound to fast except on Fridays. But in times of manifest necessity the brothers are not obliged to corporal fasting.

I counsel, admonish and exhort my brothers in the Lord Jesus Christ, that, when they go about the world, they do not quarrel or fight with words (cf. 2 Tim 2:14), or judge others; rather, let them be meek, peaceful and unassuming, gentle and humble, speaking courteously to everyone, as is becoming. And they should not ride horseback unless they are forced by manifest necessity or infirmity. In whatever house they enter, let them say: "Peace to this house" (cf. Lk 10:5). And, according to the holy Gospel, they are free to eat of whatever food is set before them (cf. Lk 10:8).

CHAPTER IV

The Brothers are never to receive money

I firmly command all the brothers that they in no way receive coins or money, either personally or through an intermediary. Nonetheless let the ministers and custodians alone take special care to provide for the needs of the sick and the clothing of the other brothers through spiritual friends according to [diversity of] places and sons and cold climates, as they may judge the demands of necessity; excepting always, as stated above, they do not receive coins or money.

CHAPTER V

The Manner of working

Those brothers to whom the Lord has given the grace of working should do their work faithfully and devotedly so that, avoiding idleness, the enemy of the soul, they do not extinguish the Spirit of holy prayer and devotion to which all other things of our earthly existence must contribute. As payment for their work they may receive whatever is necessary for their own bodily needs and [those of] their brothers, but not money in any form; and they should do this humbly as is fitting for servants of God and followers of most holy poverty.

Chapter VI

The Brothers shall not acquire anything as their own, begging alms; the sick brothers

The brothers shall not acquire anything as their own, neither a house nor a place nor anything at all. Instead, as pilgrims and strangers (cf. I Pet 2:11) in this world who serve the Lord in poverty and humility, let them go begging for alms with full trust. Nor should they feel ashamed since the Lord made Himself poor for us in this world (cf. 2 Cor 8:9). This is that summit of highest poverty which has established you, my most beloved brothers, as heirs and kings of the kingdom of heaven; it has made you poor in the things [of this world] but exalted you in virtue (cf. Ja 2:5). Let this be your portion, which leads into the land of the living (cf. Ps 141:6). Dedicating yourselves totally to this, my most beloved brothers, do not wish to have anything else forever under heaven for the sake of our Lord Jesus Christ. And wherever the brothers may be together or meet [other] brothers, let them give witness that they are members of one family. And let each one confidently make known his need to the other, for, if a mother has such care and love for her son born according to the flesh (cf. I Thes 2:7), should not someone love and care for his brother according to the Spirit even more diligently? And if any of them becomes sick, the other brothers should serve him as they would wish to be served themselves (cf. Mt 7:12).

Chapter VII

The Penance to be imposed on the Brothers who sin

If any of the brothers, at the instigation of the enemy, sin mortally in regard to those sins about which it may have been decreed among the brothers to have recourse only to the ministers provincial, such brothers must have recourse to them as soon as possible, without delay. If these ministers are priests, they shall impose a penance upon them with mercy; but if they are not priests, they shall have imposed by other priests of the Order as it seems best to them according to God. They must take care not to become angry or disturbed because of the sin of another, since anger and disturbance hinder charity in themselves and in others.

Chapter VIII

The Election of the Minister General
of this Fraternity and the Chapter of Pentecost

All the brothers are bound always to have one of the brothers of this Order as the minister general and servant of the entire fraternity and they are bound strictly to obey him. Should he die, the election of a successor should be made by the ministers provincial and the custodians at the Chapter of Pentecost, for which the ministers provincial are always bound to convene in whatever place it has been decided by the minister general; and they shall do this once every three years or at a longer or shorter interval as decided by the aforesaid minister. And if at any time it should become evident to the body of the ministers provincial and the custodians that the aforesaid minister is not qualified for the service and general welfare of the brothers, then the same brothers, to whom the election is entrusted are bound in the name of the Lord to elect another for themselves as custodian. After the Chapter of Pentecost each minister and custodian may call his brothers to a Chapter once in the same year in their territories—if they wish and if it seems expedient to them.

CHAPTER IX

Preachers

The brothers shall not preach in the diocese of any bishop when he has opposed their doing so. And none of the brothers shall dare to preach to the people unless he has been examined and approved by the minister general of this fraternity and has received from him the office of preaching. I also admonish and exhort those brothers that, in their preaching, their words be "well chosen and chaste" (cf. Ps 11:7; 17:31), for the instruction and edification of the people, speaking to them of vices and virtues, punishment and glory in a discourse that is brief, because it was in few words that the Lord preached while on earth.

CHAPTER X

The Admonition and Correction of the Brothers

The brothers who are the ministers and servants of the other brothers should visit and admonish their brothers and humbly and charitably correct them, not commanding them anything which might be against their conscience and our Rule. On the other hand, the brothers who are subject to them should remember that they have given up their own wills for God. Therefore I strictly command them to obey their ministers in all those things which they have promised the Lord to observe and which are not against [their] conscience and our Rule. And wherever there are brothers who know and realize that they cannot observe the Rule spiritually, it is their duty and right to go to the minister for help. The ministers on their part should receive them with great kindness and love and should be so approachable that these brothers can speak and deal with [the ministers] as masters with their servants; for this is the way it should be: The ministers shall be the servants of all the brothers. At the same time I admonish and exhort the brothers in the Lord Jesus Christ that they beware of all pride, vainglory, envy, avarice (cf. 12:15), cares and worries of this world (cf. Mt. 13:22), detraction and complaint. And those who are illiterate should not be eager to learn. Instead let them pursue what they must desire above all things: have the Spirit of the Lord and His holy manner of working, pray always to

Him with a pure heart and to have humility, patience, in persecution and weakness, and to love those who persecute us, find fault with us, or rebuke us, because the Lord says: "Love your enemies, and pray for those who persecute and slander you" (Mt 5:44). "Blessed are those who suffer persecution for the sake of justice for theirs is the kingdom of heaven" (Mt 5:10). "But whoever perseveres to the end, he will be saved" (Mt 10:22).

CHAPTER XI

The Brothers are not to enter the monasteries of nuns

I firmly command all the brothers not to have any associations or meetings with women which could arouse suspicion. Moreover, they should not enter the monasteries of nuns, except those [brothers] to whom special permission has been granted by the Apostolic See. They should not be godfathers of men or women so that scandal not arise on this account among the brothers or concerning them.

CHAPTER XII

Those who go among the Saracens and other nonbelievers

Those brothers who, by divine inspiration, desire to go among the Saracens and other nonbelievers should ask permission from their ministers provincial. But the ministers should not grant permission except to those whom they consider fit to be sent.

In addition, I command the ministers through obedience to petition the Lord Pope for one of the cardinals of the holy Roman Church, who would be the governor, protector, and corrector of this fraternity, so that, always submissive and prostrate at the feet of the same holy Church, and steadfast in the Catholic faith, we may observe the poverty and the humility and the holy Gospel (cf. Col 1:23) of our Lord Jesus Christ which we have firmly promised.

No one, therefore, is in any way permitted to tamper with this decree of our confirmation or to oppose it rashly. If anyone, however, should presume to attempt this, let it be known that he shall incur the indignation of Almighty God and of His blessed Apostles Peter and Paul.

Given at the Lateran, the twenty-ninth day of November in the eighth year of our Pontificate.

The Canticle of Brother Sun

Most High, all-powerful, good Lord,
Yours are the praises, the glory, the honor, and all blessing.
To You alone, Most High, do they belong
and no man is worthy to mention Your name.
Praised be You, my Lord, with all your creatures,
especially Sir Brother Sun,
Who is the day and through whom You give us light.
And he is beautiful and radiant with great splendor;
and bears a likeness of You, Most High One.
Praised be You, my Lord, through Sister Moon and the stars,
in heaven You formed them clear and precious and beautiful.
Praised be You, my Lord, through Brother Wind,
and through the air, cloudy and serene, and every kind of weather
through which You give sustenance to Your creatures.
Praised be You, my Lord, through Sister Water,
which is very useful and humble and precious and chaste.
Praised be You, my Lord, through Brother Fire,
through whom You light the night
and he is beautiful and playful and robust and strong.
Praised be You, my Lord, through our Sister Mother Earth,
who sustains and governs us,
and who produces varied fruits with colored flowers and herbs.
Praised be You, my Lord, through those who give pardon for Your love
and bear infirmity and tribulation.
Blessed are those who endure in peace
for by You, Most High, they shall be crowned.
Praised be You, my Lord, through our Sister Bodily Death,
from whom no living man can escape.
Woe to those who die in mortal sin.
Blessed are those whom death will find in Your most holy will,
for the second death shall do them no harm.
Praise and bless my Lord and give Him thanks
and serve him with great humility.

St. Clare of Assisi

1193-1253

Born into a household of pious and charitable noblewomen in the medieval walled city of Assisi, young Clare Offreduccio was forced to flee into the nearby city of Perugia when class warfare erupted in 1199. Francis Bernadone, known to us as St. Francis, was a member of the merchant class that was razing the imperial fortress and the castles of the nobility. Despite the social and political animosity that separated them, Clare and Francis came to share a vision of spiritual renewal for the medieval church through a radical return to early Christian values. Refusing a marriage arranged by her family, Clare established a community of women living a life of absolute poverty under the protection of Francis and his "little brothers," the Franciscan friars. Clare's unwavering dedication to the spiritual ideal of absolute poverty was put to the test after the death of Francis. Pope Gregory IX wanted the "Poor Ladies" to follow the Benedictine model of individual poverty buffered by the security of communal ownership of property. Finally, in 1228, he granted Clare and her sisters "the privilege of poverty" in a special papal bull. Clare had to fight another pope, Innocent IV, to maintain this radical form of monastic poverty for her order. Two days before her death in 1253, the pope approved her Rule for the "Poor Ladies," the first rule for a religious order written by a woman.

Clare's *Testament* recounts the history of her order and is intended to guide its spiritual direction. Not yet knowing if her Rule would be approved by the pope, she wanted her spiritual vision written down to guide her sisters. Central to this vision was radical poverty. St. Francis's friars had already strayed from this ideal, as had some of the "Poor Ladies" in other European communities. Clare wanted to be sure that her community at San Damiano, a small church outside the city walls, would never deviate from absolute poverty. She wanted her community of "Poor Ladies" to mirror the poverty and humility of Christ and St. Francis. Although cloistered, St. Clare believed that a communal life of poverty and humility provided a mirror of spiritual perfection for the secular world.

Poverty was central to the spirituality of St. Clare and St. Francis, yet Franciscans strive to alleviate poverty in the world. Can you explain this apparent paradox? St. Francis created a new kind of monasticism by taking the gospel values of early Christianity into the secular medieval world. Why was St. Clare's Franciscan spirituality lived within a cloister? Why was the medieval church so opposed to the Franciscan ideal of absolute personal and communal poverty?

The Testament

In the name of the Lord! Amen.

Among the other gifts that we have received and do daily receive from our benefactor, "the Father of mercies" (2 Cor 1:3), and for which we must express the deepest thanks to the glorious Father of Christ, there is our vocation, for which, all the more by way of its being more perfect and greater, do we owe the greatest thanks to Him. Therefore the Apostle [writes]: "Know your vocation" (1 Cor 1:26). The Son of God has been made for us "the Way" (cf. Jn 14:6), which our blessed father Francis, His true lover and imitator, has shown and taught us by word and example.

Therefore, beloved sisters, we must consider the immense gifts that God has bestowed on us, especially those that He has seen fit to work in us through His beloved servant, our blessed father Francis, not only after our conversion but also while we were still [living among] the vanities of the world. In fact, almost immediately after his conversion, when he had neither brothers nor companions, while he was building the church of San Damiano, where he was totally visited by divine consolation and impelled to completely abandon the world, through the great joy and enlightenment of the Holy Spirit, the holy man made a prophecy about us that the Lord later fulfilled.

For at that time, climbing the wall of that church, he shouted in French to some poor people who were standing nearby: "Come and help me in the work [of building] the monastery of San Damiano, because ladies are yet to dwell here who will glorify "our heavenly Father" (cf. Mt 5:16) throughout His holy, universal Church by their celebrated and holy manner of life.

We can consider in this, therefore, the abundant kindness of God to us. Because of His mercy and love, He saw fit to speak these words through His saint about our "vocation and choice" (cf. 2 Pt 1:10) through His saint. And our most blessed father prophesied not only for us, but also for those who would come to this [same] holy vocation to which the Lord has called us.

With what eagerness and fervor of mind and body, therefore, must we keep the commandments of our God and Father, so that, with the help of Lord, we may return to Him an increase of His "talent" (cf. Mt 25:15–23)! For the Lord Himself has placed us not only as a form for others in being an example and mirror, but even for our sisters whom the Lord has called to our way of life as well, that they in turn might be a mirror and example to those living in the world. Since the Lord has called us to such great things that those who are to be a mirror and example to others may be reflected in us, we are greatly bound to bless and praise God and be all the more strengthened to do good in the Lord. Therefore, if we live according to the form mentioned above, we shall leave others a noble "example" (cf. 2 Mac 6:28, 31) and gain, with very little effort, "the prize" of eternal happiness (cf. Phil 3:14).

After the most high heavenly Father saw fit in His mercy and grace to enlighten my heart, that I should do penance according to the example and teaching of our most blessed father Francis, a short while after his conversion, I, together with a few sisters whom the Lord had given me after conversion, willingly promised him obedience, as the Lord gave us the light of His grace through his wonderful life and teaching. When the blessed Francis saw, however, that, although we were physically weak and frail, we did not shirk deprivation, poverty, hard work, trial, or the shame or contempt of the world—rather, we considered them as great delights, as he had frequently examined us according to the example of the saints and his brothers—he greatly rejoiced in the Lord. And moved by compassion for us, he bound himself, both through himself and through his Order, to always have the same loving care and special solicitude for us as for his own brothers.

And thus, by the will of God and our most blessed father Francis, we went to dwell in the Church of San Damiano, where, in a little while, the Lord, through His mercy and grace, made our number increase so that He would fulfill what He had foretold through His saint. In fact, we had stayed in another place [before this], but only for a short while.

Afterwards he wrote a form of life for us, especially that we always persevere in holy poverty. While he was living he was not content to encourage us with many words and examples to the love of holy poverty and its observance, but he gave us many writings that, after his death, we would in no way turn away from it, as the Son of God never wished to abandon this holy poverty while He lived in the world. And our most blessed father Francis, having imitated His footprints, never departed either in example or in teaching from this holy poverty that he had chosen for himself and his brothers.

Therefore, I, Clare, a handmaid of Christ and of the Poor Sisters of the Monastery of San Damiano—although unworthy—and the little plant of the holy father, consider together with my sisters so lofty a profession and the command of such a father and also the frailty of some others that we feared in ourselves after the passing of our holy father Francis, who was our pillar [of strength] and, after God, our one consolation and support. Time and again we willingly bound ourselves to our Lady, most holy Poverty, that after my death, the sisters, those present and those to come, would never turn away from her.

And as I have always been most zealous and solicitous to observe and to have the others observe the holy poverty that we have promised to the Lord and our holy father Francis, so, too, the others who will succeed me in office should be always bound to observe holy poverty with the help of God and have it observed by the other sisters. Moreover, for greater security, I took care to have our profession of the most holy poverty that we promised our father strengthened with privileges by the Lord Pope Innocent, during whose pontificate we had our beginning, and by his other successors, that we would never nor in any way turn away from her.

For this reason, on bended knees and bowing low with both [body and soul], I commend all my sisters, both those present and those to come, the holy Mother the Roman Church, the supreme Pontiff, and, especially, the Lord Cardinal who has been appointed for the Order of Friars Minor and for us, that out of love of the God Who was placed poor in the crib, lived poor in the world, and remained naked on the cross, [our Protector] may always see to it that his little flock (cf. Lk 12:32), which the Lord Father has begotten in His holy Church by the word and example of our blessed father Francis by following the poverty and humility of His beloved Son and His glorious Virgin Mother, observe the holy poverty that we have promised to God and our most blessed father Saint Francis. May he always encourage and support them in these things.

And as the Lord gave us our most blessed father Francis as a founder, planter, and helper in the service of Christ and in those things we have promised to God and to our blessed father, who while he was living was always solicitous in word and in deed to cherish and take care of us, his plant, so I commend and leave my sisters, both those present and those to come, to the successor of our blessed Father Francis and to the entire Order, that they may always help us to progress in serving God more perfectly and, above all, to observe more perfectly most holy poverty.

If the sisters spoken of ever leave and go elsewhere, let them be bound, after my death, wherever they may be, to observe that same form of poverty that we have promised God and our most blessed father Francis.

Nevertheless, let both [the sister] who is in office, as well as the other sisters, exercise such care and farsightedness that they do not acquire or receive more land about the place than extreme necessity requires for a vegetable garden. But if, for the integrity and privacy of the monastery, it becomes necessary to have more land beyond the limits of the garden, no more should be acquired than extreme necessity demands. This land should not be cultivated or planted but remain always untouched and undeveloped.

In the Lord Jesus Christ, I admonish and exhort all my sisters, both those present and those to come, to strive always to imitate the way of holy simplicity; humility and poverty and [to preserve] the integrity of our holy way of living, as we were taught from the beginning of our conversion by Christ, and our blessed father Francis. May the Father of mercies (2 Cor 1:3) always spread the fragrance of a good name from them (cf. 2 Cor 2:15), both among those who are far away as well as those who are near, not by any merits of ours but by the sole mercy and grace of His goodness. And loving one another with the charity of Christ, may the love you have in your hearts be shown outwardly in your deeds so that, compelled by such an example, the sisters may always grow in love of God and in charity for one another.

I also beg that [sister] who will be in an office of the sisters to strive to exceed the others more by her virtues and holy life than by her office, so that, stimulated by her example, they obey her not so much because of her office as because of love. Let her also be discerning and attentive to her sisters as a good mother is to her daughters, and let her take care especially to provide for them according to the needs of each one out of the alms that the Lord shall give. Let her also be so kind and available that they may safely reveal their needs and confidently have recourse to her at any hour, as they see fit both for themselves and their sisters.

Let the sisters who are subjects, however, keep in mind that they have given up their own wills for the sake of the Lord. Therefore I want them to obey their mother of their own free will as they have promised the Lord, so that, seeing the charity, humility and unity they have toward one another, their mother might bear all the burdens of her office more easily, and, through their way of life, what is painful and bitter might be changed into sweetness.

And because the way and path is "difficult and the gate" through which one passes and enters "to life is narrow, there are both few who" walk it and enter through it (cf. Mat 7:14). And if there are some who walk that way for a while, there are very few who persevere on it. But how blessed are those to whom it has been given "to walk" that way and "to persevere till the end" (cf. Ps 118:1; Mt 10:22).

Let us be very careful, therefore, that, if we have set out on the path of the Lord, we do not at any time turn away from it through our own fault or negligence or ignorance, nor that we offend so great a Lord and His Virgin Mother, and our blessed father Francis, the Church Triumphant and even the Church Militant. For it is written: "Those who turn away from your commands are cursed" (Ps 118:21).

For this reason I "bend my knee to the Father of our Lord Jesus Christ" (cf. Eph 3:14) that, through the supporting merits of the glorious and holy Virgin Mary, His Mother, and of our most blessed father Francis and all the saints, the Lord Himself, Who has given a good beginning, will also give the increase and "final perseverance" (cf. 2 Cor 8:6, 1 1). Amen.

So that it may be better observed, I leave you this writing, my very dear and beloved sisters, those present and those to come, as a sign of the blessing of the Lord and of our most blessed father Francis and of my blessing, your mother and servant.

Rabbi Moses ben Maimon
known as
Maimonides

1135-1204

Born into a scholarly Jewish family, Maimonides left his Spanish homeland because of religious persecution and traveled throughout the Middle East until he settled in Egypt under the religiously tolerant Sultan Saladin. By profession he was a court physician, but Maimonides is known as the foremost rabbinic authority in the medieval world. When he died at sixty-nine, both Jews and Moslems observed three days of public mourning.

The Talmud is a body of Jewish civil and religious law, including commentaries on the Torah, or Pentateuch. The Talmud consists of a codification of laws, called the *Mishnah*, and a commentary on the *Mishnah*, called the *Gemara*. Maimonides's greatest work in the field of Jewish law is his study of the Torah, *Mishnah Torah* or *Repetition of the Torah* (1180) which is a fourteen-volume abstract in Hebrew of all the rabbinical legal literature in existence at his time. In his other great work, *Guide for the Perplexed*, written in Arabic (1190), Maimonides sought to harmonize faith and reason by reconciling the tenets of rabbinical Judaism with the rationalism of Aristotelian philosophy in its modified Arabic form. This work is considered to have influenced Thomas Aquinas and other great European scholastics.

Compare the ideas of evil and of the Messianic Age with both Christian and Islamic teaching. How is Maimonides's epistemology—his way of knowing—similar to and different from the scholasticism of Aquinas and the mysticism of Hildegard of Bingen?

Selections from Philosophical Writings

On the Existence of Evil

Men frequently think that the evils in the world are more numerous than the good things; many sayings and songs of the nations dwell on this belief. They say that a good thing is found only exceptionally, whilst evil things are numerous and enduring. Not only common people make this mistake, but even many who imagine they are wise. . . . The origin of the error is to be found in the circumstance that people judge the whole Universe on the basis of what happens to one particular individual. An ignorant man is prone to believe that the whole Universe only exists for him, and therefore if any disappointment comes to him, he immediately concludes that the whole Universe is evil. If, however, he would take the whole Universe into consideration, and realize how small a part of it he is, then he would know the real truth. . . .

The numerous evils to which individual persons are exposed are due to the defects existing in the persons themselves. We complain and seek relief from our own faults; we suffer from the evils which we, by our own free will, inflict on ourselves. Why then ascribe them to God, who has no part in them? . . .

The evils which befall men are of three kinds:

The first kind of evil is that which comes to man because he is subject to birth and death, being possessed of a physical body.

. . . Now, it is in accordance with the divine wisdom that there can be no birth without death, for unless the individuals die, how can the species continue? Thus the true beneficence of God is proved. Whoever thinks he can have flesh and bones without being subject to external influences—to physical accidents, and so forth—unconsciously wishes to reconcile two opposites: viz., to be at the same time subject and not subject to change. If man were never subject to change, there could be no generation; there would be one single being, but no individuals forming a species. . . .

The second class of evils comprises such as people cause to each other: e.g., when some of them use their strength against others. These evils are more numerous than those of the first kind, and originate in ourselves rather than in the outside elements. Nevertheless, against them too the individual is helpless. . . .

The third class of evils, however, comprises those which a man causes to himself by his own action. This is the largest class, and . . . originates in man's vices, such as excessive desire for eating, drinking, and love. Indulgence in these things in undue measure or in improper manner, brings disease and affliction to body and soul alike.

The sufferings brought to the body are familiar. The sufferings of the soul are twofold: First, those directly due to the afflictions of the body, since the properties of the soul depend on the condition of the body. Secondly, the soul, when accustomed to superfluous things, acquires a strong habit of desiring things which are neither necessary for the preservation of the individual nor for that of the species. This desire is without a limit, whilst things which are necessary are few in number and restricted within certain limits. For example, you desire to have your vessels of silver, but golden vessels are still better; others have even vessels of sapphire, or perhaps they can be made of emeralds or rubies, or any other substance that might be suggested. Those who are ignorant and perverse in their thought are therefore constantly in trouble and pain, because they cannot get as much of superfluous things as others possess. They are wont to expose themselves to great dangers—e.g., by sea-voyage, or service of kings—and all this for the purpose of obtaining that which is superfluous and not necessary. And when they incur the consequences of their folly, they blame the decrees and judgments of God! . . .

How many trials and tribulations are due to the lust for superfluous things! In our frantic search for them, we lose even those which are indispensable. For the more we strive after that which is superfluous, the less strength have we left to grasp that which is truly needed.

Observe how Nature proves the correctness of this assertion. The more necessary a thing is for living beings, the more easily it is found and the cheaper it is; the less necessary it is, the rarer and dearer it is. For example, air, water, and food are indispensable to man. Air is most necessary, for if man is without air a short time he dies, whilst he can be without water a day or two. And is not air more abundant and easily obtained than water? Again, water is more necessary than food, for some people can be four or five days without food, provided they have water. And is not water more abundant everywhere, and cheaper, than food? The same proportion can be noticed in the different kinds of food: that which is more necessary in a certain place exists there in larger quantities and is cheaper than that which is less necessary. No intelligent person, I think, considers musk, amber, rubies, and emeralds as very necessary for man except perhaps as medicines; and they, as well as other like substances, can be replaced for this purpose by herbs and minerals. This shows the kindness of God to his creatures, even to us weak beings . . . *Guide* III:12

ALL THAT GOD MADE IS GOOD

I contend that no intelligent person can assume that any of the actions of God can be in vain, purposeless, or unimportant. According to our view and the view of all who follow the Torah of Moses, all actions of God are "exceedingly good." Thus Scripture says, "And God saw everything that he had made, and behold, it was very good" (Gen. 1:31). And that which God made for a certain thing is necessary, or at least very useful, for the existence of that thing. Thus food is necessary for the existence of living beings; the possession of eyes is very useful to man during his life. . . . This is assumed also by the philosophers, for they declare that nothing in Nature is purposeless. *Guide* III: 25

CONCERNING GENTILES

The teachers of truth, our Rabbis, declared, "The pious of the Gentiles have a portion in the World-to-Come," if they have attained what is due from them to attain relative to a knowledge of the Creator, and corrected their soul with the virtues. And there is no doubt about the matter that whoever corrects his soul with purity of morals and purity of knowledge in the faith of the Creator will assuredly be of the children of the World-to-Come. On that account our Rabbis stated, "Even the Gentile who occupies himself with the Torah of Moses is equal to the High Priest."

Responsa II:23[d] et seq.

WHO CAN BE A PROPHET?

Among those who believe in Prophecy, and even among our co-religionists, there are some ignorant people who think as follows: God selects any person He pleases, inspires him with the spirit of Prophecy, and entrusts him with a mission. It makes no difference whether that person be wise or stupid, old or young, so long as he is to some extent morally good. (They have not yet gone so far as to maintain that God might inspire even a wicked person with His spirit. They admit that this is impossible, unless God has previously caused him to improve his ways.)

The philosophers, on the other hand, hold that Prophecy is a certain faculty of man in a state of perfection, which can only be obtained by study. Although the faculty is common to the whole race, yet it is not fully developed in each individual, either on account of the individual's defective constitution, or on account of some other external cause. . . . Accordingly, it is impossible that an ignorant person should be a Prophet; or that a person being no Prophet in the evening should, unexpectedly on the following morning, discover himself to be a Prophet. But if a person, perfect in his intellectual and moral faculties, and also perfect, as far as possible, in his imaginative faculty, prepares himself in the manner which will be described, he must become a Prophet; since Prophecy is a natural faculty of man. It is impossible that a man who has the capacity for Prophecy should prepare himself for it without attaining it, just as it is impossible that a person with a healthy constitution should be fed well and yet not properly assimilate his food.

But there is a third view taught in Scripture, and this forms one of the principles of our faith. It coincides with the opinion of the philosophers in all points except one. For we believe that, even if one has the capacity for Prophecy and has duly prepared himself, it may yet happen that he does not actually prophesy. In that case the will of God keeps him from the use of the faculty. (In my own opinion, however, such a case would be as exceptional as any other miracle, since the laws of Nature demand that whoever has a proper physical constitution, and has been duly prepared as regards education and training, can be a Prophet.) *Guide* II:32

PROPHETS VS. SCIENTISTS

In the realm of science the Prophet is like the rest of men. If a Prophet expresses an opinion in this realm, and a non-Prophet likewise expresses an opinion, and should the former declare "The Holy One, blessed be He, has informed me that my view is correct"—do not believe him. If a thousand Prophets, all of the status of Elijah and Elisha, were to entertain an opinion and thousand plus one Sages held the opposite, we must abide by the majority and reject the view of the thousand distinguished Prophets. *C. Mishna*, Introduction

WHY THE DIETARY LAWS?

I maintain that the food which is forbidden by the Torah is unwholesome. . . . The principal reason why the Torah forbids swine's flesh is to be found in the circumstance that the swine's habits and food are very dirty and loathsome. It has already been pointed out how emphatically the Torah enjoins the removal of the sight of loathsome objects, even in the field and in the camp; how much more objectionable is such a sight in towns. But if the eating of swine's flesh were permitted, the streets and houses would be dirtier than any cesspool, as may be seen at present in the country of the Franks. A saying of our Sages declares, "The mouth of a swine is as dirty as dung itself."

The fat of the intestines makes us full, interrupts our digestion, and produces cold and thick blood; it is more fit for fuel than for human food.

Blood (Lev. 17:12) and also the flesh of a diseased animal (Exod. 22:30), or of an animal that died of itself (Dent. 14:21), are indigestible and injurious as food.

The characteristics given in the Torah (Lev. ii and Deut. 14) of the permitted animals—viz., cud-chewing and divided hoofs for cattle, fins and scales for fish—are in themselves neither the cause of the permission when they are present, nor of the prohibition when they are absent. They are merely signs by which the recommended species of animals can be discerned from those that are forbidden. . . .

It is prohibited to cut off a limb of a living animal and eat it, because such an act would be cruel and would encourage cruelty. Besides, the heathens used to do that, for it was a form of idolatrous worship to cut a certain limb off a living animal and eat it.

Meat boiled in milk is undoubtedly gross food and makes overfull; but I think that most probably it is also prohibited because it is somehow connected with idolatry, forming perhaps part of the service, or being used during some heathen festival. . . .

The commandment concerning the slaughter of animals is necessary since meat is a natural food of man—as any doctor knows full well—and the Torah therefore enjoins that animals should be put to death as mercifully as possible. It is forbidden to torment the animal by cutting the throat in a clumsy manner, by poleaxing it, or by cutting off a limb whilst the animal is alive. *Guide* III: 48

CONCERNING FREE WILL

Free will is granted to every man. If he wishes to direct himself toward the good way and become righteous, the will to do so is in his hand; and if he wishes to direct himself toward the bad way and become wicked, the will to do so is likewise in his hand. Thus it is written in the Torah, "Behold, the man is become as one of us, knowing good and evil" (Gen. 3:22)—that is to say, the human species has become unique in the world in that it can know of itself, by its own wit and reflection, what is good and what is evil, and in that it can do whatever it wishes.

Let there not enter your mind the belief of the fools among other peoples and also of the many uninformed men among Israelites, that the Holy One, blessed be He, decrees concerning the human being, from his birth, whether he is to be righteous or wicked. The matter is not so. Every man has the possibility becoming as righteous as Moses our teacher, or as wicked as Jeroboam—wise or stupid, kind or cruel, miserly or generous, and similarly with all the other qualities. That is what Jeremiah said, "Out of the mouth of the Most High proceedeth not evil and good" (Lam. 3:38), meaning, the Creator does not decree concerning a man that he should be either good or bad. It consequently follows that the sinner caused his own downfall, and it behooves him to weep and lament over his sins and for having done violence to his soul. . . .

This subject is a most important Principle of Faith; it is a pillar of the Torah and of the commandments. . . . If God decided whether a man is to be righteous or wicked . . . as the foolish astrologers imagine, how could He have commanded us through the Prophets, Do this and avoid that, mend your ways and go not after your wickedness? If from the outset of man's existence his fate had been decreed for him . . . what place would there have been for the whole of the Torah? And by what justice, or by what right, could God punish the wicked or reward the righteous? "Shall not the Judge of all the earth do justly?" (Gen. 18:25).

Do not say in surprise, "How can a man do all that he desires and his actions be under his control? Can he do anything in the world without the permission and will of his Creator; as Scripture declares, 'Whatsoever the Lord pleased, that hath He done in heaven and in earth' (Ps. 135:6)?" Know that even though everything is done according to God's will, our actions remain under our own control. How is this? In the same way that the Creator willed that . . . all created things should have the tendency which He desired, so did He desire that a man should be possessed of free will, that all his actions should be under his control, and that there should not be anything to compel or withhold him, but that of his own accord and by the mind with which God had endowed him, he should do all that man is able to do. For this reason is a man judged according to his actions. If he has done good, good is done to him; and if he has done evil, evil is done to him. *Yad,* Teshuba V,1-4

ON THE MESSIANIC AGE

Let it not enter the mind that anything in the world's system will cease to exist when the Messiah comes, or that any novelty will be introduced into the scheme of the Universe. The world will go on as usual. The statement of Isaiah, "The wolf shall dwell with the lamb, and the leopard shall lie down with the kid" (11:6), is a metaphorical expression signifying that Israel will dwell in safety among the wicked of the heathens who are likened to wolves and leopards (c. Jer. 5:6). They will be converted to the true religion, and will no more plunder and destroy, but will live honestly and quietly like Israel . . .

The Sages and Prophets did not long for the days of the Messiah for the purpose of wielding dominion over all the world, or of ruling over the heathens, or being exalted by the peoples, or of eating and drinking and rejoicing. Their desire was to be free to devote themselves to the Torah and its wisdom, without anyone to oppress and disturb them, in order that they might merit the life of the World-to-Come.

In that era there will be neither famine nor war, neither jealousy nor strife. Prosperity will be widespread, all comforts found in abundance. The sole occupation throughout the world will be to know the Lord. And men will then be very wise, learned in things that are now hidden; they will attain all the knowledge of the Creator that is within the capacity of mortals—as it is said, "For the earth shall be full of the knowledge of the Lord, as the waters cover the sea" (Isa. 11:9).

Yad, Alelaclum XI, 1; XII, 1

WHAT CAN A MAN BELIEVE?

Know that it is not proper for a man to believe except these three things: (1) that for which the mind offers clear proof—e.g., arithmetic, geometry, and astronomy; (2) that which he can grasp through the five senses—e.g., he knows and sees that this is black and that red, etc., through the vision of the eye; or he tastes that this is bitter and that sweet; or he feels that this is hot and that cold; or he hears that this sound is clear and that blurred; or he smells that this is malodorous and that pleasant; and so on; (3) that which is received from the Prophets and righteous men.

It is necessary that a man should be mentally able to classify in his mind all that he believes, and say, "This I believe because it is handed down from the Prophets; this I believe from my senses; and this I believe from reason." But whoever believes anything which does not fall within these three categories, to him applies the dictum, "The thoughtless believeth every word" (Prov. 14:1 5).

Responsa II, 25a

WHAT CAN A MAN KNOW?

I declare that there is a limit to man's capacity for knowledge, since so long as the mind is in the body, it cannot know what is beyond Nature. Therefore when the mind essays to contemplate what is beyond, it attempts that which is impossible. However, it certainly can know and reflect on all that is in Nature, and should try its utmost to do so. *Responsa* II, 23b

There are three causes which prevent men from discovering exact truth: first, arrogance and vainglory; second, the subtlety, depth and difficulty of any subject which is being examined; third, ignorance and want of capacity to comprehend what might be comprehended.

And there is a fourth cause: viz., habit and training. We naturally like whatever is familiar, and dislike whatever is strange. This may be observed amongst rustics. Though they can rarely take a bath, have few enjoyments, and live a life of wretchedness, they abhor city life. The privations with which they are familiar seem to them better than the comforts to which they are foreign. It would give them no satisfaction to live in palaces, to be clothed in silk, and to indulge in baths, ointments, and perfumes.

The same is true of the opinions to which a man has been accustomed from his youth. He likes them, defends them, and shuns the opposite views. This is likewise one of the causes which prevent men from finding truth, and which make them cling to their habitual opinions. *Guide* I:31

Men are Not Born Good or Evil

It is impossible for man to be endowed by nature from his very birth with either virtue or vice, just as it is impossible that he should be born skilled by nature in any particular art. It is possible, however, that through natural causes he may from birth be so constituted as to have a predilection for a particular virtue or vice so that he will more readily practice it than any other. For instance a man whose natural constitution inclines toward dryness, whose brain-matter is clear and not overloaded with fluids, finds it much easier to learn, remember, and understand things than the phlegmatic man whose brain is encumbered with a great deal of humidity. But if one who inclines constitutionally toward a certain excellence is left entirely without instruction, and if his faculties are not stimulated, he will undoubtedly remain ignorant. On the other hand, if one by nature dull and phlegmatic, possessing an abundance of humidity, is instructed and enlightened, he will, though of course with difficulty, gradually succeed in acquiring knowledge and understanding.

In exactly the same way, he whose blood is especially warm has the requisite quality to become a brave man. But another whose heart is colder than it should be, is naturally inclined toward cowardice and fear, so that if he should be encouraged to be a coward, he would easily become one. If, however, it be desired to make a brave man of him, he can without doubt become one, providing he receive the proper training which would require, of course, great exertion.

I have entered into this subject so that thou mayest not believe the absurd ideas of astrologers, who falsely assert that the constellation at the time of one's birth determines whether one is to be virtuous or vicious, the individual being thus necessarily compelled to follow out a certain line of conduct. We, on the contrary, are convinced that our Torah agrees with Greek philosophy, which substantiates with convincing proofs the contention that man's conduct is entirely in his own hands, that no compulsion is exerted, and that no external influence is brought to bear upon him that constrains him to be either virtuous or vicious—except inasmuch as, according to what we have said above, he may be by nature so constituted as to find it easy or hard, as the case may be, to do a certain thing. But that he must necessarily do, or refrain from doing, a certain thing is absolutely untrue.

Comm. Mishna, Eight Chapters VIII

THE MEDIEVAL CHURCH

1215

In 1215 two events defined the axis around which the High Middle Ages in Europe pivoted. At Runnymede in England, feudal aristocrats assembled to impose a contract upon their king which guaranteed their rights and freedoms: The Magna Carta. In Rome, the Fourth Lateran Council of the Catholic Church met to articulate the major doctrines and beliefs of the medieval church. Lateran Councils are the five ecumenical councils of the Roman Catholic Church, named after the palace in Rome, the Lateran, where they took place. The Fourth Lateran Council, held in 1215 under Pope Innocent III, is the most important because it clarified many of the beliefs and practices of the medieval church. Included in its 70 decrees are a condemnation of heresies, a confession of faith, a definition of transubstantiation, a requirement that all members of the Western church confess and communicate at least once a year, arrangements for the calling of a new Crusade, and the institution of marriage as one of the sacraments of the Church. In addition, it promulgated a practice which altered the consciences of believers in the West: the doctrine of private penitence.

Compare Constitutions 1 and 21 with what you have learned about Islam and Judaism. How are the beliefs and practices of these religions similar and different? In addition to outlining important aspects of faith, this document also examines the problems and abuses of actual practice in the medieval church. What are the important issues, and what other texts have we seen that reflect these same concerns? In addition to considering the workings of the church, the text also shows considerable attention to perceived threats to the church. What were they? From what quarter did they come?

from the *Constitutions of the Fourth Lateran Council*

1 Confession of Faith

We firmly believe and simply confess that there is only one true God, eternal and immeasurable, almighty, unchangeable, incomprehensible and ineffable, Father, Son and Holy Spirit, three persons but one absolutely simple essence, substance or nature. The Father is from none, the Son from the Father alone, and the Holy Spirit from both equally, eternally without beginning or end; the Father generating, the Son being born, and the holy Spirit proceeding; consubstantial and coequal, co-omnipotent and coeternal; one principle of all things, creator of all things invisible and visible, spiritual and corporeal; who by his almighty power at the beginning of time created from nothing both spiritual and corporeal creatures, that is to say angelic and earthly, and then created human beings composed as it were of both spirit and body in common. The devil and other demons were created by God naturally good, but they became evil by their own doing. Man, however, sinned at the prompting of the devil.

This holy Trinity, which is undivided according to its common essence but distinct according to the properties of its persons, gave the teaching of salvation to the human race through Moses and the holy prophets and his other servants, according to the most appropriate disposition of the times. Finally the only-begotten Son of God, Jesus Christ, who became incarnate by the action of the whole Trinity in common and was conceived from the ever virgin Mary through the cooperation of the Holy Spirit, having become true man, composed of a rational soul and human flesh, one person in two natures, showed more clearly the way of life. Although he is immortal and unable to suffer according to his divinity, he was made capable of suffering and dying according to his humanity. Indeed, having suffered and died on the wood of the cross for the salvation of the human race, he descended to the underworld, rose from the dead and ascended into heaven. He descended in the soul, rose in the flesh, and ascended in both. He will come at the end of time to judge the living and the dead, to render to every person according to his works, both to the reprobate and to the elect. All of them will rise with their own bodies, which they now wear, so as to receive according to their deserts, whether these be good or bad; for the latter perpetual punishment with the devil, for the former eternal glory with Christ.

There is indeed one universal church of the faithful, outside of which nobody at all is saved, in which Jesus Christ is both priest and sacrifice. His body and blood are truly contained in the sacrament of the altar under the forms of bread and wine, the bread and wine having been changed in substance, by God's power, into his body and blood, so that in order to achieve this mystery of unity we receive from God what he received from us. Nobody can effect this sacrament except a priest who has been properly ordained according to the church's keys, which Jesus Christ himself gave to the apostles and their successors. But the sacrament of baptism is consecrated in water at the invocation of the undivided Trinity (namely Father, Son and Holy Spirit) and brings salvation to both children and adults when it is correctly carried out by anyone in the form laid down by the church. If someone falls into sin after having received baptism, he or she can always be restored through true penitence. For not only virgins and the continent but also married persons find favour with God by right faith and good actions and deserve to attain to eternal blessedness.

21 ON YEARLY CONFESSION TO ONE'S OWN PRIEST, YEARLY COMMUNION, THE CONFESSIONAL SEAL

All the faithful of either sex, after they have reached the age of discernment, should individually confess all their sins in a faithful manner to their own priest at least once a year, and let them take care to do what they can to perform the penance imposed on them. Let them reverently receive the sacrament of the eucharist at least at Easter unless they think, for a good reason and on the advice of their own priest, that they should abstain from receiving it for a time. Otherwise they shall be barred from entering a church during their lifetime and they shall be denied a Christian burial at death. Let this salutary decree be frequently published in churches, so that nobody may find the pretence of an excuse in the blindness of ignorance. If any persons wish, for good reasons, to confess their sins to another priest let them first ask and obtain the permission of their own priest; for otherwise the other priest will not have the power to absolve or to bind them. The priest shall be discerning and prudent, so that like a skilled doctor he may pour wine and oil over the wounds of the injured one. Let him carefully inquire about the circumstances of both the sinner and the sin, so that he may prudently discern what sort of advice he ought to give and what remedy to apply, using various means to heal the sick person. Let him take the utmost care, however, not to betray the sinner at all by word or sign or in any other way. If the priest needs wise advice, let him seek it cautiously without any mention of the person concerned. For if anyone presumes to reveal a sin disclosed to him in confession, we decree that he is not only to be deposed from his priestly office but also to be confined to a strict monastery to do perpetual penance.

32 PARISH PRIESTS TO HAVE ADEQUATE INCOMES

There has grown up in certain parts a vicious custom which should be eradicated, namely that patrons of parish churches and certain other people claim the incomes from the churches wholly for themselves and leave to the priests, for the appointed services, such a small portion that they cannot live fittingly on it. For in some regions, as we have learnt for certain, parish priests receive for their sustenance only a quarter of a quarter, that is to say a sixteenth, of the tithes. Whence it comes about in these regions that almost no parish priest can be found who is even moderately learned. As the mouth of the ox should not be muzzled when it is treading out the grain, and he who serves at the altar should live from it, we therefore decree that, notwithstanding any custom of a bishop or a patron or anyone else, a sufficient portion is to be assigned to the priest. He who has a parish church is to serve it not through a vicar but in person, in the due form which the care of that church requires, unless by chance the parish church is annexed to a prebend or a dignity. In that case we allow that he who has such a prebend or dignity should make it his business, since he must serve in the greater church, to have a suitable and permanent vicar canonically instituted in the parish church; and the latter is to have, as has been said, a fitting portion from the revenues of the church. Otherwise let him know that by the authority of this decree he is deprived of the parish church, which is freely to be conferred on someone else who is willing and able to do what has been said. We utterly forbid anyone to dare deceitfully to confer a pension on another person, as it were as a benefice, from the revenues of a church which has to maintain its own priest.

62 REGARDING SAINTS' RELICS

The Christian religion is frequently disparaged because certain people put saints' relics up for sale and display them indiscriminately. In order that it may not be disparaged in the future, we ordain by this present decree that henceforth ancient relics shall not be displayed outside a reliquary or be put up for sale. As for newly discovered relics, let no one presume to venerate them publicly unless they have previously been approved by the authority of the Roman pontiff. Prelates, moreover, should not in future allow those who come to their churches, in order to venerate, to be deceived by lying stories or false documents, as has commonly happened in many places on account of the desire for profit. We also forbid the recognition of alms-collectors, some of whom deceive other people by proposing various errors in their preaching, unless they show authentic letters from the apostolic see or from the diocesan bishop. Even then they shall not be permitted to put before the people anything beyond what is contained in the letters.

We have thought it good to show the form of letter which the apostolic see generally grants to alms-collectors, in order that diocesan bishops may follow it in their own letters. It is this: "Since, as the Apostle says, we shall all stand before the judgment seat of Christ to receive according to what we have done in the body, whether it be good or bad, it behooves us to prepare for the day of the final harvest with works of mercy and to sow on earth, with a view to eternity, that which, with God returning it with multiplied fruit, we ought to collect in heaven; keeping a firm hope and confidence, since he who sows sparingly reaps sparingly, and he who sows bountifully shall reap bountifully unto eternal life. Since the resources of a hospital may not suffice for the support of the brethren and the needy who flock to it, we admonish and exhort all of you in the Lord, and enjoin upon you for the remission of your sins, to give pious alms and grateful charitable assistance to them, from the goods that God has bestowed upon you; so that their need may be cared for through your help, and you may reach eternal happiness through these and other good things which you may have done under God's inspiration."

Let those who are sent to seek alms be modest and discreet, and let them not stay in taverns or other unsuitable places or incur useless or excessive expenses, being careful above all not to wear the garb of false religion. Moreover, because the keys of the church are brought into contempt and satisfaction through penance loses its force through indiscriminate and excessive indulgences, which certain prelates of churches do not fear to grant, we therefore decree that when a basilica is dedicated, the indulgence shall not be for more than one year, whether it is dedicated by one bishop or by more than one, and for the anniversary of the dedication the remission of penances imposed is not to exceed forty days. We order that the letters of indulgence, which are granted for various reasons at different times, are to fix this number of days, since the Roman pontiff himself, who possesses the plenitude of power, is accustomed to observe this moderation in such things.

63 ON SIMONY

As we have certainly learnt, shameful and wicked exactions and extortions are levied in many places and by many persons, who are like the sellers of doves in the temple, for the consecration of bishops, the blessing of abbots and the ordination of clerics. There is fixed how much is to be paid for this or that and for yet another thing. Some even strive to defend this disgrace and wickedness on the grounds of long-established custom, thereby heaping up for themselves still further damnation. Wishing therefore to abolish so great an abuse, we altogether reject such a custom which should rather be termed a corruption. We firmly decree that nobody shall dare to demand or extort anything under any pretext for the conferring of such things or for their having been conferred. Otherwise both he who receives and he who gives such an absolutely condemned payment shall be condemned with Gehazi and Simon.

67 JEWS AND EXCESSIVE USURY

The more the Christian religion is restrained from usurious practices, so much the more does the perfidy of the Jews grow in these matters, so that within a short time they are exhausting the resources of Christians. Wishing therefore to see that Christians are not savagely oppressed by Jews in this matter, we ordain by this synodal decree that if Jews in future, on any pretext, extort oppressive and excessive interest from Christians, then they are to be removed from contact with Christians until they have made adequate satisfaction for the immoderate burden. Christians too, if need be, shall be compelled by ecclesiastical censure, without the possibility of an appeal, to abstain from commerce with them. We enjoin upon princes not to be hostile to Christians on this account, but rather to be zealous in restraining Jews from so great oppression. We decree, under the same penalty, that Jews shall be compelled to make satisfaction to churches for tithes and offerings due to the churches, which the churches were accustomed to receive from Christians for houses and other possessions, before they passed by whatever title to the Jews, so that the churches may thus be preserved from loss.

68 JEWS APPEARING IN PUBLIC

A difference of dress distinguishes Jews or Saracens from Christians in some provinces, but in others a certain confusion has developed so that they are indistinguishable. Whence it sometimes happens that by mistake Christians join with Jewish or Saracen women, and Jews or Saracens with Christian women. In order that the offence of such a damnable mixing may not spread further, under the excuse of a mistake of this kind, we decree that such persons of either sex, in every Christian province and at all times, are to be distinguished in public from other people by the character of their dress (seeing moreover that this was enjoined upon them by Moses himself, as we read). They shall not appear in public at all on the days of lamentation and on passion Sunday; because some of them on such days, as we have heard, do not blush to parade in very ornate dress and are not afraid to mock Christians who are presenting a memorial of the most sacred passion and are displaying signs of grief. What we most strictly forbid, however, is that they dare in any way to break out in derision of the Redeemer. We order secular princes to restrain with condign punishment those who do so presume, lest they dare to blaspheme in any way him who was crucified for us, since we ought not to ignore insults against him who blotted out our wrongdoings.

71 CRUSADE TO RECOVER THE HOLY LAND

It is our ardent desire to liberate the Holy Land from infidel hands. We therefore declare, with the approval of this sacred council and on the advice of prudent men who are fully aware of the circumstances of time and place, that crusaders are to make themselves ready so that all who have arranged to go by sea shall assemble in the kingdom of Sicily on 1 June after next: some as necessary and fitting at Brindisi and others at Messina and places neighbouring it on either side, where we too have arranged to be in person at that time, God willing, so that with our advice and help the Christian army may be in good order to set out with divine and apostolic blessing. Those who have decided to go by land should also take care to be ready by the same date. They shall notify us meanwhile so that we may grant them a suitable *legate a latere* for advice and help. Priests and other clerics who will be in the Christian army, both those under authority and prelates, shall diligently devote themselves to prayer and exhortation, teaching the crusaders by word and example to have the fear and love of God always before their eyes, so that they say or do nothing that might offend the divine majesty. If they ever fall into sin, let them quickly rise up again through true penitence. Let them be humble in heart and in body, keeping to moderation both in food and in dress, avoiding altogether dissensions and rivalries, and putting aside entirely any bitterness or envy, so that thus armed with spiritual and material weapons they may the more fearlessly fight against the enemies of the faith, relying not on their own power but rather trusting in the strength of God. We grant to these clerics that they may receive the fruits of their benefices in full for three years, as if they were resident in the churches, and if necessary they may leave them in pledge for the same time.

To prevent this holy proposal being impeded or delayed, we strictly order all prelates of churches, each in his own locality, diligently to warn and induce those who have abandoned the cross to resume it, and them and others who have taken up the cross, and those who may still do so, to carry out their vows to the Lord. And if necessary they shall compel them to do this without any backsliding, by sentences of excommunication against their persons and of interdict on their lands, excepting only those persons who find themselves faced with an impediment of such a kind that their vow deservedly ought to be commuted or deferred in accordance with the directives of the apostolic see. In order that nothing connected with this business of Jesus Christ be omitted, we will and order patriarchs, archbishops, bishops, abbots and others who have the care of souls to preach the cross zealously to those entrusted to them. Let them beseech kings, dukes, princes, margraves, counts, barons and other magnates, as well as the communities of cities, vills and towns—in the name of the Father, Son and Holy Spirit, the one, only, true and eternal God—that those who do not go in person to the aid of the Holy Land should contribute, according to their means, an appropriate number of fighting men together with their necessary expenses for three years, for the remission of their sins in accordance with what has already been explained in general letters and will be explained below for still greater assurance. We wish to share in this remission not only those who contribute ships of their own but also those who are zealous enough to build them for this purpose. To those who refuse, if there happen to be any who are so ungrateful to our lord God, we firmly declare in the name of the apostle that they should know that they will have to answer to us for this on the last day of final judgment before the fearful judge. Let them consider beforehand, however, with what conscience and with what security it was that they were able to confess before the only-begotten Son of God, Jesus Christ, to whom the Father gave all things into his hands, if in this business, which is as it were peculiarly his, they refuse to serve him who was crucified for sinners, by whose beneficence they are sustained and indeed by whose blood they have been redeemed.

Lest we appear to be laying on men's shoulders heavy and unbearable burdens which we are not willing to lighten, like those who say yes but do nothing, behold we, from what we have been able to save over and above necessities and moderate expenses, grant and give thirty thousand pounds to this work, besides the shipping which we are giving to the crusaders of Rome and neighbouring districts. We will assign for this purpose, moreover, three thousand marks of silver, which we have left over from the alms of certain of the faithful, the rest having been faithfully distributed for the needs and benefit of the aforesaid Land by the hands of the abbot patriarch of Jerusalem, of happy memory, and of the masters of the Temple and of the Hospital. We wish, however, that other prelates of churches and all clerics may participate and share both in the merit and in the reward. We therefore decree, with the general approval of the council, that all clerics, both those under authority and prelates, shall give a twentieth of their ecclesiastical revenues for three years to the aid of the Holy Land, by means of the persons appointed by the apostolic see for this purpose; the only exceptions being certain religious who are rightly to be exempted from this taxation and likewise those persons who have taken or will take the cross and so will go in person. We and our brothers, cardinals of the holy Roman church, shall pay a full tenth. Let all know, moreover, that they are obliged to observe this faithfully under pain of excommunication, so that those who knowingly deceive in this matter shall incur the sentence of excommunication. Because it is right that those who persevere in the service of the heavenly ruler should in all justice enjoy special privilege, and because the day of departure is somewhat more than a year ahead, crusaders shall therefore be exempt from taxes or levies and other burdens. We take their persons and goods under the protection of St Peter and ourself once they have taken up the cross. We ordain that they are to be protected by archbishops, bishops and all prelates of the church, and that protectors of their own are to be specially appointed for this purpose, so that their goods are to remain intact and undisturbed until they are known for certain to be dead or to have returned. If anyone dares to act contrary to this, let him be curbed by ecclesiastical censure.

If any of those setting out are bound by oath to pay interest, we ordain that their creditors shall be compelled by the same punishment to release them from their oath and to desist from exacting the interest; if any of the creditors does force them to pay the interest, we command that he be forced by similar punishment to restore it. We order that Jews be compelled by the secular power to remit interest, and that until they do so all intercourse shall be denied them by all Christ's faithful under pain of excommunication. Secular princes shall provide a suitable deferral for those who cannot now pay their debts to Jews, so that after they have undertaken the journey and until there is certain knowledge of their death or of their return, they shall not incur the inconvenience of paying interest. The Jews shall be compelled to add to the capital, after they have deducted their necessary expenses, the revenues which they are meanwhile receiving from property held by them on security. For such a benefit seems to entail not much loss, inasmuch as it postpones the repayment but does not cancel the debt. Prelates of churches who are negligent in showing justice to crusaders and their families should know that they will be severely punished.

Furthermore, since corsairs and pirates greatly impede help for the Holy Land, by capturing and plundering those who are travelling to and from it, we bind with the bond of excommunication everyone who helps or supports them. We forbid anyone, under threat of anathema, knowingly to communicate with them by contracting to buy or to sell; and we order rulers of cities and their territories to restrain and curb such persons from this iniquity. Otherwise, since to be unwilling to disquiet evildoers is none other than to encourage them, and since he who fails to oppose a manifest crime is not without a touch of secret complicity, it is our wish and command that prelates of churches exercise ecclesiastical severity against their persons and lands. We excommunicate and anathematize, moreover, those false and impious Christians who, in opposition to Christ and the Christian people, convey arms to the Saracens and iron and timber for their galleys. We decree that those who sell them galleys or ships, and those who act as pilots in pirate Saracen ships, or give them any advice or help by way of machines or anything else, to the detriment of the Holy Land, are to be punished with deprivation of their possessions and are to become the slaves of those who capture them. We order this sentence to be renewed on Sundays and feast-days in all maritime towns; and the bosom of the church is not to be opened to such persons unless they send in aid of the Holy Land the whole of the damnable wealth which they received and the same amount of their own, so that they are punished in proportion to their offence. If perchance they do not pay, they are to be punished in other ways in order that through their punishment others may be deterred from venturing upon similar rash actions. In addition, we prohibit and on pain of anathema forbid all Christians, for four years, to send or take their ships across to the lands of the Saracens who dwell in the east, so that by this a greater supply of shipping may be made ready for those wanting to cross over to help the Holy Land, and so that the aforesaid Saracens may be deprived of the not inconsiderable help which they have been accustomed to receiving from this.

Although tournaments have been forbidden in a general way on pain of a fixed penalty at various councils, we strictly forbid them to be held for three years, under pain of excommunication, because the business of the crusade is much hindered by them at this present time. Because it is of the utmost necessity for the carrying out of this business that rulers of the Christian people keep peace with each other, we therefore ordain, on the advice of this Holy general synod, that peace be generally kept in the whole Christian world for at least four years, so that those in conflict shall be brought by the prelates of churches to conclude a definitive peace or to observe inviolably a firm truce. Those who refuse to comply shall be most strictly compelled to do so by an excommunication against their persons and an interdict on their lands, unless their wrongdoing is so great that they ought not to enjoy peace. If it happens that they make light of the church's censure, they may deservedly fear that the secular power will be invoked by ecclesiastical authority against them as disturbers of the business of him who was crucified.

We therefore, trusting in the mercy of almighty God and in the authority of the blessed apostles Peter and Paul, do grant, by the power of binding and loosing that God has conferred upon us, albeit unworthy, unto all those who undertake this work in person and at their own expense, full pardon for their sins about which they are heartily contrite and have spoken in confession, and we promise them an increase of eternal life at the recompensing of the just; also to those who do not go there in person but send suitable men at their own expense, according to their means and status, and likewise to those who go in person but at others' expense, we grant full pardon for their sins. We wish and grant to share in this remission, according to the quality of their help and the intensity of their devotion, all who shall contribute suitably from their goods to the aid of the said Land or who give useful advice and help. Finally, this general synod imparts the benefit of its blessings to all who piously set out on this common enterprise in order that it may contribute worthily to their salvation.

English Civil Liberties

1215

The *Magna Carta* (or "Great Charter") sets out the rights granted by King John of England to the English barons on June 15, 1215, and is considered the basis of English constitutional liberties. A number of political events, including high taxes and abuses of power, led the English barons to draw up a charter protecting their rights against royal authority. When John refused to sign it, the barons captured London, forcing John to meet them at Runnymede to sign and seal the charter. The *Magna Carta* is important because it details, for the first time, the relative powers of the king and the barons. In order to regularize the judicial system, it sets up the Courts of Common Pleas, rules for court procedures, and standard penalties. The historical basis for English civil liberties is contained in the statement: "No freeman shall be taken and imprisoned or disseized or exiled or in any way destroyed, nor shall we go upon him nor send upon him, except by the lawful judgment of his peers and by the law of the land." Rules for commerce were also established, including standardized measures and rights for foreign merchants. The *Magna Carta* was thus the basis of later freedoms. In the early seventeenth century, despite some who argued that the charter applied only to a compact between the king and the barons, members of Parliament interpreted it to include all freemen. The charter was buttressed in 1628 by the Petition of Right and in 1689 by the Bill of Rights, confirming parliamentary superiority over the Crown.

What basic freedoms do you see reflected in the *Magna Carta* that have become part of America's fundamental liberties? What hierarchies are reflected in the charter? Have these changed or remained constant into the twentieth century?

from the *Magna Carta*

THE GREAT CHARTER OF ENGLISH LIBERTY
Decreed by King John at Runnymede

June 15, A.D. 1215

John, by the grace of God, King of England, Lord of Ireland, Duke of Normandy and Aquitaine, and Count of Anjou:

To the archbishops, bishops, abbots, earls, barons, justices, foresters, sheriffs, prevosts, serving men, and to all his bailiffs and faithful subjects, Greeting. Know that we, by the will of God and for the safety of our soul, and of the souls of all our predecessors and our heirs, to the honor of God and for the exaltation of the holy Church, and the bettering of our realm: by the counsel of our venerable fathers Stephen Archbishop of Canterbury, primate of all England and cardinal of the holy Roman church; of Henry Archbishop of Dublin; of the bishops William of London, Peter of Winchester, Jocelin of Bath and Glastonbury, Hugo of Lincoln, Walter of Worcester, William of Coventry and Benedict of Rochester; of master Pandulf, subdeacon and of the household of the Lord Pope; of brother Aymeric, master of the knights of the Temple in England; and of the noble men . . . and others of our faithful subjects:

1 First of all have granted to God, and, for us and for our heirs forever, have confirmed, by this our present charter, that the English church shall be free and shall have its rights intact and its liberties uninfringed upon. And thus we will that it be observed. As is apparent from the fact that we, spontaneously and of our own free will, before discord broke out between ourselves and our barons, did grant and by our charter confirm—and did cause the Lord Pope Innocent III, to confirm—freedom of elections, which is considered most important and most necessary to the church of England. Which charter both we ourselves shall observe, and we will that it be observed with good faith by our heirs forever. We have also granted to all free men of our realm, on the part of ourselves and our heirs forever, all the subjoined liberties, to have and to hold, to them and to their heirs, from us and from our heirs:

2 If any one of our earls or barons, or of others holding from us in chief through military service, shall die; and if, at the time of his death, his heir be of full age and owe a relief: he shall have his inheritance by paying the old relief;—the heir, namely, or the heirs of an earl, by paying one hundred pounds for the whole barony of an earl; the heir or heirs of a baron, by paying one hundred pounds for the whole barony; the heir or heirs of a knight, by paying one hundred shillings at most for a whole knight's fee; and he who shall owe less shall give less, according to the ancient custom of fees.

3 But if the heir of any of the above persons shall be under age and in wardship,—when he comes of age he shall have his inheritance without relief and without fine.

7 A widow, after the death of her husband, shall straightway, and without difficulty, have her marriage portion and her inheritance, nor shall she give any thing in return for her dowry, her marriage portion, or the inheritance which belonged to her, and which she and her husband held on the day of the death of that husband. And she may remain in the house of her husband, after his death, for forty days; within which her dowry shall be paid over to her.

8 No widow shall be forced to marry when she prefers to live without a husband; so, however, that she gives security not to marry without our consent, if she hold from us, or the consent of the lord from whom she holds, if she hold from another.

9 Neither we nor our bailiffs shall seize any revenue for any debt, so long as the chattels of the debtor suffice to pay the debt; nor shall the sponsors of that debtor be distrained so long as the chief debtor has enough to pay the debt. But if the chief debtor fail in paying the debt, not having the wherewithal to pay it, the sponsors shall answer for the debt. And, if they shall wish, they may have the lands and revenues of the debtor until satisfaction shall have been given them for the debt previously paid for him; unless the chief debtor shall show that he is quit in that respect towards those same sponsors.

12 No scutage or aid shall be imposed in our realm unless by the common counsel of our realm; except for redeeming our body, and knighting our eldest son, and marrying once our eldest daughter. And for these purposes there shall only be given a reasonable aid. In like manner shall be done concerning the aids of the city of London.

13 And the city of London shall have all its old liberties and free customs as well by land as by water. Moreover we will and grant that other cities and burroughs, and towns and ports, shall have all their liberties and free customs.

30 No sheriff nor bailiff of ours, no any one else, shall take the horses or carts of any freeman for transport, unless by the will of that freeman.

31 Neither we nor our bailiffs shall take another's wood for castles or for other private uses, unless by the will of him to whom the wood belongs.

35 There shall be one measure of wine throughout our whole realm, and one measure of ale and one measure of corn—namely, the London quart;—and one width of dyed and resset and hauberk cloths—namely, two ells below the selvage. And with weights, moreover, it shall be as with measures.

38 No baliff, on his own simple assertion, shall henceforth put any one to his law, without producing faithful witnesses in evidence.

39 No freeman shall be taken, or imprisoned, or disseized, or outlawed, or exiled, or in any way harmed—nor will we go upon or send upon him—save by the lawful judgment of his peers or by the law of the land.

54 No one shall be taken or imprisoned on account of the appeal of a woman concerning the death of another than her husband.

60 Moreover all the subjects of our realm, clergy as well as laity, shall, as far as pertains to them, observe, with regard to their vassals, all these aforesaid customs and liberties which we have decreed shall, as far as pertains to us, be observed in our realm with regard to our own.

63 Wherefore we will and firmly decree that the English church shall be free, and that the subjects of our realm shall have and hold all the aforesaid liberties, rights and concessions, duly and in peace, freely and quietly, fully and entirely, for themselves and their heirs, from us and our heirs, in all matters and in all places, forever, as has been said. Moreover it has been sworn, on our part as well as on the part of the barons, that all these above mentioned provisions shall be observed with good faith and without evil intent. The witnesses being the above mentioned and many others. Given through our hand, in the plain called Runnymede between Windsor and Stanes, on the fifteenth day of June, in the seventeenth year of our reign.

St. Thomas Aquinas

c.1225-1274

Thomas d'Aquino was born into a family of minor nobility at Roccasecca in Italy. He began his formal studies at the Benedictine monastery founded by St. Benedict at Monte Cassino, but around the age of fifteen he encountered members of the recently established Dominican order. Like the Franciscans, the Dominicans emphasized poverty and reform, and over the objections of his family Thomas joined the order and subsequently continued his education in Paris and Cologne. In 1256 Thomas and his great contemporary, St. Bonaventure, were appointed to the teaching faculty at Paris. Soon after this the young Dominican undertook his first work of theology, the *Summa contra Gentiles.* His greatest intellectual product, the enormously influential *Summa Theologiae*, appeared before his death at the age of 49.

In its most recent Latin and English edition, the *Summa Theologiae* contains 60 volumes. Originally delivered as university lectures, it is a challenging work of synthesis, an attempt to integrate the knowledge of what we would call separate disciplines—theology, philosophy, law psychology, even physics—into a single unified system whose author is a benevolent God. Obviously a prolific writer, Aquinas was also the foremost scholastic (or university teacher) of the High Middle Ages. As a Christian, Aquinas believed that God had revealed himself to sinful humanity through scripture and in the life of Jesus. But as a student in Cologne, Aquinas came under the influence of Albert the Great, whose enthusiasm for the works of the pagan philosopher, Aristotle, Thomas grew to share. In the *Summa Theologiae* the influence of Aristotelian thought is unmistakable. For Aquinas, natural reason and the disciplined employment of logic can secure for humankind some knowledge of God and of God's creation. But ultimately men and women must turn to revelation for truths about God which are simply beyond the compass of a human will and understanding which have been clouded by the taint of original sin.

In the selections contained here, St. Thomas addresses a large and perennial issue: God's perfection and humankind's resemblance to God. He also discusses two more specific and perhaps culturally conditioned issues: the nature of women and the problem of usury (lending money at interest). What is Aquinas's estimate of human nature in the first selection, and how might it be different from an earlier view put forward by St. Augustine at the start of our course? What conclusions does he draw about the nature of women and the practice of usury, and what evidence does he enlist in support of his arguments? Recalling Humanities 124, what is "Aristotelian" about Aquinas's method in the *Summa Theologiae?*

from *Summa Theologiae*

Third Article
Whether God Exists?

We proceed thus to the third Article:

Objection I. It seems that God does not exist; because if one of two contraries be infinite, the other would be altogether destroyed. But the name God means that He is infinite goodness. If, therefore, God existed, there would be no evil discoverable; but there is evil in the world. Therefore God does not exist.

Objection 2. Further, it is superfluous to suppose that what can be accounted for by a few principles has been produced by many. But it seems that everything we see in the world can be accounted for by other principles, supposing God did not exist. For all natural things can be reduced to one principle, which is nature; and all voluntary things can be reduced to one principle, which is human reason, or will. Therefore there is no need to suppose God's existence.

On the contrary, It is said in the person of God: "I am Who I am." (Exod. iii 14).

I answer that, The existence of God can be proved in five ways.

The first and more manifest way is the argument from motion. It is certain, and evident to our senses, that in the world some things are in motion. Now whatever is moved is moved by another, for nothing can be moved except it is in potentiality to that towards which it is moved; whereas a thing moves inasmuch as it is in act. For motion is nothing else than the reduction of something from potentiality to actuality. But nothing can be reduced from potentiality to actuality, except by something in a state of actuality. Thus that which is actually hot, as fire, makes wood, which is potentially hot, to be actually hot, and thereby moves and changes it. Now it is not possible that the same thing should be at once in actuality and potentiality in the same respect, but only in different respects. For what is actually hot cannot simultaneously be potentially hot; but it is simultaneously potentially cold. It is therefore impossible that in the same respect and in the same way a thing should be both mover and moved, i.e., that it should move itself. Therefore, whatever is moved must be moved by another. If that by which it is moved be itself moved, then this also must needs be moved by another, and that by another again. But this cannot go on to infinity, because then there would be no first mover, and, consequently, no other mover, seeing that subsequent movers move only inasmuch as they are moved by the first mover; as the staff moves only because it is moved by the hand. Therefore it is necessary to arrive at a first mover, moved by no other; and this everyone understands to be God.

The second way is from the nature of efficient cause. In the world of sensible things we find there is an order of efficient causes. There is no cause known (neither is it, indeed, possible) in which a thing is found to be the efficient cause of itself; for so it would be prior to itself, which is impossible. Now in efficient causes it is not possible to go on to infinity, because in all efficient causes following in order, the first is the cause of the intermediate cause, and the intermediate is the cause of the ultimate cause, whether the intermediate cause be several, or one only. Now to take away the cause is to take away the effect. Therefore, if there be no first cause among efficient causes, there will be no ultimate, nor any intermediate, cause. But if in efficient causes it is possible to go on to infinity, there will be no first efficient cause, neither will there be an ultimate effect, nor any intermediate efficient causes; all of which is plainly false. Therefore it is necessary to admit a first efficient cause, to which everyone gives the name of God.

The third way is taken from possibility and necessity, and runs thus. We find in nature things that are possible to be and not to be, since they are found to be generated, and to be corrupted, and consequently, it is possible for them to be and not to be. But it is impossible for these always to exist, for that which can not-be at some time is not. Therefore, if everything can not-be, then at one time there was nothing in existence. Now if this were true, even now there would be nothing in existence, because that which does not exist begins to exist only through something already existing. Therefore, if at one time nothing was in existence, it would have been impossible for anything to have begun to exist; and thus even now nothing would be in existence—which is absurd. Therefore, not all beings are merely possible, but there must exist something the existence of which is necessary. But every necessary thing either has its necessity caused by another, or not. Now it is impossible to go on to infinity in necessary things which have their necessity caused by another, as has been already proved in regard to efficient causes. Therefore we cannot but admit the existence of some being having of itself its own necessity, and not receiving it from another, but rather causing in others their necessity. This all men speak of as God.

The fourth way is taken from the gradation to be found in things. Among beings there are some more and some less good, true, noble, and the like. But *more* and *less* are predicated of different things according as they resemble in their different ways something which is the maximum, as a thing is said to be hotter according as it more nearly resembles that which is hottest; so that there is something which is truest, something best, something noblest, and, consequently, something which is most being, for those things that are greatest in truth are greatest in being, as it is written in Metaph. ii. Now the maximum in any genus is the cause of all in that genus, as fire, which is the maximum of heat, is the cause of all hot things, as is said in the same book. Therefore there must also be something which is to all beings the cause of their being, goodness, and every other perfection; and this we call God.

The fifth way is taken from the governance of the world. We see that things which lack knowledge, such as natural bodies, act for an end, and this is evident from their acting always, or nearly always, in the same way, so as to obtain the best result. Hence it is plain that they achieve their end not fortuitously, but designedly. Now whatever lacks knowledge cannot move towards an end, unless it be directed by some being endowed with knowledge and intelligence; as the arrow is directed by the archer. Therefore some intelligent being exists by whom all natural things are directed to their end; and this being we call God.

Reply Objection 1. As Augustine says: "Since God is the highest good, He would not allow any evil to exist in His works, unless His omnipotence and goodness were such as to bring good even out of evil." This is part of the infinite goodness of God, that He should allow evil to exist, and out of it produce good.

Reply Objection 2. Since nature works for a determinate end under the direction of a higher agent, whatever is done by nature must be traced back to God as to its first cause. So likewise whatever is done voluntarily must be traced back to some higher cause other than human reason and will, since these can change and fail; for all things that are changeable and capable of defect must be traced back to an immovable and self-necessary first principle, as has been shown.

ON THE CAUSE OF SIN, IN SO FAR AS ONE SIN IS THE CAUSE OF ANOTHER
In Four Articles

We must now consider the cause of sin, in so far as one sin is the cause of another. Under this head there are four points of inquiry: (1) Whether covetousness is the root of all sins? (2) Whether pride is the beginning of every sin? (3) Whether other special sins should be called capital vices, besides pride and covetousness? (4) How many capital vices there are, and which are they?

First Article
WHETHER COVETOUSNESS IS THE ROOT OF ALL SINS?

We proceed thus to the First Article:
Objection 1. It would seem that covetousness is not the root of all sins. For covetousness, which is an immoderate desire for riches, is opposed to the virtue of liberality. But liberality is not the root of all virtues. Therefore covetousness is not the root of all sins.

Objection 2. Further, the desire for the means proceeds from the desire for the end. Now riches, the desire for which is called covetousness, are not desired except as being useful for some end, as is stated in *Ethics* I. Therefore covetousness is not the root of all sins, but proceeds from some deeper root.

Objection 3. Further, it often happens that avarice, which is another name for covetousness, arises from other sins; as when a man desires money through ambition, or in order to sate his gluttony. Therefore it is not the root of all sins.

"On the contrary," the Apostle says (I Tim. vi. 10): "The desire of money is the root of all evil."

I answer that, According to some, covetousness may be understood in three ways.

First, as denoting inordinate desire for riches; and thus it is a special sin. Secondly, as denoting inordinate desire for any temporal good; and thus it is a genus comprising all sins, because every sin includes an inordinate turning to a mutable good, as was stated above. Thirdly, as denoting an inclination of a corrupt nature to desire corruptible goods inordinately; and they say that in this sense covetousness is the root of all sins, comparing it to the root of a tree, which draws its sustenance from the earth, just as every sin grows out of the love of temporal things.

Now, though all this is true, it does not seem according to the mind of the Apostle when he states that covetousness is the root of all sins. For in that passage he clearly speaks against those who, because they "will become rich, fall into temptation, and into the snare of the devil for covetousness is the root of all evils." Hence it is evident that he is speaking of covetousness as denoting the inordinate desire for riches. Accordingly, we must say that covetousness, as denoting a special sin, is called the root of all sins, in likeness to the root of a tree, in furnishing sustenance to the whole tree. For we see that by riches a man acquires the means of committing any sin whatever, and of sating his desire for any sin whatever, since money helps a man to obtain all manner of temporal goods, according to Eccles. x. 19: "All things obey money." Hence, in this sense the desire for riches is the root of all sins.

Reply Objection 1. Virtue and sin do not arise from the same source. For sin arises from the desire of a mutable good; and consequently the desire of that good which helps one to obtain all temporal goods is called the root of all sins. But virtue arises from the desire for the immutable Good; and consequently charity, which is the love of God, is called the root of the virtues, according to Ephes. iii. 17: "Rooted and founded in charity."

Reply Objection 2. The desire for money is said to be the root of sins, not as though riches were sought for their own sake, as being the last end, but because they are much sought after as useful for any temporal end. And since a universal good is more desirable than a particular good, it moves the appetite more than any individual goods, which along with many others can be procured by means of money.

Reply Objection 3. Just as in natural things we do not aim at knowing what always happens, but what happens most frequently, for the reason that the nature of corruptible things can be hindered so as not to act always in the same way, so also in moral matters we consider what happens in the majority of cases, not what happens invariably, for the reason that the will does not act of necessity. So when we say that covetousness is the root of all evils, we do not assert that no other evil can be its root, but that other evils more frequently arise from it, for the reason given.

Second Article
Whether Pride is the Beginning of Every Sin?

We proceed thus to the Second Article:

Objection 1. It would seem that pride is not the beginning of every sin. For the root is a beginning of a tree, so that the beginning of a sin seems to be the same as the root of sin. Now covetousness is the root of every sin, as was stated above. Therefore it is also the beginning of every sin, and not pride.

Objection 2. Further, it is written (Ecclus. x. 14): "The beginning of the pride of man is apostasy from God." But apostasy from God is a sin. Therefore another sin is the beginning of pride, so that the latter is not the beginning of every sin.

Objection 3. Further, the beginning of every sin would seem to be that which causes all sins. Now this is inordinate self-love, which according to Augustine, "builds up the city of Babylon." Therefore self-love, and not pride, is the beginning of every sin.

On the contrary, It is written (Ecclus. x. 15): "Pride is the beginning of all sin."
I answer that, Some say that pride is to be taken in three ways.

First, as denoting inordinate desire to excel: and thus it is a special sin. Secondly, as denoting actual contempt of God, in so far as this means that they are not subject to His commandment; and thus, they say, it is a generic sin. Thirdly, as denoting an inclination to this contempt, owing to the corruption of nature; and in this sense they say that it is the beginning of every sin, and that it differs from covetousness, because covetousness regards sin as turning towards the mutable good by which sin is, as it were, nourished and fostered (for which reason covetousness is called the *root*), whereas pride regards sin as turning away from God, to Whose commandment man refuses to be subject (for which reason it is called the *beginning*, because the beginning of evil consists in turning away from God).

Now though all this is true, nevertheless, it is not according to the mind of the wise man who said, "Pride is the beginning of all sin." For it is evident that he is speaking of pride as denoting inordinate desire to excel, as is clear from what follows (verse 17): "God hath overturned the thrones of proud princes"; indeed, this is the point of nearly the whole chapter. We must therefore say that pride, even as denoting a special sin, is the beginning of every sin. For we must note that, in voluntary actions, such as sins, there is a twofold order, namely, of intention and of execution. In the former order, the principle is the end, as we have stated many times before. Now man's end in acquiring all temporal goods is that, through their means, he may have some distinction perfection and excellence. Therefore, from this point of view, pride, which is the desire to excel, is said to be the beginning of every sin.—On the other hand, in the order of execution, the first place belongs to that which, by furnishing the opportunity of fulfilling all desires of sin, has the character of a root; and such are riches. Hence, from this point of view, covetousness is said to be the root of all evils, as we have stated above.

This suffices for the Reply to the First Objection.
Reply Objection 2. Apostasy from God is stated to be the beginning of pride in so far as it denotes a turning away from God; because, from the fact that man wishes not to be subject to God, it follows that he desires inordinately his own excellence in temporal things. Therefore, in the passage quoted, apostasy from God does not denote the special sin, but rather that general condition of every sin, consisting in a turning away from the immutable good.—It may also be said that apostasy from God is said to be the beginning of pride because it is the first species of pride. For it is characteristic of pride to be unwilling to be subject to any superior, and especially to God; and from this it happens that a man is unduly lifted up in relation to the other species of pride.

Reply Objection 3. In desiring to excel, man loves himself, for to love oneself is the same as to desire some good for oneself. Consequently, it amounts to the same whether we reckon pride or self-love as the beginning of every evil.

Fourth Article
WHETHER THE SEVEN CAPITAL VICES ARE SUITABLY RECKONED?

We proceed thus to the Fourth Article:
Objection 1. It would seem that we ought not to reckon seven capital vices, viz., vainglory, envy, anger, covetousness, sloth, gluttony, lust. For sins are opposed to virtues. But there are four principal virtues, as was stated above. Therefore there are only four principal or capital vices.

Objection 2. Further, the passions of the Soul are causes of sin, as was stated above. But there are four principal passions of the soul, two of which, viz., hope and fear, are not mentioned among the above sins, whereas certain vices are mentioned to which pleasure and sadness belong, since pleasure belongs to gluttony and lust, and sadness to sloth and envy. Therefore the principal sins are unfittingly enumerated.

Objection 3. Further, anger is not a principal passion. Therefore it should not be placed among the principal vices.

Objection 4. Further, just as covetousness or avarice is the root of sin, so pride is the beginning of sin, as was stated above. But avarice is reckoned to be one of the capital vices. Therefore pride also should be placed among the capital vices.

Objection 5. Further, some sins are committed which cannot be caused through any of these, as, for instance, when one sins through ignorance, or when one commits a sin with a good intention, e.g., steals in order to give an alms. Therefore the capital vices are insufficiently enumerated.

On the contrary stands the authority of Gregory who enumerates them in this way.

I answer that, As was stated above, the capital vices are those which give rise to others, especially in the manner of a final cause. Now this kind of origin may take place in two ways.

First, because of the condition of the sinner, who is so disposed as to have a strong inclination for one particular end, with the result that he frequently goes forward to other sins. But this kind of origin does not come under the consideration of art, because man's particular dispositions are infinite in number.—Secondly, because of a natural relationship of the ends to one another; and it is in this way that most frequently one vice arises from another, so that this kind of origin can come under the consideration of art.

Accordingly, therefore, those vices are called capital whose ends have certain fundamental modes of moving the appetite; and it is in respect of these fundamental modes that the capital vices are differentiated. Now a thing moves the appetite in two ways. First, directly and of its very nature. Thus, good moves the appetite to seek it, while evil, for the same reason, moves the appetite to avoid it. Secondly, indirectly and because of something else, as it were. Thus one seeks an evil because of some attendant good, or avoids a good because of some attendant evil.

Now man's good is threefold. For, in the first place, there is a certain good of the soul, which derives its aspect of appetibility merely through being apprehended, viz., the excellence of honor and praise; and this good is sought inordinately by vainglory. Secondly, there is the good of the body, and this pertains either to the preservation of the individual, e.g., meat and drink, which good is pursued inordinately by gluttony,—or the preservation of the species, e.g., sexual intercourse, which good is sought inordinately by lust. Thirdly, there is external good, viz., riches, to which covetousness is directed. These same four vices avoid inordinately the contrary evils.

Or, again, the good moves the appetite chiefly through possessing some property of happiness, which all men seek naturally. Now, in the first place, it is of the nature of happiness to contain perfection, since happiness is a perfect good, to which belongs excellence or renown, that is desired by pride or vainglory. Secondly, it is of the nature of happiness to contain satiety, which covetousness seeks in riches that give promise thereof. Thirdly, it is of its nature to contain pleasure, without which happiness is impossible, as is stated in *Ethics i* and *x*., and this gluttony and lust pursue.

On the other hand, the avoidance of good because of an attendant evil occurs in two ways. For this happens either in respect of one's own good, and thus we have sloth, which is sadness about one's spiritual good because of the attendant bodily labor; or else it happens in respect of another's good, and this, if it be without recrimination, belongs to envy, which is sadness about another's good as being a hindrance to one's own excellence, while if it be with recrimination with a view to vengeance, it is anger. Furthermore, these same vices attack the contrary evils.

Reply Objection 1. Virtue and vice do not originate in the same way, since virtue is caused by the subordination of the appetite to reason, or to the immutable good, which is God, whereas vice arises from the appetite for a mutable good. Therefore there is no need for the principal vices to be contrary to the principal virtues.

Reply Objection 2. Fear and hope are irascible passions. Now all the passions of the irascible part arise from the passions of the concupiscible part; and these are all, in a way, directed to pleasure or sorrow. Hence pleasure and sorrow have a prominent place among the capital sins, as being the most important of the passions, as was stated above.

Reply Objection 3. Although anger is not a principal passion, yet it has a distinct place among the capital vices because it implies a special kind of movement in the appetite, in so far as one attacks the good of another as though to do so were a virtuous good, i.e., as though to do so were a vindication of justice.

Reply Objection 4. Pride is said to be the beginning of every sin according to the nature of an end, as was stated above; and it is according to the same nature of an end, that we are to consider the capital sin as being principal. Therefore pride is not counted along with the others as a universal vice, but is reckoned as the "queen of them all," as Gregory states. But "covetousness is said to be the root from another point of view," as we have stated above.

Reply Objection 5. These vices are called capital because others arise from them most frequently; so that nothing prevents some sins from arising out of other causes—Nevertheless, we might say that all the sins which are due to ignorance can be reduced to sloth, to which pertains the negligence by which a man refuses to acquire spiritual goods because of the attendant labor; for the ignorance that can cause sin is due to negligence, as we have stated above. As for the fact that a man commits a sin with a good intention, this seems to point to ignorance, in so far as he does not know that evils should not be done that good may come of them.

QUESTION XCII

IN SO FAR AS ONE SIN IS THE CAUSE OF ANOTHER
In Four Articles

We must next consider the production of the woman. Under this head there are four points of inquiry: (1) Whether woman should have been made in the first production of things? (2) Whether woman should have been made from man? (3) Whether of man's rib? (4) Whether woman was made immediately by God?

First Article
WHETHER WOMAN SHOULD HAVE BEEN MADE IN THE FIRST PRODUCTION OF THINGS?

We proceed thus to the First Article:

Objection 1. It would seem that woman should not have been made in the first production of things. For the Philosopher says that "the female is misbegotten male." But nothing misbegotten or defective should have been made in the first production of things. Therefore woman should not have made at that first production.

Objection 2. Further, subjection and limitation were a result of sin, for to the woman was it said after sin (Gen. iii. 16): "Thou shalt be under the man's power"; and Gregory says that, "Where there is no sin, there is no inequality." But woman is naturally of less strength and dignity than man, "for the agent is always more honorable than the patient," as Augustine says. Therefore woman should not have been made in the first production of things before sin.

Objection 3. Further, occasions of sin should be cut off. But God foresaw that "woman" would be an occasion of sin to man. Therefore He should not have made woman.

On the contrary, It is written (Gen. ii. 18): "It is not good for man to be alone; let us make him a helper like to himself."

I answer that, It was necessary for woman to be made, as the Scripture says as a helper to man; not, indeed, as a helpmate in other works, as some say, since man can be more efficiently helped by another man in other works; but as a helper in the work of generation. This can be made clear if we observe the mode of generation carried out in various living things.

Some living things do not possess in themselves the power of generation, but are generated by an agent of another species; and such are those plants and animals which are generated, without seed, from suitable matter through the active power of the heavenly bodies. Others possess the active and passive generative power together, as we see in plants which are generated from seed. For the noblest vital function in plants is generation, and so we observe that in these the active power of generation invariably accompanies the passive power. Among perfect animals, the active power of generation belongs to the male sex, and the passive power to the female. And as among animals there is a vital operation nobler than generation, to which their life is principally directed, so it happens that the male sex is not found in continual union with the female in perfect animals, but only at the time of coition; so that we may consider that by coition the male and female are one, as in plants they are always united, even though in some cases one of them preponderates, and in some the other. But man is further ordered to a still nobler work of life, and that is intellectual operation. Therefore there was greater reason for the distinction of these two powers in man; so that the female should be produced separately from the male, and yet that they should be carnally united for generation. Therefore directly after the formation of woman, it was said: "And they shall be two in one flesh" (Gen. ii.24).

Reply Objection 1. As regards the individual nature, woman is defective and misbegotten, for the active power in the male seed tends to the production of a perfect likeness according to the masculine sex; while the production of woman comes from defect in the active power, or from some material indisposition, or even from some external influence such as that of a south wind, which is moist, as the Philosopher observes. On the other hand, as regards universal human nature, woman is not misbegotten, but is included in nature's intention as directed to the work of generation. Now the universal intention of nature depends on God, Who is the universal Author of nature. Therefore, in producing nature, God formed not only the male but also the female.

Reply Objection 2. Subjection is twofold. One is servile, by virtue of which a superior makes use of a subject for his own benefit; and this kind of subjection began after sin. There is another kind of subjection, which is called economic or civil, whereby the superior makes use of his subjects for their own benefit and good; and this kind of subjection existed even before sin. For the good of order would have been wanting in the human family if some were not governed by others wiser than themselves. So by such a kind subjection woman is naturally subject to man, because in man the discernment of reason predominates. Nor is inequality among men excluded by the state of innocence, as we shall prove.

Reply Objection 3. If God had deprived the world of all those things which proved an occasion of sin, the universe would have been imperfect. Nor was it fitting for the common good to be destroyed in order that individual evil might be avoided; especially as God is so powerful that He can direct any evil to a good end.

Second Article
WHETHER WOMAN SHOULD HAVE BEEN MADE FROM MAN?

We proceed thus to the Second Article:
Objection I. It would seem that woman should not have been made from man. For sex belongs both to man and animals. But in the other animals the female was not made from the male. Therefore neither should it have been so with man.

Objection 2. Further, things of the same species are of the same matter. But male and female are of the same species. Therefore, as man was made of the slime of the earth, so woman should have been made of the same, and not from man.

Objection 3. Further, woman was made to be a helpmate to man in the work of generation. But close relationship makes a person unfit for that office; and hence near relations are debarred from intermarriage, as is written (Lev xviii. 6). Therefore woman should not have been made from man.

On the contrary, It is written (Ecce. xvii. 5): "He created of him," that is, out of man, "a helpmate like to himself," that is, woman.

I answer that, When all things were first made, it was more suitable for woman to be formed from man than for this to happen in other animals.

First, in order thus to give the first man a certain dignity consisting in this, that as God is the principle of the whole universe, so the first man, in likeness to God, was the principle of the whole human race. Hence Paul says that "God made the whole human race from one" (Acts xvii. 26). Secondly, that man might love woman all the more, and cleave to her more closely, knowing her to be fashioned from himself. Hence it is written (Gen. ii. 23, 34): "She was taken out of man, wherefore a man shall leave father and mother, and shall cleave to his wife." This was most necessary in the human species, in which the male and female live together for life; which is not the case with other animals. Thirdly, because, as the Philosopher says, the human male and female are united, not only for generation, as with other animals, but also for the purpose of domestic life, in which each has his or her particular duty, and in which the man is the head of the woman. Therefore it was suitable for the woman to be made out of man, as out of her principle. Fourthly, there is a sacramental reason for this. For by this is signified that the Church takes her origin from Christ. Therefore the Apostle says (Ephes.v 32): "This is a great sacrament; but I speak in Christ and the Church."

Reply Objection 1 is clear from the foregoing.

Reply Objection 2. Matter is that from which something is made. Now created nature has a determinate principle, and since it is determined to one thing, it also has a determinate mode of proceeding. Therefore from determinate matter it produces something in a determinate species. On the other hand, the divine power, being infinite, can produce things of the same species out of any matter, such as a man from the slime of the earth, and a woman from a man.

Reply Objection 3. A certain affinity arises from natural generation, and this is an impediment to matrimony. Woman, however, was not produced from man by natural generation, but by the divine power alone. Hence Eve is not called the daughter of Adam. And so this argument does not prove.

ORIGINS OF HIGHER EDUCATION

Perhaps the greatest legacy of the Middle Ages has been the university. Of course, there were great centers of higher learning in Damascus, Baghdad, Fez, and Timbuktu, long before the rise of European universities in the late 1100s and early 1200s. But the term 'university' has a specific meaning, the rough connotation of which is 'guild' or 'trade union.' The distinctive feature of a medieval university was that teachers and students were granted certain privileges of self-government by both civil and ecclesiastical authorities. One of the privileges of the masters was the authority to determine who would be awarded a license to teach, i.e. receive a "degree," and "commence to teach." The masters also had the privilege of determining whether a program of studies undertaken at one center would be credited at another institution. This practice, of institutions recognizing work completed elsewhere, is why it is difficult, if not impossible, to state which university was the first (even though the University of Bologna usually claims the title).

The following readings are taken from documents of the university in Paris. The first of these, from 1215, provides an early look at how studies were organized at the university. Notice that in 1215 the papal legate wrote that at Paris Aristotle's logic was to be taught, but his natural philosophy and metaphysics were not. The second, from 1269, indicates that the behavior of students ('scholars' in the text) was a problem from the very beginning. The third, from Alvarus Pelagius, criticizes the behavior and practices of professors. The fourth demands that teachers lecture at a speed too rapid for students comfortably to copy the lecture. The fifth passage, from the documents of the university in Paris, comes from a council of bishops in 1210. Notice the attitude toward Aristotle. The sixth reading, from Pope Gregory IX in 1231, modified the papal position on reading Aristotle. Aristotle's works were to be expurgated before they were read in the universities. A commission was appointed to expurgate Aristotle, but it never completed its work. By 1255 all the books of Aristotle, formerly condemned in their original, unexpurgated form, were listed as required readings at Paris, as is indicated in the last selection.

The reception of Aristotle in the European universities thus had a stormy history. The problem was that some points of Aristotle's science (e.g., the "cosmos" did not have a beginning and was thus eternal) seemed to conflict with the orthodox faith of Islam and Christianity, both of which maintained that God created the cosmos in time. The stage was set for one of the classic conflicts between science and religion.

Readings on the Rise of the Universities

RULES OF THE UNIVERSITY OF PARIS, 1215

Robert, servant of the cross of Christ by divine pity cardinal priest of the title, St. Stephen in Mons Caelius, legate of the apostolic see, to all the masters and scholars of Paris eternal greeting in the Lord. Let all know that, since we have had a special mandate from the Pope to take effective measures to reform the state of the Parisian scholars for the better, wishing with the counsel of good men to provide for the tranquillity of the scholars in the future, we have decreed and ordained in this wise:

No one shall lecture in the arts at Paris before he is twenty-one years of age, and he shall have heard lectures for at least six years before he begins to lecture, and he shall promise to lecture for at least two years, unless a reasonable cause prevents, which he ought to prove publicly or before examiners. He shall not be stained by any infamy, and when he is ready to lecture, he shall be examined according to the form which is contained in the writing of the lord bishop of Paris, where is contained the peace confirmed between the chancellor and scholars by judges delegated by the pope, namely, by the bishop and dean of Troyes and by P., the bishop and J., the chancellor of Paris approved and confirmed. And they shall lecture on the books of Aristotle on dialectic old and new in the schools ordinarily and not *ad cursum*. They shall also lecture on both Priscians ordinarily, or at least on one. They shall not lecture on feast days except on philosophers and rhetoric and the quadrivium and *Barbarismus* and ethics, if it please them, and the fourth book of the *Topics*. They shall not lecture on the books of Aristotle on metaphysics and natural philosophy or on summaries of them or concerning the doctrine of master David of Dinant or the heretic Amaury or Mauritius of Spain.

In the *principia* and meetings of the masters and in the responsions or oppositions of the boys and youths there shall be no drinking. They may summon some friends or associates, but only a few. Donations of clothing or other things as has been customary, or more, we urge should be made, especially to the poor. None of the masters lecturing in arts shall have a cope except one round, black and reaching to the ankles, at least while it is new. Use of the pallium is permitted. No one shall wear with the round cope shoes that are ornamented or with elongated pointed toes. If any scholar in arts or theology dies, half of the masters of arts shall attend the funeral at one time, the other half the next time, and no one shall leave until the sepulture is finished, unless he has reasonable cause. If any master in arts or theology dies, all the masters shall keep vigils, each shall read or cause to be read the Psalter, each shall attend the church where is celebrated the watch until midnight or the greater part of the night, unless reasonable cause prevent. On the day when the master is buried, no one shall lecture or dispute.

We fully confirm to them the meadow of St. Germain in that condition in which it was adjudicated to them.

Each master shall have jurisdiction over his scholar. No one shall occupy a classroom or house without asking the consent of the tenant, provided one has a chance to ask it. No one shall receive the licentiate from the chancellor or another for money given or promise made or other condition agreed upon. Also, the masters and scholars can make both between themselves and with other persons obligations and constitutions supported by faith or penalty or oath in these cases: namely, the murder or mutilation of a scholar or atrocious injury done a scholar, if justice should not be forthcoming, arranging the prices of lodging, costume, burial, lectures and disputations, so, however, that the university be not thereby dissolved or destroyed.

As to the status of the theologians, we decree that no one shall lecture at Paris before his thirty-fifth year and unless he has studied for eight years at least, and has heard the books faithfully and in classrooms, and has attended lectures in theology for five years before he gives lectures himself publicly. And none of these shall lecture before the third hour on days when masters lecture. No one shall be admitted at Paris to formal lectures or to preachings unless he shall be of approved life and science. No one shall be a scholar at Paris who has no definite master.

Moreover, that these decrees may be observed inviolate, we by virtue of our legatine authority have bound by the knot of excommunication all who shall contumaciously presume to go against these our statutes, unless within fifteen days after the offense they have taken care to emend their presumption before the university of masters and scholars or other persons constituted by the university. Done in the year of Grace 1215, the month of August.

PROCLAMATION OF THE OFFICIAL OF THE EPISCOPAL COURT OF PARIS AGAINST CLERKS AND SCHOLARS WHO GO ABOUT PARIS ARMED BY DAY AND NIGHT AND COMMIT CRIMES

The official of the court of Paris to all the rectors of churches, masters and scholars residing in the city and suburb of Paris, to whom the present letters may come, greeting in the Lord. A frequent and continual complaint has gone the rounds that there are in Paris some clerks and scholars, likewise their servants, trusting in the folly of the same clerks, unmindful of their salvation, not having God before their eyes, who, under pretense of leading the scholastic life, more and more often perpetrate unlawful and criminal acts, relying on their arms: namely, that by day and night they atrociously wound or kill many persons, rape women, oppress virgins, break into inns, also repeatedly committing robberies and many other enormities hateful to God. And since they attempt these and other crimes relying on their arms, we . . . do excommunicate in writing clerks and scholars and their servants who go about Paris by day or night armed, unless by permission of the reverend bishop of Paris or ourselves. We also excommunicate in writing those who rape women, break into inns, oppress virgins, likewise all those who have banded together for this purpose. . . .

But inasmuch as some clerks and scholars and their servants have borne arms in Paris, coming there from their parts or returning to their parts, and likewise certain others, knowing that clerks, scholars and their servants have borne arms in Paris, fear that for said reasons they have incurred the said penalty of excommunication we do declare herewith that it neither is nor was our intention that those clerks, scholars and their servants should be liable to the said sentence who, coming to Paris for study and bearing arms on the way, on first entering the city bear the same to their lodgings, nor, further, those, wishing to return home or setting out on useful and honest business more than one day's journey from the city of Paris, who have borne such arms going and returning while they were outside the city. . . . Given in the year 1268 A.D., the Friday following Epiphany.

ON THE VICES OF THE MASTERS

By Alvarus Pelagius

The first [vice] is that, although they be unlearned and insufficiently prepared, they get themselves promoted to be masters by prayers and gifts. . . . And when they are called upon to examine others, they admit inept and ignorant persons to be masters.

Second, moved by envy, they scorn to admit well-prepared subordinates to professorial chairs, and, full of arrogance, they despise others and censure their utterances unreasonably. . . .

Third, they despise simple persons who know how to avoid faults of conduct better than those of words. . . .

Fourth, they teach useless, vain, and sometimes false doctrines, a most dangerous course in doctrine of faith and morals, yet one especially characteristic of doctors of theology. These are fountains without water and clouds driven by whirlwinds and darkening the landscape. . . .

Fifth, they are dumb dogs unable to bark, as Isaiah inveighs against them, 66:10. Seeing the faults of peoples and lords, they keep silent lest they displease them, when they ought to argue at least in secret—which they also sometimes omit to do because they are involved in like vices themselves. . . .

Sixth, they retain in their classes those who have been excommunicated, or do not reprove scholars who are undisciplined and practice turpitudes publicly. For they ought to impress morality along with science.

Seventh, although receiving sufficient salaries, they avariciously demand beyond their due or refuse to teach the poor unless paid for it, and want pay whether they teach on feast days or not, or fail to lecture when they should, attending to other matters, or teach less diligently.

Eighth, they try to say what is subtle, not what is useful, so that they may be seen of men and called rabbis, which is especially reprehensible in masters of theology. And in this especially offend, remarks the aforesaid Alvarus, the masters of Paris and those in England at Oxford, secular as well as regular, Dominicans as well as Franciscans, and others, of whom the arrogance of some is inexplicable. In their classes not the prophets, nor the Mosaic law, nor the wisdom of the Father, nor the Gospel of Christ, nor the doctrine of the apostles and holy doctors are heard, but Reboat, the idolatrous philosopher, and his commentator, with other teachers of the liberal arts, so that in classes in theology not holy writ but philosophy is taught. Nay more, now doctors and bachelors do not even read the text of the *Sentences* in class but hurry on to curious questions which have no apparent connection with the text.

METHOD OF LECTURING IN THE LIBERAL ARTS PRESCRIBED, PARIS

In the name of the Lord, amen. Two methods of lecturing on books in the liberal arts having been tried, the former masters of philosophy uttering their words rapidly so that the mind of the hearer can take them in but the hand cannot keep up with them, the latter speaking slowly until their listeners can catch up with them with the pen; having compared these by diligent examination, the former method is found the better. Wherefore, the consensus of opinion warns us that we imitate it in our lectures. We, therefore, all and each, masters of the faculty of arts, teaching and not teaching, convoked for this specially by the venerable man, master Albert of Bohemia, then rector of the university, at St. Julien le Pauvre, have decreed in this wise, that all lecturers, whether masters or scholars of the same faculty, whenever and wherever they chance to lecture on any text ordinarily or cursorily in the same faculty, or to dispute any question concerning it, or anything else by way of exposition, shall observe the former method of lecturing to the best of their ability, so speaking forsooth as if no one was taking notes before them, in the way that sermons and recommendations are made in the university and which the lectures in other faculties follow. Moreover, transgressors of this statute, if the lecturers are masters or scholars, we now deprive henceforth for a year from lecturing, honors, offices and other advantages of our faculty. Which if anyone violates, for the first relapse we double the penalty, for the second we quadruple it, and so on. Moreover, listeners who oppose the execution of this our statute by clamor, hissing, noise, throwing stones by themselves or by their servants and accomplices, or in any other way, we deprive of and cut off from our society for a year, and for each relapse we increase the penalty double and quadruple as above.

BANNING OF ARISTOTLE'S WORKS

Neither the books of Aristotle on natural philosophy nor their commentaries are to be read at Paris in public or secret, and this we forbid under penalty of excommunication.

GREGORY IX ON BOOKS OFFENSIVE TO THE CATHOLIC FAITH

Since other sciences ought to render service to the wisdom of holy writ, they are to be in so far embraced by the faithful as they are known to conform to the good pleasure of the Giver, so that anything virulent or otherwise vicious, by which the purity of the Faith might be derogated from, be quite excluded. . . .

But since, as we have learned, the books on nature which were prohibited at Paris in provincial council are said to contain both useful and useless matter, lest the useful be vitiated by the useless, we command your discretion, in which we have full faith in the Lord, firmly bidding by apostolic writings under solemn adjuration of divine judgment, that, examining the same books as is convenient subtly and prudently, you entirely exclude what you shall find there erroneous or likely to give scandal or offense to readers, so that, what are suspect being removed, the rest may be studied without delay and without offense. Given at the Lateran, April 23, in the fifth year of our pontificate.

COURSES IN ARTS, PARIS

In the year of the Lord 1254. Let all know that we, all and each, masters of arts by our common assent, no one contradicting, because of the new and incalculable peril which threatens in our faculty—some masters hurrying to finish their lectures sooner than the length and difficulty of the texts permits, for which reason both masters in lecturing and scholars in hearing make less progress—worrying over the ruin of our faculty and wishing to provide for our status, have decreed and ordained for the common utility and the reparation of our university to the honor of God and the church universal that all and single masters of our faculty in the future shall be required to finish the texts which they shall have begun on the feast of St. Remy at the times below noted, not before.

The *Physics* of Aristotle, *Metaphysics*, and *De animalibus* on the feast of St. John the Baptist; *De celo et mundo*, first book of *Meteorology* with the fourth, on Ascension day; *De anima*, if read with the books on nature, on the feast of the Ascension, if with the logical texts, on the feast of the Annunciation of the blessed Virgin; *De generatione* on the feast of the Chair of St. Peter; *De causis* in seven weeks; *De sensu et sensato* in six weeks; *De sompno et vigilia* in five weeks; *De plantis* in five weeks; *De memoria et reminiscentia* in two weeks; *De differentia spiritus et animae* in two weeks; *De morte et vita* in one week. Moreover, if masters begin to read the said books at another time than the feast of St. Remy, they shall allow as much time for lecturing on them as is indicated above. Moreover, each of the said texts, if read by itself, not with another text, can be finished in half the time of lecturing assigned above. It will not be permitted anyone to finish the said texts in less time, but anyone may take more time.

PETER ABELARD

1079-1142

Peter Abelard was a monk, logician, and perhaps the most brilliant teacher of his times. Although he is perhaps best known today for his love affair with Heloise, his work *Sic et Non* ("Yes and No") had a profound affect on the development of teaching, the use of logic in theology, and the increased interest in Aristotle during the High Middle Ages. He was born in Le Pallet in Brittany and became a knight, only to abandon that life to pursue dialectic, or logic. He studied under many teachers, but because he himself was such an electric teacher he frequently attracted more students than did his own teachers. However, he had an unfortunate habit of attacking and abandoning his teachers, some of whom seem to have then treated Abelard jealously, if not antagonistically. Because of his popularity as a teacher, he directed the cathedral school in Paris. It was in Paris that he met Heloise and began the famous love affair. By 1118, Heloise had been sent to a convent, their son was being cared for by Abelard's sister, and Abelard himself became a monk at the abbey of St. Denys, just outside of Paris. Before 1120 he produced some short works on logic and in 1120 he wrote a treatise on the divine unity and the trinity, which was quickly condemned by the Church in 1121. For his heterodoxy Abelard was confined briefly. Upon his release, he returned to St. Denys, but soon antagonized the monks by discovering that the patron saint of the monastery, St. Denys ("Dionysius" in Latin), a follower of St. Paul, was not the St. Denys to whom the good monks of the abbey attributed certain theological works (a fifth century writer now known as "Pseudo-Dionysius"). Abelard had to flee from the monks for debunking their cherished beliefs about their patron. He spent the next few years in rural solitude and wrote *Sic et Non* during this period. Abelard eventually returned to Brittany to reform a monastery there, but left after an unsuccessful attempt on his life. By 1136 he was again teaching at Paris, and again making enemies. In 1140 he tangled with St. Bernard of Clairvaux, a formidable opponent who had Abelard condemned by Rome. Abelard spent his final years at the abbey of Cluny.

Abelard's *Sic et Non* contains 156 questions. Each question is posed so that a "pro" or "con" position must be taken, for example, "That God is one—and the contrary," "That the Son is without beginning—and the contrary," etc. For each question, Abelard then lists statements from the church Fathers that support the "pro" position *and* statements from the church Fathers that support the "con" position. Abelard is certainly suggesting that a scholar could not accept all of these statements uncritically, because they are contradictory. Note that Abelard juxtaposes contradictory statements, making no effort to resolve the contradictions. This has led some to wonder if Abelard did not write the whole work "tongue in cheek."

Abelard's *Sic et Non* is significant for many reasons. First, it gave many medieval readers a first-hand acquaintance with some important sayings from the church Fathers. One must remember that at this time "books" were hand-written manuscripts—expensive, labor-intensive products. Few had access to such a rich source of information from the church Fathers. Second, Abelard's method in *Sic et Non* was the point of departure for Peter Lombard's *Four Books of Sentences*. Like Abelard, Lombard raised questions which required a yes or no answer and gave pro and con quotes from the church Fathers, but unlike Abelard, Lombard took a stance on the posed question and resolved difficulties of the contrary position. In the 1200s, Lombard's *Four Books of Sentences* became the standard textbook in theology curriculum at the universities. Everyone who became a master in theology had to write a commentary on it. (Imagine for a moment that every student at every university would be required to write a senior research paper on the same book!) Third, because of Abelard's *Sic et Non* and Lombard's *Four Books of Sentences*, it became necessary for masters and students to be able to argue both sides of an issue: pro and con. In order to do this, they needed to know techniques of successful argumentation, i.e. Aristotelian logic. Fourth, the demand for Aristotle's logical works, prompted by the need for students to argue in their classroom exercises, soon emerged as a demand in the universities for all of Aristotle, including his works on natural philosophy and metaphysics. This sets the stage for the grand medieval conflicts over, and syntheses of, Christian religious beliefs and the best "science" of the day, that of Aristotle.

from *Sic et Non*

Among the multitudinous words of the holy Fathers some sayings seem not only to differ from one another but even to contradict one another. Hence it is not presumptuous to judge concerning those by whom the world itself will be judged, as it is written, "They shall judge nations" (Wisdom 3:8) and, again, "You shall sit and judge" (Luke 22:30). We do not presume to rebuke as untruthful or to denounce as erroneous those to whom the Lord said; "He who hears you hears me; he who despises you despises me" (Luke 10:26). Bearing in mind our foolishness we believe that our understanding is defective rather than the writing of those to whom the Truth Himself said, "It is not you who speak but the spirit of your Father who speaks in you" (Matthew 10:20). Why should it seem surprising if we, lacking the guidance of the Holy Spirit through whom those things were written and spoken, the Spirit impressing them on the writers, fail to understand them? Our achievement of full understanding is impeded especially by unusual modes of expression and by the different significances that can be attached to one and the same word, as a word is used now in one sense, now in another. Just as there are many meanings so there are many words. Tully says that sameness is the mother of satiety in all things, that is to say it gives rise to fastidious distaste and so it is appropriate to use a variety of words in discussing the same thing and not to express everything in common and vulgar words. . . .

We must also take special care that we are not deceived by corruptions of the text or by false attributions when sayings of the Fathers are quoted that seem to differ from the truth or to be contrary to it; for many apocryphal writings are set down under names of saints to enhance their authority, and even the texts of divine Scripture are corrupted by the errors of scribes. That most faithful writer and true interpreter, Jerome, accordingly warned us, "Beware of apocryphal writings. . . " Again, on the title of Psalm 77 which is "An Instruction of Asaph," he commented, "It is written according to Matthew that when the Lord had spoken in parables and they did not understand, he said, 'These things are done that it might be fulfilled which was written by the prophet Isaias, *I will open my mouth in parables*.' The Gospels still have it so. Yet it is not Isaias who says this but Asaph." Again, let us explain simply why in Matthew and John it is written that the Lord was crucified at the third hour but in Mark at the sixth hour. There was a scribal error, and in Mark too the sixth hour was mentioned, but many read the Greek *epismo* as *gamma*. So too there was a scribal error where "Isaias" was set down for "Asaph." We know that many churches were gathered together from among ignorant gentiles. When they read in the Gospel, "That it might be fulfilled which was written by the prophet Asaph," the one who first wrote down the Gospel began to say, "Who is this prophet Asaph?" for he was not known among the people. And what did he do? In seeking to amend an error he made an error. We would say the same of another text in Matthew. "He took," it says, "the thirty pieces of silver, the price of him that was prized, as was written by the prophet Jeremias." But we do not find this in Jeremias at all. Rather it is in Zacharias. You see then that here, as before, there was an error. If in the Gospels themselves some things are corrupted by the ignorance of scribes, we should not be surprised that the same thing has sometimes happened in the writings of later Fathers who are of much less authority. . . .

It is no less important in my opinion to ascertain whether texts quoted from the Fathers may be ones that they themselves have retracted and corrected after they came to a better understanding of the truth as the blessed Augustine did on many occasions; or whether they are giving the opinion of another rather than their own opinion. . . or whether, in inquiring into certain matters, they left them open to question rather than settled them with a definitive solution. . . .

In order that the way be not blocked and posterity deprived of the healthy labor of treating and debating difficult questions of language and style, a distinction must be drawn between the work of later authors and the supreme canonical authority of the Old and New Testaments. If, in Scripture, anything seems absurd you are not permitted to say, "The author of this book did not hold to the truth"—but rather that the codex is defective or that the interpreter erred or that you do not understand. But if anything seems contrary to truth in the works of later authors, which are contained in innumerable books, the reader or auditor is free to judge, so that he may approve what is pleasing and reject what gives offense, unless the matter is established by certain reason or by canonical authority (of the Scriptures). . . .

In view of these considerations we have undertaken to collect various sayings of the Fathers that give rise to questioning because of their apparent contradictions as they occur to our memory. This questioning excites young readers to the maximum of effort in inquiring into the truth, and such inquiry sharpens their minds. Assiduous and frequent questioning is indeed the first key to wisdom. Aristotle, that most perspicacious of all philosophers, exhorted the studious to practice it eagerly, saying, "Perhaps it is difficult to express oneself with confidence on such matters if they have not been much discussed. To entertain doubts on particular points will not be unprofitable." For by doubting we come to inquiry; through inquiring we perceive the truth, according to the Truth Himself. "Seek and you shall find," He says, "Knock and it shall be opened to you." In order to teach us by His example He chose to be found when He was about twelve years old sitting in the midst of the doctors and questioning them, presenting the appearance of a disciple by questioning rather than of a master by teaching, although there was in Him the complete and perfect wisdom of God. Where we have quoted texts of Scripture, the greater authority attributed to Scripture, the more they should stimulate the reader and attract him to the search for truth. Hence I have prefixed to this my book, compiled in one volume from the saying of the saints, the decree of Pope Gelasius concerning authentic books, from which it may be known that I have cited nothing from apocryphal books. I have also added excerpts from the Retractions of St. Augustine, from which it will be clear that nothing is included which he later retracted and corrected.

[*Abelard then presents 156 questions dealing with topics such these: "That God is one—and the contrary," "That the Son is without beginning—and the contrary," "That God can do all things—and the contrary," "That God knows all things—and the contrary," "That our first parents were created mortal—and the contrary," "That Adam was saved—and the contrary," "That Peter and Paul and all the apos-*

tles were equal—and the contrary," "That Christ alone is the foundation of the church—and the contrary," "That Peter did not deny Christ—and the contrary," "That without baptism of water no one can be saved—and the contrary," "That all are permitted marry—and the contrary," "That saintly works do not justify man—and the contrary," "That it is permitted to kill men—and the contrary," The first question is given here.]

THAT FAITH SHOULD BE BASED ON HUMAN REASON—AND THE CONTRARY

GREGORY, Homily XXVI. We know that the works of the Lord would not excite wonder if they were understood by reason; nor is there any merit in faith where human reason offers proof.

GREGORY, Homily V. At one word of command Peter and Andrew left their nets and followed the Redeemer. They had seen him work no miracles; they had heard nothing from him about eternal retribution; and nevertheless, at one command of the Lord, they forgot what they had seemed to possess. . . .

From the *First Book of Augustine against Faustus,*
FAUSTUS. It is a weak profession of faith if one does not believe in Christ without evidence and argument. You yourself are accustomed to say that Christian belief is simple and absolute and should not be inquired into too curiously. Why then are you destroying the simplicity of the faith by buttressing it with judgments and evidences?

From *The Life of St. Sylvester,*
where, disputing with the Jews, he said to the Rabbi Roasus, "Faith is not submitted to human reason, and faith teaches us that this God, whom you confess to be one God, is Father, Son, and Holy Spirit."

AUGUSTINE,From *On the Morals of the Church Against the Manicheans.*
The order of nature is such that, when we state anything, authority precedes reason for a reason might seem weak if, after it has been presented, authority is cited to confirm it. . . .

AMBROSE. If I am convinced by reason I give up faith.

GREGORY to Bishop Dominicus. Although these things are so I wish that all heretics be held in check by Catholic priests vigorously and always by reasoning.

GREGORY in *Pastoral Care*. The wise of this world and the dull are to be admonished differently. The former are for the most part converted by the arguments of reason, the latter sometimes better by examples . . . .

HILARY, from *On the Trinity, Book XII.* It is fitting for those who preach Christ to the world to refute the irreligious and unsound doctrines of the world through their knowledge of omnipotent wisdom, according as the Apostle says, "Our weapons are not carnal but mighty before God for the destruction of strongholds and the destroying of arguments and of every obstacle raised up against the knowledge of God. . . ." (2 Corinthians 10:4.)

AUGUSTINE to Count Valerian, discussing marriage and concupiscence.
While you satirize with a most robust faith it is good nevertheless that you also know how to support what we believe by defending it; for the Apostle Peter commanded us to be always ready to give satisfaction to anyone asking us the reason for our faith and hope. . . . We should give an account of our faith and hope to enquirers in a two-fold fashion. We should always explain the just grounds of our faith and hope to questioners, whether they ask honestly or dishonestly, and we should hold fast to the pure profession of our faith and hope even amid the pressures of our adversaries.

John Peckham

1225-1292

John Peckham was a Franciscan thinker, scholar, and teacher. He held the Franciscan chair in theology at the university in Paris from 1269-1270, and taught at Oxford from 1272-1275 before being called to Rome to give lectures to the cardinals in the Curia from 1277-1279. In 1279 he was named Archbishop of Canterbury. He wrote on a variety of subjects, from optics to astronomy. A recent editor of some of his works has described him as "one of the most interesting and multi-faceted personalities of the late thirteenth century."

The Franciscans were frequently at odds with the Dominicans, another mendicant order that also had a chair in theology at the university in Paris. When Peckham was teaching in Paris, Thomas Aquinas held the Dominican chair. As can be imagined, Peckham, the leading Franciscan teacher, had his disagreements with Thomas, the leading Dominican. Another Franciscan named Roger Marston witnessed and described the details of a meeting of the masters in Paris around 1270 in which Peckham and other masters confronted Thomas. Marston wrote that in the presence of Thomas Aquinas, one of Thomas's theories (based largely on Aristotelian principles) was solemnly excommunicated by John Peckham and twenty-four other doctors in theology because the theory was contrary to the teaching of the saints. Peckham, in a letter dated June 1, 1285, described this same meeting. His account, which may be somewhat self-serving, maintains that he alone stood by Thomas during (one is led to believe) a polite and courteous exchange, and that Thomas, the humble doctor, modified his positions once shown the truth. Peckham may not have been as polite in 1270 as he remembered in 1285. In 1276 Peckham attacked even the revised position of Thomas, and in 1286 as archbishop of Canterbury, Peckham issued a condemnation of eight propositions which formed the basis for Thomas's "erroneous" position. In 1323, in the disposition concerning the canonization of Thomas Aquinas, Peckham is described as repeatedly attempting to exasperate Thomas with "pompous and bombastic speech," but Thomas always responded with kindness and humility.

In the following passage, which is from a collection of Peckham's letters, note that "Brother Alexander" is Alexander of Hales, a Franciscan, and "Brother Bonaventure" is St. Bonaventure, also a Franciscan. The diversity of ideas reflected in this passage further reconfirms Peckham's observation on Dec. 20, 1284, that the two orders, Dominicans and Franciscans, were at odds on virtually every debatable point of doctrine.

from a Letter to Pope Gregory III

We do not reject philosophical studies in so far as they serve the cause of theology. But we do reject the profane novelties contrary to philosophical truth that have been introduced in these last twenty years by those who reject and despise the teachings of the saints of old. Which is the more sound and solid doctrine, that of the sons of St. Francis like Brother Alexander of holy memory and Brother Bonaventure, whose works are based on irreproachable saints and philosophers; or this newfangled system [of Thomas Aquinas], which is wholly contrary to the teaching of Augustine . . . and which strives to destroy it, filling the world with a war of words? Let the wise doctors of old look on this; let God in heaven look on it and correct it. May God grant to the pope the opportunity and inclination to separate the weeds from the grain and root them up by the power of the keys entrusted to him.

Marsilius of Padua

c. 1275-1342

An Italian physician who became rector of the University of Paris in 1313, Marsilius was declared a heretic by the Avignon Pope John XXII in 1327 after it became public that Marsilius was the author of *The Defender of Peace* (1324). The book contains a forceful antipapalist argument, repudiating the Roman pontiff's claim to a plenitude of power, or supreme spiritual and temporal authority throughout Christendom. According to Marsilius, secular rulers were not subject to the pope and could not be deposed by the head of the Church. Indeed for the author, ecclesiastical authorities must be made subordinate to secular government. In what some scholars have viewed as an anticipation of the sixteenth-century Protestant Reformation, Marsilius wrote that ordained clergy should not own property and should limit themselves exclusively to spiritual duties.

In a radical departure from traditional medieval views, Marsilius insists that legitimate political leaders are elected and must enforce laws agreed upon by the wider community. This concept is especially applicable to high church leaders, for Marsilius maintains that a general council of the Church is superior to the pope and to individual members of the ecclesiastical hierarchy. The very fact that the papacy was an elective office gave added force to his argument. This "ascending" view of government in both Church and state may be familiar to the modern mind, but in the early fourteenth century such notions stood in opposition to the hierarchical principle which dominated so many compartments of life: social theory, natural philosophy and cosmology, political theory, and domestic governance.

The ideas presented in this selection from *The Defender of Peace* did not originate in a vacuum. Conflict between church and state had been a constant feature of the medieval experience in the West since the time of Charlemagne, and the conflict would continue down into the seventeenth century. When reading Marsilius, consider his views on the origins of the state, the role of lawmaking, limits on the secular ruler, and the power of the papacy. How did *The Defender of Peace* advance the cause of plural authorities in Western Europe? To what extent is the principle of plural authorities (in opposition to theocracy) at the core of modern democratic practice?

from the *Defender of Peace*

CHAPTER III: ON THE ORIGIN OF THE CIVIL COMMUNITY

Having defined tranquillity as the good disposition of the state for the functioning of its parts, we must now examine what the state is in itself, and why; what and how many are its primary parts; what is the function appropriate to each part, their causes, and their order in relation to one another. For these are the main points required for the perfect determination of tranquillity and its opposite.

However, before discussing the state and its species or kinds, since the state is the perfect community we must first trace the origin of civil communities and of their regimes and modes of living. From the imperfect kinds, men have advanced to perfect communities, regimes, and modes of living in them. For from the less to the more perfect is always the path of nature and of its imitator, art. And men do not think that they have scientific knowledge of each thing unless they "know its first causes and first principles down to the elements."

Following this method, then, we must note that civil communities had small beginnings in diverse regions and times, and growing gradually came at length to completion, just as we said happens in every process of nature or of art. For the first and smallest combination of human beings, wherefrom the other combinations emerged, was that of male and female, as the foremost of the philosophers says in the *Politics*, Book I, Chapter I, and as appears more fully from his *Economics*. From this combination there were generated other humans, who first occupied one household; from these, more combinations of the same kind were formed, and so great was the procreation of children that a single household did not suffice for them, but many households had to be made. A number of these households was called a village or hamlet, and this was the first community, as is also written in the above-cited treatise.

So long as men were in a single household, all their actions, especially those we shall henceforth call "civil," were regulated by the elder among them as being more discerning, but apart from laws or customs, because these could not yet have been discovered. Not only were the men of a single household ruled in this way, but so too was the first community, called the village. However, in some villages the case was different. For although the head of a single household might have been allowed to pardon or to punish domestic injuries entirely according to his own will and pleasure, this would not have been allowed the head of the first community called the village. For in this community the elder had to regulate matters of justice and benefit by some reasonable ordinance or quasi-natural law, because thus it seemed appropriate to all by a certain equity, not as a result of prolonged inquiry, but solely by the common dictate of reason and a certain duty of human society.

The cause of this difference of regime in a single household and in a village is and was as follows. If someone in the single and first household or domestic family had killed or otherwise offended his brother, then the head of the household, if he so desired, was allowed not to give the wrongdoer the extreme penalty without any dangerous consequences resulting therefrom because the injury seemed to have been done to the father alone, who forgave it; and because of the paucity of men; and again because it was less unfortunate and sorrowful for the father to lose one son than two. Our first ancestor, Adam, seems to have acted in this way when his firstborn son, Cain, killed his brother Abel. For there is properly no civil justice of a father in relation to his son, as Aristotle wrote in Book IV of the *Ethics*, the treatise on justice. On the other hand, in the first community, the village or hamlet, such procedure was not and would not be allowed, because the case here was different from that of the family; indeed, unless injuries were avenged or equalized by the elder, there would have arisen fighting and the separation of the villagers.

Villages having multiplied and the community grown larger because of increasing procreation, they were still ruled by one man, either because of a lack of many prudent men or through some other cause, as is written in the *Politics*, Book III, Chapter 9. The ruler, however, was the elder or the man who was regarded as better, although the regulations of these communities were less imperfect than those by which the single village or hamlet was ordered. Those first communities, however, did not have so great a differentiation and ordering of parts, or so large a quantity of necessary arts and rules of living, as were gradually to be found afterwards in perfect communities. For sometimes the same man was both ruler and farmer or shepherd, like Abraham and several others after him; but in perfect communities this was not expedient nor would it be allowed.

These communities having gradually increased, men's experience became greater, more perfect arts and rules and ways of living were discovered, and also the parts of communities were more fully differentiated. Finally, the things which are necessary for living and for living well were brought to full development by men's reason and experience, and there was established the perfect community called the state, with the differentiation of its parts, to the discussion of which we shall now proceed.

Let this much suffice, then, concerning the rise of the civil community.

CHAPTER XII: ON THE DEMONSTRABLE EFFICIENT CAUSE OF HUMAN LAWS, AND ALSO ON THAT CAUSE WHICH CANNOT BE PROVED BY DEMONSTRATION: WHICH IS TO INQUIRE INTO THE LEGISLATOR. Whence it Appears Also that Whatever is Established by Election Derives its Authority from Election Alone Apart from Any Other Confirmation

We must next discuss that efficient cause of the laws which is capable of demonstration. For I do not intend to deal here with that method of establishing laws which can be effected by the immediate act or oracle of God apart from the human will, or which has been so effected in the past. It was by this latter method, as we have said, that the Mosaic law was established; but I shall not deal with it here even insofar as it contains commands with regard to civil acts for the status of the present world. I shall discuss the establishment of only those laws and governments which emerge immediately from the decision of the human mind.

Let us say, to begin with, that it can pertain to any citizen to discover the law taken materially and in its third sense, as the science of civil justice and benefit. Such inquiry, however, can be carried on more appropriately and be completed better by those men who are able to have leisure, who are older and experienced in practical affairs, and who are called "prudent men," than by the mechanics who must bend all their efforts to acquiring the necessities of life. But it must be remembered that the true knowledge or discovery of the just and the beneficial, and of their opposites, is not law taken in its last and most proper sense, whereby it is the measure of human civil acts, unless there is given a coercive command as to its observance, or it is made by way of such a command, by someone through whose authority its transgressors must and can be punished. Hence, we must now say to whom belongs the authority to make such a command and to punish its transgressors. This, indeed, is to inquire into the legislator or the maker of the law.

Let us say, then, in accordance with the truth and the counsel of Aristotle in the *Politics*, Book III, Chapter 6, that the legislator, or the primary and proper efficient cause of the law, is the people or the whole body of citizens, or the weightier part thereof, through its election or will expressed by words in the general assembly of the citizens, commanding or determining that something be done or omitted with regard to human civil acts, under a temporal pain or punishment. By the "weightier part" I mean to take into consideration the quantity and the quality of the persons in that community over which the law is made. The aforesaid whole body of citizens or the weightier part thereof is the legislator regardless of whether it makes the law directly by itself or entrusts the making of it to some person or persons, who are not and cannot be the legislator in the absolute sense, but only in a relative sense and for a particular time and in accordance with the authority of the primary legislator. And I say further that the laws and anything else established through election must receive their necessary approval by that same primary authority and no other, whatever be the case with regard to certain ceremonies or solemnities, which are required not for the being of the matters elected but for their well-being, since the election would be no less valid even if these ceremonies were not performed. Moreover, by the same authority must the laws and other things established through election undergo addition, subtraction, complete change, interpretation, or suspension, insofar as the exigencies of time or place or other circumstances make any such action opportune for the common benefit. And by the same authority, also, must the laws be promulgated or proclaimed after their enactment, so that no citizen or alien who is delinquent in observing them may be excused because of ignorance.

A citizen I define in accordance with Aristotle in the *Politics*, Book III, Chapters 1, 3, and 7, as one who participates in the civil community in the government or the deliberative or judicial function according to his rank. By this definition, children, slaves, aliens and women are distinguished from citizens, although in different ways. For the sons of citizens are citizens in proximate potentiality, lacking only in years. The weightier part of the citizens should be viewed in accordance with the honorable custom of polities, or else it should be determined in accordance with the doctrine of Aristotle in the *Politics*, Book VI, Chapter 2.

Having thus defined the citizen and the weightier part of the citizens, let us return to our proposed objective, namely, to demonstrate that the human authority to make laws belongs only to the whole body of the citizens or to the weightier part thereof. Our first proof is as follows. The absolutely primary human authority to make or establish human laws belongs only to those men from whom alone the best laws can emerge. But these are the whole body of the citizens, or the weightier part thereof, which represents that whole body; since it is difficult or impossible for all persons to agree upon one decision, because some men have a deformed nature, disagreeing with the common decision through singular malice or ignorance. The common benefit should not, however, be impeded or neglected because of the unreasonable protest or opposition of these men. The authority to make or establish laws, therefore, belongs only to the whole body of the citizens or to the weightier part thereof.

The first proposition of this demonstration is very close to self-evident, although its force and its ultimate certainty can be grasped from Chapter V of this discourse. The second proposition, that the best law is made only through the hearing and command of the entire multitude, I prove by assuming with Aristotle in the *Politics*, Book III, Chapter 7, that the best law is that which is made for the common benefit of the citizens. As Aristotle said: "That is presumably right," that is, in the laws, "which is for the common benefit of the state and the citizens." But that this is best achieved only by the whole body of the citizens or by the weightier part thereof, which is assumed to be the same thing, I show as follows: That at which the entire body of the citizens aims intellectually and emotionally is more certainly judged as to its truth and more diligently noted as to its common utility. For a defect in some proposed law can be better noted by the greater number than by any part thereof, since every whole, or at least every corporeal whole, is greater in mass and in virtue than any part of it taken separately. Moreover, the common utility of a law is better noted by the entire multitude, because no one knowingly harms himself. Anyone can look to see whether a proposed law leans toward the benefit of one or a few persons more than of the others or of the community, and can protest against it. Such, however, would not be the case were the law made by one or a few persons, considering their own private benefit rather than that of the community. This position is also supported by the arguments which we advanced in Chapter XI of this discourse with regard to the necessity of having laws.

Another argument to the principal conclusion is as follows. The authority to make the law belongs only to those men whose making of it will cause the law to be better observed or observed at all. Only the whole body of the citizens are such men. To them, therefore, belongs the authority to make the law. The first proposition of this demonstration is very close to self-evident, for a law would be useless unless it were observed. Hence Aristotle said in the *Politics*, Book IV, Chapter 6: "Laws are not well ordered when they are well made but not obeyed." He also said in Book VI, Chapter 5: "Nothing is accomplished by forming opinions about justice and not carrying them out." The second proposition I prove as follows. That law is better observed by every citizen which each one seems to have imposed upon himself. But such is the law which is made through the hearing and command of the entire multitude of the citizens. The first proposition of this prosyllogism is almost self-evident; for since "the state is a community of free men," as is written in the *Politics*, Book III, Chapter 4, every citizen must be free, and not undergo another's despotism, that is, slavish dominion. But this would not be the case if one or a few of the citizens by their own authority made the law over the whole body of citizens. For those who thus made the law would be despots over the others, and hence such a law, however good it was, would be endured only with reluctance, or not at all, by the rest of the citizens, the more ample part. Having suffered contempt, they would protest against it, and not having been called upon to make it, they would not observe it. On the other hand, a law made by the hearing or consent of the whole multitude, even though it were less useful, would be readily observed and endured by every one of the citizens, because then each would seem to have set the law upon himself, and hence would have no protest against it, but would rather tolerate it with equanimity. The second proposition of the first syllogism I also prove in another way, as follows. The power to cause the laws to be observed belongs only to those men to whom belongs coercive force over the transgressors of the laws. But these men are the whole body of citizens or the weightier part thereof. Therefore, to them alone belongs the authority to make the laws.

The principal conclusion is also proved as follows. That practical matter whose proper establishment is of greatest importance for the common sufficiency of the citizens in this life, and whose poor establishment threatens harm for the community, must be established only by the whole body of the citizens. But such a matter is the law. Therefore, the establishment of the law pertains only to the whole body of the citizens. The major premise of this demonstration is almost self-evident, and is grounded in the immediate truths which were set forth in Chapters IV and V of this discourse. For men came together to the civil community in order to attain what was beneficial for sufficiency of life, and to avoid the opposite. Those matters, therefore, which can affect the benefit and harm of all ought to be known and heard by all, in order that they may be able to attain the beneficial and to avoid the opposite. Such matters are the laws, as was assumed in the minor premise. For in the laws being rightly made consists a large part of the whole common sufficiency of men, while under bad laws there arise unbearable slavery, oppression, and misery of the citizens, the final result of which is that the polity is destroyed.

Again, and this is an abbreviation and summary of the previous demonstrations: The authority to make laws belongs only to the whole body of the citizens, as we have said, or else it belongs to one or a few men. But it cannot belong to one man alone for the reasons given in Chapter XI and in the first demonstration adduced in the present chapter; for through ignorance or malice or both, this one man could make a bad law, looking more to his own private benefit than to that of the community, so that the law would be tyrannical. For the same reason, the authority to make laws cannot belong to a few; for they too could sin, as above, in making the law for the benefit of a certain few and not for the common benefit, as can be seen in oligarchies. The authority to make the laws belongs, therefore, to the whole body of citizens or to the weightier part thereof, for precisely the opposite reason. For since all the citizens must be measured by the law according to due proportion, and no one knowingly harms or wishes injustice to himself, it follows that all or most wish a law conducing to the common benefit of the citizens.

From these same demonstrations it can also be proved, merely by changing the minor term, that the approval, interpretation, and suspension of the laws, and the other matters set forth in paragraph three of this chapter, pertain to the authority of the legislator alone. And the same must be thought of everything else which is established by election. For the authority to approve or disapprove rests with those who have the primary authority to elect, or with those to whom they have granted this authority of election, For otherwise, if the part could dissolve by its own authority what had been established by the whole, the part would be greater than the whole, or at least equal to it.

CHAPTER XVII: ON THE CORRECTION OF THE RULER, AND FOR WHAT CAUSE, HOW, AND BY WHOM HE MUST BE PUNISHED WHEN HE TRANSGRESSES THE LAW

We have previously stated that it pertains to the legislator to correct governments or to change them completely, just as to establish them. In this connection, someone may well wonder whether it is expedient that rulers be corrected by coercive judgment and force; and if it is expedient, whether they should be corrected for every kind of excess, or only for some and not for others; also who should make such judgments against the rulers, and execute them by coercive force—for it was said above that it pertains to the rulers alone to issue civil sentences and to punish transgressors of the laws by coercive force.

Let us say that the ruler through his action in accordance with the law and the authority given to him is the standard and measure of every civil act, like the heart in an animal, as was sufficiently shown in Chapter XV. Now if the ruler received no other form beside the law and the authority and the desire to act in accordance with it, he would never perform any action which was wrong or corrigible or measurable by someone else. And therefore he and his action would be the measure of every civil act of men other than himself, in such manner that he would never be measured by others, like the well-formed heart in an animal. For since the heart receives no form that inclines it to an action contrary to the action which has to emerge from its natural virtue and heat, it always does naturally the appropriate action and never the contrary. Hence it regulates and measures, through its influence or action, the other parts of the animal, in such manner that it is not regulated by them nor does it receive any influence from them.

But since the ruler is a human being, he has understanding and appetite, which can receive other forms, like false opinion or perverted desire or both, as a result of which he comes to do the contraries of the things determined by the law. Because of these actions, the ruler is rendered measurable by someone else who has the authority to measure or regulate him, or his unlawful actions, in accordance with the law. For otherwise every government would become despotic, and the life of the citizens slavish and insufficient. This is an evil to be avoided, as is apparent from our discussions in Chapters V and XI.

Now the judgment, command, and execution of any correction of the ruler, in accordance with his demerit or transgression, must be done by the legislator, or by a person or persons appointed for this purpose by the authority of the legislator, as was demonstrated in Chapters XII and XV. And it is well to suspend for some time the office of the ruler who is to be corrected, especially in relation to the person or persons who must judge of his transgression, because otherwise there would then be a plurality of governments in the community, from which would result schism, agitation, and fighting; and also because he is corrected not as a ruler but as subject who has transgressed the law.

Coming now to the questions which were raised above, let us say that the ruler's excess is either grave or slight; it may occur frequently or only rarely; and it is among the things determined by law or it is not. If the ruler's excess be grave, such as against the commonwealth or against a notable or any other person, from failure to correct which there could likely arise scandal or agitation among the people, then whether the excess be one which occurs frequently or rarely, the ruler must be corrected for it. For if the excess be not avenged, agitation might arise among the people, and upheaval and destruction of the polity. If the excess is determined by law, it must be corrected according to the law; but if not, then it must be corrected according to the sentence of the legislator; and it must be determined by law as much as possible, as we showed in Chapter XI.

If the ruler's excess be small, then its occurrence and its commission by the ruler may be either rare or frequent. If it is rarely committed or rarely capable of being committed by the ruler, then it must be allowed to pass and be glossed over rather than having the ruler corrected for it. For if the ruler is corrected for every small and infrequent excess, he will be made an object of contempt, which will result in no slight harm to the community, since the citizens then exhibit less respect and obedience for the law and the ruler. Again, since the ruler is unwilling to undergo correction for every slight offense, because he will regard this as bringing him into low repute, there will be a possibility of grave scandal. But such a condition must not be stirred up in communities when no evident utility can emerge therefrom, but rather harm.

Such was clearly the view of Aristotle on this question, in the *Politics* Book II, Chapter 4, where he said: "It is manifest that some errors of both legislators and rulers should be allowed to pass. For one will do less good by making changes than one will do harm by becoming accustomed to rebelling against the rulers." By "legislator" Aristotle meant an established law; and he says that if men have become accustomed to observing it, then it must not be changed in order to make a slight correction in it, but must rather be allowed to pass. For frequent changing of the laws saps their strength, which is the custom of obeying and observing what the laws command. As Aristotle said in the same book and chapter: "The law has no power for persuasion except that of custom," that is, for the law to be observed by the subjects, the most important factor is custom. And the case is very similar with regard to respecting and obeying the ruler.

But if the ruler's excess, while slight in extent, is capable of frequent occurrence, then it must be determined by law, and the ruler who frequently commits the offense must be given the appropriate punishment. For an offense, however slight, would be of notable harm to the polity if it were frequently committed, just as "small expenses frequently incurred consume a fortune," that is, in riches. "For the whole sum is not small, although it is made up of small sums," as it is written in the *Politics*, Book V, Chapter 4.

Such then are our conclusions concerning the correction of rulers, by whom it should be done, and for what reasons.

CHAPTER XXII: IN WHAT SENSE THE ROMAN BISHOP AND HIS CHURCH ARE THE HEAD AND LEADER OF THE OTHERS; AND BY WHAT AUTHORITY THIS HEADSHIP BELONGS TO THEM

Now that we have determined these matters, we wish to show that it is expedient and very useful to appoint a single bishop and a single church or priestly college as the head or leader of the others. But first we must differentiate the ways or senses in which one church or bishop can be understood to be the head of all the others, so that we may separate the proper way from the ways which are improper and inexpedient. For one bishop and church to be the head of all the others can in one sense be understood to mean that all churches and individuals in the world are obliged to believe in their definitions or interpretations of doubtful senses of Scripture (especially with regard to what it is necessary to believe and observe for salvation), and to perform the church ritual or divine worship in accordance with their decrees. But in this sense no one bishop or church of any province, as such, nor any college of priests, is the head of the others, according to divine law, nor does the example of the primitive church show that it is expedient to have a head church of such a kind, nor, similarly, is such headship authorized by any decree of the faithful human legislator. For if there were such a head, one of the many evils that would follow therefrom would be this: that it would be necessary for salvation that all rulers, communities, and peoples believe, in accordance with the definition or decree of Boniface VIII, that they were all subject in coercive jurisdiction to the Roman pope, and believe further, in accordance with the ordinances of a certain so-called Roman pope, that Christ did not counsel that the possession (in private or in common) of temporal goods in excess of present needs be spurned or renounced, and likewise the ownership of such goods, that is, the power lawfully to sue for them or to lay claim to them before a coercive judge. The first of these assertions is the most horrible falsehood; and the second must be denied as heretical, as has been clearly shown above in Chapters XIII, XIV, XVI, XX, and XXI of this discourse.

Another sense in which one bishop and church or college can be regarded as the head or leader of all the rest, is this: that all the clergymen or clerical colleges in the world are subject to their coercive jurisdiction. But this kind of headship belongs to no bishop or church according to divine law, but is rather forbidden by counsel or command, as has been adequately shown in Chapters IV, V, VIII, IX, and XI of this discourse.

This priority can be understood in still another sense: that to one bishop or church or college pertains the appointment of all church officials and the distribution, deposit, and withdrawal of temporal goods or benefices. But that some one bishop or church is in this sense prior to the others cannot be proved by divine law, but rather the opposite. And in a word, by virtue of the words of Scripture it cannot be proved that some one bishop or church is the head or leader of the others with respect to any authority or power, as has been shown in Chapters XV, XVI, XVII, XX, and XXI of this discourse.

Consequently, one bishop can no more excommunicate another than the other can excommunicate him; nor can one bishop interdict the reception of divine sacraments or services by the people or province entrusted to the care of another bishop, any more than the other bishop can do so to the former's people or province; nor, with regard to any other authority, does one bishop have more of it over another bishop, or over this other bishop's province, than the latter has over the former bishop or over his province, unless such authority or power shall have been granted by the general council or the faithful human legislator. For all bishops are of equal merit and authority insofar as they are bishops, as we showed in Chapter XV of this discourse from Jerome's epistle to Evander. Nor is one bishop more perfect than another simply because a more perfect apostle or bishop laid his hands on him. For "let no man glory in men," wrote the Apostle; "for all things are yours, whether Paul, or Apollo, or Cephas, etc., and ye are Christ's." Whereon the gloss: "'And ye are Christ's, not man's, in creation or re-creation." For this reason, it makes no difference with regard to any sacrament whether the priest who lays on his hands is more or less perfect, so long as he has the authority, because God alone gives the effect of a sacrament. And hence the Apostle, in the same chapter of Corinthians settles this question by saying: "I have planted, Apollo watered, but God gave the increase." For just as a tree's power of germination or of life-functioning is bestowed not by him who plants or waters the tree but rather by him who gives to the plant its vegetative soul, so too does the Apostle show that meritorious works are bestowed not by those who lay on their hands, and teach or give blessing, but rather by him who bestows the internal character or grace, God himself; although the former are of assistance, like those who water the plant. And since there is only one giver of internal authority, of character (of the same species), and of grace, namely, God himself, it follows that all bishops or priests are of equal authority and merit bestowed by God, which was the view held by Jerome.

By virtue of the words of Scripture, therefore, no bishop or church is the head or leader of the rest, as such. For the only absolute head of the church and foundation of the faith, by immediate ordainment of God, according to the Scripture or truth, is Christ himself, and not any apostle, bishop, or priest, as the Apostle very clearly says in Ephesians, Chapters 4 and 5, in Colossians, Chapter I, and in I Corinthians, Chapter 10. And hence he says that all the apostles, prophets, teachers, and other believers constitute the "body of Christ," which is the church as meaning the other members; but no one is the "head" except Christ alone. Whence in Ephesians, Chapter 4, it is written: "And he gave some, apostles; and some, prophets; and some, evangelists; and some, pastors and teachers; for the perfecting of the saints, for the work of the ministry, for the edifying of the body of Christ: till we all come in the unity of the faith," etc. And a little below the Apostle adds: "But speaking the truth in love, let us grow up into him in all things, which is the head, Christ: from whom the whole body fitly joined together and compacted by that which every joint supplieth, according to the effectual working in the measure of every part, maketh increase of the body unto the edifying of itself in love." And again in Chapter 5 of the same epistle: "For the husband is the head of the wife, even as Christ is the head of the church: and he is the savior of the body. Therefore as the church is subject unto Christ, so let the wives be to their own husbands in everything." But never did Paul say that Cephas was the head of the church, or that the church was subject to him as its head, although such statements were made after Christ rose up from the dead and ascended the heavens. And hence the Apostle, speaking in the person of all believers, writes a little below in the same chapter: "For no man ever yet hated his own flesh, but nourisheth and cherisheth it, even as Christ the church, for we are members of his body." Again, in Colossians, Chapter I: "And he is the head of the body, the church: who is the beginning, the first-born from the dead; that in all things he might have the preeminence." The same is clearly shown by St. Peter in his first epistle, Chapter 5: "And when the chief shepherd," Christ, "shall appear, ye shall receive a crown of glory that fadeth not away." But besides being the head, Christ alone is and was the foundation and rock of the church or faith. Whence in I Corinthians, Chapter 3, it is written: "For other foundation can no man lay than that is laid, which is Jesus Christ." And again in Chapter 10 of the same epistle: "And that rock was Christ."

CHRISTINE DE PISAN

1364-1430

Although Christine de Pisan was born in Venice, she spent most of her life in France, where her father was a physician and astrologer in the court of King Charles V. At her father's insistence, and over her mother's objections, Christine received an excellent education. In 1380, when she was about fifteen, Christine married Étienne du Castel, a court secretary, and with him she had an exceptionally happy marriage. The unexpected deaths of her father and her husband left Christine a widow at the age of twenty-five with three small children, her mother, and a niece to support. Responding to this necessity, she became the first female professional writer in Europe. Over the course of her career her output was large and well received, but after her death Christine's reputation faded.

Only recently has her contribution to literary history been recognized again. A striking element of Christine's work is the wide variety of writings she produced: allegorical tales, philosophical arguments, biographies, autobiography, romances, prose tracts, and dream visions. One of her most popular works was *The Book of Arms and Chivalry*, a handbook for knightly conduct which William Caxton (1422-1491), England's first printer, translated and published for Henry VII. Many readers assumed the author to be a man. In the early 1400s she became embroiled in a notorious literary debate with some of the most famous writers of her time over *The Romance of the Rose*, an extremely popular text which she attacked for defaming women. In the same vein, she produced *The City of Ladies* in 1405, an allegorical collection of stories which rewrites history from the woman's viewpoint. At the end of her life, she retired to live in a convent where she dedicated her last known poem, "Hymn," to Joan of Arc in 1429.

Throughout her career, Christine opposed courtly and clerkly traditions that suppressed women. She wrote that "God has demonstrated that he has truly placed language in women's mouths so that He might be thereby served." The following selections from *The City of Ladies* show Christine re-examining famous women in history through a sympathetic feminine lens. Think about other versions of Eve, the Amazons, and Empress Theodora that you have already encountered. How does Christine suggest a new way to view each of them?

from *The City of Ladies*

"My lady, one of the Catos—who was such a great orator—said, nevertheless, that if this world were without women, we would converse with the gods."

She replied, "You can now see the foolishness of the man who is considered wise, because, thanks to a woman, man reigns with God. And if anyone would say that man was banished because of Lady Eve, I tell you that he gained more through Mary than he lost through Eve when humanity was conjoined to the Godhead, which would never have taken place if Eve's misdeed had not occurred. Thus man and woman should be glad for this sin, through which such an honor has come about. For as low as human nature fell through this creature woman, was human nature lifted higher by this same creature. And as for conversing with the gods, as this Cato has said, if there had been no woman, he spoke truer than he knew, for he was a pagan, and among those of this belief, gods were thought to reside in Hell as well as Heaven, that is, the devils whom they called the gods of Hell—so that it is no lie that these gods would have conversed with men, if Mary had not lived."

HERE SHE SPEAKS OF ZENOBIA, QUEEN OF THE PALMYRENES.

"The women of Amazonia were not the only valorous women, for no less celebrated is Zenobia, queen of the Palmyrenes, a lady of noble blood and offspring of the Ptolemies, kings of Egypt. The great courage of this lady and the chivalrous inclination she possessed were obvious throughout her childhood. As soon as she was even slightly strong, no one could keep her from leaving the residence of walled cities, palaces, and royal chambers in order to live in the woods and forests, where, armed with sword and spear, she eagerly hunted wild game. After stags and hinds, she began to fight with lions and bears and all other wild beasts which she would attack fearlessly and conquer marvelously. This lady did not consider it a hardship to sleep in the woods, on the hard ground in cold and in heat, for she feared nothing, nor did she mind traveling through forest passes, climbing mountains, going down into villages as she pursued the various beasts. This maiden despised all physical love and refused to marry for a long time, for she was a woman who wished to keep her virginity for life. In the end, under pressure from her parents, she took as husband the king of the Palmyrenes, who had a handsome face and body. The noble Zenobia was always possessed of supreme self-control and paid little attention to her own beauty, and Fortune was extremely favorable to Zenobia's inclinations by allowing her to have a husband who corresponded so well to her own mores. This king, who was quite brave, desired to conquer by force all the Orient and nearby empires. In this time Valerianus, the ruler of the Roman Empire, was captured by Sapor, the king of the Persians. The king of the Palmyrenes assembled his great army; whereupon Zenobia, who did not give a thought to preserving the freshness of her beauty, resolved to suffer the exercise of arms with her husband, to arm herself and to participate with him in all the labors of the exercise of chivalry. The king, who was named Odenatus, appointed a son, named Herod, whom he had had by another woman, to lead a part of his army in the advance guard against the Persian king Sapor, who then occupied Mesopotamia. He then ordered Zenobia his wife to advance from the one flank, in all boldness; he would then advance from the other flank with a third of his army; and they set out under these orders. But what should I tell you? The end of this affair, just as you can read in history books, was as follows: this lady Zenobia conducted herself so bravely and courageously and with such boldness and strength that she won several battles against this Persian king, and so decisively, thanks to her prowess, that she placed Mesopotamia under her husband's rule. In the end she lay siege to Sapor in his city and captured him with his concubines and great treasure. After this victory it happened that her husband was killed by one of his own relatives out of jealousy, but it did not help the relative at all because this noblehearted lady kept him out of power; she bravely and valiantly took possession of the empire on behalf of her children, who were still small. She placed herself on the royal throne as empress, took over the government, exercised great strength and care, and, to tell the entire story, governed so well, so wisely, and with so much chivalric discipline that Gallienus, and after him, Claudius, emperors of Rome, although they occupied a large part of the Orient on behalf of Rome, never dared to undertake anything against her. The same was true for the Egyptians, the Arabians, and the Armenians: they so feared her power and bravery that they were all happy to maintain the boundaries of their lands. So wisely did this lady govern that she was honored by her princes, obeyed and loved by her people, and feared and respected by her knights. When she rode out in arms, which happened frequently, she did not speak to the members of her army unless she was in armor, with her helmet on her head, nor did she ever have herself carried in a litter, although the kings of that time all had themselves transported in this manner, but she was always mounted on a war-charger, and sometimes, to spy on her enemies, she would ride *incognito* in front of her troops. Just as she surpassed in discipline and chivalry all the knights of her time in the world, this noble lady Zenobia surpassed all other ladies in her noble and upright conduct and integrity of living. In her entire life-style she was extraordinarily sober. But, notwithstanding this, she often held great assemblies and feasts with her barons and with foreigners, and on these occasions she spared nothing in magnificence and royal generosity and bestowed large and beautiful gifts, for she knew well how to attract beautiful people to her love and benevolence. This woman was supremely chaste. Not only did she avoid other men, but she also slept with her husband only to have children, and demonstrated this clearly by not sleeping with her husband when she was pregnant. And to make certain that her entire outward appearance corresponded and joined with her inner character, she refused to allow any lecherous man or man of vile morals to frequent her court and insisted that all who wished to have her favor were virtuous and well-bred. She bestowed honor upon people according to their goodness, bravery, and strength and never on account of their wealth or noble birth, and she loved men with roughhewn manners who were, nevertheless, proven in chivalry. She lived in the magnificent and lavish royal custom of an empress, in the Persian manner, which was the most stately ever to have prevailed among kings. She was served in vessels of gold and precious stones, adorned with every decoration. She amassed great treasures from her revenues and her own goods without extorting wealth from any of her subjects, and so generously did she give, when it was reasonable, that there was never seen a prince of greater generosity nor of greater magnificence.

"With all this having been said, the high point of her virtues which I have to tell you was, in summary, her profound learnedness in letters, both in those of the Egyptians and in those of her own language. When she rested, she diligently applied herself to study and wished to be instructed by Longinus the philosopher, who was her master and introduced her to philosophy. She knew Latin as well as Greek, through the aid of which she organized and arranged all historical works in concise and very careful form. Similarly, she desired that her children, whom she raised with strict discipline, be introduced to learning. Therefore, my dear friend, note and recall if you have ever seen or read of any prince or knight more complete in every virtue."

CONCERNING ANTONIA WHO BECAME EMPRESS

"It was no small secret which God revealed through a woman's vision to Justinian, who subsequently became emperor of Constantinople. This Justinian was a guard of the treasures and coffers of Emperor Justin. One day, when Justinian went out to relax in the fields and brought along a woman named Antonia, whom he loved to keep him company, the noon hour arrived and he was overcome with fatigue. Justinian lay down under a tree to sleep and placed his head in his girl friend's lap. Just as he fell asleep, Antonia saw a large eagle come and fly over their heads, spreading its wings to shield Justinian's face from the heat of the sun. Antonia was wise and understood the significance of this sign. When Justinian awoke, she spoke to him with fair words and said, 'Sweet friend, I have loved and I love you very much. You are the master of my body and my love, and you know it. Since it is right that a beloved lover should refuse his mistress nothing, in exchange for my virginity and my love, I want to ask you for a boon, which, although quite important to me, will seem quite insignificant to you.' Justinian answered his girl friend that she should ask boldly and that she would never lack for anything which he could grant. Then Antonia asked, 'The boon which I am asking from you is that, when you are emperor, you will not disdain your poor friend Antonia but will let her be the companion of your honor and your empire through faithful marriage. And so from this moment on, promise me this.' When Justinian heard the maiden speak this way, he began to laugh, thinking that she had said this as a joke. Since he considered it impossible that it could ever happen that he would be emperor, he promised her that he would without fail take her as his wife when he was emperor; he swore it to her by all the gods, and she thanked him for it. As a sign of this promise, she made him give her his ring and she gave him hers. Thereupon she said, 'Justinian, I tell you in all certainty that you will be emperor and that this will happen to you in a short time.' And with that, they left. Shortly afterward, after the emperor Justin had assembled his army to attack the Persians, he caught an illness from which he died. Later, when the barons and princes assembled to elect a new emperor and could not reach a consensus, it happened that out of spite for one another they elected Justinian emperor, who did not waste time dreaming but immediately moved in great strength with a large army against the Persians and won the battle, captured the king of the Persians, and won great honor and booty. After he had returned to the palace, his girlfriend Antonia was not out amusing herself but through great subtleness she had managed to make her way to where he sat on the throne surrounded by princes. And there, kneeling before him, she began her plea, explaining that she was a maiden who had come to him to ask for justice from a young man who was engaged to her and who had given her his ring and taken hers. The emperor, not thinking of her at all, replied that if a young man was engaged to her as she said, the right thing was for him to take her as his wife and that he, the emperor, would gladly see that she receive justice, provided that she could prove her claim. Antonia then took the ring from her finger and handed it to him, saying, 'Noble Emperor, I can prove it with this ring. See whether you recognize it.' At this point the emperor realized that he had been caught by his own words, yet all the same he wished to keep his promise to her and immediately had her led to his chambers and dressed in noble garments, and he took her as his wife."

RECTITUDE GIVES EXAMPLES OF MEN WHO WERE FAVORED WITH GOOD FORTUNE BECAUSE THEY BELIEVED THEIR WIVES.

"I will tell you about those men favored with good fortune because they followed the advice given by their wives, and let this proof suffice, for I could say so much that it would be an endless process, and what I told you before about many wise and virtuous ladies on this subject applies here, too. The emperor Justinian, whom I mentioned to you before, had a baron as his companion whom he loved as much as himself. This baron was named Belisarius, and he was a very brave knight. Therefore, the emperor made him the master and commander of his cavalry, and had him sit at his table and served with the same dignity, and, in short, he showed Belisarius so many signs of love that his other barons became quite jealous and told the emperor that Belisarius intended to put him to death and assume control of the empire. The emperor believed this report too readily and, intending to put Belisarius to death covertly, commanded him to fight against a people called the Vandals whom he would not be able to defeat because of their overwhelming strength. When Belisarius heard this command, he realized and knew for sure that the emperor would not have charged him with this mission unless he had surely fallen from the emperor's favor and good will. He was grieved he could do nothing more and he left for home. When his wife, who was named Antonia and who was the empress' sister, saw him lying in bed, pale and pensive his eyes filled with tears, she took pity on him and repeatedly asked him what the matter was, so that, in great pain, he told her the cause of his sorrow. After having listened to him, the wise lady pretended to be very joyful and consoled him, saying, 'What! Is that all that is bothering you? You must not be so upset!' As this happened during the time when the faith of Jesus Christ was still quite new, the good lady, who was a Christian, then said, 'Have faith in Jesus Christ, the crucified, and through this faith and with His help, you will surely triumph. If the envious desire to destroy you with their false words, you will show with your good deeds that they are liars and taken in by their own lies. So trust in me and do not disparage my words. Let all your hope be in the Living God, and I promise you that you will conquer. Take care not to give the slightest appearance of being burdened by this matter or of being sad, but instead seem glad, like someone who is quite happy. I will tell you when to assemble your army as hastily as possible. In addition, take care that no one knows where you wish to go. Also arrange to have plenty of ships and then divide your army into two parts, and, as quickly and as secretly as you can, invade Africa with one part of your army and immediately attack your enemies. I will have the other part of your troops with me, and we will arrive by sea from the other side of the port, and, while the enemy will be trying to join battle with you, we will come in from the other flank into the cities and towns and will put everyone to death and everything to the torch and destroy them all.' Belisarius followed this advice and so acted like a wise man and organized the expedition according to what she had said, no more, no less. Everything turned out so well for him that he was able to conquer and subjugate his enemies. He captured the king of the Vandals and won such a noble victory through the good counsel, sense, and valiance of his wife that the emperor loved him more than ever.

"Likewise, a second time it happened that, because of false gossip spread by envious courtiers, Belisarius again fell from the emperor's grace and was completely stripped of his duties with the cavalry. Nevertheless, his wife comforted him and gave him hope. Then the emperor himself was deposed from his rule over the empire by the same envious courtiers. However, because of his wife's advice, Belisarius managed with all his power intact to return the emperor to his throne, even though the emperor had done him great wrong. Thus the emperor realized the loyalty of his knight and the treason of the others, and this all thanks to the wisdom and sound advice of the shrewd lady."

Margery Kempe

1373-1438

Margery Burnham, daughter of the mayor of Bishop's Lynne in Norfolk, England, was born into a comfortable merchant family in 1373 and married John Kempe in 1393. Because of a traumatic incident connected with the birth of her first child, Kempe began a life-long search for holiness and an emotional union with God. After the births of their fourteen children, Kempe persuaded her husband to take a vow of chastity, and in 1414 she embarked on a series of pilgrimages to Jerusalem, Rome, Canterbury, and sites in Germany. Kempe's devotional life included: visions in which she conversed with Jesus and members of the holy family, meditations on Christ's life which resulted in loud weeping, and constant struggles with her bodily desires. Although it is uncertain if Kempe could read or write, she had a wide knowledge of religious literature in English and Latin. Later in her life, Kempe dictated her story to two clerks; the result, *The Book of Margery Kempe,* is the first spiritual autobiography in English. Selections of Kempe's text appeared anonymously in early printed devotional materials, but the complete manuscript of her *Book* was not discovered until 1934.

Kempe's story shows her to be a very real person struggling to have her religious expression validated by her community. Her extravagantly pious displays of weeping and devotion won her both admiration and ridicule, the same reactions many modern readers have to her. Although her devotional practice was orthodox, imitating models in religious handbooks of her day, she was nevertheless accused of being a Lollard. Lollards, members of a persecuted religious sect in fourteenth- and fifteenth-century England, were influenced by the English theologian and religious reformer John Wycliffe. Along with a belief in the primacy of the Bible, Lollards encouraged the religious participation and education of women. Thus, Kempe's active witnessing (which she insisted was not "preaching") brought her before suspicious authorities, who eventually acquitted her of heresy.

In Chapter 1, Kempe begins her story of religious awakening. Her word "stirrings" is also frequently used by Richard Rolle, the enormously popular and influential mid-fourteenth-century devotional writer, to describe the physical symptoms of his passionate spiritual ecstasy. It also reflects Kempe's personal struggle between physical and spiritual desires. How do you see this conflict played out in the following selections? What have we read in Humanities 124 and this semester which sheds light on Kempe's feelings that she has been contaminated by marriage and childbirth? In Kempe's visions she practices "affective piety." Based on your reading of Chapter 64, how would you define this term?

from *The Book of Margery Kempe*

CHAPTER 1

When this creature was twenty years of age, or somewhat more, she was married to a worshipful burgess [of Lynn] and was with child within a short time, as nature would have it. And after she had conceived, she was troubled with severe attacks of sickness until the child was born. And then, what with the labour-pains she had in childbirth and the sickness that had gone before, she despaired of her life, believing she might not live. Then she sent for her confessor, for she had a thing on her conscience which she had never revealed before that time in all her life. For she was continually hindered by her enemy—the devil—always saying to her while she was in good health that she didn't need to confess but to do penance by herself alone, and all should be forgiven, for God is merciful enough. And therefore this creature often did great penance in fasting on bread and water, and performed other acts of charity with devout prayers, but she would not reveal that one thing in confession.

And when she was at any time sick or troubled, the devil said in her mind that she should be damned, for she was not shriven of that fault. Therefore, after her child was born, and not believing she would live, she sent for her confessor, as said before, fully wishing to be shriven of her whole lifetime, as near as she could. And when she came to the point of saying that thing which she had so long concealed, her confessor was a little too hasty and began sharply to reprove her before she had fully said what she meant, and so she would say no more in spite of anything he might do. And soon after, because of the dread she had of damnation on the one hand, and his sharp reproving of her on the other, this creature went out of her mind and was amazingly disturbed and tormented with spirits for half a year, eight weeks and odd days.

And in this time she saw, as she thought, devils opening their mouths all alight with burning flames of fire, as if they would have swallowed her in, sometimes pawing at her, sometimes threatening her, sometimes pulling her and hauling her about both night and day during the said time. And also the devils called out to her with great threats, and bade her that she should forsake her Christian faith and belief, and deny her God, his mother, and all the saints in heaven, her good works and all good virtues, her father, her mother, and all her friends. And so she did. She slandered her husband, her friends, and her own self. She spoke many sharp and reproving words; she recognized no virtue nor goodness; she desired all wickedness; just as the spirits tempted her to say and do, so she said and did. She would have killed herself many a time as they stirred her to, and would have been damned with them in hell, and in witness of this she bit her own hand so violently that the mark could be seen for the rest of her life. And also she pitilessly tore the skin on her body near her heart with her nails, for she had no other implement, and she would have done something worse, except that she was tied up and forcibly restrained both day and night so that she could not do as she wanted.

And when she had long been troubled by these and many other temptations, so that people thought she should never have escaped from them alive, then one time as she lay by herself and her keepers were not with her, our merciful Lord Christ Jesus—ever to be trusted, worshipped be his name, never forsaking his servant in time of need—appeared to his creature who had forsaken him, in the likeness of a man, the most seemly, most beauteous, and most amiable that ever might be seen with man's eye, clad in a mantle of purple silk, sitting upon her bedside, looking upon her with so blessed a countenance that she was strengthened in all her spirits, and he said to her these words: 'Daughter, why have you forsaken me, and I never forsook you?' And as soon as he had said these words, she saw truly how the air opened as bright as any lightning, and he ascended up into the air, not hastily and quickly, but beautifully and gradually, so that she could clearly behold him in the air until it closed up again.

And presently the creature grew as calm in her wits and her reason as she ever was before, and asked her husband, as soon as he came to her, if she could have the keys of the buttery to get her food and drink as she had done before. Her maids and her keepers advised him that he should not deliver up any keys to her, for they said she would only give away such goods as there were, because she did not know what she was saying, as they believed.

Nevertheless, her husband, who always had tenderness and compassion for her, ordered that they should give her the keys. And she took food and drink as her bodily strength would allow her, and she once again recognized her friends and her household, and everybody else who came to her in order to see how our Lord Jesus Christ had worked his grace in her—blessed may he be, who is ever near in tribulation. When people think he is far away from them he is very near through his grace. Afterwards this creature performed all her responsibilities wisely and soberly enough, except that she did not truly know our Lord's power to draw us to him.

CHAPTER 3

One night, as this creature lay in bed with her husband, she heard a melodious sound so sweet and delectable that she thought she had been in paradise. And immediately she jumped out of bed and said 'Alas that ever I sinned! It is full merry in heaven.' This melody was so sweet that it surpassed all the melody that might be heard in this world, without any comparison, and it caused this creature when she afterwards heard any mirth or melody to shed very plentiful and abundant tears of high devotion, with great sobbings and sighings for the bliss of heaven, not fearing the shames and contempt of this wretched world. And ever after her being drawn towards God in this way, she kept in mind the joy and the melody that there was in heaven, so much so that she could not very well restrain herself from speaking of it. For when she was in company with any people she would often say, 'It is full merry in heaven!'

And those who knew of her behaviour previously and now heard her talk so much of the bliss of heaven said to her, 'Why do you talk so of the joy that is in heaven? You don't know it, and you haven't been there any more than we have.' And they were angry with her because she would not hear or talk of worldly things as they did, and as she did previously.

And after this time she never had any desire to have sexual intercourse with her husband, for paying the debt of matrimony was so abominable to her that she would rather, she thought, have eaten and drunk the ooze and muck in the gutter than consent to intercourse, except out of obedience.

And so she said to her husband, 'I may not deny you my body, but all the love and affection of my heart is withdrawn from all earthly creatures and set on God alone.' But he would have his will with her, and she obeyed with much weeping and sorrowing because she could not live in chastity. And often this creature advised her husband to live chaste and said that they had often (she well knew) displeased God by their inordinate love, and the great delight that each of them had in using the other's body, and now it would be a good thing if by mutual consent they punished and chastised themselves by abstaining from the lust of their bodies. Her husband said it was good to do so, but he might not yet—he would do so when God willed. And so he used her as he had done before, he would not desist. And all the time she prayed to God that she might live chaste, and three or four years afterwards, when it pleased our Lord, her husband made a vow of chastity, as shall be written afterwards, by Jesus's leave.

And also, after this creature heard this heavenly melody, she did great bodily penance. She was sometimes shriven two or three times on the same day, especially of that sin which she had so long concealed and covered up, as is written at the beginning of this book. She gave herself up to much fasting and keeping of vigils; she rose at two or three of the clock and went to church, and was there at her prayers until midday and also the whole afternoon. And then she was slandered and reproved by many people because she led so strict a life. She got herself a hair-cloth from a kiln—the sort that malt is dried on—and put it inside her gown as discreetly and secretly as she could, so that her husband should not notice it. And nor did he, although she lay beside him every night in bed and wore the hair-shirt every day, and bore him children during that time.

Then she had three years of great difficulty with temptations, which she bore as meekly as she could, thanking our Lord for all his gifts, and she was as merry when she was reproved, scorned or ridiculed for our Lord's love, and much more merry than she was before amongst the dignities of this world. For she knew very well that she had sinned greatly against God and that she deserved more shame and sorrow than any man could cause her, and contempt in this world was the right way heavenwards, for Christ himself chose that way. All his apostles, martyrs, confessors and virgins and all those who ever came to heaven, passed by the way of tribulation, and she desired nothing as much as heaven. Then she was glad in her conscience when she believed that she was entering upon the way which would lead her to the place that she most desired.

And this creature had contrition and great compunction, with plentiful tears and much loud and violent sobbing, for her sins and for her unkindness towards her maker. She reflected on her unkindness since her childhood, as our Lord would put it into her mind, very many times. And then when she contemplated her own wickedness, she could only sorrow and weep and ever pray for mercy and forgiveness. Her weeping was so plentiful and continual that many people thought that she could weep and leave off when she wanted, and therefore many people said she was a false hypocrite, and wept when in company for advantage and profit. And then very many people who loved her before while she was in the world abandoned her and would not know her, and all the while she thanked God for everything, desiring nothing but mercy and forgiveness of sin.

CHAPTER 64

The creature said to her Lord Christ Jesus, 'Ah, blessed Lord, I wish I knew in what I might best love you and please you; and that my love were as sweet to you as I think your love is to me.'

Then our sweet Lord Jesus, answering his creature, said 'Daughter, if you knew how sweet your love is to me, you would never do anything else but love me with all your heart. And therefore, do believe, daughter, that my love is not so sweet to you as your love is to me. Daughter, you do not know how much I love you, for it may not be known in this world how much it is, nor be felt as it is, for you would fail and burst and never endure it, for the joy that you would feel. And therefore I measure it as I wish to your greatest ease and comfort.

'But daughter, you shall well know in another world how much I loved you on earth, for there you will have great reason to thank me. There you will see without end every good day that I ever gave you on earth of contemplation, of devotion, and of all the great charity that I have given you to the profit of your fellow Christians. For this shall be your reward when you come home into heaven.

'There is no clerk in all this world who can, daughter, teach you better than I can do, and, if you will be obedient to my will, I shall be obedient to your will. Where is a better token of love than to weep for your Lord's love? You know very well, daughter, that the devil has no charity, for he is very angry with you, and he might hurt you somewhat, but he shall not injure you, except a little, in this world, in sometimes making you afraid, so that you should pray all the more strongly to me for grace, and direct your love all the more towards me. There is no clerk who can speak against the life which I teach you, and, if he does so, he is not God's clerk, he is the devil's clerk. I tell you truly that there is no man in this world—if he would willingly suffer as much humiliation for my love as you have done, and cleave as steadfastly to me, not willing to forsake me for anything that may be said or done against him—but I shall treat him fairly and show him much grace, both in this world, and in the other.'

Then the creature said, 'Ah, my beloved Lord, you should show this life to religious men and priests.'

Our Lord replied to her, 'No, no, daughter, for that thing which I love best they do not love—and that is shame, contempt, scorn and rebukes from people—and therefore they shall not have this grace. For, daughter, I tell you, he that dreads the shame of the world may not perfectly love God. And, daughter, under the habit of holiness is covered much wickedness. Daughter, if you saw the wickedness that is done in the world as I do, you would be amazed that I do not take utter vengeance upon them. But, daughter, I desist because of your love. You weep so every day for mercy that I have to grant it, and people will not believe the goodness that I work in you for them.

'Nevertheless, daughter, there shall come a time when they shall be very glad to believe the grace that I have given you for them. And I shall say to them when they are passed out of this world, "Look, I ordained her to weep for her sins, and you held her in great contempt, but her charity for you would never cease." And therefore, daughter, those who are good souls shall highly thank me for the grace and goodness that I have given you, those who are wicked shall protest and have great pain to endure the grace that I show to you. And therefore I shall chastise them as it were for myself.'

She prayed, 'No, beloved Lord Jesus, do not chastise any creature for me. You well know, Lord, that I desire no vengeance, but I ask mercy and grace for all men if it be your will to grant it. Nevertheless, Lord, rather than that they should be separated from you without end, chastise them as you wish yourself. It seems, Lord, in my soul, that you are full of charity, for you say you do not wish the death of a sinful man. And you also say that you wish all men to be saved. Then Lord, since you wish all men to be saved, I must wish the same, and you say yourself that I must love my fellow Christians as my own self. And, Lord, know that I have wept and sorrowed many years because I would be saved, and so must I do for my fellow Christians.'

Islam

ARAB ORAL TRADITION

1400s

'ANTARA IBN SHADDAD
Warrior and Poet

'Antara ibn Shaddad is a historical figure who lived in the second half of the sixth century in pre-Islamic southern Arabia or Yemen. His father, Shaddad, was the chief of his nomadic desert tribe, and his mother, Zabiba, was a black slave. 'Antar was a great warrior who won his freedom through acts of bravery, but it is his poetic ability, as reflected in his ode to Abla, which won him his lasting renown. For centuries, *Sirat 'Antar*, the epic version of 'Antar's life, has been an important part of Arabic legend, and even today 'Antar is a popular prototype of the heroic ideal in the Arab world. Although the famous medieval Arab philologist 'Abd al-Malik ibn Quraib al-Asmai (d. 823) claims authorship of the epic, the version we have today comes from an extensive tradition of oral storytelling and multiple manuscript revisions. *Sirat 'Antar* is one of the longest works of Arabic fiction: the fifteenth century version from which this excerpt is taken covers 5600 pages. The complete *Sirat 'Antar* recounts 'Antar's childhood, his courage in varied circumstances, his numerous love affairs, his involvement with magic, and his extensive travels. In the excerpt here, 'Antar begins his torturously long, but eventually successful, courtship of his cousin Abla.

'Antar provides an interesting contrast to other famous warriors. In what ways could you compare him to Roland, also the subject of oral epic? Much later, when you read Shakespeare's *Othello*, recall the convention of the great black Arabic warrior. Although 'Antar is a pre-Islamic work, it has maintained its popularity in Islamic countries through the centuries. Why might that be?

from the epic *Sirat 'Antar*

The Fourth Story

'Abla

It was the custom in those far-off days that the Arab women should drink sheep's milk as they arose in the early morning, and this milk would be brought to the tents of the leaders of the tribe by a servant who had seen to it that the warm milk had been cooled in the dawn breeze. 'Antar performed this service for Samiya, wife of his father Sheddad, and for Sheriya, the wife of Malec, son of Karad, uncle of 'Antar. Malec was a man of suspicious nature, and one in whom envy and jealousy strove with arrogance for mastery of his soul. He lacked the graces of magnanimity so precious to the Arab people. His son, Amr, inherited his father's meanness, but his daughter, 'Abla, displayed in her person and in her personality all the gifts most admired in a daughter of the desert. Her merry humour, her kindness to the unfortunate and her respect for her elders rendered her a byword in the tribe; and as she emerged from childhood to womanhood her beauty was fast becoming legendary.

Yet, for all her good humour, there was little love between sister and brother, 'Abla and Amr. Indeed, he disliked what he considered to be her lack of dignity. For Amr was proud of the nobility of his family which he shared by birth, and he had not realized, as had his sister, that noble behaviour should accompany a high position. Moreover, as children, 'Abla had far excelled him as a rider of horses, for in those days she had sought to emulate Robab, and the Princess Zenobia, who led her father's men into battle in the days when Palmyra was still a fair city at the height of its beauty; and 'Abla would still recount the story of the conception of the mare, Dahis, the Thruster, and of the Great Race, but Amr did not like these stories.

And it happened at this time—and it was springtime—that when 'Antar entered the women's tent to serve the cool milk, he surprised his cousin 'Abla at her toilet, for she sat unveiled and only half-dressed while her mother combed and plaited her long black hair. 'Abla cried out in her embarrassment and fled across the tent, her hair flowing behind her as a silken pennant floats in the wind; and 'Antar, though almost bereft of his senses by her beauty, yet retained enough of them to observe the loveliness of her form—her ivory skin, and her firm breasts rising cleanly as do the desert dunes in the moonlight; and the rustle of her dress was soft as the wings of starlings flocking to the wadi [a dry stream bed] in the evening hours. So 'Antar lost his heart to his cousin 'Abla, who was yet so far above him in rank that never could he aspire to marriage with her, being but a slave although of noble blood.

On the following morning, as he entered the tent again, he was overcome with embarrassment, for 'Abla cried in her merry way, "It seems, friend, that I must rise earlier than you to preserve my modesty! See how well I have done today, almost beating the dawn itself!" And she laughed, and her aunt and her mother laughed too; but as for poor 'Antar, his love and his confusion were so great that he offered the sheep's milk to his fair cousin before he had served it to the elder women. Then Samiya, wife of Sheddad, was furious, and drove him from the tent. But 'Abla smiled to herself and was not unaware of 'Antar's strength and comeliness for all that his colour was black as the pitch which oozes over the sand foot of the Persian mountains in the far desert.

In those days, as in our own, there were plots and intrigues among the slaves and servants, and among their masters too. Samiya's anger with 'Antar was exploited now by Zajir, slave of Rabia, who bore a grudge against 'Antar. Zajir told Samiya how 'Antar had learned camel-riding and his horse-riding at the expense of the herds, and how he had injured the few and precious trees of the desert fringes by aiming at them his javelins and spears. And Samiya sought her husband and complained to him of the black slave who could not care for the animals in his charge nor appreciate the true position of an elder woman's rank compared to that of young 'Abla.

And Sheddad was angry, and seizing his son he beat him cruelly. But 'Antar, although he was already as strong as his father, suffered the beating in all humility because he respected his father and his father's position in the tribe. Zebeeba came also to her son and warned him to remember his lowly position. But 'Antar, who lay bound after the beating, burst his bonds simply by flexing his muscles, and seizing a horse he followed the slave Zajir into the desert, and there killed him for his treachery. "For," he said to himself, "a man should, if he have a grievance, speak openly to his opponent of the quarrel, nor should he secretly persuade a woman to speak for him."

Among the leaders of the tribe, too, there were feuds and dissension, for Rabia, clever and ambitious as he was, disliked the Prince and his brothers, and Sheddad and Malec swayed to one side or the other side, but all respected and feared, or loved, lord Zuhair.

Now when 'Antar had killed the second slave he sought protection from the Prince against Rabia's wrath, and the Prince made up his mind to settle the affair with no further bloodshed, for the Prince was a kindly man. He sought the elders in their assembly, and all rose as he entered, giving and receiving the greetings. And the Prince, still standing, turned to Rabia and said, "Cousin, I greet you, and if you love me I would ask a favour of you." "Indeed I love you," growled Rabia, who did no such thing, but to whom the courtesies were important as they are to all true Arabs. "Give me then, I pray, your slave Zajir," continued the Prince. Now Rabia valued Zajir, and thought he was still alive, and to give himself time to think he reproached the Prince, saying, "Sit down in your place, I beg of you, my cousin, for are we not all standing because you continue so?" "Do you wish I should sit down, and do you love me?" queried the Prince. "Then favour me with your slave, else I remain standing and may disbelieve your love." Rabia had no choice but to agree, and the company was seated, and when Zuhair joined them, then did the Prince reveal Zajir's death, and he explained to Rabia that this unfortunate fact was now of little consequence to the dishonest slave's former master. And Zuhair and his elders smiled at the Prince's trick, and Rabia appeared pacified by the gift of two new slaves.

But afterwards, Rabia sought out his brother, Amara the Coxcomb, who hated the Prince, and together they approached Sheddad, and they persuaded Sheddad that his Negro son was becoming a menace to the unity of the tribe, and Sheddad agreed, and a plot was laid to kill 'Antar when he was alone and unprotected in the desert. "For," said these uncles of his, and his father, "Lord Zuhair and the Prince think well of 'Antar, but may we not be overwhelmed by a veritable ocean of calamities and misfortunes if he continues to live among us? He must die."

Now 'Antar's flocks were grazing in a secluded valley far from the camp, and 'Antar was composing to himself a poem in praise of his beautiful cousin 'Abla, when an enormous lion burst through the bushes and confronted him. And behind the rocks, on the other side of the valley, 'Antar's father and his two uncles crept up in hiding, planning to murder him. But 'Antar thrust the crook he carried between the lion's teeth and, advancing, seized the animal's upper jaw in one hand and its lower jaw in the other hand, and tore the lion in two. Then he skinned the lion and burned its flesh, and started scraping its pelt for his own use; and as he scraped he sang:

O lion, father of lion cubs and king of the sandy
 wastes and of the animals which dwell there,
How strong thou art, how proud of thy strength.

But thou art brought low.

And I—I did not use my sword or my lance,
With my bare hands I brought about thy downfall.
Of the two of us, is it not I that am the lion?"

And the men hidden behind the rocks shuddered and said, "Which of us would dare to attack this youth? Prudence demands we abandon our plan and return whence we came." And this they did, and when 'Antar returned with his flocks and his lion's skin, they joined in the rejoicing at his exploit and appeared as friendly and as deeply impressed as Zuhair himself.

So when, in a few days, the elders of the tribe and the fighting men went off upon a desert raid, Sheddad repented his harshness and left 'Antar, of whom he was secretly proud, in charge of his tents and of the flocks and of the women, and he warned 'Antar not to let any of them wander far, and 'Antar answered proudly, "O my master, should the smallest object be missing on your return, let me, for the remainder of my life, be kept in chains and bondage."

But when the warriors had departed, and after a few days constrained within the camp the women became bored, and Samiya, wife of Sheddad, proposed that a feast should be held on the shores of Dhat al Arsad's pools, not far from the camp, and 'Antar dared not hinder her; and indeed rejoiced with the women, for he would be for a whole day in 'Abla's company.

When the pleasure-seekers reached the lakeside on the following day, the sun sparkled upon the waters and was not too hot to hinder their preparations. The servants fanned the charcoal to a steady glow, and lambs were put to roast over it; and the two kids, which had been baking overnight buried in clay pots beneath the soil, were uncovered and distributed with rice and leben among the hungry children. Birds sang among the reeds, and the broad beaches of the lake were bright with flowers. Flushed with wine, some among the girls danced for their elders' delight, discarding their veils; and, among them all, 'Abla was the most beautiful.

Then suddenly a cry rang down the valley, "The Qahtan, the Qahtan!" And seventy horsemen armed to the teeth seemed to pour like a torrent from the crest of the eastern hill down to the waterside. Each horseman seized one of the girls or the women, and the children scattered, and the servants fled. And 'Antar? As he saw his beloved seized by one of the armed men and dragged to the saddle, 'Antar sprang like a panther and threw the marauder to the dust where death welcomed him as her own. 'Antar seized the warrior's arms and his horse, and pausing only to shelter 'Abla behind some rocks, outstripped the raiders and faced them, crying: "A curse upon you, evil ones, who dare only to attack women, the daughters and the wives of noble men. Now must you reckon with 'Antar!" Twenty men fell to his lance and sword, and the remainder fled, calling to each other, "If the slaves of this tribe display such strength and courage, what can the warriors be like!" So the women were saved and returned to camp, praising 'Antar with smiles and tears of gratitude, and 'Antar himself drove before him the arms and the horses of the twenty-one raiders he had slain, and he was elated, remembering 'Abla's heartfelt thanks at her rescue. Only Samiya feared the wrath of Sheddad, her husband, at having so wantonly exposed the tribeswomen to danger, so she swore all to secrecy; and only 'Abla and 'Antar remembered what looks had passed between them after the encounter.

But after a few days, when the warriors also had returned to the camp, Sheddad noticed the twenty-one new horses among his own horses, and he reproached 'Antar unjustly with having organized some raiding party of his own instead of minding the womenfolk—so winning for his tribe the slur of troublemaking. And 'Antar, bound by his promise, gritted his teeth and bore upon his body the whipping his father inflicted, and in his mind the humiliation he so little deserved. But Samiya's heart melted towards him, and in confessing all she saved him further punishment and, indeed, won for him Sheddad's good opinion, for he thought, In truth I have a noble son who has saved all the women of the tribe from rapine and who has allowed himself to suffer unjustly rather than betray a promise. Sheddad rewarded 'Antar with presents, as did the lord Zuhair. And Samiya praised 'Antar in poetry, saying:

> It is right that I respect him, that I protect him,
> For did not his strength and valour preserve my honour,
> His courage preserve honour among us all?

'Antar replied with a poem of gratitude, describing also his own steadfastness, for he said:

> Men are of two kinds—those whose hearts
> Crack with fear as a glass goblet crazes in the heat,
> And those whose hearts are of rock.

So was Sheddad charmed, as 'Abla had been charmed by a poem on her gaiety and beauty on the day of the picnic by the lake.

Ibn Khaldun

1332-1395

Abd al-Rahman Ibn Mohammad is generally known as Ibn Khaldun after a remote ancestor. Born into a Spanish Arab family in Tunisia, Khaldun spent a lifetime of turbulent government service in Arab capitols such as Cairo and Fez. While in retreat in Algeria, he wrote *Muqaddimah*, the first volume of his world history which earned him the title "father of modern social science and cultural history." After an analysis of historiography, *Muqaddimah* identifies psychological, economic, environmental and social facts which have helped shape human civilization. Khaldun argues that those things mandated by God can be shown scientifically to be the best social policies, and that this is the natural consequence of the fact that economic principles and the foundation of the good life were both created by God. Other volumes deal with histories, both contemporary and ancient, of the Arabs, Hebrews, Greeks, Romans, and Persians. These also include histories of Muslim and European rulers. The last volume, *Al-Tasrif,* mostly recounts the stories of his life including meeting the Mongol conqueror Tamerlane.

What are the important methods Khaldun urges us to use in reading and interpreting history? What, for example, might he say about reading Procopius or Babur?

from *The Muqaddimah*

The Introduction

The excellence of historiography. An appreciation of the various approaches to history. A glimpse of the different kinds of errors to which historians are liable. Why these errors occur.

It should be known that history is a discipline that has a great number of approaches. Its useful aspects are very many. Its goal is distinguished.

History makes us acquainted with the conditions of past nations as they are reflected in their national character. It makes us acquainted with the biographies of the prophets and with the dynasties and policies of rulers. Whoever so desires may thus achieve the useful result of being able to imitate historical examples in religious and worldly matters.

The (writing of history) requires numerous sources and much varied knowledge. It also requires a good speculative mind and thoroughness, which lead the historian to the truth and keep him from slips and errors. If he trusts historical information in its plain transmitted form and has no clear knowledge of the principles resulting from custom, the fundamental facts of politics, the nature of civilization, or the conditions governing human social organization, and if, furthermore, he does not evaluate remote or ancient material through comparison with near or contemporary material, he often cannot avoid stumbling and slipping and deviating from the path of truth. Historians, Qur'ân commentators and leading transmitters have committed frequent errors in the stories and events they reported. They accepted them in the plain transmitted form, without regard for its value. They did not check them with the principles underlying such historical situations, nor did they compare them with similar material. Also, they did not probe with the yardstick of philosophy, with the help of knowledge of the nature of things, or with the help of speculation and historical insight. Therefore, they strayed from the truth and found themselves lost in the desert of baseless assumptions and errors.

This is especially the case with figures, either of sums of money or of soldiers, whenever they occur in stories. They offer a good opportunity for false information and constitute a vehicle for nonsensical statements. They must be controlled and checked with the help of known fundamental facts.

For example, al-Mas'ûdî and many other historians report that Moses counted the army of the Israelites in the desert. He had all those able to carry arms, especially those twenty years and older, pass muster. There turned out to be 600,000 or more. In this connection, al-Mas'ûdî forgets to take into consideration whether Egypt and Syria could possibly have held such a number of soldiers. Every realm may have as large a militia as it can hold and support, but no more. This fact is attested by well-known customs and familiar conditions. Moreover, an army of this size cannot march or fight as a unit. The whole available territory would be too small for it. If it were in battle formation, it would extend two, three, or more times beyond the field of vision. How, then, could two such parties fight with each other, or one battle formation gain the upper hand when one flank does not know what the other flank is doing! The situation at the present day testifies to the correctness of this statement. The past resembles the future more than one drop of water another.

Furthermore, the realm of the Persians was much greater than that of the Israelites. This fact is attested by Nebuchadnezzar's victory over them. He swallowed up their country and gained complete control over it. He also destroyed Jerusalem, their religious and political capital. And he was merely one of the officials of the province of Fârs. It is said that he was the governor of the western border region. The Persian provinces of the two 'Irâqs, Khurâsân, Transoxania, and the region of Derbend on the Caspian Sea were much larger than the realm of the Israelites. Yet, the Persian army did not attain such a number or even approach it. The greatest concentration of Persian troops, at al-Qâdisîyah, amounted to 120,000 men all of whom had their retainers. This is according to Sayf; who said that with their retainers they amounted to over 200,000 persons. According to 'Â'ishah and az-Zuhrî, the troop concentration with which Rustum advanced against Sa'd at al-Qâdisîyah amounted to only 60,000 men, all of whom had their retainers.

Then, if the Israelites had really amounted to such a number, the extent of the area under their rule would have been larger, for the size of administrative units and provinces under a particular dynasty is in direct proportion to the size of its militia and the groups that support the dynasty. Now, it is well known that the territory of the Israelites did not comprise an area larger than the Jordan province and Palestine in Syria and the region of Medina and Khaybar in the Hijâz. Also, there were only three generations between Moses and Israel, according to the best-informed scholars. Moses was the son of Amram, the son of Kohath, the son of Levi, the son of Jacob who is Israel-Allâh. This is Moses' genealogy in the Torah. The length of time between Israel and Moses was indicated by al-Mas'ûdî when he said: 'Israel entered Egypt with his children, the tribes, and the children, when they came to Joseph numbering seventy souls. The length of their stay in Egypt until they left with Moses for the desert was two hundred and twenty years. During those years, the kings of the Copts, the Pharaohs, passed them on (as their subjects) one to the other.' It is improbable that the descendants of one man could branch out into such a number within four generations.

It has been assumed that this number of soldiers applied to the time of Solomon and his successors. Again, this is improbable. Between Solomon and Israel, there were only eleven generations, that is: Solomon, the son of David, the son of Jesse, the son of Obed, the son of Boaz, the son of Salmon, the son of Nahshon, the son Amminadab, the son of Ram, the son of Hezron, the son of Perez, the son of Judah, the son of Jacob. The descendants of one man in eleven generations would not branch out into such a number, as has been assumed. They might, indeed, reach hundreds or thousands. This often happens. But an increase beyond that to higher figures is improbable. Comparison with observable present-day and well-known nearby facts proves the assumption and report to be untrue. According to the definite statement of the Israelite stories, Solomon's army amounted to 12,000 men, and his horses numbered 1,400, which were stabled at his palace. This is the correct information. No attention should be paid to nonsensical statements by the common run of informants. In the days of Solomon, the Israelite state saw its greatest flourishing and their realm its widest extension.

Whenever contemporaries speak about the dynastic armies of their own or recent times, and whenever they engage in discussions about Muslim or Christian soldiers, or when they get to figuring the tax revenues and the money spent by the government, the outlays of extravagant spenders, and the goods that rich and prosperous men have in stock, they are quite generally found to exaggerate, to go beyond the bounds of the ordinary, and to succumb to the temptation of sensationalism. When the officials in charge are questioned about their armies, when the goods and assets of wealthy people are assessed, and when the outlays of extravagant spenders are looked at in ordinary light, the figures will be found to amount to a tenth of what those people have said. The reason is simple. It is the common desire for sensationalism, the ease with which one may just mention a higher figure, and the disregard of reviewers and critics. This leads to failure to exercise self-criticism about one's errors and intentions, to demand from oneself moderation and fairness in reporting, to reapply oneself to study and research. Such historians let themselves go and made a feast of untrue statements. 'They procure for themselves entertaining stories in order to lead others away from the path of God.' This is a bad enough business.

It may be said that the increase of descendants to such a number would be prevented under ordinary conditions which, however do not apply to the Israelites. The increase in their case would be a miracle in accordance with the tradition which said that one of the things revealed to their forefathers, the prophets Abraham, Isaac, and Jacob, was that God would cause their descendants to increase until they were more numerous than the stars of heaven and the pebbles of the earth. God fulfilled this promise to them as an act of divine grace bestowed upon them and as an extraordinary miracle in their favour. Thus, ordinary conditions could not hinder it and nobody should speak against it.

Someone might come out against this tradition with the argument that it occurs only in the Torah which, as is well known, was altered by the Jews. The reply to this argument would be that the statement concerning the alteration of the Torah by the Jews is unacceptable to thorough scholars and cannot be understood in its plain meaning, since custom prevents people who have a revealed religion from dealing with their divine scriptures in such a manner. Thus, great increase in numbers in the case of the Israelites would be an extraordinary miracle. Custom, in the proper meaning of the word, would prevent anything of the sort from happening to other peoples.

It is true that a movement of (such a large group) would hardly be possible, but none took place, and there was no need for one. It is also true that each realm has only its particular number of militia. But the Israelites at first were no militiamen and had no dynasty. Their numbers increased that much, so that they could gain power over the land of Canaan which God had promised them and territory of which He had purified for them. All these things are miracles. God guides to the truth.

Another fictitious story of the historians, which they all report, concerns the reason for ar-Rashîd's destruction of the Barmecides. It is the story of al-'Abbâsah, ar-Rashîd's sister, and Ja'far b. Yahyâ b. Khâlid, his minister. Ar-Rashîd is said to have worried about where to place them when he was drinking wine with them. He wanted to receive them together in his company. Therefore, he permitted them to conclude a marriage that was not consummated. Al-'Abbâsah then tricked Ja'far in her desire to be alone with him, for she had fallen in love with him. Ja'far finally had intercourse with her—it is assumed, when he was drunk—and she became pregnant. The story was reported to ar-Rashîd who flew into a rage.

This story is irreconcilable with al-'Abbâsah's position, her religiousness, her parentage, and her exalted rank. She was a descendant of 'Abdallâh b. 'Abbâts and separated from him by only four generations, and they were the most distinguished and greatest men in Islam after him. Al-'Abbâsah was the daughter of Muhammad al-Mahdi, the son of Abû Ja'far 'Abdallâh al-Mansûr, the son of Muhammad as-Sajjâd, the son of the Father of the Caliphs 'Alî. 'Alî was the son of 'Abdallâh, the Interpreter of the Qur'ân, the son of the Prophet's uncle, al-'Abbâs. Al-'Abbâsah was the daughter of a caliph and the sister of a caliph. She was born to royal power, into the prophetical succession (the caliphate), and was descended from the men around Muhammad and his uncles. She was connected by birth with the leadership of Islam, the light of the revelation, and the place where the angels descended to bring the revelation. She was close in time to the desert attitude of true Arabism, to that simple state of Islam still far from the habits of luxury and lush pastures of sin. Where should one look for chastity and modesty, if she did not possess them? Where could cleanliness and purity be found, if they no longer existed in her house? How could she link her pedigree with that of Ja'far b. Yahyâ and stain her Arab nobility with a Persian client? His Persian ancestor had been acquired as a slave, or taken as a client, by one of her ancestors, an uncle of the Prophet and noble Qurashite, and all Ja'far did was that he together with his father was drawn along (by the growing fame of) the 'Abbâsid dynasty and thus prepared for and elevated to a position of nobility. And how could it be that ar-Rashîd, with his high-mindedness and great pride, would permit himself to become related by marriage to Persian clients! If a critical person looks at this story in all fairness and compares al-'Abbâsah with the daughter of a great ruler of his own time, he must find it disgusting and unbelievable that she could have done such a thing with one of the clients of her dynasty and while her family was in power. He would insist that the story be considered untrue. And who could compare with al-'Abbâsah and ar-Rashîd in dignity!

The reason for the destruction of the Barmecides was their attempt to gain control over the dynasty and their retention of the tax revenues. This went so far that when ar-Rashîd wanted even a little money, he could not get it. They took his affairs out of his hands and shared with him in his authority. He had no say with them in the affairs of his realm. Their influence grew, and their fame spread. They filled the positions and ranks of the government with their own children and creatures who became high officials, and thus barred all others from the positions of wazir, secretary, army commander, doorkeeper, and from the military and civilian administration. It is said that in the palace of ar-Rashîd, there were twenty-five high officials, both military and civilian, all children of Yahyâ b. Khâlid. There, they crowded the people of the dynasty and pushed them out by force. They could do that because of the position of their father, Yahyâ, mentor to Hârûn both as crown prince and as caliph. Hârûn run practically grew up in his lap and got all his education from him. Hârûn let him handle his affairs and used to call him 'father'. As a result, the Barmecides, and not the government, wielded all the influence. Their presumption grew. Their position became more and more influential. They became the centre of attention. All obeyed them. All hopes were addressed to them. From the farthest borders, presents and gifts of rulers and amirs were sent to them. The tax money found its way into their treasury, to serve as an introduction to them and to procure their favour. They gave gifts to and bestowed favours upon the men of the Shî'ah and upon important relatives of the Prophet. They gave the poor from the noble families related to the Prophet something to earn. They freed the captives. Thus, they were given praise as was not given to their caliph. They showered privileges and gifts upon those who came to ask favours from them. They gained control over villages and estates in the open and near the main cities in every province.

Eventually, the Barmecides irritated the inner circle. They caused resentment among the elite and aroused the displeasure of high officials. Jealousy and envy of all sorts began to show themselves, and the scorpions of intrigue crept into their soft beds in the government. The Qahtabah family, Ja'far's maternal uncles, led intrigues against them. Feelings for blood ties and relationship could not move or sway the Qahtabahs from the envy which was so heavy on their hearts. This joined with their master's incipient jealousy, with his dislike of restrictions and high-handedness, and with his latent resentment aroused by small acts of presumptuousness on the part of the Barmecides. When they continued to flourish, as they did, they were led to gross insubordination.

Ja'far himself paved the way for his own and his family's undoing, which ended with the collapse of their exalted position, with the heavens falling in upon them and the earth's sinking with them and their house. Their days of glory became a thing of the past, an example to later generations.

Close examination of their story, scrutinizing the ways of government and their own conduct, discloses that all this was natural and is easily explained. One understands that it was only jealousy and struggle for control on the part of the caliph and his subordinates that killed them. Another factor was the verses that enemies of the Barmecides among the inner circle surreptitiously gave the singers to recite, with the intention that the caliph should hear them and his stored-up animosity against them be aroused. These are the verses:

Would that Hind could fulfil her promise to us
And deliver us from our predicament,
And for once act on her own.
The impotent person is he who never acts on his own.

When ar-Rashîd heard these verses, he exclaimed: 'Indeed, I am just such an impotent person.' By this and similar methods, the enemies of the Barmecides eventually succeeded in arousing ar-Rashîd's latent jealousy and in bringing his terrible vengeance upon them. God is our refuge from men's desire for power and from misfortune.

The stupid story of ar-Rashid's winebibbing and his getting drunk in the company of boon companions is really abominable. It does not in the least agree with ar-Rashîd's attitude toward the fulfilment of the requirements of religion and justice incumbent upon caliphs. He consorted with religious scholars and saints. He wept when he heard their sermons. Then, there is his prayer in Mecca when he circumambulated the Ka'bah. He was pious, observed the times of prayer, and attended the morning prayer at its earliest hour. He used to go on raids (against unbelievers) one year and to make the pilgrimage to Mecca the next. He once rebuked his jester, Ibn Abî Maryam, who made an unseemly remark to him during prayer. When Ibn Abî Maryam heard ar-Rashîd recite: 'How is it that I should not worship Him who created me?' he said: 'Indeed, I do not know why.' 'Jokes even at prayer?' he said. 'Beware, beware of the Qur'ân and Islam. Apart from that, you may do whatever you wish.'

Furthermore, ar-Rashîd possessed a good deal of learning and simplicity, because his epoch was close to that of his forebears who had those qualities. The time between him and his grandfather, al-Mansûr, was not a long one. He was a young lad when al-Mansûr died. Al-Mansûr possessed a good deal of learning and religion.

His son, al-Mahdî, ar-Rashîd's father, experienced the austerity of al-Mansûr, who would not use public funds to provide new clothes for his family. One day, al-Mahdî came to him when he was at his office discussing with the tailors the patching of his family's worn garments. Al-Mahdî did not relish that and said: 'O Commander of the Faithful, this year I shall pay for the family's clothes from my own income.' Al-Mansûr's reply was: 'Do that.' He did not prevent him from paying himself but would not permit any public Muslim money to be spent for that purpose.

ZAHIRUDDIN MUHAMMAD BABUR

1483-1530

Zahiruddin Muhammad Babur was born a prince of Fergana in Transoxiana which is now modern Uzbekistan and Tajikistan. Babur was a member of the ruling family descended from the great conqueror Amir Temur (1336-1405), whose name was popularized in the West as "Tamerlane." From a life of conquest begun when he took the throne of Samarkand at twelve, Babur initiated what became the great Mughal Empire of India. The last of that line left India in 1858. Not only a great soldier and strategist, Babur was also a remarkably frank and prolific author. His autobiography, *The Baburnama,* is the first in Islamic literature and ranks among the great historical memoirs. Babur tells his tale in his own dialect of Turkish, rather than in Persian, the international language of culture of his time.

The text of *The Baburnama* opens with Babur's inheritance of the throne after the accidental death of his father, Umar-Shaukh Mirza, who had been at odds with his brother, Sultan-Ahmad Mirza, and his brother-in-law, Sultan-Mahmud Khan. Babur's personal narrative is mixed with general observations on the peoples of the region, their families, their households, and the landscape.

What do you notice about the dynamics of Babur's family? How is power derived in this dynasty? How trustworthy is Babur as a narrator?

from *The Baburnama*

[Memoirs of Babur, Prince and Emperor]

In the month of Ramadan in the year 899 [June 1494], in the province of Fergana, in my twelfth year I became king.

Since Umar-Shaykh Mirza was a *padishah* of exalted ambition with great claims, he was always bent on territorial expansion. Several times he led his army against Samarkand: sometimes he was defeated, and sometimes he returned disappointed. Several times also he invited his father-in-law, Yunus Khan, who was a descendant of Genghis Khan's second son, Chaghatay Khan, and was at that time the khan of the Moghul nation in Chaghatay Khan's territory. Each time Umar-Shaykh Mirza brought in Yunus Khan, he gave him lands. But Yunus Khan did not always agree with Umar-Shaykh Mirzra's ambitions, sometimes owing to Umar-Shaykh Mirza's misconduct and at other times to the rebelliousness of the Moghul nation, so Yunus Khan, unable to remain in the province, left for Moghulistan. The last time he brought in Yunus Khan, he gave him Tashkent, a province at that time under Umar-Shaykh Mirza's control. (In books Tashkent is called Shash and Chach, from which derives the "Chachi" bow.) From that date until 908 [1503] the territory of Tashkent and Shahrukhiyya was under the control of the Chaghatayid khans.

At that date the khanate of the Moghul nation was held by Yunus Khan's eldest son, my maternal uncle Sultan-Mahmud Khan. Umar-Shaykh Mirza's elder brother, the *padishah* of Samarkand, Sultan-Ahmad Mirza, and the khan of the Moghul nation, Sultan-Mahmud Khan, made a pact because they were suffering from Umar-Shaykh Mirza's misconduct. Sultan-Ahmad Mirza married one of his daughters to Sultan-Mahmud Khan, and on the above-mentioned date Sultan-Ahmad Mirza from the south of the Khodzhent River and Sultan-Mahmud Khan from the north led their armies out against Umar-Shaykh Mirza.

At this point a strange event occurred. It has been mentioned that the Akhsi fortress is situated atop a high ravine, with the buildings at its edge. On Monday, the fourth of Ramadan of this year [June 8, 1494], Umar-Shaykh Mirza toppled into the ravine with his doves and dovecote and gave up the ghost. He was thirty-nine years old.

UMAR-SHAYKH MIRZA

His birth and lineage. He was born in 860 [1456] in Samarkand. He was Sultan-Abusa'id Mirza's fourth son, younger than Sultan-Ahmad Mirza, Sultan-Muhammad Mirza, and Sultan-Mahmud Mirza. Sultan-Abusa'id Mirza was Sultan-Muhammad Mirza's son. Sultan-Muhammad Mirza was the son of Miranshah Mirza, Temur Beg's third son, who was younger than Umar-Shaykh Mirza and Jahangir Mirza, and older than ShaliruIch Mirza.

His realm. First Sultan-Abusa'id Mirza gave Kabul to Umar-Shaylth Mirza and sent him off with Baba Kabuli as his *beg atäkä*. He recalled him from Daragaz to Samarkand for the mirzas' circumcision feast. Since Temür Beg had given Fergana to the elder Umar-Shaykh Mirza, he gave him the province of Andizhan and sent him off with Khudaberdi Tughchï Temürtash as his *beg atäkä*.

His appearance and habits. He was short in stature, had a round beard and a fleshy face, and was fat. He wore his tunic so tight that to fasten the ties, he had to hold in his stomach; if he let himself go, it often happened that the ties broke. He was unceremonious in both dress and speech. He wore his turban over a *dastarpech*. At that time, all turbans were twisted four times, but he wrapped his without twisting and left the fringe hanging. In the summertime, except when he was holding court, he wore a Mongol cap.

His character. He was a Hanafi by sect and orthodox of belief. He never neglected the five prayer times. Throughout his lifetime he always made up missed prayers and often recited the Koran. He was devoted to Khwaja Ubaydullah and considered it an honor to participate in his gatherings.The khwaja addressed him as "my son." He was well read and literate and read both *Khamsas*, the volumes of the *Mathnawi*; and histories. He often read the *Shahnama*. He had some poetic talent, but he paid no attention to composing poetry. His sense of justice was great: Once when he learned that a caravan from Cathay with a thousand beasts of burden had been trapped by heavy snow at the foot of the mountains to the east of Andizhan and only two persons had survived, he sent his revenuers to make a record of all the goods in the caravan. Although he himself was in need, he kept the goods until, a year or two later, the heirs could be brought from Samarkand Khurasan and the goods could be turned over to them.

He was liberal, and his moral character was equal to his liberality. He was a good-natured, talkative, eloquent, and well-spoken man. He was brave and valiant. Twice he performed more courageously than any of his warriors in wielding the sword. Once was at the gate of Akhsi, and another was at the gate of Shahrukhiyya. He was a middling shot. He packed quite a punch, however, and no one was ever hit by him who did not bite the dust. On account of his urge to expand his territory he turned many a truce into battle and many a friend into a foe.

He used to drink a lot. Later in life he held drinking parties once or twice a week. He was fun to be with in a gathering and was good at reciting poetry for his companions. He grew rather fond of *ma'jun*, and under its influence would lose his head. He was of an scrappy temperament and had many scars and brands to show for it. He played backgammon a lot and occasionally gambled.

His offspring. Three sons and five daughters survived. The eldest of all the sons was I, Zahiruddin Muhammad Babur. My mother was Qutlugh Nigar Khanïm.

EVENTS OF THE YEAR 900 [1494-95]

An emissary named Abdul-Quiddus beg came to me from Sultan-Mahmud Mirza. He brought gifts from the celebration of the marriage of Sultan-Mahmud Mirza's eldest son, Sultan-Mas'ud Mirza, to Sultan-Ahmad Mirza's second daughter, Aq Begim: gold and silver ornaments in the shapes of almonds and pistachios.

The emissary, who was probably related to Hasan Ya'qub, must have been sent to make promises to entice Hasan Ya'qub to look favorably upon Mirza Sultan-Mahmud. Hasan Ya'qub gave him smooth replies and making as though he had been won over, gave him leave to withdraw. Five or six months later Hasan Ya'qub's manner changed for the worse, and he began to quarrel with the men around me. His disposition was so altered that he would have dismissed me and installed Jahangir Mirza as *padishah*. But he was on bad terms with all the officers and military men too, and everyone knew what was on his mind. Khwaja Qazi, Qasim Qauchin, Ali Dost Taghayï, Uzun Hasan, and some of my other supporters met with my grandmother Esän Dawlat Begim and decided to depose Hasan Ya'qub and put down the conspiracy. (For tactics and strategy, there were few women like my grandmother, Esän Dawlat Begim. She was intelligent and a good planner. Most affairs were settled with her counsel.) Hasan Ya'qub was in the citadel. My mother and grandmother were in the gatehouse in the outer fortress. Intent upon deposing Hasan Ya'qub, I mounted and headed toward the citadel. Hasan Ya'qub had ridden out to go hunting, but as soon as he heard of my approach he left immediately, straight for Samarkand. All the men and begs who were with him were arrested, including Muhammad Baqir Beg, Sultan Muhammad Dulday's father Sultan-Mahmud Dulday, and some others. Some were given leave to go to Samarkand. The lordship of the gate and the governorship of Andizhan were settled upon Qasim Qauchin.

While on his way to Samarkand, Hasan Ya'qub stopped at Kanibadam and set out a few days later with ill intentions for Akhsi and the Kokand Orchin region. When his route was learned, some begs and warriors were dispatched to attack him, but only after a detachment of warriors was sent as an advance party. Hasan Ya'qub, however, surprised the party in the dark of night and attacked Uy Müngüzi with a barrage of arrows. One of Hasan Ya'qub's own men shot him in the cheek; before he could flee, he fell prey to his own action.

> When you have done evil, be not secure from calamity, for
> retribution is a law of nature.

This year I began to abstain from suspect food. I was careful about knives, spoons, and tablecloths. Even the after-midnight prayer was seldom omitted.

In the month of Rabi' II [December 30, 1494—January 27, 1495], Sultan-Mahmud Mirza was stricken with a severe illness and within six days passed from this world. He was forty-three years old.

A DESCRIPTION OF SAMARKAND

Few cities in the civilized world are as pleasant as Samarkand. It is in the fifth clime, 99° 56′ longitude, 40° 40′ latitude. Samarkand is the seat of the province, which is Transoxiana. Because it has not been stormed and seized by enemies, Samarkand is called *balda-i-mahfuza*. Samarkand became Muslim during the time of the caliph Uthman. One of the Companions, Qutham son of Abbas, went there, and his tomb outside the Iron Gate is now called Mazar-i-Shah. Samarkand is supposed to have been built by Alexander. The Moghuls and Turks call it "Semizkand" (Fat City). Temür Beg was the first to make it his capital.

I ordered that the fortress be paced off atop the wall; the count came to 10,700 paces.

The people are all Sunnis and orthodox followers of the religious law. Ever since the time of the Prophet, no province has been known to have produced so many leaders of Islam as Transoxiana. Shaykh Abu-Mansur, who is one of the great exponents of dialectic theology, was from a suburb of Samarkand called Maturid. Theologians are divided into two groups, the Maturidites and the Ash'arites. The attribution of the Maturidites is to this Shaykh Abu-Mansur. Another, the author of the *Sahih of Bukhari*, Khwaja Isma'il, was also from Transoxiana. The author of the *Hidaya*, a book of jurisprudence that holds a high place of distinction in the sect of Abu-Hanifa, was from the Margilan area of Fergana, which is within Transoxiana.

Samarkand lies on the edge of the civilized world. To the east are Fergana and Kashghar, to the west Bukhara and Khwarazm, to the north Tashkent and Shahrukhiyya, which are also called Shash and Banakath respectively, and to the south Balkh and Termez.

In Samarkand and its suburbs are many of Temür Beg's and Ulughbeg Mirza's buildings and gardens. In the Samarkand citadel, Temür Beg had constructed a large four-story pavilion known as the Kök Saray. It is a superb building. Near the Iron Gate, inside the walls, he had a Friday mosque built of stone. Most of the stonemasons sent from Hindustan worked there. The inscription on the mosque, the Koranic verse, "And Abraham and Ishmael raised the foundations of the house" etc., is written in script so large that it can be read from nearly a league away. This too is a superb building. To the east of Samarkand he had two gardens constructed. The farther of the two is called Bagh-i-Dulday and the nearer Bagh-i-Dilgusha. An avenue was made from the Dilgusha garden to the Turquoise Gate, and on both sides poplar trees were planted. In the Dilgusha a large pavilion was constructed and in it Temür Beg's India campaign was depicted. At the foot of Kohak Hill, above the still river at Kan-i-Gil, which is known as the Ab-i-Rahmat River, a garden called Naqsh-i-Jahan was constructed. When I saw it the garden was in ruins, nothing more than a name remained. To the south of Samarkand near the fortress is the Bagh-i-Chanar; on the lower side of Samarkand are the Bagh-i-Shimal and the Bagh-i-Bihisht. Temür Beg's grandson, Jahangir Mirza's son Muhammad-Sultan Mirza, had a *madrasa* constructed in the gateway to the outer wall of Samarkand. The tombs of Temür Beg and all of his descendants who ruled Samarkand are there.

Of Ulughbeg Mirza's buildings inside the walls of Samarkand are a *madrasa* and a *khanaqah*. The dome over the *khanaqah* is huge—few domes in the world are so large. Near the *madrasa* and *khanaqah* is a beautiful bathhouse known as the Mirza's Bath. It is paved in all sorts of stone. In all of Khurasan and Samarkand no such bath is known to exist. To the south of the *madrasa* was constructed a mosque called the Muqatta' Mosque, because many little pieces of wood are carved in floral and geometric patterns. All the walls and ceiling are in this style. The *kiblah* of this mosque differs from that of the *madrasa*, probably because the *kiblah* of Muqatta' was determined astronomically.

Another superb building on Kohak Hill is the observatory, which is an instrument for compiling astronomical tables. It is three stories tall. Ulughbeg Mirza used this observatory to compile the Zij-i-Gurkani, which is the table used throughout the world now, others being little used. Prior to it the zij-i-Ilkhani, which was done by Khwaja Nasir Tusi in Maragha in the time of Hülägü Khan, was current. It was Hülägü Khan who was called the Ilkhan.

Probably not more than seven or eight observatories have been constructed in the whole world. One was made for the Caliph Ma'mun, for whom the Zij-i-Ma'muni was compiled. Another was made by Ptolemy. Another currently in use by the Hindus, was compiled in India in the time of Raja Vikramaditya the Hindu in Ujjain and Dhar, which is the kingdom of Malwa, now known as Mandu. Compiled 1,584 years ago, it is the least complete of all these catalogues.

On the western side of Kohak Hill was constructed a garden called Bagh-i-Maydan, in the middle of which was built a superb building called Chil Sutun, two stories high with columns of stone. On its four towers are raised four towers, like minarets, through which are the passageways to the top. In all other places there are columns of stone, some fluted in spirals, and on the four sides of the upper story are porticos with columns of stone. In the middle is *chardara*. The building's plinth is paved in stone. Going from this building toward Kohak Hill is another small garden where yet another portico was built. Inside the portico was placed a large stone slab—approximately fourteen or fifteen yards long, seven or eight yards wide, and a yard thick—brought from a great distance. In the middle is a crack that people say developed after the stone was brought here. In this same small garden is a *chardara*, called the Chinikhana, with porcelain all around the dado. Someone was sent to Cathay to bring the porcelain. Inside the Samarkand city wall is yet another ancient building called the Laqlaqa Mosque. If one stamps in a certain place under the middle of the dome, the whole dome reverberates with a clacking sound. No one knows the secret behind this strange phenomenon.

During the time of Sultan-Ahmad Mirza, men of high rank and low constructed many gardens, large and small. For pleasure, good air, and superb vista, few are like Darwesh Muhammad Tarkhan's *charbagh*. It is situated below the Bagh-i-Maydan on a rise overlooking the Qolba meadow, so that the entire meadow lies stretched out below it. Planted in straight lines in the *charbagh* are beautiful ornamental trees, cypresses, and poplars. It is a truly magnificent spot, the only flaw being the lack of a great stream.

The city of Samarkand is an amazingly ornamented city. One peculiarity here is found in few other cities: every trade has a separate market, and they are not commingled. This is a wonderful custom. There are excellent bakeries and cook shops. The best paper in the world comes from Samarkand. The water for the paper factories comes from the beautiful Kan-i-Gil meadow, beside which is a still water, the Qara Su, which is also called Ab-i-Rahmat. Another product of Samarkand is red velvet, which is exported everywhere.

All around the city are exquisite meadows, including the famous Kan-i-Gil, one league to the east and slightly to the north of the city. The Qara Su, a seven- or eight-mill stream, which is also called Ab-i-Rahmat, flows through it. Beside the river are reservoirs. Some say that the original name of this meadow was Kan-i-Abgir, but in histories it is always called Kan-i-Gil. The rulers of Samarkand have always made this meadow a protected reserve and come out every year to stay for a month or two.

I have not written all this to complain: I have simply written the truth. I do not intend by what I have written to compliment myself: I have simply set down exactly what happened. Since I have made it a point in this history to write the truth of every matter and to set down no more than the reality of every event, as a consequence I have reported every good and evil I have seen of father and brother and set down the actuality of every fault and virtue of relative and stranger. May the reader excuse me; may the listener take me not to task.

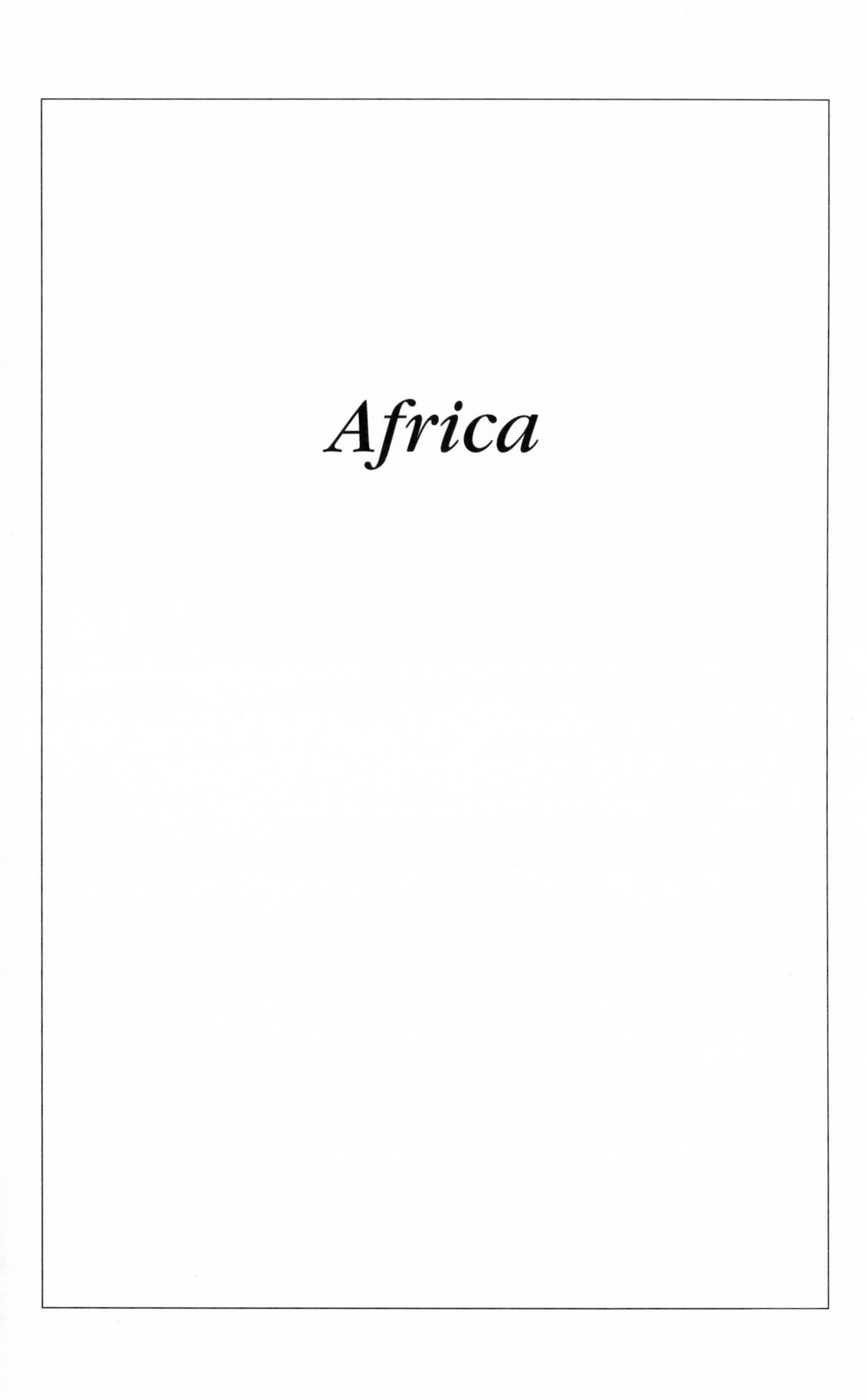

Africa

AL 'OMARI

1301-1349

One of the best sources for information respecting the political, military, and social organization of fourteenth-century Mali is provided by al 'Omari, a Muslim traveller who was born in Damascus, Syria. A potential difficulty with this source is that al 'Omari visited Cairo some twelve years after the events he recorded. His account relies heavily upon the memoirs of a court functionary who had visited Mali and whose task it had been to greet the emperor Mansa Musa at the gates of Cairo. The orderly system of law and government, together with the healthy economy described in this selection, may not be unrelated to the fact that those promoting this picture of Mali were themselves Sudanese Muslims of the ruling class or from mercantile families situated in urban centers.

We know a great deal less about the non-Muslim who made up the majority of the population of Mali. al 'Omari tells us that "pagan and magical practices" were widespread throughout the kingdom, and that the ruler did not wish to proselytize too strongly lest the economy suffer as workers resisted the new faith. It is probably fair to conclude that the empire was held together ultimately through the use of force (al 'Omari says that there was an army of 100,000 and a cavalry consisting of 10,000 horsemen). Traditional African kinship units doubtless persisted below the veneer of centralized statecraft. Nevertheless, this account provides a useful glimpse into the workings of this prosperous Sudanic state.

Can we draw any comparisons between political organization in Mali and its European counterpart in the fourteenth century? Are the qualities of leadership described here similar or different from those we have examined in Europe?

Mali in the Fourteenth Century

In 1324 the renowned emperor of Mali, Mansa Kankan Musa, left his capital on the Upper Niger for a pilgrimage to Mecca, taking with him, it was said, five hundred slaves each bearing a staff weighing five hundred *mitqals* of gold, a *mitqal* being then about one eighth of an ounce. His passage through Cairo long echoed in memory.

Ibn Fadi Allah al Omari, who was in Cairo twelve years after this glittering event, has left a secondhand account which reads with a marvellous veracity, no doubt because he was able to draw on the intimate memoirs of a court functionary whose task it had been to greet the Mali emperor on his arrival at the gates of Cairo. Omari also wrote a description of the empire from information provided by a learned friend who had lived in Mali for thirty-five years.

TRAVELLING THROUGH CAIRO

During my first journey to Cairo and sojourn there I heard talk of the arrival of the Sultan Musa [Mansa Musa, emperor of Mali] and I found the Cairenes very glad to talk of the large expenditures of those people. I questioned the Emir Abu'l 'Abbas Ahmed ben Abi'l Haki, el Mehmendar, who spoke of the sultan's noble appearance, dignity and trustworthiness. "When I went out to greet him in the name of the glorious Sultan el Malik en Nasir [of Egypt]," he told me, "he gave me the warmest of welcomes and treated me with the most careful politeness. But he would talk to me only through an interpreter [that is, his spokesman or linguist] although he could speak perfect Arabic. He carried his imperial treasure in many pieces of gold, worked or otherwise.

"I suggested that he should go up to the palace and meet the Sultan [of Egypt]. But he refused, saying: 'I came for the pilgrimage, and for nothing else, and I do not wish to mix up my pilgrimage with anything else.' He argued about this. However, I well understood that the meeting was repugnant to him because he was loath to kiss the ground [before the Sultan] or to kiss his hand. I went on insisting and he went on making excuses. But imperial protocol obliged me to present him, and I did not leave him until he had agreed. When he came into the Sultan's presence we asked him to kiss the ground. But he refused and continued to refuse, saying: 'However can this be?' Then a wise man of his suite whispered several words to him that I could not understand. 'Very well,' he thereupon declared, 'I will prostrate myself before Allah who created me and brought me into the world.' Having done so he moved towards the Sultan. The latter rose for a moment to welcome him and asked him to sit beside him: then they had a long conversation. After Sultan Musa had left the palace the Sultan of Cairo sent him gifts of clothing for himself, his courtiers and all those who were with him; saddled and bridled horses for himself and his chief officers. . . .

"When the time of pilgrimage arrived, [the Sultan of Egypt] sent him a large quantity of drachmas, baggage camels and choice riding camels with saddles and harness. [The Sultan of Egypt] caused abundant quantities of foodstuffs to be brought for his suite and his followers, established posting stations for the feeding of the animals, and gave to the emirs of the pilgrimage a written order to look after and respect [the Emperor of Mali]. When the latter returned it was I who went to greet him and settle him into his quarters. . . .

"This man," el Mehmendar also told me, "spread upon Cairo the flood of his generosity: there was no person, officer of the [Cairo] court or holder of any office of the [Cairo] sultanate who did not receive a sum in gold from him. The people of Cairo earned incalculable sums from him, whether by buying and selling or by gifts. So much gold was current in Cairo that it ruined the value of money.

Let me add [continues Omari] that gold in Egypt had enjoyed a high rate of exchange up to the moment of their arrival. The gold *mitqal* that year had not fallen below twenty-five drachmas. But from that day [of their arrival] onward, its value dwindled; the exchange was ruined, and even now it has not recovered. The *mitqal* scarcely touches twenty-two drachmas. That is how it has been for twelve years from that time, because of the great amounts of gold they brought to Egypt and spent there.

THE EMPIRE OF MALI

The king of this country is known to the people of Egypt as the king of Tekrur [roughly, inland Senegal]; but he himself becomes indignant when he is called thus, since Tekrur is only one of the countries of his empire. The title he prefers is that of lord of Mali, the largest of his states; it is the name by which he is most known. He is the most important of the Muslim Negro kings; his land is the largest, his army the most numerous; he is the king who is the most powerful, the richest, the most fortunate, and the most feared by his enemies and the most able to do good to those around him.

His kingdom consists of the lands of Gana, Zagun, Tirakka, Tekrur, Bambugu, Zarquatabana, Darmura, Zaga, Kabora, Baraguri, Gao-gao. The inhabitants of Gao-gao are of the tribes of Yarten. The region of Mali is that where the residence of the king is situated [in] the town of Niane, and all the other regions are dependent on it; it has the official name of Mali because it is the capital of this kingdom which also includes towns, villages and centers of population to the number of fourteen.

The honorable and truthful Sheikh Abu Sa'id Otman ed Dukkali, who has lived in the town of Niane for thirty-five years and travelled throughout the kingdom, has told me that this is square in shape, being four months [of travel] in length and at least as much in breadth. . . .

The sultan of this country has sway over the land of the "desert of native gold," whence they bring him gold every year. The inhabitants of that land are savage pagans whom the sultan would subject to him if he wished. But the sovereigns of this kingdom have learned by experience that whenever one of them has conquered one of these gold towns, established Islam there and sounded the call to prayer, the harvest of gold dwindles and falls to nothing, meanwhile it grows and expands in neighboring pagan countries. When experience had confirmed them in this observation, they left the gold country in the hands of its pagan inhabitants, and contented themselves with assuring their obedience and paying tribute.

Reception at Court

The sultan of this kingdom presides in his palace on a great balcony called *bembe* where he has a great seat of ebony that is like a throne fit for a large and tall person: on either side it is flanked by elephant tusks turned towards each other. His arms stand near him, being all of gold, sabre, lance, quiver, bow and arrows. He wears wide trousers made of about twenty pieces [of stuff] of a kind which he alone may wear. Behind him there stand about a score of Turkish or other pages which are bought for him in Cairo: one of them, at his left, holds a silk umbrella surmounted by a dome and a bird of gold: the bird has the figure of a falcon. His officers are seated in a circle about him, in two rows, one to the right and one to the left; beyond them sit the chief commanders of his cavalry. In front of him there is a person who never leaves him and who is his executioner; also another who serves as intermediary [that is, official spokesman] between the sovereign and his subjects, and who is named the herald. In front of them again, there are drummers. Others dance before their sovereign, who enjoys this, and make him laugh. Two banners are spread behind him. Before him they keep two saddled and bridled horses in case he should wish to ride.

The Importance of Horses

Arab horses are brought for sale to the kings of this country, who spend considerable sums in this way. Their army numbers one hundred thousand men of whom there are about ten thousand horse-mounted cavalry: the others are infantry having neither horses nor any other mounts. They have camels in this country but do not know the art of riding them with a saddle. . . .

The officers of this king, his soldiers and his guard receive gifts of land and presents. Some among the greatest of them receive as much as fifty thousand *mitqals* of gold a year, besides which the king provides them with horses and clothing. He is much concerned with giving them fine garments and making his cities into capitals.

Royal Bureaucracy

It is one of their customs that whenever someone charged with a certain task or important affair reports to the king, the latter questions him on everything that has happened from the time of his departure to the time of his return, and in great detail. Legal cases and appeals also go up to the sovereign who examines them himself. Generally he writes nothing; but gives his orders, most of the time, orally. He has *qadis*, secretaries, offices.

OCEAN TRAVELS

The emir Abu Hasan Ali b. Amir Hajib told me that he was often in the company of sultan Musa, the king of this country (of Mali), when he came to Egypt on the Pilgrimage. . . . A friendship grew up between them, and this sultan Musa told him a great deal about himself and his country and the people of the Sudan who were his neighbors. One of the things which he told him was that his country was very extensive and contiguous with the [Atlantic] ocean. . . .

Ibn Amir Hajib continued: "I asked sultan Musa how the kingdom fell to him, and he said: 'We belong to a house which hands on the kingship by inheritance. The king who was my predecessor did not believe that it was impossible to discover the furthest limit of the Atlantic ocean and wished vehemently to do so. So he equipped 200 ships filled with men and the same number filled with gold, water and provisions enough to last them for years, and said to the man deputed to lead them: "Do not return until you reach the end of it, or your provisions and water give out." They departed and a long time passed before anyone came back. Then one ship returned and we asked the captain what news they brought. He said: "Yes, O Sultan, we travelled for a long time until there appeared in the open sea (as it were) a river with a powerful current. Mine was the last of those ships. The (other) ships went on ahead but when they reached that place they did not return and no more was seen of them and we do not know what became of them. As for me, I went about at once and did not enter that river." But the sultan disbelieved him.

"'Then that sultan got ready 2,000 ships, 1,000 for himself and the men whom he took with him and 1,000 for water and provisions. He left me to deputize for him and embarked on the Atlantic ocean with his men. That was the last we saw of him and all those who were with him, and so I became king in my own right.'"

DUARTE PIRES

b. Fourteenth century

Direct European interaction with West Africa began in the middle of the fifteenth century, when the first Portuguese traders made contact with established African kingdoms like Benin. From about 1487 until 1507, the Portuguese maintained a trading post at the Benin river port of Ughoton. Exchanging European textile and metalware products for gold, ivory and peppers, the Portugese slowly eroded the monopoly previously enjoyed by trans-Saharan Muslim traders. Perhaps the most interesting feature of these early contacts was the absence of slaving; both sides enjoyed a profitable commercial relationship on the basis of commodity trade, not the sale of war captives. Indeed by 1516 the king of Benin prohibited the Portuguese from buying male slaves, although the numbers of war captives in the kingdom was rising.

Something of this climate of mutual (if at times grudging) respect is indicated in the letter of Duarte Pires to the king of Portugal in 1516. Two years earlier the king of Benin sent an embassy to Portugal in order to discuss trade and to inquire about the Christian religion. The Portuguese were apparently intrigued by the fact that the kings of Benin contacted another ruler in the interior in order to confirm their accession. The Benin messengers brought back with them insignia in the shape of metal crosses. Initially the Portuguese concluded that this potentate must be Prester John, although in fact the unnamed ruler was probably the Oni (king) of Ife. Still, the emphasis on prospects for the spread of Christianity in this letter is significant. After 1516, when the Portuguese king refused to sell arms to the Benin military, all trade relations came to an end, and by the mid-sixteenth century Benin cut itself off from all contact with Europeans.

What does the tone of this letter reveal of Pires's estimate of the king—and kingdom—of Benin? Does the letter reflect a strong desire on the part of the Portuguese to enhance the bilateral relationship?

from a Letter to a king about the King of Benin

[1516] Most high and mighty king and prince, our lord. May God increase your royal estate. Sir, your highness will be pleased to know how Pero Baroso gave me a letter from your highness, which made me rejoice that your highness should be mindful of so humble a man as I; and now I render account to your highness in regard to the letter which you sent me. Sir, with reference to what you say about my being in very great favour with the king of Benin, it is truly so; because the king of Benin is pleased with what I said in favour of your highness, and he desires to be your very good friend and speaks of nothing save what concerns Our Lord and your interest; and so he is very glad, and likewise all his noblemen and his people; and your highness will shortly know about this.

The favour which the king of Benin accords us is due to his love of your highness; and thus he pays us high honor and sets us at table to dine with his son, and no part of his court is hidden from us but all the doors are open. Sir, when these priests arrived in Benin, The delight of the king of Benin was so great that I do not know how to describe it, and likewise that of all his people; and he sent for them at once; and they remained with him for one whole year in war. The priests and we reminded him of the embassy of your highness, and he replied to us that he was very satisfied with it; but since he was at war, that he could do nothing until he returned to Benin, because he needed leisure for such a deep mystery as this; as soon as he was in Benin, he would fulfill his promise to your highness, and he would so behave as to give great pleasure to your highness and to all your kingdom.

So it was that, at the end of one year, in the month of August, the king gave his son and some of his noblemen—the greatest in his kingdom—so that they might become Christians; and also he ordered a church to be built in Benin; and they made them Christians straightway; and also they are teaching them to read, and your highness will be pleased to know that they are very good learners. Moreover, sir, the king of Benin hopes to finish his war this summer, and we shall return to Benin, and I shall give your highness an account of everything that happens. Sir, I Duarte Pires, and Joham Sobrynho, a resident in The island of O Principe, and Grygoryo Lourenco, a black man and formerly the servant of Francysquo Lourenco, all remain in the service of your highness, and we have submitted proposals on your behalf to the king of Benin, and we have described to him how your highness is a great lord and how you can make him a great lord. Done in this war, on 20 October 1516.

To the lord the king.

Duarte Pires

Affonso of Kongo
King Mvemba Nzinga

Ruled 1506–1543

Portuguese involvement in the slave trade began in the late fifteenth century as a plantation economy centered on sugar production developed on various tropical islands off the west coast of Africa. By the mid-sixteenth century, the demand for slaves shifted to Spanish and Portuguese holdings in the Americas, and Portuguese traders began to look further afield than the Niger delta for slaves. These traders were drawn to the Kongo kingdom located just south of the lower Congo river. Impressed by the political organization of this African state, the Portuguese sent emissaries, priests and artisans to Kongo in hopes of cementing an alliance. In return for "technological" assistance, the Portuguese hoped to secure a monopoly of trade, including trade in slaves, with Kongo.

In 1506 Mvemba Nzinga was elected king by the provincial rulers of the kingdom. The new monarch had been converted to Christianity by Portuguese missionaries, and he seems to have welcomed Portuguese support as a means of strengthening the monarchy against the nobility. In particular, he hoped to limit the succession to his own direct descendants. By the 1530s, almost one third of all slaves taken out of Africa were coming from Kongo. The king attempted to end this relationship, but many of his own subjects were actively involved in trading and raiding, and Mvemba Nzinga turned to the Portuguese king for help in restraining the European traders.

Reading the selection included here, think about how the relationship between African leaders and their European counterparts changed in the wake of the emerging slave trade. In what respect, if at all, did the conversion of the king of Kongo to Christianity facilitate the advancement of African interests?

from a Letter on the Evils of the Slave Trade

[1526] Sir, Your Highness [of Portugal] should know how our Kingdom is being lost in so many ways that it is convenient to provide for the necessary remedy, since this is caused by the excessive freedom given by your factors and officials to the men and merchants who are allowed to come to this Kingdom to set up shops with goods and many things which have been prohibited by us, and which they spread throughout our Kingdoms and Domains in such an abundance that many of our vassals, whom we had in obedience, do not comply because they have the things in greater abundance than we ourselves; and it was with these things that we had them content and subjected under our vassalage and jurisdiction, so it is doing a great harm not only to the service of God, but the security and peace of our Kingdoms and State as well.

And we cannot reckon how great the damage is, since the mentioned merchants are taking every day our natives, sons of the land and the sons of our noblemen and vassals and our relatives, because the thieves and men of bad conscience grab them wishing to have the things and wares of this Kingdom which they are ambitious of; they grab them and get them to be sold; and so great, Sir, is the corruption and licentiousness that our country is being completely depopulated, and Your Highness should not agree with this nor accept it as in your service. And to avoid it we need from those [your] Kingdoms no more than some priests and a few people to teach in schools, and no other goods except wine and flour for the holy sacrament. That is why we beg of Your Highness to help and assist us in this matter, commanding your factors that they should not send here either merchants or wares, because it is our will that in these Kingdoms there should not be any trade of slaves nor outlet for them. Concerning what is referred above, again we beg of Your Highness to agree with it, since otherwise we cannot remedy such an obvious damage. Pray Our Lord in His mercy to have Your Highness under His guard and let you do for ever the things of His service. I kiss your hands many times.

At our town of Congo, written on the sixth day of July.

João Teixeira did it in 1526.

The King. Dom Affonso.[1]

HOW SLAVING BEGAN

[1526] Moreover, Sir, in our Kingdoms there is another great inconvenience which is of little service to God, and this is that many of our people [naturaes], keenly desirous as they are of the wares and things of your Kingdoms, which are brought here by your people, and in order to satisfy their voracious appetite, seize many of our people, freed and exempt men; and very often it happens that they kidnap even noblemen and the sons of noblemen, and our relatives, and take them to be sold to the white men who are in our Kingdoms; and for this purpose they have concealed them; and others are brought during the night so that they might not be recognized.

And as soon as they are taken by the white men they are immediately ironed and branded with fire, and when they are carried to be embarked, if they are caught by our guards' men the whites allege that they have bought them but they cannot say from whom, so that it is our duty to do justice and to restore to the freemen their freedom, but it cannot be done if your subjects feel offended, as they claim to be.

And to avoid such a great evil we passed a law so that any white man living in our Kingdoms and wanting to purchase goods in any way should first inform three of our noblemen and officials of our court whom we rely upon in this matter, and these are Dom Pedro Manipanza and Dom Manuel Manissaba, our chief usher, and Goncala Pires our chief freighter, who should investigate if the mentioned goods are captives or free men, and if cleared by them there will be no further doubt nor embargo for them to be taken and embarked. But if the white men do not comply with it they will lose the aforementioned goods. And if we do them this favor and concession it is for the part Your Highness has in it, since we know that it is in your service too that these goods are taken from our Kingdom, otherwise we should not consent to this. . . .

A CALL FOR AID (NEVER ANSWERED)

[1526] Sir, Your Highness has been kind enough to write to us saying that we should ask in our letters for anything we need, and that we shall be provided with everything, and as the peace and the health of our Kingdom depend on us, and as there are among us old folks and people who have lived for many days, it happens that we have continuously many and different diseases which put us very often in such a weakness that we reach almost the last extreme; and the same happens to our children, relatives and natives owing to the lack in this country of physicians and surgeons who might know how to cure properly such diseases. And as we have got neither dispensaries nor drugs which might help us in this forlornness, many of those who had been already confirmed and instructed in the holy faith of Our Lord Jesus Christ perish and die; and the rest of the people in their majority cure themselves with herbs and breads and other ancient methods, so that they put all their faith in the mentioned herbs and ceremonies if they live, and believe that they are saved if they die; and this is not much in the service of God.

And to avoid such a great error and inconvenience, since it is from God in the first place and then from your Kingdoms and from Your Highness that all the good and drugs and medicines have come to save us, we beg of you to be agreeable and kind enough to send us two physicians and two apothecaries and one surgeon, so that they may come with their drug stores and all the necessary things to stay in our kingdoms because we are in extreme need of them all and each of them. We shall do them all good and shall benefit them by all means since they are sent by Your Highness, whom we thank for your work in their coming. We beg of Your Highness as a great favor to do this for us, because besides being good in itself it is in the service of God as we have said above.

NOTES

[1]The address on the reverse of this letter reads "To the most powerful and excellent prince Dom Joao, King our Brother."

China, Japan and India in the Medieval Period

Shu Yüeh-hsiang
1217-1301

Wen T'ung
1018-1079

While it once seemed that few documents had survived about women's daily experience in medieval Asia and Europe, it is now clear that many historical texts are witness to women's participation in economic, social, religious, and political life. Below are two examples of poems which provide specifics about women's work. The first, by Shu Yüeh-hsiang, depicts a number of vocations, and the second, by Wen T'ung, reveals the hardship of female weavers. In all of these instances, the women's work is arduous. What do you think are the poets's intentions in writing the poems?

By the front hill the woman picking tea
Quickly takes up her basket, revealing her take.
The work is hard but she knows her task
And sings and laughs without sign of sadness.
Her eyebrows, reflected in the water, she doesn't paint.
A flower is stuck in her hair, but she doesn't blush.
Everyone cares about appearance,
So why doesn't she comb her hair?

At the edge of the field the waterwheel woman
Draws the water to let it circulate.
Her black hat is pushed to the side in the burning sun.
Her blue skirt flaps noisily in the evening breeze.
Over and over she repeats the same steps,
Treading away on what seems to be empty space.
I catch the sense of her work song:
As long as you live, don't marry into a peasant family.

The woman by the river pulling up fish
Every morning goes to the city.
Leaving her young child to watch the boat,
She trades her catch for wine for her drunkard husband.
Not one to wear fancy socks,
The edge of her long skirt is wet with water.

Shu Yüeh-hsiang

She does not dare leave the loom
Through the night, after the fire and candles are out.
She has to finish the tax [cloth].
How is there time to worry about her own clothes?
She has long known bone-piercing cold.
She willingly exposes her arms and legs.
The local government runner is squatting at the door,
Cursing them for handing [the cloth] over late.
How can the feelings of the weaving woman
Catch the attention of the officials in charge?

Wen T'ung

CH'ENG I
1061–1085 C.E.

While the Sung Dynasty (960–1279 C.E.) was a thriving culture, famous for its beautiful artistic productions and strengthened civil service, it was also a time of tremendous social and political upheaval. By reacting against the militaristic tradition of the Tang dynasty, the Sung faced administrative difficulties. Consequently, in the early 1120s the Northern Sung allied themselves with the Chin dynasty of northern Manchuria; later, in 1279, the Southern Sung fell to Kublai Khan. Sung Dynasty China seems to be a negative moment in Chinese women's history. Issues such as foot binding, loss of property rights, and remarriage prohibitions reflect the troubled female experience during that time. In contrast, Ch'eng I, a Confucian scholar of the eleventh century, relates a story of his niece which reflects his family's love and high regard for their female child. Although an important proponent of values both Confucian and male-centered, Ch'eng I nevertheless encouraged female education and discouraged foot binding.

This selection from Ch'eng I shows the love Chinese families have for their daughters and their hopes for a good marriage, although the definition of a good marriage may vary from the modern idea. How does this reading define the "good" match and how does it compare to European ideas on marriage of the same time? What values does the niece exhibit which make her exemplary?

On his Niece's Marriage

When young [my niece] was sedate and calm and did not speak or laugh foolishly. Her style was lofty and her interests high-minded. She was exceptionally far-sighted when she discussed affairs. She could sit calmly all day, dignified and correct. She was never taught to read books, but on her own learned the meanings of texts. Everyone in the family loved and cherished her.

For a husband we wished to get someone who would be her match. Her father [Ch'eng Hao, 1032–1085] was famous in his age, known throughout the realm, and men of discernment all frequented his home. And yet although we looked for a husband for seven or eight years, we never found a suitable one. Our relatives considered this sad, and our friends considered it wrong, saying that since antiquity they had never heard of a woman not marrying because she was too worthy. With no alternative, we set our sights lower. Once, we were in the process of negotiating but could not bear to let her know, for we knew the man was not up to her. Then her mother died, and she mourned her to the full extent of her grief; not one of the filial gentlemen of the past exceeded her [in mourning]. She ruined her health and died. . . .

All of the others deplored the fact that she had not married; only I disagreed. Her father and I took the sages as our teachers and tried to do the appropriate thing. If we matched her to an ordinary fellow because we had not come across a worthy one, that would bring disgrace to her to the end of her life. I deplore her death, but not her failure to marry.

Tu Fu
710–770 C.E.

The Chinese poet Tu Fu, who wrote during China's Tang Dynasty (618–907 C.E.), is regarded by many as the greatest Chinese poet. The later Tang's famous cultural flowering produced three of China's greatest poets: Li Po, Tu Fu, and Po Chi-I. In the late Tang, the decline of Buddhism and a revival of Confucianism created the vigorous new Confucian tradition which guided Tu Fu's upbringing. An important contribution to Chinese government from this era of unprecedented strength and brilliance is the system of civil service examinations. Although Tu Fu was raised in a family known for its scholarly interests, he failed the government examination and did not receive a government post until he was 43. Ironically, in that same year, the Emperor's abdication and subsequent civil upheavals caused Tu Fu, his wife, and children to flee their home. During much of his remaining life, he was forced to become an itinerant wanderer. Tu Fu's early poetry is lyrical, much like that of his model Li Po. However, his later poetry, represented here, shows his reactions to the harsh realities of his life.

Much of Tu Fu's poetry is intensely personal. What important differences can you see between his poetry and that of his contemporary, Li Po? How does Tu Fu represent the Confucian sensibility, and in what ways can you see his deep interrogation of that philosophical system? Many critics comment that his poetry is "densely packed with meaning." Identify one such meaningful passage and discuss.

Poems

On the Border
First Series

1.
We recruits have our commanders to send us off,
but, bound for distant duty, we're people too!
From here we go out to face life or death—
no cause for the officers to scowl at us so!
Along the route we come on someone we know,
give him a letter to hand to close kin.
Sad as it is, we and they are parted now,
no longer to share the same troubles and pain.

2.
If you draw a bow, draw a strong one;
if you use an arrow, use one that's long.
If you want to shoot a man, shoot his horse first;

if you want to seize the enemy, seize their leader first.
But killing people has limits too,
and when you guard a state, there are boundaries to be observed.
Just so you manage to keep invaders out—
Seeing how many you can slaughter—that's not the point!

SONG OF THE BEAUTIFUL LADIES

Third month, third day, in the air a breath of newness;
by Ch'ang-an riverbanks the beautiful ladies crowd,
warm-bodied, modest-minded, mild and pure,
with clear sleek complexions, bone and flesh well matched,
in figured gauze robes that shine in the late spring,
worked with golden peacocks, silver unicorns.
On their heads what do they wear?
Kingfisher glinting from hairpins that dangle by sidelock borders.
On their back what do I see?
Pearls that weight the waistband and subtly set off the form.
Among them, kin of the lady of cloud screen and pepper-scented halls,
granted titles to the great fiefs of Kuo and Ch'in.
Humps of purple camel proffered from blue caldrons,
platters of crystal spread with slivers of raw fish;
but ivory chopsticks, sated, dip down no more,
and phoenix knives in vain hasten to cut and serve.
Yellow Gate horses ride swiftly, leaving the dust unstirred,
bearing from royal kitchens unending rare delights.
Plaintive notes of flute and drum, enough to move the gods;
throngs of guests and lackeys, all the highest rank;
and last, another rider, with slow and measured stride,
dismounts at the tent door, ascends the brocade carpet.
The snow of willow catkins blankets the white-flowered reeds;
a bluebird flies away, in its bill a crimson kerchief—
Where power is all-surpassing, fingers may be burned;
Take care and draw no closer to His Excellency's glare!

SONG OF P'ENG-YA

I remember when we first fled the rebels,
hurrying north over dangerous trails;
night deepened on P'eng-ya Road,
the moon shone over White-water Hills.
A whole family endlessly trudging,
begging without shame from the people we met:
valley birds sang, a jangle of soft voices;

we didn't see a single traveler returning.
The baby girl in her hunger bit me;
fearful that tigers or wolves would hear her cries,
I hugged her to my chest, muffling her mouth,
but she squirmed and wailed louder than before.
The little boy pretended he knew what was happening;
importantly he searched for sour plums to eat.
Ten days, half in rain and thunder,
through mud and slime we pulled each other on.
There was no escaping from the rain,
trails slick, clothes wet and clammy;
getting past the hardest places,
a whole day advanced us no more than three or four li.
Mountain fruits served for rations,
low-hung branches were our rafter and roof.
Mornings we traveled by rock-bedded streams,
evenings camped in mists that closed in the sky.
We stopped a little while at the marsh of T'ung-chia,
thinking to go out by Lu-tzu Pass;
an old friend there, Sun Tsai,
ideals higher than the piled-up clouds;
he came out to meet us as dusk turned to darkness,
called for torches, opening gate after gate,
heated water to wash our feet,
cut strips of paper to call back our souls.
Then his wife and children came;
seeing us, their tears fell in streams.
My little chicks had gone to sleep;
he called them to wake up and eat from his plate,
said he would make a vow with me,
the two of us to be brothers forever.
At last he cleared the room where we sat,
wished us goodnight, all he had at our command.
Who is willing, in the hard, bleak times,
to break open, lay bare his innermost heart?
Parting from you, a year of months has rounded,
Tartar tribes still plotting evil,
and I think how it would be to have strong wings
that would carry me away, set me down before you.

MOONLIGHT NIGHT

From her room in Fu-chou tonight
all alone she watches the moon.
Far away, I grieve that her children

can't understand why she thinks of Ch'ang-an.
Fragrant mist in her cloud hair damp,
clear lucence on her jade arms cold—
when will we lean by chamber curtains
and let it light the two of us, our tear stains dried?

Spring Prospect

The nation shattered, hills and streams remain.
The city in spring, grass and trees deep:
feeling the times, flowers draw tears;
hating separation, birds alarm the heart.
Beacon fires three months running,
a letter from home worth ten thousand in gold—
white hairs, fewer for the scratching,
soon too few to hold a hairpin up.

Passing Chao-ling Again

From rude darkness the heroes rose;
amid songs of praise, destiny chose him;
in wind and dust, his three-foot sword,
armor donned for the altars of the land;
wings to his father, pure in civil virtue;
heir of the great charge, wielder of war's might;
his holy vision wide and huge as heaven,
in service of ancestors more radiant than the sun.
The mound-side chamber lies wrapped in empty slopes;
warriors, bearlike, to guard the blue-green hill.
Once more I gaze up the pine and cypress road,
Watching five-hued clouds drift by.

Lovely Lady

Lovely lady, fairest of the time,
hiding away in an empty valley;
daughter of a good house, she said,
fallen now among grasses of the wood.
"There was tumult and death within the passes then;
my brothers, old and young, were killed.
Office, position—what help were they?
I couldn't even gather up my brothers' bones!
The world despises you when your luck is down;
all I had went with the turn of the flame.

My husband was a fickle fellow,
his new girl as fair as jade.
Blossoms that close at dusk keep faith with the hour,
mandarin ducks will not rest apart;
but he could only see the new one laughing,
never hear the former one's tears—"
Within the mountain the stream runs clear;
out of the mountain it turns to mud.
Her maid returns from selling a pearl,
braids vines to mend their roof of thatch.
The lady picks a flower but does not put it in her hair,
gathers juniper berries, sometimes a handful.
When the sky is cold, in thin azure sleeves,
at dusk she stands leaning by the tall bamboo.

Presented to Wei Pa, Gentleman in Retirement

Life is not made for meetings;
like stars at opposite ends of the sky we move.
What night is it, then, tonight,
when we can share the light of this lamp?
Youth—how long did it last?
The two of us grayheaded now,
we ask about old friends—half are ghosts;
cries of unbelief stab the heart.
Who would have thought?—twenty years
And once again I enter your house.
You weren't married when I left you;
now suddenly a whole row of boys and girls!
merrily greeting their father's friend,
asking me what places I've been.
Before I finish answering,
you send the boys to set out wine and a meal,
spring scallions cut in night rain,
new cooked rice mixed with yellow millet.
Meetings are rare enough, you say;
pour the wine till we've downed ten cups!
But ten cups do not make me drunk;
your steadfast love is what moves me now.
Tomorrow hills and ranges will part us,
the wide world coming between us again.

Sei Shonagon

966–?

Sei Shonagon was the daugher of Kiyohara no Motosuke (908–990 C.E.), a distinguished *waka* poet. From 993–1001 she was in the court service of Empress Teishi, the first consort of Emperor Ichijo. At the same time, Ichijo's second consort, Empress Shoshi, was served by Murasaki Shikibu. The only recorded events of Shonagon's life are her visits to various temples and shrines. However, the final section of *Pillow Book* offers information on the circumstances under which she began writing the book, how it first came into circulation, and how the book was celebrated by the court. Like other women of her time, even her name is something of a mystery. "Sei" is the Sino-Japanese pronunciation of the first character in Kiyohara, her father's name. While "Shonagon" means lesser counselor, neither her father nor husband had that title. Sei Shonagon wrote during the great mid-Heian period of feminine vernacular literature that produced not only the world's first psychological novel, Murasaki Shikibu's *Genji Monogatari*, but also much poetry and a series of diaries mostly by court ladies. These illustrate the life of upper-class Japanese women a thousand years ago. In the Heian Period, when the educated male was expected to write both public documents and private memoirs in kamban Chinese, women took the lead in developing prose writing in Japanese *hirangana*.

Makura no Soshi ("Notes of the Pillow" or *Pillow Book*) is probably a generic name referring to a miscellany, a group of literary jottings, or an informal book of notes which both men and women composed when they retired to their rooms in the evening. The term *Pillow Book* may refer to books kept in the drawers of wooden pillows used by ladies of the court who had elaborate hairdos, or perhaps it alludes to a writer's sketchbook of topics for poetry and prose composition, as a kind of thesaurus to be consulted when writing. Two elements distinguish *Pillow Book*: the obvious wit and learning of the author and its beauty in Japanese. The miscellany contains one hundred and sixty-four catalogues of places, plants, and familiar objects. Some of the most famous lists concern those items Sei has an opinion about, such as "things that look pretty but are bad inside," "things that cannot be compared," and "things that have lost their power." In addition to her lists, Sei provides numerous descriptions of nature, diary entries, character sketches, and court anecdotes. Entries range in length from a line or two to several pages with no obvious attempt to unify or arrange the various components. The celebrated opening of her work, which catalogues the best times of day for admiring the four seasons, sets a tradition to which numbers of other poets responded. Her epithets, such as the "dawn of spring" and "evening of autumn," became standard aesthetic cliches in later *waka* and *monogatari* poetry.

What aspects of Heian life seem similar to European medieval life and which seem substantially different? In particular, how is the female writer in Heian courtly life like her European counterparts Marie de France and Hildegard of Bingen?

from *The Pillow Book* of Sei Shonagon

1. In Spring It Is the Dawn

In spring it is the dawn that is most beautiful. As the light creeps over the hills, their outlines are dyed a faint red and wisps of purplish cloud trail over them.

In summer the nights. Not only when the moon shines, but on dark nights too, as the fireflies flit to and fro, and even when it rains, how beautiful it is!

In autumn the evenings, when the glittering sun sinks close to the edge of the hills and the crows fly back to their nests in threes and fours and twos; more charming still is a file of wild geese, like specks in the distant sky. When the sun has set, one's heart is moved by the sound of the wind and the hum of the insects.

In winter the early mornings. It is beautiful indeed when snow has fallen during the night, but splendid too when the ground is white with frost; or even when there is no snow or frost, but it is simply very cold and the attendants hurry from room to room stirring up the fires and bringing charcoal, how well this fits the season's mood! But as noon approaches and the cold wears off, no one bothers to keep the braziers alight, and soon nothing remains but piles of white ashes.

5. Different Ways of Speaking

A priest's language.

The speech of men and of women.

The common people always tend to add extra syllables to their words.

6. That Parents Should Bring Up Some Beloved Son

That parents should bring up some beloved son of theirs to be a priest is really distressing. No doubt it is an auspicious thing to do; but unfortunately most people are convinced that a priest is as unimportant as a piece of wood, and they treat him accordingly. A priest lives poorly on meagre food, and cannot sleep without being criticized. While he is young, it is only natural that he should be curious about all sorts of things, and, if there are women about, he will probably peep in their direction (though, to be sure, with a look of aversion on his face). What is wrong about that? Yet people immediately find fault with him for even so small a lapse.

The lot of an exorcist is still more painful. On his pilgrimages to Mitake, Kumano, and all the other sacred mountains he often undergoes the greatest hardships. When people come to hear that his prayers are effective, they summon him here and there to perform services of exorcism: the more popular he becomes, the less peace he enjoys. Sometimes he will be called to see a patient who is seriously ill and he has to exert all his powers to cast out the spirit that is causing the affliction. But if he dozes off, exhausted by his efforts, people say reproachfully, 'Really this priest does nothing but sleep. ' Such comments are most embarrassing for the exorcist, and I can imagine how he must feel.

That is how things used to be; nowadays priests have a somewhat easier life.

11. THE SLIDING SCREEN IN THE BACK OF THE HALL

The sliding screen in the back of the hall in the north-east corner of Seiryo Palace is decorated with paintings of the stormy sea and of the terrifying creatures with long arms and long legs that live there. When the doors of the Empress's room were open, we could always see this screen. One day we were sitting in the room, laughing at the paintings and remarking how unpleasant they were. By the balustrade of the veranda stood a large celadon vase, full of magnificent cherry branches; some of them were as much as five foot long, and their blossoms overflowed to the very foot of the railing. Towards noon the Major Counsellor, Fujiwara no Korechika, arrived. He was dressed in a cherry-coloured Court cloak, sufficiently worn to have lost its stiffness, a white under-robe, and loose trousers of dark purple; from beneath the cloak shone the pattern of another robe of dark red damask. Since His Majesty was present, Korechika knelt on the narrow wooden platform before the door and reported to him on official matters.

A group of ladies-in-waiting was seated behind the bamboo blinds. Their cherry-coloured Chinese jackets hung loosely over their shoulders with the collars pulled back; they wore robes of wistaria, golden yellow, and other colours, many of which showed beneath the blind covering the half-shutter. Presently the noise of the attendants' feet told us that dinner was about to be served in the Daytime Chamber, and we heard cries of 'Make way. Make way.'

The bright, serene day delighted me. When the Chamberlains had brought all the dishes into the Chamber, they came to announce that dinner was ready, and His Majesty left by the middle door. After accompanying the Emperor, Korechika returned to his previous place on the veranda beside the cherry blossoms. The Empress pushed aside her curtain of state and came forward as far as the threshold. We were overwhelmed by the whole delightful scene. It was then that Korechika slowly intoned the words of the old poem,

> The days and the months flow by,
> But Mount Mimoro lasts forever.

Deeply impressed, I wished that all this might indeed continue for a thousand years.

As soon as the ladies serving in the Daytime Chamber had called for the gentlemen-in-waiting to remove the trays, His Majesty returned to the Empress's room. Then he told me to rub some ink on the inkstone. Dazzled, I felt that I should never be able to take my eyes off his radiant countenance. Next he folded a piece of white paper. 'I should like each of you,' he said, 'to copy down on this paper the first ancient poem that comes into your head.'

'How am I going to manage this?' I asked Korechika, who was still out on the veranda.

'Write your poem quickly,' he said, 'and show it to His Majesty. We men must not interfere in this.' Ordering an attendant to take the Emperor's inkstone to each of the women in the room, he told us to make haste. 'Write down any poem you happen to remember,' he said. 'The Naniwazu or whatever else you can think of.'

For some reason I was overcome with timidity; I flushed and had no idea what to do. Some of the other women managed to put down poems about the spring, the blossoms, and such suitable subjects; then they handed me the paper and said, 'Now it's your turn.' Picking up the brush, I wrote the poem that goes,

> The years have passed
> And age has come my way.
> Yet I need only look at this fair flower
> For all my cares to melt away.

I altered the third line, however, to read, 'Yet I need only look upon my lord.'

When he had finished reading, the Emperor said, 'I ask you to write these poems because, I wanted to find out how quick you really were.

'A few years ago, he continued, 'Emperor Enyu ordered all his courtiers to write poems in a notebook. Some excused themselves on the grounds that their handwriting was poor; but the Emperor insisted, saying that he did not care in the slightest about their handwriting or even whether their poems were suitable for the season. So they all had to swallow their embarrassment and produce something for the occasion. Among them was His Excellency, our present Chancellor, who was then Middle Captain of the Third Rank. He wrote down the old poem,

> Like the sea that heats
> Upon the shores of Izurno
> As the tide sweeps in,
> Deeper it grows and deeper—
> The love I hear for you.

But he changed the last line to read, "The love I bear my lord!", and the Emperor was full of praise.'

When I heard His Majesty tell this story, I was so overcome that I felt myself perspiring. It occurred to me that no younger woman would have been able to use my poem and I felt very lucky. This sort of test can be a terrible ordeal: it often happens that people who usually write fluently are so overawed that they actually make mistakes in their characters.

Next the Empress placed a notebook of *Kokin Shu* poems before her and started reading out the first three lines of each one, asking us to supply the remainder. Among them were several famous poems that we had in our minds day and night; yet for some strange reason we were often unable to fill in the missing lines. Lady Saisho, for example, could manage only ten, which hardly qualified her as knowing her *Kokin Shu*. Some of the other women, even less successful, could remember only about half a dozen poems. They would have done better to tell the Empress quite simply that they had forgotten the lines; instead they came out with great lamentations like 'Oh dear, how could we have done so badly in answering the questions that Your Majesty was pleased to put to us?,—all of which I found rather absurd.

When no one could complete a particular poem, the Empress continued reading to the end. This produced further wails from the women: 'Oh, we all knew that one! How could we be so stupid?'

'Those of you,' said the Empress, 'who had taken the trouble to copy out the *Kokin Shu* several times would have been able to complete every single poem I have read. In the reign of Emperor Murakami there was a woman at Court known as the Imperial Lady of Senyo Palace. She was the daughter of the Minister of the Left who lived in the Smaller Palace of the First Ward, and of course you have all heard of her. When she was still a young girl, her father gave her this advice: "First you must study penmanship. Next you must learn to play the seven-string zither better than anyone else. And also you must memorize all the poems in the twenty volumes of the *Kokin Shu*."

'Emperor Murakami,' continued Her Majesty, 'had heard this story and remembered it years later when the girl had grown up and become an Imperial Concubine. Once, on a day of abstinence, he came into her room, hiding a notebook of *Kokin Shu* poems in the folds of his robe. He surprised her by seating himself behind a curtain of state; then, opening the book, he asked, "Tell me the verse written by such-and-such a poet, in such-and-such a year and on such-and-such an occasion." The lady understood what was afoot and that it was all in fun, yet the possibility of making a mistake or forgetting one of the poems must have worried her greatly. Before beginning the test, the Emperor had summoned a couple of ladies-in-waiting who were particularly adept in poetry and told them to mark each incorrect reply by a go stone. What a splendid scene it must have been! You know, I really envy anyone who attended that Emperor even as a lady-in-waiting.

'Well,' Her Majesty went on, 'he then began questioning her. She answered without any hesitation, just giving a few words or phrases to show that she knew each poem. And never once did she make a mistake. After a time the Emperor began to resent the lady's flawless memory and decided to stop as soon as he detected any error or vagueness in her replies. Yet, after he had gone through ten books of the *Kokin Su*, he had still not caught her out. At this stage he declared that it would be useless to continue. Marking where he had left off, he went to bed. What a triumph for the lady!

'He slept for some time. On waking, he decided that he must have a final verdict and that if he waited until the following day to examine her on the other ten volumes, she might use the time to refresh her memory. So he would have to settle the matter that very night. Ordering his attendants to bring up the bedroom lamp, he resumed his questions. By the time he had finished all twenty volumes, the night was well advanced; and still the lady had not made a mistake.

'During all this time His Excellency, the lady's father, was in a state of great agitation. As soon as he was informed that the Emperor was testing his daughter, he sent his attendants to various temples to arrange for special recitations of the Scriptures. Then he turned in the direction of the Imperial Palace and spent a long time in prayer. Such enthusiasm for poetry is really rather moving.'

The Emperor, who had been listening to the whole story, was much impressed. 'How can he possibly have read so many poems?' he remarked when Her Majesty had finished. 'I doubt whether I could get through three or four volumes. But of course things have changed. In the old days even people of humble station had a taste for the arts and were interested in elegant pastimes. Such a story would hardly be possible nowadays, would it?'

The ladies in attendance on Her Majesty and the Emperor's own ladies-in-waiting who had been admitted into Her Majesty's presence began chatting eagerly, and as I listened I felt that my cares had really 'melted away'.

14. HATEFUL THINGS

One is in a hurry to leave, but one's visitor keeps chattering away. If it is someone of no importance, one can get rid of him by saying, 'You must tell me all about it next time'; but, should it be the sort of visitor whose presence commands one's best behaviour, the situation is hateful indeed.

One finds that a hair has got caught in the stone on which one is rubbing one's inkstick, or again that gravel is lodged in the inkstick, making a nasty, grating sound.

Someone has suddenly fallen ill and one summons the exorcist. Since he is not at home, one has to send messengers to look for him. After one has had a long fretful wait, the exorcist finally arrives, and with a sigh of relief one asks him to start his incantations. But perhaps he has been exorcizing too many evil spirits recently; for hardly has he installed himself and begun praying when his voice becomes drowsy. Oh, how hateful!

A man who has nothing in particular to recommend him discusses all sorts of subjects at random as though he knew everything.

An elderly person warms the palms of his hands over a brazier and stretches out the wrinkles. No young man would dream behaving in such a fashion; old people can really be quite shameless. I have seen some dreary old creatures actually resting their feet on the brazier and rubbing them against the edge while they speak. These are the kind of people who in visiting someone's house first use their fans to wipe away the dust from the mat and, when they finally sit on it, cannot stay still but are forever spreading out the front of their hunting costume or even tucking it up under their knees. One might suppose that such behaviour was restricted to people of humble station; but I have observed it in quite well-bred people, including a Senior Secretary of the Fifth Rank in the Ministry of Ceremonial and a former Governor of Suruga.

I hate the sight of men in their cups who shout, poke their fingers in their mouths, stroke their beards, and pass on the wine to their neighbours with great cries of 'Have some more! Drink up!' They tremble, shake their heads, twist their faces, and gesticulate like children who are singing, 'We're off to see the Governor.' I have seen really well-bred people behave like this and I find it most distasteful.

To envy others and to complain about one's own lot; to speak badly about people; to be inquisitive about the most trivial matters and to resent and abuse people for not telling one, or, if one does manage to worm out some facts, to inform everyone in the most detailed fashion as if one had known all from the beginning—oh, how hateful!

One is just about to be told some interesting piece of news when a baby starts crying.

A flight of crows circle about with loud caws.

An admirer has come on a clandestine visit, but a dog catches sight of him and starts barking. One feels like killing the beast.

One has been foolish enough to invite a man to spend the night in an unsuitable place—and then he starts snoring.

A gentleman has visited one secretly. Though he is wearing a tall, lacquered hat, he nevertheless wants no one to see him. He is so flurried, in fact, that upon leaving he bangs into something with his hat. Most hateful! It is annoying too when he lifts up the Iyo blind that hangs at the entrance of the room, then lets it fall with a great rattle. If it is a head-blind, things are still worse, for being more solid it makes a terrible noise when it is dropped. There is no excuse for such carelessness. Even a head-blind does not make any noise if one lifts it up gently on entering and leaving the room; the same applies to sliding-doors. If one's movements are rough, even a paper door will bend and resonate when opened; but, if one lifts the door a little while pushing it, there need be no sound.

One has gone to bed and is about to doze off when a mosquito appears, announcing himself in a reedy voice. One can actually feel the wind made by his wings and, slight though it is, one finds it hateful in the extreme.

A carriage passes with a nasty, creaking noise. Annoying to think that the passengers may not even be aware of this! If I am travelling in someone's carriage and I hear it creaking, I dislike not only the noise but also the owner of the carriage.

One is in the middle of a story when someone butts in and tries to show that he is the only clever person in the room. Such a person is hateful, and so, indeed, is anyone, child or adult, who tries to push himself forward.

One is telling a story about old times when someone breaks in with a little detail that he happens to know, implying that one's own version is inaccurate—disgusting behaviour!

Very hateful is a mouse that scurries all over the place.

Some children have called at one's house. One makes a great fuss of them and gives them toys to play with. The children become accustomed to this treatment and start to come regularly forcing their way into one's inner rooms and scattering one's furnishings and possessions. Hateful!

A certain gentleman whom one does not want to see visits one at home or in the Palace, and one pretends to be asleep. But a maid comes to tell one and shakes one awake, with a look on her face that says, 'What a sleepyhead!' Very hateful.

A newcomer pushes ahead of the other members in a group; with a knowing look, this person starts laying down the law and forcing advice upon everyone—most hateful.

A man with whom one is having an affair keeps singing the praises of some woman he used to know. Even if it is a thing of the past, this can be very annoying. How much more so if he is still seeing the woman! (Yet sometimes I find that it is not as unpleasant as all that.)

A person who recites a spell himself after sneezing. In fact I detest anyone who sneezes except the master of the house

Fleas, too, are very hateful. When they dance about under someone's clothes, they really seem to be lifting them up.

The sound of dogs when they bark for a long time in chorus is ominous and hateful.

I cannot stand people who leave without closing the panel behind them.

How I detest the husbands of nurse-maids! It is not so bad if the child in the maid's charge is a girl, because then the man will keep his distance. But, if it is a boy, he will behave as though he were the father. Never letting the boy out of his sight, he insists on managing everything. He regards the other attendants in the house as less than human, and, if anyone tries to scold the child, he slanders him to the master. Despite this disgraceful behaviour, no one dare accuse the husband; so he strides about the house with a proud, self-important look, giving all the orders.

I hate people whose letters show that they lack respect for worldly civilities, whether by discourtesy in the phrasing or by extreme politeness to someone who does not deserve it. This sort of thing is, of course, most odious if the letter is for oneself; but it is bad enough even if it is addressed to someone else.

As a matter of fact, most people are too casual, not only in their letters but in their direct conversation. Sometimes I am quite disgusted at noting how little decorum people observe when talking to each other. It is particularly unpleasant to hear some foolish man or woman omit the proper marks of respect when addressing a person of quality; and, when servants fail to use honorific forms of speech in referring to their masters, it is very bad indeed. No less odious, however, are those masters who, in addressing their servants, use such phrases as 'When you were good enough to do such-and-such' or 'As you so kindly remarked'. No doubt there are some masters who, in describing their own actions to a servant, say, 'I presumed to do so-all-so'!

Sometimes a person who is utterly devoid of charm will try to create a good impression by using very elegant language; yet he only succeeds in being ridiculous. No doubt he believes this refined language to be just what the occasion demands, but, when it goes so far that everyone bursts out laughing, surely something must be wrong.

It is most improper to address high-ranking courtiers, Imperial Advisers, and the like simply by using their names without titles or marks of respect; but such mistakes are fortunately rare.

If one refers to the maid who is in attendance on some lady-in-waiting as 'Madam' or 'that lady', she will be surprised, delighted, and lavish in her praise.

When speaking to young noblemen and courtiers of high rank, one should always (unless Their Majesties are present) refer to them by their official posts. Incidentally, I have been shocked to hear important people use the word 'I' while conversing in Their Majesties' presence. Such a breach of etiquette is really distressing, and I fail to see why people cannot avoid it.

A man who has nothing in particular to recommend him but who speaks in an affected tone and poses as being elegant.

An inkstone with such a hard, smooth surface that the stick glides over it without leaving any deposit of ink.

Ladies-in-waiting who want to know everything that is going on.

Sometimes one greatly dislikes a person for no particular reason—and then that person goes and does something hateful.

A gentleman who travels alone in his carriage to see a procession or some other spectacle. What sort of a man is he? Even though he may not be a person of the greatest quality, surely he should have taken along a few of the many young men who are anxious to see the sights. But no, there he sits by himself (one can see his silhouette through the blinds), with a proud look on his face, keeping all his impressions to himself.

A lover who is leaving at dawn announces that he has to find his fan and his paper. 'I know I put them somewhere last night,' he says. Since it is pitch dark, he gropes about the room, bumping into the furniture and muttering, 'Strange! Where on earth can they be?' Finally he discovers the objects. He thrusts the paper into the breast of his robe with a great rustling sound; then he snaps open his fan and busily fans away with it. Only now is he ready to take his leave. What charmless behaviour! 'Hateful' is an understatement.

Equally disagreeable is the man who, when leaving in the middle of the night, takes care to fasten the cord of his headdress. This is quite unnecessary; he could perfectly well put it gently on his head without tying the cord. And why must he spend time adjusting his cloak or hunting costume? Does he really think someone may see him at this time of night and criticize him for not being impeccably dressed?

A good lover will behave as elegantly at dawn as at any other time. He drags himself out of bed with a look of dismay on his face. The lady urges him on: 'Come, my friend, it's getting light. You don't want anyone to find you here.' He gives a deep sigh, as if to say that the night has not been nearly long enough and that it is agony to leave. Once up, he does not instantly pull on his trousers. Instead he comes close to the lady and whispers whatever was left unsaid during the night. Even when he is dressed, he still lingers, vaguely pretending to be fastening his sash.

Presently he raises the lattice, and the two lovers stand together by the side door while he tells her how he dreads the coming day, which will keep them apart; then he slips away. The lady watches him go, and this moment of parting will remain among her most charming memories.

Indeed, one's attachment to a man depends largely on the elegance of his leave-taking. When he jumps out of bed, scurries about the room, tightly fastens his trouser-sash, rolls up the sleeves of his Court cloak, over-robe, or hunting costume, stuffs his belongings into the breast of his robe and then briskly secures the outer sash—one really begins to hate him.

HINDU FOLKLORE

1200s

The Indian folktale, *Prithvi Rai*, reflects the important age in Indian history when India, predominately Hindu, was being conquered by Islamic empires. The word 'Hindu,' derived from the Sanskrit word for river, was first applied to the people of the Indus River by the Persians in the Fifth century B.C.E. This geographical reference for the peoples of Hinduism reflects that the religion is a syncretism of what all the people of India have believed and done. From such a synthesis, Hinduism developed a social and doctrinal system that extended to every aspect of human life. The Gupta Empire (320–480 C.E.) was the period of great Hindu classical literatures, while the eras which followed produced eclectic blends of literature, including the vernacular folk tale below. The last Hindu monarchy was founded in 606 by Harsha, but at his death, division and anarchy prevailed until 1025 when the Muslem conqueror Mahmud of Ghazni brought about the dramatic change of social and religious culture which culminated in the founding of the Mughal dynasty in 1526.

This short romance is clearly a nostalgic piece about the vanquished Hindu rulers. What attributes of the ideal male warrior and the female heroine does this tale celebrate? In what ways are they different from or the same as European models?

Prithvi Rai: Last of the Hindu Knights

The Indian *Romeo and Juliet*
retold by Sister Nivedita

Now in the days of the old Hindu knighthood of India, there were four great cities where strong kings lived, who claimed that between them they ruled the whole of the country. And some of these cities you can find on the map quite easily, for three of them at least are there to this day. They were Delhi, Ajmere, Gujarat, and Kanauj, and one of them, Gujarat, is now known as Ahmedabad.

The King who sat on the throne of Delhi was the very flower of Hindu knights. Young, handsome, and courageous, a fearless horseman and a brave fighter, all the painters in India painted the portrait, and all the minstrels sang the praises, of Prithvi Rai; but loudest of all sang his own dear friend, Chand, the court-bard of Delhi.

Prithvi Rai's life had not been all play by any means. His duty, as a king, was greater than that of other knights, since he had of course to defend his people. And already he had had to fight great battles. For across the border lived a Saracen people under a chief called Mahmud of Ghazni, and six times this chieftain had invaded India, and six times Prithvi Rai had met and overcome him. Only, fighting as good knight should, for glory and not for greed, each time he had conquered him he had also set him free, and Mahmud had gone home again. And the last of these battles had been fought at Thaneswar, where the Afghan was badly wounded.

Just at this time, it very unfortunately happened that the King of Ajmere died, and left no son or grandson to succeed him. But he had had a daughter who had married the King of Delhi, and Prithvi Rai was her son. So, as the old man had no son's son to leave his throne to, it seemed natural enough to leave it to his daughter's son, Prithvi Rai, who thus became King of Delhi and Ajmere, and in this way the most powerful monarch in India. But this made one man very angry. The King of Kanauj claimed that he ought to have had Ajmere, for he had been married to a sister of the old King. Probably he had always been jealous of Prithvi Rai, but now he began to hate him with his whole heart.

In all countries always it has been believed that the bravest knight should wed the fairest lady. Now in the India of that day it was accepted on all hands that Prithvi Rai was the bravest knight, but, alas, every one also knew that the most beautiful princess in the world was the daughter of Kanauj! She was tall graceful and lovely. Her long, thick hair was black, with a blue light on it, and her large eyes were like the black bee moving in the petals of the white lotus. Moreover, it was said that the maiden was as high-souled and heroic as she was beautiful. So Prithvi Rai, King of Delhi, determined to win Samyukta, Princess of Kanauj and daughter of his mortal foe for his own. How was it to be done?

First he went to his old nurse who had brought him up. He prostrated himself before her and touched her feet, calling her "Mother," and she, with a smile, first put her fingers under his chin, and then kissed her own hand. For so mothers and children salute each other in India. Then the King sat down on the floor before her, and told her all that was in his heart.

She listened, and sat without speaking for a few minutes when he had finished. "Well" she said, after a while, "give me only your portrait. I shall send you hers. And I can promise you, that when you win your way to the girl's side, you will find her just as determined as yourself, to marry no one but you."

That evening the old nurse left Delhi with a party of merchants bound for another of the royal cities. And in her baggage, unknown to her humble fellow-travellers, was a tiny portrait on ivory of the King. It was a week or two afterwards, that the ladies of the King's household, at Kanauj, took an old woman into their service who claimed that she had been born at the court of Ajmere, and had waited, in her childhood, on the late Queen of Kanauj. This old lady soon grew specially fond of the Princess, and was gradually allowed to devote herself to her. In the long, hot hours she would sit fanning and chatting with her, or she would prepare the bath, with its scents and unguents, and herself brush the soles of Samyukta's feet with vermilion paint. Or at night, when the heat made it difficult to sleep, she would steal into some marble pavilion on the roof, and coax the Princess to come out there into the starlight, while she would crouch by her side, with the peacock fan, and tell her tales of Delhi, and of Prithvi Rai, and his love for her. And often they gazed together at a miniature, which had been sent, said the old woman, by her hand, to ask if the Princess would deign to accept it. For as we all have guessed, of course, it was the old nurse of Prithvi Rai's mother, and of Prithvi Rai himself, who was here, serving the maiden whom he hoped to make his bride.

In a few months came the time when the King of Kanauj must announce his daughter's marriage. And he determined to call a Swayamvara, that is, a gathering of princes and nobles, amongst whom the princess might come and choose her husband. She would carry a necklace of flowers in her hand, and heralds would go before. At each candidate's throne as they came to it, the praises of that prince, and all his great deeds in battle and tournament, would be declared by the heralds. Then the Princess would pause a moment, and if she decided that this was the knight whom she desired to choose for her husband, she would signify the fact by throwing her garland round his neck. And then the Swayamvara would turn into a wedding, and all the rival princes would take their places as guests. This was a ceremony only used for a royal maiden, and naturally no one was ever asked whom it would not be desirable for her to choose.

In this case, invitations were sent to the kin and princes of all the kingdoms, save only of Delhi, and all India knew that the most beautiful princess in the world was about to hold her Swayannara.

This was the time for Prithvi Rai to act. So he and his friend Chand, the court-bard, disguised themselves as minstrels, and rode all the way to Kanauj, determined to be present at the Swayamvara, whatever it might cost.

At last the great day dawned, and Samyukta made ready for the bridal choice. Very sad at heart was she, for she knew not what the day might bring forth, only she was sure that of her own free will she would marry none but Prithvi Rai, and he had not even been asked to the ceremony.

The insult thus done to the knight of whom she dreamed, burned like fire in the heart of the Princess, and she wondered contemptuously which of the princes whom she would meet in the hall of choice could dare to stand before the absent King of Delhi on the field of battle. And something of her father's own pride and courage rose in her against her father himself, as the hour drew near for the Swayarnvara to open. Yet behind all this lay the dull misery of the question: What could she possibly do to announce her silent choice in the absence of the hero? A princess might choose amongst those present, but to speak the name of one who was absent would be a fall unheard of from the royal dignity! How the brow of the Rajput maiden throbbed as they bound on it the gold fillets of her marriage-day! How the wrists burned, on which they fastened the bridal ornaments! And the feet and ankles, loaded with their tiny golden bells, which would tinkle as their owner walked, like "running water" in the bed of the streamlet, how glad they would have been to carry Samyukta away into seclusion, where she might do anything rather than face the ordeal before her!

At last, however, the dreaded hour had come. Seated on thrones in the hall of choice, the long array of knights and princes held their breath as they caught the first distant sounds of the blare of trumpets preceding the princess. Nearer and nearer came the heralds, and so silent was the company that presently, underneath all the noise and clang of the procession without, could be heard distinctly, throughout the great hall, the tinkle of anklets, and they knew that the queen of that bridal day was approaching.

As for Samyukta herself, as with slow footsteps and bent head she paced along the pathway from the castle to the doorway of the hall, she saw no one amongst the many thousands, on foot and on horseback, beside the path. Had she but once looked up, the whole scene would have been changed for her, and in a moment she might have made her choice. But this was not to be. Lower and lower bent the head of the royal maiden beneath her long rich veil. Tighter and tighter were clasped the hands that with their firm hold on the marriage-garland, hung down before her. And slower and slower were the footsteps with which she drew near to the hall of choice, till she had reached the door itself. But there the proud daughter of king raised her head high, to lower it never again. For one moment she paused, startled, dismayed, incredulous, and then, with flushed cheeks and haughty air, drawing herself up to her full height, she entered the hall of choice with perfect calm. For here at the entrance to the pavilion stood a grotesque wooden figure of the King of Delhi, made to stand like a doorkeeper to wait at the marriage of the chosen knight. At first Samyukta could not believe her own eyes. The image was hideous, mean, and dwarfish, but it was unmistakably intended for Prithvi Rai. Had it not been insult enough to the gallant knight that his name had been omitted from the list of guests, that Kanauj should add to this the madness of mockery? Yet so it was. And as soon as she had realised it, the daughter of the King knew also her own part in the day's great ceremonies, and whatever might be the outcome for herself, she would play it to the end. The princes rose to their feet as the veiled maiden entered, and then sat down once more on their various thrones. The heralds fell back at the entrance, making room now for the Princess to precede them. And then, with slow firm steps, she, whose each footfall was music, passed on from throne to throne, waiting quietly for the questioning cry of her own heralds, and the answering salutation of those about the enthroned prince, before she could listen to the tale of brave deeds by which each bard sought to glorify his own master in the eyes of the fair lady. But at each throne, after patiently listening, after giving every opportunity to its adherents to urge their utmost, the veiled Princess paused a moment and passed on. And something in her bearing or quiet disdain told each whom she left behind her, that she required more of the knight she would choose than he had yet attained. But the sadness of disappointment gave place to astonishment, as Samyukta drew near to the last throne, and stood listening as patiently and as haughtily as ever. This prince, as all thought, she must perforce accept. Round his neck she must throw the marriage-garland. With veil knotted to his cloak, she must at his side step forward to the sacred fire. These things she must do, for now there was no alternative. Yet none of these things did the daughter of the King attempt. Her slender form looked right queenly, and even beneath her veil her courage and triumph were plain to be seen as she turned her back on the whole assembly, as if to pass out of the lull of choice, and then stood a moment in the open door way, and threw the garland round the neck of the caricature of Prithvi Rai!

Her father, seated at the end of the hall high above the guests, sprang to his feet with a muttered oath! From the marriage-bower to the darkness of the dungeon, was this the choice that his daughter would make? What else could she mean by such a defiance? But scarcely had he strode a foot's length from his place when a tall horseman from amongst the crowd was seen to stoop down over the form of the Princess, and, lifting her to his saddle, gallop off out of sight, followed by another. For Prithvi Rai and his friend Chand had not failed to be present at Samyukta's Swamvara, knowing well that though the King of Delhi was not amongst the guests, yet no other than he to whom her heart was given would be chosen by the peerless daughter of Kanauj.

And then the festive hall became the scene of a council of war. The King of Kanauj swore a mighty oath that to the enemies of Delhi he would henceforth prove a friend. The outraged princes added their promises to his, and runners were sent across the border with letters to Mahmud of Ghazni, offering him the alliance of Kanauj in his warfare against Prithvi Rai. The day that had dawned so brightly went down in darkness amidst mutterings of the coming storm. For the wedding day of Samyukta was to prove the end of all the ages of the Hindu knighthood.

A year had passed. To Prithvi Rai and his bride it had passed like a dream. Amongst the gardens and pavilions of the palace they had wandered hand in hand. And Prithvi Rai, lost in his happiness, had forgotten, as it seemed, the habits of the soldier. Nor did Samyukta remember the wariness and alertness that are proper to great kings. It was like a cup of rich wine drunk before death. Yet were these two right royal souls, and knew well how to meet the end. Suddenly broke the storm of war. Suddenly came the call to meet Mahmud of Ghazni on the field of action. And then, without a tear, did Samyukta fasten her husband's armour, and buckle on his sword, and kiss the royal jewel that she was to place in the front of his helmet. And while the battle raged around the standard of Delhi, she waited, cold and collected in the palace. What had she to fear? The funeral fire stood ready, if the worst news should come. Not for her to see the downfall of her country. Was she not the daughter and the wife of kings?

Hours passed away, and ever on and farther onwards rolled the tide of battle—on one side the infuriated Kanauj, fighting by the side of the alien in faith and race, and on the other Prithvi Rai with his faithful troops. Splendidly fought the adherents of the King of Delhi. But in the end the advantage of numbers prevailed, and Prithvi Rai fell, pierced to the heart, at the foot of his own banner.

It was dark when they brought the news to Samyukta, waiting in the shadows of the palace. But red grew the night with the funeral fire, when she had heard. For her eye brightened when they told her, and her lips smiled. "Then must I haste to my lord where he awaits me," said this Rajput queen gaily, and with the words she sprang into the flames.

So passed away the old Hindu kings and queens of Delhi, and all things were changed in India, and Mohammedan sovereigns reigned in their stead.

The Renaissance and Reformation

ISOTTA NOGAROLA

1418-1466

According to scholars of the period, Isotta Nogarola was one of the most famous and admired "women humanists." She was taught Latin and Greek by a humanist tutor, and she began to write letters to a number of well-known scholars such as Guarino of Verona. Although her efforts to join the humanist circle of men failed, she continued to study throughout her life.

In the selection that follows, Nogarola argues for a defense of Eve, though her idea of a defense may seem, by our twentieth-century standards, to read more like a condemnation. How can you compare Nogarola's defense of Eve to Christine de Pisan's? Why might Nogarola have used the strategy of "ignorance" as a defense, and how does her strategy reflect some of the dominant principles of humanism? What makes Eve continue to be such a compelling figure to explore?

[1]Information for this introduction was taken from Margaret King and Albert Rabil, Jr. eds., *Her Immaculate Hand: Selected Works By and About the Women Humanists of Quattrocento Italy.* (Asheville, NC: Pegasus Press, 1997) 16–18.

Letter to Ludovico Foscarini

OF THE EQUAL OR UNEQUAL SIN OF ADAM AND EVE

An honorable disputation between the illustrious lord Ludovico Foscarini, Venetian doctor of arts and both laws, and the noble and learned and divine lady Isotta Nogarola of Verona, regarding this judgment of Aurelius Augustine: They sinned unequally according to sex, but equally according to pride.

LUDOVICO begins: If it is in any way possible to measure the gravity of human sinfulness, then we should see Eve's sin as more to be condemned than Adam's [for three reasons]. [First], she was assigned by a just judge to a harsher punishment than was Adam. [Second], she believed that she was made more like God, and that is in the category of unforgiveable sins against the Holy Spirit. [Third], she suggested and was the cause of Adam's sin—not he of hers; and although it is a poor excuse to sin because of a friend, nevertheless none was more tolerable than the one by which Adam was enticed.

ISOTTA: But I see things—since you move me to reply—from quite another and contrary viewpoint. For where there is less intellect and less constancy, there there is less sin; and Eve [lacked sense and constancy] and therefore sinned less. Knowing [her weakness] that crafty serpent began by tempting the woman, thinking the man perhaps invulnerable because of his constancy. [For it says in] *Sentences* 2: Standing in the woman's presence, the ancient foe did not boldly persuade, but approached her with a question: "Why did God bid you not to eat of the tree of paradise?" She responded: "Lest perhaps we die." But seeing that she doubted the words of the Lord, the devil said: "You shall not die," but "you will be like God, knowing good and evil."

[Adam must also be judged more guilty than Eve, secondly] because of his greater contempt for the command. For in Genesis 2 it appears that the Lord commanded Adam, not Eve, where it says: "The Lord God took the man and placed him in the paradise of Eden to till it and to keep it," (and it does not say, "that they might care for and protect it") ". . . and the Lord God commanded the man" (and not "them"): "From every tree of the garden you may eat" (and not "you" [in the plural sense]), and, [referring to the forbidden tree], "for the day you eat of it, you must die," [again, using the singular form of "you"]. [God directed his command to Adam alone] because he esteemed the man more highly than the woman.

Moreover, the woman did not [eat from the forbidden tree] because she believed that she was made more like God, but rather because she was weak and [inclined to indulge in] pleasure. Thus: "Now the woman saw that the tree was good for food, pleasing to the eyes, and desirable for the knowledge it would give. She took of its fruit and ate it, and also gave some to her husband and he ate," and it does not say [that she did so] in order to be like God. And if Adam had not eaten, her sin would have had no consequences. For it does not say: "If Eve had not sinned Christ would not have been made incarnate," but "If Adam had not sinned." Hence the woman, but only because she had been first deceived by the serpent's evil persuasion, did indulge in the delights of paradise; but she would have harmed only herself and in no way endangered human posterity if the consent of the first-born man had not been offered. Therefore Eve was no danger to posterity but [only] to herself; but the man Adam spread the infection of sin to himself and to all future generations. Thus Adam, being the author of all humans yet to be born, was also the first cause of their perdition. For this reason the healing of humankind was celebrated first in the man and then in the woman, just as [according to Jewish tradition], after an unclean spirit has been expelled from a man, as it springs forth from the synagogue, the woman is purged [as well].

Moreover, that Eve was condemned by a just judge to a harsher punishment is evidently false, for God said to the woman: "I will make great your distress in childbearing; in pain shall you bring forth children; for your husband shall be your longing, though he have dominion over you." But to Adam he said: "Because you have listened to your wife and have eaten of the tree of which I have commanded you not to eat" (notice that God appears to have admonished Adam alone [using the singular form of "you"] and not Eve) "Cursed be the ground because of you; in toil shall you eat of it all the days of your life; thorns and thistles shall it bring forth to you, and you shall eat the plants of the field. In the sweat of your brow you shall eat bread, till you return to the ground, since out of it you were taken; for dust you are and unto dust you shall return." Notice that Adam's punishment appears harsher than Eve's; for God said to Adam: "to dust you shall return," and not to Eve, and death is the most terrible punishment that could be assigned. Therefore it is established that Adam's punishment was greater than Eve's.

I have written this because you wished me to. Yet I have done so fearfully since this is not a woman's task. But you are kind, and if you find any part of my writing clumsy you will correct it.

LUDOVICO: You defend the cause of Eve most subtly, and indeed defend so [well] that, if I had not been born a man, you would have made me your champion. But sticking fast to the truth, which is attached by very strong roots, I have set out [here] to assault your fortress with your own weapons. I shall begin by attacking its foundations, which can be destroyed by the testimony of Sacred Scripture, so that there will be no lack of material for my refutation.

Eve sinned from ignorance and inconstancy, from which you conclude that she sinned less seriously. [But] ignorance—especially of those things which we are obligated to know—does not excuse us. For it is written: "If anyone ignores this, he shall be ignored." The eyes which guilt makes blind punishment opens. He who has been foolish in guilt will be wise in punishment especially when the sinner's mistake occurs through negligence. For the woman's ignorance, born of arrogance, does not excuse her, in the same way that Aristotle and the [lawyers], who teach a true philosophy, find the drunk and ignorant deserving of a double punishment. Nor do I understand how in the world you, so many ages distant from Eve, fault her intellect, when her knowledge divinely created by the highest craftsman of all things, daunted that clever serpent lurking in paradise. For, as you write, he was not bold enough to attempt to persuade her but approached her with a question.

But the acts due to inconstancy are even more blameworthy [than those due to ignorance]. For to the same degree that the acts issuing from a solid and constant mental attitude are more worthy and distinct from the preceding ones, so should those issuing from inconstancy be punished more severely since inconstancy is an evil in itself and when paired with an evil sin makes the sin worse.

Nor is Adam's companion excused because Adam was appointed to protect her, [contrary to your contention that] thieves who have been trustingly employed by a householder are not punished with the most severe punishment like strangers or those in whom no confidence has been placed. Also the woman's frailty was not the cause of sin, as you write, but her pride, since the demon promised her knowledge, which leads to arrogance and inflates [with pride], according to the apostle. For it says in Ecclesiasticus: "Pride was the beginning of every sin." And though the other women followed, yet she was the first since, when man existed in a state of innocence, the flesh was obedient to him and [did not struggle] against reason. The first impulse [of sin], therefore, was an inordinate appetite for seeking that which was not suited to its own nature, as Augustine wrote to Orosius: "Swollen by pride, man obeyed the serpent's persuasion and disdained God's commands." For the adversary said to Eve: "Your eyes will be opened and you will be like God, knowing good and evil." Nor would the woman have believed the demon's persuasive words, as Augustine says [in his commentary] on Genesis, unless a love of her own power had overcome her, which [love is] a stream sprung from the well of pride. [I shall continue to follow Augustine in his view that at the moment] when Eve desired to capture divinity, she lost happiness. And those words: "If Adam had not sinned, etc." confirm me in my view. For Eve sinned perhaps in such a way that, just as the demons did not merit redemption, neither perhaps did she. I speak only in jest, but Adam's sin was fortunate, since it warranted such a redeemer.

And lest I finally stray too far from what you have written, [I shall turn to your argument that Adam's punishment was more severe than Eve's and his sin, accordingly, greater. But] the woman suffers all the penalties [inflicted on] the man, and since her sorrows are greater than his, not only is she doomed to death, condemned to eat at the cost of sweat, denied by the cherubim and flaming swords entry to paradise, but in addition to all these things which are common [to both], she alone must give birth in pain and be subjected to her husband. [Her punishment is thus harsher than Adam's, as her sin is greater.]

But because in such a matter it is not sufficient to have refuted your arguments without also putting forward my own, [I shall do so now]. Eve believed that she was made similar to God and, out of envy, desired that which wounds the Holy Spirit. Moreover, she must bear responsibility for every fault of Adam because, as Aristotle testifies, the cause of a cause is the cause of that which is caused. Indeed, every prior cause influences an outcome more than a secondary cause, and the principle of any genus, according to the same Aristotle, is seen as its greatest [component]. In fact, [it] is considered to be more than half the whole. And in the *Posterior Analytics* he writes: "That on account of which any thing exists is that thing and more greatly so." Now [since] Adam sinned on account of Eve, it follows that Eve sinned much more than Adam. Similarly, just as it is better to treat others well than to be well-treated, so it is worse to persuade another to evil than to be persuaded to evil. For he sins less who sins by another's example, inasmuch as what is done by example can be said to be done according to a kind of law, [and thus justly]. For this reason it is commonly said that "the sins that many commit are [without fault]." [Thus Eve, who persuaded her husband to commit an evil act, sinned more greatly than Adam, who merely consented to her example]. And if Adam and Eve both had thought that they were worthy of the same glory, Eve, who was inferior [by nature], more greatly departed from the mean, and consequently sinned more greatly. Moreover, as a beloved companion she could deceive her husband [vulnerable to her persuasion because of his love for her] more easily than the shameful serpent could deceive the woman. And she persevered longer [in sin] than Adam, because she began first, and offenses are that much more serious (according to Gregory's decree) in relation to the length of time they hold the unhappy soul in bondage. Finally, to bring my discourse to a close, Eve was the cause and the example of sin, and Gregory greatly increases the guilt in the case of the example. And Christ, who could not err, condemned more severely the pretext of the ignorant Jews, because it came first, than he did the sentence of the learned Pilate, when he said: "They who have betrayed me to you have greater sin, etc." All who wish to be called Christians have always agreed with this judgment, and you, above all most Christian, will approve and defend it. Farewell, and do not fear, but dare to do much, because you have excellently understood so much and write so learnedly.

ISOTTA: I had decided that I would not enter further into a contest with you because, as you say, you assault my fortress with my own weapons. [The propositions] you have presented me were so perfectly and diligently defended that it would be difficult not merely for me, but for the most learned men to oppose them. But since I recognize that this contest is useful for me, I have decided to obey your honest wish. Even though I know I struggle in vain, yet I will earn the highest praise if I am defeated by so mighty a man as you.

Eve sinned out of ignorance and inconstancy, and hence you contend that she sinned more gravely, because the ignorance of those things which we are obligated to know does not excuse us, since it is written: "He who does not know will not be known." I would concede your point if that ignorance were crude or affected. But Eve's ignorance was implanted by nature, of which nature God himself is the author and founder. In many people it is seen that he who knows less sins less, like a boy who sins less than an old man or a peasant less than a noble. Such a person does not need to know explicitly what is required for salvation, but implicitly, because [for him] faith alone suffices. The question of inconstancy proceeds similarly. For when it is said that the acts which proceed from inconstancy are more blameworthy, [that kind of] inconstancy is understood which is not innate but the product of character and sins.

The same is true of imperfection. For when gifts increase, greater responsibility is imposed. When God created man, from the beginning he created him perfect, and the powers of his soul perfect, and gave him a greater understanding and knowledge of truth as well as a greater depth of wisdom. Thus it was that the Lord led to Adam all the animals of the earth and the birds of heaven, so that Adam could call them by their names. For God said: "Let us make mankind in our image and likeness, and let them have dominion over the fish of the sea, and the birds of the air, the cattle, over all the wild animals and every creature that crawls on the earth," making clear his own perfection. But of the woman he said: "It is not good that the man is alone; I will make him a helper like himself." And since consolation and joy are required for happiness, and since no one can have solace and joy when alone, it appears that God created woman for man's consolation. For the good spreads itself, and the greater it is the more it shares itself. Therefore, it appears that Adam's sin was greater than Eve's. [As] Ambrose [says]: "In him to whom a more indulgent liberality has been shown is insolence more inexcusable."

"But Adam's companion," [you argue], "is not excused because Adam was appointed to protect her, because thieves who have been trustingly employed by a householder are not punished with the most severe punishment like strangers or those in whom the householder placed no confidence." This is true, however, in temporal law, but not in divine law, for divine justice proceeds differently from temporal justice in punishing [sin].

[You argue further that] "the fragility of the woman was not the cause of sin, but rather her inordinate appetite for seeking that which was not suited to her nature," which [appetite] is the product, as you write, of pride. Yet it is clearly less a sin to desire the knowledge of good and evil than to transgress against a divine commandment, since the desire for knowledge is a natural thing, and all men by nature desire to know. And even if the first impulse [of sin] were this inordinate appetite, which cannot be without sin, yet it is more tolerable than the sin of transgression, for the observance of the commandments is the road which leads to the country of salvation. [It is written] "But if thou wilt enter into life, keep the commandments"; and likewise: "What shall I do to gain eternal life? Keep the commandments." And transgression is particularly born of pride, because pride is nothing other than rebellion against divine rule, exalting oneself above what is permitted according to divine rule by disdaining the will of God and displacing it with one's own. Thus Augustine [writes] in *On Nature and Grace*: "Sin is the will to pursue or retain what justice forbids, that is, to deny what God wishes." Ambrose agrees with him in *On Paradise*: "Sin is the transgression against divine law and disobedience the heavenly commandments." Behold! See that the transgression against a disobedience to the heavenly commandments is the greatest sin, whereas you have thus defined sin: "Sin is the inordinate desire to know." Thus clearly sin of transgression against a command is greater than [the sin of] desiring knowledge of good and evil. So even if inordinate desire be a sin, as with Eve, yet she did not desire to be like God in power but only in the knowledge of good and evil, which by nature she was actually inclined to desire.

[Next, as to your statement] that those words, "if Adam had not sinned" confirm you in your view [of Eve's damnability], since Eve may have so sinned that, like the demons, she did not merit redemption, I reply that she also was redeemed with

Adam, because [she was] "bone of my bone and flesh of my flesh." And if it seems that God did not redeem her, this was undoubtedly because God held her sin as negligible. For if man deserved redemption, the woman deserved it much more because of the slightness of the crime. For the angel cannot be excused by ignorance as can the woman. For the angel understands without investigation or discussion and has an intellect more in the likeness of God's—to which it seems Eve desired to be similar—than does man. Hence the angel is called intellectual and the man rational. Thus where the woman sinned from her desire for knowledge, the angel sinned from a desire for power. While knowledge of an appearance in some small way can be partaken of by the creature, in no way can it partake in the power of God and of the soul of Christ. Moreover, the woman in sinning thought she would receive mercy, believing certainly that she was committing a sin, but not one so great as to warrant God's inflicting such a sentence and punishment. But the angel did not think [of mercy]. Hence Gregory [says in the] fourth book of the *Moralia*: "The first parents were needed for this, that the sin which they committed by transgressing they might purge by confessing." But that persuasive serpent was never punished for his sin, for he was never to be recalled to grace. Thus, in sum, Eve clearly merited redemption more than the angels.

[As to your argument] that the woman also suffers all the penalties inflicted on the man, and beyond those which are common [to both] she alone gives birth in sorrow and has been subjected to man, this also reinforces my earlier point. As I said, the good spreads itself, and the greater it is the more it shares itself. So also evil, the greater it is the more it shares itself, and the more it shares itself the more harmful it is, and the more harmful it is the greater it is. Furthermore, the severity of the punishment is proportional to the gravity of the sin. Hence Christ chose to die on the cross, though this was the most shameful and horrible kind of death, and on the cross he endured in general every kind of suffering by type. Hence Isidore writes concerning the Trinity: "The only-born Son of God in executing the sacrament of his death, in himself bears witness that he consummated every kind of suffering when, with lowered head, he gave up his spirit." The reason was that the punishment had to correspond to the guilt. Adam took the fruit of the forbidden tree; Christ suffered on the tree and so made satisfaction [for Adam's sin]. [As] Augustine [writes]: "Adam disdained God's command" (and he does not say Eve) "accepting the fruit from the tree, but whatever Adam lost Christ restored." [For Christ paid the penalty for sin he had not committed, as it says in] Psalm 64: "For what I have not taken, then I atoned." Therefore, Adam's sin was the greatest [possible], because the punishment corresponding to his fault was the greatest [possible] and was general in all men. [As the] apostle [says]: "All sinned in Adam."

"Eve," [you say], "must bear responsibility for every fault of Adam because, as Aristotle shows, whatever is the cause of the cause is the cause of the thing caused." This is true in the case of things which are, as you know better [than I], in themselves the causes of other things, which is the case for the first cause, the first principle, and "that on account of which anything is what it is." But clearly this was not the case with Eve, because Adam either had free will or he did not. If he did not have it, he did not sin; if he had it, then Eve forced the sin [upon him], which is impossible. For as Bernard says: "Free will, because of its inborn nobility, is forced by no necessity," not even by God, because if that were the case it would be to concede that two contradictories are true at the same time. God cannot do, therefore, what would cause an act proceeding from free will and remaining free to be not free but coerced. [As] Augustine [writes in his commentary] on Genesis: "God cannot act against that nature which he created with a good will." God could himself, however, remove that condition of liberty from any person and bestow some other condition on him. In the same way fire cannot, while it remains fire, not burn, unless its nature is changed and suspended for a time by divine force. No other creature, such as a good angel or devil can do this, since they are less than God; much less a woman, since she is less perfect and weaker than they. Augustine clarifies this principle [of God's supremacy] saying: "Above our mind is nothing besides God, nor is there anything intermediary between God and our mind." Yet only something which is superior to something else can coerce it; but Eve was inferior to Adam, therefore she was not herself the cause of sin. [In] Ecclesiasticus 15 [it says]: "God from the beginning created man and placed him in the palm of his counsel and made clear his commandments and precepts. If you wish to preserve the commandments, they will preserve you and create in you pleasing faith." Thus Adam appeared to accuse God rather than excuse himself when he said: "The woman you placed at my side gave me fruit from the tree and I ate it."

[Next you argue] that the beloved companion could have more easily deceived the man than the shameful serpent the woman. To this I reply that Eve, weak and ignorant by nature, sinned much less by assenting to that astute serpent who was called "wise," than Adam—created by God with perfect knowledge and understanding—in listening to the persuasive words and voice of the imperfect woman.

[Further, you say] that Eve persevered in her sin a longer time and therefore sinned more, because crimes are that much more serious according to the length of time they hold the unhappy soul in bondage. This is no doubt true, when two sins are equal, and in the same person or in two similar persons. But Adam and Eve were not equals, because Adam was a perfect animal and Eve imperfect and ignorant. [Therefore, their sins were not comparable, and Eve who persevered longer in sin, was not on that account more guilty than Adam].

Finally, if I may quote you: "The woman was the example and the cause of sin, and Gregory emphatically extends the burden of guilt to [the person who provided] an example, and Christ condemned the cause of the ignorant Jews, because it was first, more than the learned Pilate's sentence when he said: 'Therefore he who betrayed me to you has greater sin.'" I reply that Christ did not condemn the cause of the ignorant Jews because it was first, but because it was vicious and devilish due to their native malice and obstinacy. For they did not sin from ignorance. The gentile Pilate was more ignorant about these things than the Jews, who had the law and the prophets and read them and daily saw signs concerning [Christ]. For John 15 says: "If I had not come and spoken to them, they would have no sin. But now they have no excuse for their sin." Thus they themselves said: "What are we doing? for this man is working signs." And: "Art thou the Christ, the Son of the Blessed One?" For the [Jewish] people was special to God, and Christ himself [said]: "I was not sent except to the lost sheep of the house of Israel. It is not fair to take the children's bread and cast it to the dogs." Therefore the Jews sinned more, because Jesus loved them more.

Let these words be enough from me, an unarmed and poor little woman.

LUDOVICO: So divinely have you encompassed the whole of this problem that I could believe your words were drawn not from the fonts of philosophy and theology but from heaven. Hence they are worthy of praise rather than contradiction. Yet, lest you be cheated of the utility [you say you have begun to receive from this debate], attend to these brief arguments which can be posed for the opposite view, that you may sow the honey-sweet seeds of paradise which will delight readers and surround you with glory.

Eve's ignorance was very base, because she chose to put faith in a demon rather than in the creator. This ignorance actually is due to her sin, as sacred writings attest, and certainly does not excuse her sin. Indeed, if the truth be plainly told, it was extreme stupidity not to remain within the boundaries which the excellent God had set for her, [but] to fall prey to vain hope and lose what she had had and what she aspired to.

The issues which you have cleverly joined I shall not divide. The inconstancy of Eve which has been condemned was not an inconstancy of nature but of habit. For those qualities which are in us by nature we are neither praised nor blamed, according to the judgment of the wisest philosophers. Actually, the woman's nature was excellent and concordant with reason, genus and time. For just as teeth were given to wild beasts, horns to oxen, feathers to birds for their survival, to the woman mental capacity was given sufficient for the preservation and pursuit of the health of her soul.

If [as you say] Eve was naturally created to aid, perfect, console and gladden man, she conducted herself contrary to the laws [of her nature], providing him with toil, imperfection, sadness and sorrow, which the holy decrees had ordained would be serious crimes. And human laws, too, ordered through long ages by the minds of great men, by sure reasoning have established that seizure of someone else's goods merits the more serious punishment the more it injures the owner.

Your argument about [Adam's] transgression of God's commandments does not acquit Eve [of responsibility], because neither did she keep them. As to your distinction between the sin of the angel and of man, [by means of which you argue that Eve's sin was less serious than that of the rebellious angels, thus redeemable], that is a huge issue, and though it provides worthy for your brilliant mind, it is too abundant to consider in this brief space. And how you can consider it to be concordant with the principle of the highest God's goodness that greater punishments are poured out upon those who sinned less [—for you argue that the evil consequences of Adam's sin, when diffused to Eve, whose being had derived from his, were intensified—] I cannot understand.

You push too far Aristotle's views on first causes. [You agree that] every cause of a cause is a cause of the thing caused, [but argue that since Adam had free will his act could not have been caused by Eve]. But since Adam had free will, I do not consider him free from obligation to sin, and even though I have assigned Adam's whole fault in some degree to Eve, yet [I do not contend] that Adam's sin was entirely and in every way caused by Eve.

I agree [with what you say] concerning free will and the [essential] goodness of [human] nature.

As to the ease of the man's consent to the woman's words, [which you see as indicating his sinful weakness], I want, since I am writing to you, to pass by in silence the matter of the deceitfulness of the [female] sex. But this ancient proverb states: "There is no plague more deadly than an intimate enemy." The first mother kindled a great fire, which to our ruin has not yet been extinguished. This demonstrates the extreme seriousness of her sin. For just as those sicknesses of the body are more serious which are less curable, so the [diseases] of the soul [which Eve brought upon us are serious indeed].

Though I have spoken, you may not hear. You may spurn and disdain [my words because of] Augustine's conclusion that they were equally guilty: "The principle of how much longer, etc." Let us read the history of the passion and the dreams of the wife, the words of Pilate, the washing of hands, the avoidance of judgment, and we shall confess that he understood better than the Jews that the sentence was unjust. These things make it quite clear that the force of my arguments has not been weakened.

I have explained my views with these few words, both because I was ordered not to exceed the paper [you] sent me, and because I speak to you who are most learned. For I do not wish to be a guide on such a road to you for whom, because of your great goodness, all things stand open in the brightest light. I, indeed—a single man and a mere mortal, as it were, a reflection of the celestial life—have only pointed a finger, so to speak, in the direction of the sources. And although others may find that my writings suffer from the defect of obscurity, if you, most brilliant, accept them and join them to what you and I have already written, our views will become very evident and clear, and will shine amid the shadows. And if what I have written is clumsy, by your skill you will make it worthy of your mind, virtue, and glory. For you march forward to new battles to the sound of sacred eloquence (as do soldiers to the clamour of trumpets), always more learned and more ready. And you march forward, against me, who has applied the whole sum of my thinking to my reading all at the same time, and to my writing, that I might present my case and defend myself against yours, although the many storms and floods of my obligations toss me about at whim. Farewell.

Laura Cereta

1469-1499

Like Isotta Nogarola, Laura Cereta came from a home in which learning was valued, and she seems to have been supported in her scholarly activities by her father, Silvestro Cereta, a member of the Brescian aristocracy.[1] She was interested in astrology and the zodiac, Latin and Greek rhetorical texts and Petrarch. Her hopes to style herself after Petrarch led to an interest in studying moral philosophy, theology, and literature. After her marriage, at the age of fifteen, she was able to continue her studies (this was rare; usually marriage signaled the end of a learned life for women fortunate enough to study in the first place). Her husband died a year and a half after their marriage, and she used the study of literature to comfort her during this time of grief.

Cereta's vast knowledge and passion for the scholarly life can be seen in her published letters, a distinct literary form employed by Italian humanists of this period. Her letter-writing received strong responses, mostly from male humanists who believed the letters were actually written by her father. The selections reprinted below focus on Cereta's ideas concerning women's roles in the society of Quattrocento Italy. What can we learn about the values of this society through Cereta's letters? How has Cereta herself absorbed the dominant ideology of her culture? How does her defense of women as writers compare to that of Marie de France's defense of her own writing?

[1]Information for this introduction was taken from Margaret King and Albert Rabil, Jr. eds., *Her Immaculate Hand: Selected Works by and about the Women Humanists of Quattrocento Italy.* (Asheville, NC: Pegasus Press, 1997) 21-25.

Letters

LETTER TO AUGUSTINUS AEMILIUS, CURSE AGAINST THE ORNAMENTATION OF WOMEN

Alone, I fled to the country, and in tranquil leisure delighted in [humane] studies. But you, meanwhile, were disturbed by my retreat, as if you seemed to consider me, a nonentity, important.

I came at the end when my husband was feverish. Dying myself, I saw him half dead. I cheered him when he seemed to revive, I wept over him when he died, I fell lifeless on his dead body, and the fatal house which awaited me for marriage admitted me to lamentation. Thus one, and that an abominable year, saw me a girl, bride, widow, and pauper. These events were ordered by fate, not by you; you were mortal and died.

I thank you for esteeming me so highly, and more so than I deserve, for I cannot be compared to women like Sarah, Esther, Sephora and Susanna, any more than a glowworm shining at night can be compared to the brilliant stars in heaven. I fear that your lofty opinion of me may spring from some other source than a carefully balanced judgment. Conjure up in your mind an ordinary woman, drab of face and drably dressed—for I care more for letters than for flashy clothes. Moreover, I have committed myself absolutely to that cultivation of virtue which can profit me not only when alive but also after death. There are those who are captivated by beauty. I myself should give the greater prize to grey-haired chastity, since in the lovely company of comely youth blaze up enticements to passion. For virtue excels the brilliance of beauty, elaborate polished artifice, and precious flowers of every tenderness. Let Mark Antony be attracted by bejewelled Cleopatra; I shall imitate the innocence of Rebecca. Let Paris seek the wandering Helen; I choose to imitate the modesty of Rachel. Wives are bewitched by rich display; more witless still are those who, to satisfy the appetite of their wives, destroy their patrimonies. Today men's love for women has made our commonwealth the imitator or rather the plunderer of the East. Luxury has thrived in this age, more than all others prodigiously vain. Let those who do not believe me attend the services of the church. Let them observe weddings packed with seated matrons. Let them gaze at these women who, with majestic pride, promenade amidst crowds through the piazzas. Among them, here and there, is one who ties a towering knot—made of someone else's hair—at the very peak of her head; another's forehead is submerged in waves of crimped curls; and another, in order to bare her neck, binds with a golden ribbon her golden hair. One suspends a necklace from her shoulder, another from her arm, another from neck to breast. Others choke themselves with pearl necklaces; born free, they boast to be held captive. And many display fingers glistening with jewels. One, lusting to walk more mincingly, loosens her girdle, while another tightens hers to make her breasts bulge. Some drag from their shoulders silken tunics. Others, sweet-scented with perfumes, cover themselves with an Arabian hood. Some boost themselves with high-heeled shoes. And all think it particularly modish to swathe their legs with fine soft cotton. Many press softened bread on their faces, many artificially smooth their skin, stretched with wrinkles; there are few whose ruddy faces are not painted with the lustre of white lead. In one way or another they strive by means of exquisite artistry to seem more beautiful than the Author of their beauty decreed. The impudence of some women is shameful. They paint their white cheeks with purple and, with furtive winks and smiling mouths, pierce the poisoned hearts of those who gaze on them. O the bold wantonness of lost modesty! O the weakness of our sex, stooping to voluptuousness! We have only to hang from our ears little ornaments trembling with precious stones and emeralds, and we shall not differ from pagans. Was it for this, by chance, that we were begotten, that we might worship in shameless devotion the idols of our mirrored faces? Did we renounce display in baptism so that, as Christian women, we might imitate Jews and barbarians?

Even the feeblest desire [for honor] should make us blush over this longing for magnificence. These insane and lustful cravings, born of arrogance, should frighten us. Mindful of the ashes from which we come, we should renounce sins born from desires. How will our lamentations prevail if heavenly anger and indignation should rage against us miserable women? If those who rebel against the king commit their necks to the axe, why should we women marvel, rebels, indeed, warriors against God, if, to avenge our sin, an army rise up against us? Rome mourns to this day the Gauls' assault. Italy, vanquished, bewails the Gothic sword. Greece suffers Mahomet's tyranny. These vicious devastations are not caused by human might but ordained by heaven [as a punishment for sins]. Let each woman dress and heal the wound from which we languish. We should seek the adornment of honor, not vulgar display, and we should pursue this life mindful of our mortality. For God the Father has decreed that the good die well.

Therefore, Augustine, you have had ample opportunity to see that I consider this splendid magnificence foolish, and I wish you would pay no attention to my age or at least my sex. For [woman's] nature is not immune to sin; nature produced our mother [Eve], not from earth or rock, but from Adam's humanity. To be human is, however, to incline sometimes to good, but sometimes to pleasure. We are quite an imperfect animal, and our puny strength is not sufficient for mighty battles. [But] you great men, wielding such authority, commanding such success, who justly discern among your number so many present-day Brutuses, so many Curiuses, Fabriciuses, Catos, and Aemiliuses, be careful: do not therefore be taken by the snare of this carefully arranged elegance. For where there is greater wisdom, there lies greater guilt. February 12 [1487]

LAURA CERETA TO BIBULUS SEMPRONIUS: DEFENSE OF THE LIBERAL INSTRUCTION OF WOMEN

My ears are wearied by your carping. You brashly and publicly not merely wonder but indeed lament that I am said to possess as fine a mind as nature ever bestowed upon the most learned man. You seem to think that so learned a woman has scarcely before been seen in the world. You are wrong on both counts, Sempronius, and have dearly strayed from the path of truth and disseminate falsehood. I agree that you should be grieved; indeed, you should be ashamed, for you have ceased to be a living man, but have become an animated stone; having rejected the studies which make men wise, you rot in torpid leisure. Not nature but your own soul has betrayed you, deserting virtue for the easy path of sin.

You pretend to admire me as a female prodigy, but there lurks sugared deceit in your adulation. You wait perpetually in ambush to entrap my lovely sex, and overcome by your hatred seek to trample me underfoot and dash me to the earth. It is a crafty ploy, but only a low and vulgar mind would think to halt Medusa with honey. You would better have crept up on a mole than on a wolf. For a mole with its dark vision can see nothing around it, while a wolf's eyes glow in the dark. For the wise person sees by [force of] mind, and anticipating what lies ahead, proceeds by the light of reason. For by foreknowledge the thinker scatters with knowing feet the evils which litter her path.

I would have been silent, believe me, if that savage old enmity of yours had attacked me alone. For the light of Phoebus cannot be befouled even in the mud. But I cannot tolerate your having attacked my entire sex. For this reason my thirsty soul seeks revenge, my sleeping pen is aroused to literary struggle, raging anger stirs mental passions long chained by silence. With just cause I am moved to demonstrate how great a reputation for learning and virtue women have won by their inborn excellence, manifested in every age as knowledge, the [purveyor] of honor. Certain, indeed, and legitimate is our possession of this inheritance, come to us from a long eternity of ages past.

[To begin], we read how Sabba of Ethiopia, her heart imbued with divine power, solved the prophetic mysteries of the Egyptian Salomon. And the earliest writers said that Amalthea, gifted in foretelling the future, sang her prophecies around the banks of Lake Avernus, not far from Baiae. A sibyl worthy of the pagan gods, she sold books of oracles to Priscus Tarquinius. The Babylonian prophetess Eriphila, her divine mind penetrating the distant future, described the fall and burning of Troy, the fortunes of the Roman Empire, and the coming birth of Christ. Nicostrata also, the mother of Evander, learned both in prophecy and letters, possessed such great genius that with sixteen symbols she first taught the Latins the art of writing. The fame of mach Inachian Isis will also remain eternal who, an Argive goddess, taught her alphabet to the Egyptians. Zenobia of Egypt was so nobly learned, not only in Egyptian, but also in Greek and Latin, that she wrote histories of strange and exotic places. Manto of Thebes, daughter of Tiresias, although not learned, was skilled in the arts of divination from the remains of sacrificed animals or the behavior of fire and other such Chaldaean techniques. [Examining] the fire's flames, the bird's flight, the entrails and innards of animals, she spoke with spirits and foretold future events. What was the source of the great wisdom of the Tritonian Athena by which she taught so many arts to the Athenians, if not the secret writings, admired by all, of the philosopher Apollo? The Greek women Philiasia and Lasthenia, splendors of learning, excite me, who often tripped up, with tricky sophistries, Plato's clever disciples. Sappho of Lesbos sang to her stone-hearted lover doleful verses, echoes, I believe, of Orpheus' lyre or Apollo's lute. Later, Leontia's Greek and poetic tongue dared sharply to attack, with a lively and admired style, the eloquence of Theophrastus. I should not omit Proba, remarkable for her excellent command of both Greek and Latin and who, imitating Homer and Virgil, retold the stories from the Old Testament. The majesty of Rome exalted the Greek Semiamira, [invited] to lecture in the Senate on laws and kings. Pregnant with virtue, Rome also gave birth to Sempronia, who imposingly delivered before an assembly a fluent poem and swayed the minds of her hearers with her convincing oratory. Celebrated with equal and endless praise for her eloquence was Hortensia, daughter of Hortensius, an oratrix of such power that, weeping womanly and virtuous tears, she persuaded the Triumvirs not to retaliate against women. Let me add Cornificia, sister of the poet Cornificius, to whose love of letters so many skills were added that she was said to have been nourished by waters from the Castalian spring; she wrote epigrams always sweet with Heliconian flowers. I shall quickly pass by Tulliola, daughter of Cicero, Terentia, and Cornelia, all Roman women who attained the heights of knowledge. I shall also omit Nicolosa [Sanuto] of Bologna, Isotta Nogarola and Cassandra Fedele of our own day. All of history is full of these examples. Thus your nasty words are refuted by these arguments, which compel you to concede that nature imparts equally to all the same freedom to learn.

Only the question of the rarity of outstanding women remains to be addressed. The explanation is clear: women have been able by nature to be exceptional, but have chosen lesser goals. For some women are concerned with parting their hair correctly, adorning themselves with lovely dresses, or decorating their fingers with pearls and other gems. Others delight in mouthing carefully composed phrases, indulging in dancing, or managing spoiled puppies. Still others wish to gaze at lavish banquet tables, to rest in sleep, or, standing at mirrors, to smear their lovely faces. But those in whom a deeper integrity yearns for virtue restrain from the start their youthful souls, reflect on higher things, harden the body with sobriety and trials, and curb their tongues, open their ears, compose their thoughts in wakeful hours, their minds in contemplation, to letters bonded to righteousness. For knowledge is not given as a gift, but [is gained] with diligence. The free mind, not shirking effort, always soars zealously toward the good, and the desire to know grows ever more wide and deep. It is because of no special holiness, therefore, that we [women] are rewarded by God the Giver with the gift of exceptional talent. Nature has generously lavished its gifts upon all people, opening to all the doors of choice through which reason sends envoys to the will, from which they learn and convey its desires. The will must choose to exercise the gift of reason.

[But] where we [women] should be forceful we are [too often] devious; where we should be confident we are insecure. [Even worse], we are content with our condition. But you, a foolish and angry dog, have gone to earth as though frightened by wolves. Victory does not come to those who take flight. Nor does he remain safe who makes peace with the enemy; rather, when pressed, he should arm himself all the more with weapons and courage. How nauseating to see strong men pursue a weakling at bay. Hold on! Does my name alone terrify you? As I am not a barbarian in intellect and do not fight like one, what fear drives you? You flee in vain, for traps craftily-laid rout you out of every hiding place. Do you think that by hiding, a deserter [from the field of battle], you can remain undiscovered? A penitent, do you seek the only path of salvation in flight? [If you do] you should be ashamed.

I have been praised too much; showing your contempt for women, you pretend that I alone am admirable because of the good fortune of my intellect. But I, compared to other women who have won splendid renown, am but a little mousling. You disguise your envy in dissimulation, but cloak yourself in apologetic words in vain. The lie buried, the truth, dear to God, always emerges. You stumble half-blind with envy on a wrongful path that leads you from your manhood, from your duty, from God. Who, do you think, will be surprised, Bibulus, if the stricken heart of an angry girl, whom your mindless scorn has painfully wounded, will after this more violently assault your bitter words? Do you suppose, O most contemptible man on earth, that I think myself sprung [like Athena] from the head of Jove? I am a school girl, possessed of the sleeping embers of an ordinary mind. Indeed I am too hurt, and my mind, offended, too swayed by passions, sighs, tormenting itself, conscious of the obligation to defend my sex. For absolutely everything—that which is within us and that which is without—is made weak by association with my sex.

I, therefore, who have always prized virtue, having put my private concerns aside, will polish and weary my pen against chatterboxes swelled with false glory. Trained in the arts, I shall block the paths of ambush. And I shall endeavor, by avenging arms, to sweep away the abusive infamies of noisemakers with which some disreputable and impudent men furiously, violently, and nastily rave against a woman and a republic worthy of reverence. January 13 [1488]

LAURA CERETA TO LUCILIA VERNACULA: AGAINST WOMEN WHO DISPARAGE LEARNED WOMEN

I thought their tongues should have been fine-sliced and their hearts hacked to pieces—those men whose perverted minds and inconceivable hostility [fueled by] vulgar envy so flamed that they deny, stupidly ranting, that women are able to attain eloquence in Latin. [But] I might have forgiven those pathetic men, doomed to rascality, whose patent insanity I lash with unleashed tongue. But I cannot bear the babbling and chattering women, glowing with drunkenness and wine, whose impudent words harm not only our sex but even more themselves. Empty-headed, they put their heads together and draw lots from a stockpot to elect each other [number one]; but any women who excel they seek out and destroy with the venom of their envy. A wanton and bold plea indeed for ill-fortune and unkindness! Breathing viciousness, while she strives to besmirch her better, she befouls herself; for she who does not yearn to be sinless desires [in effect] license to sin. Thus these women, lazy with sloth and insouciance, abandon themselves to an unnatural vigilance; like scarecrows hung in gardens to ward off birds, they tackle all those who come into range with a poisonous tongue. Why should it behoove me to find this barking, snorting pack of provocateurs worthy of my forebearance, when important and distinguished gentlewomen always esteem and honor me? I shall not allow the base sallies of arrogance to pass, absolved by silence, lest my silence be taken for approval or lest women leading this shameful life attract to their licentiousness crowds of fellow-sinners. Nor should anyone fault me for impatience, since even dogs are permitted to claw at pesty flies, and an infected cow must always be isolated from the healthy flock, for the best is often injured by the worst. Who would believe that a [sturdy] tree could be destroyed by tiny ants? Let them fall silent, then, these insolent little women, to whom every norm of decency is foreign; inflamed with hatred, they would noisily chew up others, [except that] mute, they are themselves chewed up within. Their inactivity of mind maddens these raving women, or rather Megaeras, who cannot bear even to hear the name of a learned woman. These are the mushy faces who, in their vehemence, now spit tedious nothings from their tight little mouths, now to the horror of those looking on spew from their lips thunderous trifles. One becomes disgusted with human failings and grows weary of these women who, [trapped in their own mental predicament], despair of attaining possession of human arts, when they could easily do so with the application of skill and virtue. For letters are not bestowed upon us, or assigned to us by chance. Virtue only is acquired by ourselves alone; nor can those women ascend to serious knowledge who, soiled by the filth of pleasures, languidly rot in sloth. For those women the path to true knowledge is plain who see that there is certain honor in exertion, labor, and wakefulness. Farewell.

November 1 [1487]

HEINRICH KRAMER AND JAKOB SPRENGER

1484

This widely used manual for the discovery, prosecution and execution of witches was written by two main religious figures of the fifteenth century, Jakob Sprenger (the Dominican inquisitor of Cologne) and Heinrich Kramer (the prior of Cologne). The following selection outlines the reasons why women are particularly "addicted" to evil, as well as how best to question and elicit a confession from the suspected witch.

While reading the *Malleus*, notice the logic behind the arguments for women's susceptibility to evil. What assumptions does this thinking reveal? How do those or similar assumptions work in the re-telling of the "Wonderful Discoveries of the Witchcrafts of Margaret and Philippa Flower"? What links can be found among the *Malleus* and the other readings which engage in an articulation of womankind? Consider St. Thomas Aquinas's treatment of the nature of woman in our selection from the *Summa Theologica*, as well as the various treatments of Eve by Christine de Pisan, Isotta Nogarola and, of course, the Bible. After reading the section on how to "examine" a suspected witch, compare it to Anne Hutchinson's 1637 examination by the court at Newton. Are there any structural similarities between the two questioning strategies? What other points of contact can you make among these two texts and the *Wonderful Discovery*?

from *Malleus Maleficarum*

Why it is that Women are Chiefly Addicted to Evil Superstitions.

There is also, concerning witches who copulate with devils, much difficulty in considering the methods by which such abominations are consummated. On the part of the devil: first, of what element the body is made that he assumes; secondly, whether the act is always accompanied by the injection of semen received from another; thirdly, as to time and place, whether he commits this act more frequently at one time than at another; fourthly, whether the act is invisible to any who may be standing by. And on the part of the women, it has to be inquired whether only they who were themselves conceived in this filthy manner are often visited by devils; or secondly, whether it is those who were offered to devils by midwives at the time of their birth; and thirdly, whether the actual venereal delectation of such is of a weaker sort. But we cannot here reply to all these questions, both because we are only engaged in a general study, and because in the second part of this work they are all singly explained by their operations, as will appear in the fourth chapter, where mention is made of each separate method. Therefore let us now chiefly consider women; and first, why this kind of perfidy is found more in so fragile a sex than in men. And our inquiry will first be general, as to the general conditions of women; secondly, particular, as to which sort of women are found to be given to superstition and witchcraft; and thirdly, specifically with regard to midwives; who surpass all other in wickedness.

As for the first question, why a greater number of witches is found in the fragile feminine sex than among men; it is indeed a fact that it were idle to contradict, since it is acredited [sic] by actual experience, apart from the verbal testimony of credible witnesses. And without in any way detracting from a sex in which God has always taken great glory that His might should be spread abroad, let us say that various men have assigned various reasons for this fact, which nevertheless agree in principle. Wherefore it is good, for the admonition of women, to speak of this matter; and it has often been proved by experience that they are eager to hear of it, so long as it is set forth with discretion.

For some learned men propound this reason; that there are three things in nature, the Tongue, an Ecclesiastic, and a Woman, which know no moderation in goodness or vice; and when they exceed the bounds of their condition they reach the greatest heights and the lowest depths of goodness and vice. When they are governed by a good spirit, they are most excellent in virtue; but when they are governed by an evil spirit, they indulge the worst possible vices.

Now the wickedness of women is spoken of in Ecclesiasticus xxv: "There is no head above the head of a serpent: and there is no wrath above the wrath of a woman. I had rather dwell with a lion and a dragon than to keep house with a wicked woman." And among much which in that place precedes and follows about a wicked woman, he concludes: "All wickedness is but little to the wickedness of a woman." Wherefore S. John Chrysostom says on the text, "It is not good to marry (*S. Matthew* xix): What else is woman but a foe to friendship, an unescapable punishment, a necessary evil, a natural temptation, a desirable calamity, a domestic danger, a delectable detriment, an evil of nature, painted with fair colors!" Therefore if it be a sin to divorce her when she ought to be kept, it is indeed a necessary torture; for either we commit adultery by divorcing her, or we must endure daily strife. Cicero in his second book of *The Rhetoric* says: "The many lusts of men lead them into one sin, but the one lust of women leads them into all sins, for the root of all woman's vices is avarice." And Seneca says in his *Tragedies*: "A woman either loves or hates; there is no third grade. And the tears of a woman are a deception, for they may spring from true grief, or they may be a snare. When a woman thinks alone, she thinks evil."

Others again have propounded other reasons why there are more superstitious women found than men. And the first is, that they are more credulous; and since the chief aim of the devil is to corrupt faith, therefore he rather attacks them. See Ecciesiaticus xix: "He that is quick to believe is lightminded, and shall be diminished. "The second reason is, that women are naturally more impressionable, and more ready to receive the influence of a disembodied spirit; and that when they use this quality well they are very good, but when they use it ill they are very evil.

The third reason is that they have slippery tongues, and are unable to conceal from their fellow-women those things which by evil arts they know; and, since they are weak, they find an easy and secret manner of vindicating themselves by witchcraft. See Ecciesiasticus as quoted above: "I had rather dwell with a lion and a dragon than to keep house with a wicked woman. All wickedness is but little to the wickedness of a woman." And to this may be added that, as they are very impressionable, they act accordingly.

There are also others who bring forward yet other reasons, of which preachers should be very careful how they make use. For it is true that in the Old Testament the Scriptures have much that is evil to say about women, and this because of the first temptress, Eve, and her imitators; yet afterwards in the New Testament we find a change of name, as from Eva to Ave (as St. Jerome says), and the whole sin of Eve taken away by the benediction of Mary. Therefore preachers should always say as much praise of them as possible.

But because in these times this perfidy is more often found in women than in men, as we learn by actual experience, if anyone is curious as to the reason, we may add to what has already been said the following: that since they are feebler both in mind and body, it is not surprising that they should come under the spell of witchcraft.

To conclude. All witchcraft comes from carnal lust, which is in women insatiable. See Proverbs xxx: "There are three things that are never satisfied, yea, fourth thing which says not, It is enough;" that is, the mouth of the womb. Wherefore for the sake of fulfilling their lusts they consort even with devils. More such reasons could be brought forward, but to the understanding it is sufficiently dear that it is no matter for wonder that there are more women than men found infected with the heresy of witchcraft. And in consequence of this, it is better called the heresy of witches than of wizards, since the name is taken from the more powerful party. And blessed be the highest who has so far preserved the male sex from so great a crime: for sins He was willing to be born and to suffer for us, therefore He has granted to men this privilege.

OF THE WAY WHEREBY A FORMAL PACT WITH EVIL IS MADE.

The method by which they profess their sacrilege through an open pact of fidelity to devils varies according to the several practices to which different witches are addicted. And to understand this it first must be noted that there are, as was shown in the first part of this treatise, three kinds of witches; namely, those who injure but cannot cure; those who cure but, through some strange pact with the devil, cannot injure; and those who both injure and cure. And among those who injure, one class in particular stands out, which can perform every sort of witchcraft and spell, comprehending all that all the others individually can do. Wherefore, if we describe the method of profession in their case, it will suffice also for all other kinds. And this class is made up of those who, against every instinct of human or animal nature, are in the habit of eating and devouring the children of their own species.

And this is the most powerful class of witches, who practice innumerable other harms also. For they raise hailstorms and hurtful tempests and lightnings; cause sterility in men and animals; offer to devils, or otherwise kill, the children whom they do not devour. But these are only the children who have not been reborn by baptism at the font, for they cannot devour those who have been baptized, nor any without God's permission. They can also, before the eyes of their parents, and when no one is in sight, throw into the water children walking by the water side; they make horses go mad under their riders; they can transport themselves from place to place through the air, either in body or in imagination; they can affect Judges and Magistrates so that they cannot hurt them; they can cause themselves and others to keep silence under torture; they can bring about a great trembling in the hands and horror in the minds of those who would arrest them; they can show to others occult things and certain future events, by the information of devils, though this may sometimes have a natural cause (see the question: *Whether devils can foretell the future*, in the *Second Book of Sentences*); they can see absent things as if they were present; they can turn the minds of men to inordinate love or hatred; they can at times strike whom they will with lightning, and even kill some men and animals; they can make of no effect the generative desires, and even the power of copulation, cause abortion, kill infants in the mother's womb by a mere exterior touch; they can at times bewitch men and animals with a mere look, without touching them, and cause death; they dedicate their own children to devils; and in short, as has been said, they can cause all the plagues with other witches can only cause in part, that is, when the Justice of God permits such things to be. All these things this most powerful of all classes of witches can do, but they cannot undo them.

But it is common to all of them to practice carnal copulation with devils; therefore, if we show the method used by this chief class in their profession of their sacrilege, anyone may easily understand the method of the other classes.

There were such witches lately, thirty years ago, in the district of Savoy, towards the State of Berne, as Nider tells in his *Formicarius*. And there are now some in the country of Lombardy, in the domains of the Duke of Austria, where the Inquisitor of Como, as we told in the former part, caused forty-one witches to be burned in one year; and he was fifty-five years old, and still continues to labor in the Inquisition.

Now the method of profession is twofold. One is a solemn ceremony, like a solemn vow. The other is private, and can be made to the devil at any hour alone. The first method is when witches meet together in conclave on a set day, and the devil appears to them in the assumed body of a man, and urges them to keep faith with him, promising them worldly prosperity and length of life; and they recommend a novice to his acceptance. And the devil asks whether she will abjure the Faith, and forsake the holy Christian religion and the worship of the Anomalous Woman (for so they call the Most Blessed Virgin Mary), and never venerate the Sacraments; and if he finds the novice or disciple willing, then the devil stretches out his hand, and so does the novice, and she swears with upraised hand to keep that covenant. And when this is done, the devil at once adds that this is not enough; and when the disciple asks what more must be done, the devil demands the following oath of homage to himself: that she give herself to him, body and soul, for ever, and do her utmost to bring others of both sexes into his power. He adds, finally, that she is to make certain unguents from the bones and limbs of children, especially those who have been baptized; by all which means she will be able to fulfill all her wishes with his help.

Of the Method of Sentencing the Accused to be Questioned: and How she must be Questioned on the First Day; and Whether she may be Promised her Life.

But if, after keeping the accused in a state of suspense, and continually postponing the day of examination, and frequently using verbal persuasions, the Judge should truly believe that the accused is denying the truth, let them question her lightly without shedding blood; knowing that such questioning is fallacious and often, as has been said, ineffective.

And it should be begun in this way. While the officers are preparing for the questioning, let the accused be stripped; or if she is a woman, let her first be led to the penal cells and there stripped by honest women of good reputation. And the reason for this is that they should search for any instrument of witchcraft sewn into her clothes; for they often make such instruments, at the instruction of devils, out of the limbs of unbaptized children, the purpose being that those children should be deprived of the beatific vision. And when such instruments have been disposed of, the Judge shall use his own persuasions and those of other honest men zealous for the faith to induce her to confess the truth voluntarily; and if she will not, let him order the officers to bind her with cords, and apply her to some engine of torture; and then let them obey at once but not joyfully, rather appearing to be disturbed by their duty. Then let her be released again at someone's earnest request, and taken on one side, and let her again be persuaded; and in persuading her, let her be told that she can escape the death penalty.

Here it is asked whether, in the case of a prisoner legally convicted by her general bad reputation, by witnesses, and by the evidence of fact, so that the only thing lacking is a confession of the crime from her own mouth, the Judge can lawfully promise her her life, whereas if she were to confess the crime she would suffer the extreme penalty.

We answer that different people have various opinions on this question. For some hold that if the accused is of a notoriously bad reputation, and gravely suspected on unequivocal evidence of the crime; and if she is herself a great source of danger, as being the mistress of other witches, then she may be promised life on the following conditions: that she be sentenced to imprisonment for life on bread and water, provided that she supply evidence which will lead to the conviction of other witches. And she is not to be told, when she is promised her life, that she is to be imprisoned in this way; but should be led to suppose that some other penance, such as exile, will be imposed on her as punishment. And without doubt notorious witches, especially such as use witches' medicines and cure the bewitched by superstitious means, should be kept in this way, both that they may help the bewitched, and that they may betray other witches. But such a betrayal by them must not be considered of itself sufficient ground for a conviction, since the devil is a liar, unless it is also substantiated by the evidence of the fact, and by witnesses.

Others think that, after she has been consigned to prison in this way, the promise to spare her life should be kept for a time, but that after a certain period she should be burned.

But if neither threats nor such promises will induce her to confess the truth, then the officers must proceed with the sentence, and she must be examined, not in any new or exquisite manner, but in the usual way, lightly or heavily according as the nature of her crimes demands. And while she is being questioned about each several point, let her be often and frequently exposed to torture, beginning with the more gentle of them; for the Judge should not be too hasty to proceed to the graver kind. And while this is being done, let the Notary write all down, how she is tortured and what questions are asked and how she answers.

And note that, if she confessed under torture, she should then be taken to another place and questioned anew, so that she does not confess only under the stress of torture.

The next step of the Judge should be that, if after being fittingly tortured she refuses to confess the truth, he should have other engines of torture brought before her, and tell her that she will have to endure these if she does not confess. If then she is not induced by terror to confess, the torture must be continued on the second or third day, but not repeated at that present time unless there should be some fresh indication of its probable success.

Argula von Grumbach

1492-c.1563

Noblewomen who sponsored and protected Protestant reformers were often successful and respected leaders, but women who began to speak or write publicly on issues of theology were thought to be operating beyond their legitimate sphere. During the first decade of the Reformation in Germany, Argula von Grumbach disregarded the injunction of St. Paul that women should be silent in the presence of men, and entered into the public controversies generated by the Reformed message. Her letters and appeals to a variety of public authorities won the tacit support of Luther and placed her at the center of discussion over the role of women in the spiritual life of the Christian community.

Born into the noble Bavarian family of Hohenstaufen, von Grumbach learned to read and to write German as a young girl. Due to the impoverishment of the family, Grumbach was employed as maid-in-waiting to the mother of the Duke of Bavaria. Upon the loss of her parents to the plague around 1505, she became a permanent member of the Duke Albrecht IV's household, and in 1516 she was married to Friedrich von Grumbach, a caretaker of ducal estates. She began to read Luther's works as they became available in German, and she corresponded with a number of early Protestant reformers. Although technically of noble birth, Grumbach considered herself to be common both in terms of education and with respect to her access to political power.

Grumbach's brief public career began in 1523 when a young instructor at the University of Ingolstadt, Arsacius Seehofer, was forced to renounce elements of the teaching which he had learned under the Protestant Philip Melanchthon. In her letter, Grumbach criticized university officials who would presume to deny a hearing to an exponent of Protestant principles. Denying the Roman Church any authority, she likened Seehofer's treatment to Rome's refusal to put the Bible into the hands of the people. She invited the faculty to discuss her position publicly, citing examples of churchman like St. Jerome who were not ashamed to write to women, and pointing to Christ's instruction of Mary Magdalene as precedent for her own exceptional activities. What does this letter tell us about the (perhaps unanticipated) radical implications of the Protestant Reformation with respect to the autonomy of the individual, human equality and issues of gender?

Letter to the University of Ingolstadt

How in God's name can you and your university expect to prevail, when you deploy such foolish violence against the word of God; when you force someone to hold the holy Gospel in their hands for the very purpose of denying it, as you did in the case of Arsacius Seehofer? When you confront him with an oath and declaration such as this, and use imprisonment and even the threat of the stake to force him to deny Christ and his word?

Yes, when I reflect on this my heart and all my limbs tremble. What do Luther or Melanchthon teach you but the word of God? You condemn them without having refuted them. Did Christ teach you so, or his apostles, prophets, or evangelists? Show me where this is written! You lofty experts, nowhere in the Bible do I find that Christ, or his apostles, or his prophets put people in prison, burnt or murdered them, or sent them into exile. . . . Don't you know what the Lord says in Matthew 10? "Have no fear of him who can take your body but then his power is at an end. But fear him who has power to despatch soul and body into the depths of hell."

One knows very well the importance of one's duty to obey the authorities. But where the word of God is concerned neither Pope, Emperor nor princes—as Acts 4 and 5 make so clear—have any jurisdiction. For my part, I have to confess, in the name of God and by my soul's salvation, that if I were to deny Luther and Melanchthon's writing I would be denying God and his word, which may God forfend for ever. Amen. . . .

My heart goes out to our princes, whom you have seduced and betrayed so deplorably. For I realise that they are ill-informed about divine Scripture. If they could spare the time from other business, I believe they, too, would discover the truth that no one has a right to exercise sovereignty over the word of God. Yes, no human being, whoever he be, can rule over it. For the word of God alone—without which nothing was made—should and must rule.

If one could enforce faith why weren't all unbelievers given instructions to believe long ago? The difficulty is that it is the word of God which has to reach us, not flesh and blood. You won't be able to gain any such fame with Arsacius Seehofer, prettying him up with his coerced and dictated oath, calling him a Master of Arts. For you have forgotten one thing: that he is only eighteen years old, and still a child. Others won't forget. From the way in which the news has come to me from other places in such a short time, you will surely be notorious throughout the entire world. . . .

Have no doubt about this: God looks mercifully on Aracius, or will do so in the future, just as he did on Peter, who tested the Lord three times. For each day the just person falls seven times and gets up on his feet again. God does not want the death of the sinner, but his conversion and life. Christ the Lord himself feared death; so much so that he sweated a bloody sweat. I trust that God will yet see much good from this young man. Just as Peter, too, did much good work later, after his denial of the Lord. And, unlike this man, he was still free, and did not suffer such lengthy imprisonment, or the threat of the stake.

A disputation is easily won when one argues with force, not Scripture. As far as I can see that means that the hangman is accounted the most learned. It's easy to see, though, that the devil helped to arrange this fine hullabaloo. God will not put up with your ways much longer. In 2 Corinthians 1 Paul says: "the devil turns himself into an angel of light." So it is no wonder that confidence tricksters turn themselves into apostles of Christ. Remember Matthew 10: "There has to be conflict, the son against the father, the daughter against the mother, the bride against the mother in law, and one's servants will become one's enemies." And John 16: "The time will come when they will kill you and think that they do God a service. For they know neither the Father nor me." And Paul in 1 Corinthians 11: "Conflict must take place, so that those who are approved may be revealed." Also 2 Corinthians 4: "If the Gospel is hidden, it is to those who are perishing."

Are you not ashamed that [Seehofer] had to deny all the writings of Martin [Luther], who put the New Testament into German, simply following the text? That means that the holy Gospel and the Epistles and the story of the Apostles and so on are all dismissed by you as heresy. It seems there is no hope of a proper discussion with you. And then there's the five books of Moses, which are being printed too. Is that nothing? It would be easier, and more profitable, to engage in discussion with a Jew. I hear nothing about any of you refuting a single article [of Arsacius] from Scripture. What I do hear is that a learned lawyer came forward to him and asked: "Why was he crying? Wasn't he a heretic?" But jurisprudence has no value here.

I beseech you for the sake of God, and exhort you by God's judgement and righteousness, to tell me in writing which of the articles written by Martin [Luther] or Melanchthon you consider heretical. In German not a single one seems heretical to me. And the fact is that a great deal has been published in German, and I've read it all. . . .

I have no Latin; but you have German, being born and brought up in this tongue. What I have written to you is no woman's chit-chat, but the word of God; and (I write) as a member of the Christian Church, against which the gates of Hell cannot prevail. Against the Roman, however, they do prevail. Just look at that church! How is it to prevail against the gates of Hell? God give us his grace, that we all may be saved, and may (God) rule us according to his will. Now may his grace carry the day. Amen.

GIORGIO VASARI

1511-1574

Vasari, himself a successful artist, is best known for recording the lives of other artists of the Renaissance. He studied under Andreas del Sarto, and worked for many distinguished patrons at a time when art had been raised from a "craft" to a "divine skill." An excellent architect as well as a painter, Vasari was acquainted with several important figures: he was a friend of Michelangelo, and a courtier of the Medici.

The full title of Vasari's work, *The Lives of the Most Eminent Architects, Painters, and Sculptors of Italy,* reflects the range of his undertaking. A thorough and accurate researcher, considering the limited resources available at the time, Vasari compiled a veritable Who's Who of Renaissance artists which is by-and-large dependable and error-free. The first edition, published in 1550, included only one living painter: the "divinissimo Michelangelo." The 1568 edition included three volumes, and detailed one hundred sixty-one lives. Still used as a resource by modern biographers, *Lives* fulfills Vasari's goal of preserving these artists from being forgotten after their deaths.

Here, following the excerpts from two lives—those of Michelangelo and Leonardo—is a letter by Michelangelo, describing some of the less sublime moments in the life of a great artist: getting paid, for example, and dealing with jealous rivals.

In these selections, compare Vasari's notions of the artist to Cellini's. Taken together, what can you learn about the role of art and the artist in Renaissance culture? How does Michelangelo's letter add to your understanding of this role?

from *The Lives of the Most Eminent Architects, Painters, and Sculptors*

LEONARDO DA VINCI 1452-1519

The most heavenly gifts seem to be showered on certain human beings. Sometimes supernaturally, marvelously, they all congregate in one individual. Beauty, grace, and talent are combined in such bounty that in whatever that man undertakes, he outdistances all other men and proves himself to be specially endowed by the hand of God. He owes his pre-eminence not to human teaching or human power. This was seen and acknowledged by all men in the case of Leonardo da Vinci, who had, besides the beauty of his person (which was such that it has never been sufficiently extolled), an indescribable grace in every effortless act and deed. His talent was so rare that he mastered any subject to which he turned his attention. Extraordinary strength and remarkable facility were here combined. He had a mind of regal boldness and magnanimous daring. His gifts were such that his celebrity was world-wide, not only in his own day, but even more after his death, and so will continue until the end of time.

Truly admirable, indeed, and divinely endowed was Leonardo da Vinci, the son of Ser Piero da Vinci. He might have been a scientist if he had not been so versatile. But the instability of his character caused him to take up and abandon many things. In arithmetic, for example, he made such rapid progress during the short time he studied it that he often confounded his teacher by his questions. He also began the study of music and resolved to learn to play the lute, and as he was by nature of exalted imagination, and full of the most graceful vivacity, he sang and accompanied himself most divinely, improvising at once both verses and music.

Though he divided his attention among pursuits so varied, Leonardo never abandoned his drawing, and also continued to model in relief, occupations which attracted him more than any others. His father, Ser Piero, observing this and taking into account the extraordinary character of his son's genius, took some of Leonardo's drawings to Andrea del Verrocchio, his intimate friend. He begged Andrea to tell him whether the boy showed promise. Verrocchio was amazed at these early efforts of Leonardo's and advised Ser Piero to see to it that his son become a painter. Leonardo was therefore sent to study in the shop of Andrea, whither he went most willingly. He studied not one branch of art only, but all. Admirably intelligent, and an excellent geometrician besides, Leonardo not only worked in sculpture—certain terra-cotta heads of smiling women and others of children done in early boyhood seem to be the work of a master—but, as an architect, designed ground plans and entire buildings; and, as an engineer, was the one who first suggested making a canal from Florence to Pisa by altering the river Arno. Leonardo also designed mills and water-driven machines. But, as he had resolved to make painting his profession, he spent most of his time drawing from life. He sometimes modeled clay figures on which he draped soft cloth dipped in plaster, and from these he made careful drawings on fine linen. He drew on paper also with so much care and so perfectly that no one has equaled him. Leonardo, imbued with power and grace, was endowed with so marvelous a facility, and his mind, his memory, and his hand were so efficient in the service of his intellect, that he confounded every antagonist.

Leonardo was frequently occupied in the preparation of plans to remove mountains or to pierce them with tunnels from plain to plain. By means of levers, cranes, and screws, he showed how to lift or move great weights. Designing dredging machines and inventing the means of drawing water from the greatest depths were among the speculations from which he never rested. Many drawings of these projects exist which are cherished by those who practice our arts.

Though his patrimony was a mere pittance, and though he worked very little, Leonardo kept many servants and horses, taking extraordinary delight in the latter. He was fond of all animals, and it is told that he used to buy caged birds only to set them free. Leonardo, in mind and spirit, gave evidence of such admirable power and perfection that whatever he did bore an impress of harmony, truthfulness, goodness, sweetness, and grace, beyond all other men.

Leonardo, with his profound comprehension of art, began many things that he never completed, because it seemed to him that perfection must elude him. He frequently formed in his imagination enterprises so difficult and so subtle that they could not be entirely realized and worthily executed by human hands. His conceptions were varied to infinity. In natural philosophy, among other things, he examined plants and observed the stars—the movements of the planets, the variations of the moon, and the course of the sun.

There is a story that a peasant on Ser Piero's country place brought a homemade shield, a piece of a fig tree he had cut down, and asked that Ser Piero have it painted for him in Florence. As the countryman was a very able huntsman and a great favorite with his master, the latter willingly promised to have it done. He took the wood, therefore, to Leonardo, not telling him for whom it was, and asked only that he paint something on it. Leonardo took the shield in hand, but since he found it crooked, coarse, and badly made, he straightened it before the fire and sent it to a turner, who returned it smooth and delicately rounded. Leonardo covered it with gypsum [gesso] and prepared it to his liking. He then considered what to put on it and thought of the head of Medusa and the terror it struck in the hearts of those who beheld it. He, therefore, assembled in a room that no one entered but himself a number of lizards, hedgehogs, newts, serpents, dragonflies, locusts, bats, glowworms, and every sort of strange animal he could lay his hands on. He fashioned a fearsome monster, hideous and appalling, breathing poison and flames and surrounded by fire issuing from a rift in a rock. He labored on while the room filled with a mortal stench, of which Leonardo was quite unaware in his interest in his work. When it was done, long after both his father and the countryman had stopped inquiring for it, Leonardo went to his father and told him he might send for the shield when he liked. Ser Piero went himself to fetch it. When he knocked, Leonardo asked him to wait a little. He darkened the room and placed the shield where a dim light would strike it, and then asked his father in. Ser Piero drew back, startled, and turned to rush out, but Leonardo stopped him, saying, "The shield will serve its purpose." The work seemed more than wonderful to Ser Piero, so he bought another shield, which was decorated with a heart transfixed with an arrow, and this he gave to the peasant who cherished it all his life. Leonardo's shield he secretly sold to a merchant for a hundred ducats. It subsequently fell into the hands of the duke of Milan, who paid three hundred ducats for it

This great genius desired to give the deepest form to his works and sought constantly to find a black darker than any known black to serve as contrast to the lights and to render them even more brilliant. He finally produced that totally dark shade in which there is no light left so that the objects have the appearance of things seen by night rather than by daylight. All this was done to give greater relief to the forms in his work, and to attain the ultimate perfection of art.

Leonardo used to follow people whose extraordinary appearance took his fancy, sometimes throughout a whole day, until he could draw them as well by memory as though they stood before him. Of heads thus drawn there exist many. Among them is the head of Amerigo Vespucci, a very beautiful old man, done in charcoal. Another was of the gypsy Scaramuccia

When Ludovico Sforza became duke of Milan in 1493, he invited Leonardo most ceremoniously to come and play the lute before him. Leonardo took an instrument he had himself constructed of silver in the shape of a horse's head, a form calculated to render the tone louder and more sonorous. Leonardo was one of the best *improvisatori* in verse of his time. He surpassed all the musicians who had assembled to perform and so charmed the duke by his varied gifts that the nobleman delighted beyond measure in his society.

For the Dominican monks of Santa Maria delle Crazie at Milan, Leonardo painted the *Last Supper*. This is a most beautiful and admirable work. The master gave so much beauty and majesty to the heads of the Apostles that he was constrained to leave the Christ unfinished, convinced as he was that he could not render the divinity of the Redeemer. Even so, this work has always been held in the highest estimation by the Milanese and by foreigners as well. Leonardo rendered to perfection the doubts and anxieties of the Apostles, their desire to know by whom their Master is to be betrayed. All their faces show their love, terror, anger, grief, or bewilderment, unable as they are to fathom the meaning of the Lord. The spectator is also struck by the determination, hatred, and treachery of Judas. The whole is executed with the most minute exactitude. The texture of the tablecloth seems actually made of linen.

The story goes that the prior was in a great hurry to see the picture done. He could not understand why Leonardo should sometimes remain before his work half a day together, absorbed in thought. He would have him work away, as he compelled the laborers to do who were digging in his garden, and never put the pencil down. Not content with seeking to hurry Leonardo, the prior even complained to the duke, and tormented him so much that at length, he sent for Leonardo and courteously entreated him to finish the work. Leonardo, knowing the duke to be an intelligent man, explained himself as he had never bothered to do to the prior. He made it clear that men of genius are sometimes producing most when they seem least to labor, for their minds are then occupied in the shaping of those conceptions to which they afterward give form. He told the duke that two heads were yet to be done: that of the Saviour, the likeness of which he could not hope to find on earth and had not yet been able to create in his imagination in perfection of celestial grace; and the other, of Judas. He said he wanted to find features fit to render the appearance of a man so depraved as to betray his benefactor, his Lord, and the Creator of the world. He said he would still search but as a last resort he could always use the head of that troublesome and impertinent prior. This made the duke laugh with all his heart. The prior was utterly confounded and went away to speed the digging in his garden. Leonardo was left in peace.

The head of Judas, as we see it finished, is indeed the image of treachery and wickedness. The nobility of this painting, in composition and in high finish, made the king of France [Francis I] wish to remove it to his own kingdom. He attempted to find architects to frame it in wood that it might be transported without injury. He was not deterred by any consideration of cost, but as the painting was on the wall, he had to forgo his desire, and the Milanese kept their picture.

Leonardo afterward gave his attention to human anatomy, in company with Messer Marcantonio della Torre, an eminent philosopher. Messer Marcantonio was then lecturing in Pavia and writing on anatomy, a subject which had, until that time, been lost in the darkness of ignorance. Leonardo filled Marcantonio's book with drawings in red crayon outlined with the pen. These were drawn with the utmost care from bodies dissected by his own hand. He set forth the structure, arrangement, and disposition of the bones. Later he added the nerves in their due order, and then the muscles. He wrote an explanation, left-handed and backward, that can be read only with a mirror. A great many of these drawings are in the possession of Messer Francesco Melzi who, in the time of Leonardo, was a beautiful child, much beloved by him, and is now a handsome and amiable old man, who treasures these drawings as relics, together with the portrait of Leonardo of blessed memory. It seems almost incredible that this sublime genius could discourse as he had done, of art, and of the muscles, nerves, veins, and every other part of the frame.

For Francesco del Giocondo, Leonardo undertook to paint the portrait of Mona Lisa, his wife [La Gioconda], but, after loitering over it for four years, he left it unfinished. It is now in the possession of Francis, king of France. Whoever desires to see how far art can imitate nature, may do so by observing this head wherein every subtlety and every peculiarity have been faithfully reproduced. The eyes are bright and moist, and around them are those pale, red, and slightly livid circles seen in life, while the lashes and eyebrows are represented with the closest exactitude with the separate hairs drawn as they issue from the skin, every turn being followed and all the pores exhibited in the most natural manner. The nose with its beautiful arid delicately red nostrils might easily be believed to be alive. The mouth, admirable in outline, is rose tinted in harmony with the carnation of the cheeks, which seems not painted, but of flesh and blood. He who looks earnestly at the pit of the throat must fancy he sees the beating of the pulse. It is a marvel of art. Mona Lisa was very beautiful, and while he painted her, Leonardo had someone near at hand to sing or play to her, or to amuse her with jests, to keep from her that look of melancholy so common in portraits. This picture, on the contrary, has so pleasing an expression and a smile so sweet that one must think it rather divine than human. It has ever been esteemed a wonderful work.

When Leo X became pope, Leonardo went to Rome with Duke Giuliano de' Medici. The pontiff was interested in philosophical inquiry and especially in alchemy. Leonardo made some fanciful figures of animals out of a wax paste, hollow and very light, which floated in the air when they were inflated, but fell to the ground as the air escaped. A gardener of the Belvedere one day brought in a curious lizard for which Leonardo made wings from the skins of other lizards. In these wings he put quicksilver, so that, when the animal walked, the wings moved with a tremulous motion. He then made eyes, horns, and a beard for the creature, which he tamed and kept in a cage. He showed it to his visitors, and all who saw it ran away terrified. More than once, he had the intestines of a sheep cleaned and scraped until they were so fine that they could be held in the hollow of the hand. Then he fastened one end to a pair of bellows in another room and blew them up so that they filled the whole room, which was a very large one. Anyone who was there had to take refuge in a corner. He made numbers of these follies and occupied himself with mirrors and optical instruments. He also made experiments in oils and varnishes for painting. Leonardo received a commission for a picture from Pope Leo and immediately began to distill oils and herbs for the varnish, whereupon the pontiff remarked, "Alas! this man will do nothing at all, since he is thinking of the end before he has made a beginning."

There was constant discord between Michelangelo Buonarroti and Leonardo. Michelangelo even left Florence because of it, and Duke Giuliano excused him by saying that the pope had summoned him to Rome. When Leonardo heard of this, he departed for France to the court of the king [Francis I] who already owned several of his works and wished him to paint the cartoon of Saint Anne. Leonardo kept him waiting, according to his custom, a long time. Finally, being old, he lay sick for many months. When he found himself near death he made every effort to acquaint himself with the doctrine of the Catholic ritual. Then he confessed himself with great penitence and devoutly received the sacrament, sustained, because he could not stand by his servants and friends. The King, who used to visit him often, came immediately afterward to his room. Leonardo was lamenting to him his fear that he had offended God and man, since he had not labored in art as he should have done, when he was seized with a violent paroxysm, the forerunner of death. The king rose and supported his head to assist him, in the hope of alleviating his pain, and Leonardo departed this life in the arms of the monarch.

The death of Leonardo caused great sorrow to all who had known him. Nor was there ever an artist who did more to honor the art of painting. The radiance of his countenance, which was splendidly beautiful, brought cheer to the most melancholy. He was most persuasive and could make a man say "yes" or "no" as he desired. He was physically so strong that he could bend a horseshoe as if it were lead. His generous liberality offered hospitality to rich or poor, provided only that his guest was distinguished by talent or excellence. The poorest or most insignificant abode was adorned by his presence, and as the city of Florence was blessed by his birth, it suffered grievously by his death. To the art of painting he contributed a mode of deepening the shadows which the moderns have used to give force and relief to their figures. His ability in sculpture is proved by three figures in bronze over the north door of San Giovanni. These were cast by Giovan Francesco Rustici, but under the direction of Leonardo, and are, without doubt, most beautiful in design and finish. We are indebted to Leonardo for a work on the anatomy of the horse and for a still more valuable one on human anatomy. For his many admirable qualities, with which he was so richly endowed, although he talked of more things than he actually accomplished, his fame can never be extinguished. Messer Giovan Battista Strozzi wrote this in his praise:—"He alone vanquished all others: he surpassed Phidias, surpassed Apelles and all their proud followers."

MICHELANGELO 1475–1564

While the artists who came after Giotto were doing their best to imitate and to understand nature, bending every faculty to increase that high comprehension sometimes called intelligence, the Almighty took pity on their often fruitless labor. He resolved to send to earth a spirit capable of supreme expression in all the arts, one able to give form to painting, perfection to sculpture, and grandeur to architecture. The Almighty Creator also graciously endowed this chosen one with an understanding of philosophy and with the grace of poetry. And because he had observed that in Tuscany men were more zealous in study and more diligent in labor than in the rest of Italy, He decreed that Florence should be the birthplace of this divinely endowed spirit.

In the Casetino, therefore, in 1475, a son was born to Signor Lodovico di Leonardo di Buonarroti Simoni, a descendant of the noble family of the counts of Canossa. The child's mother was also of a very good family. Lodovico was then mayor of Chiusi-e-Caprese, near the spot where Saint Francis of Assisi received the stigmata.[1]

Moved by compelling impulse, he named the boy Michelangelo.

When his term of office was over, Lodovico returned to Settignano near Florence. Michelangelo was given to a stonecutter's wife to nurse. In that place stone quarries provide most of the employment. Talking to Vasari one day, Michelangelo said, "Giorgio, if I am good for anything, it is because I was born in the good mountain air of your Arezzo and suckled among the chisels and hammers of the stonecutters."

Because Lodovico had many children and was far from rich, he placed his boys as apprentices in the weaver's trade. At school, Michelangelo did more drawing than studying. A friend of his, Granacci, who, though just a boy, was working for Domenico Ghirlandaio, used to bring Michelangelo drawings made by his master, who was then one of the foremost painters of all Italy. The result was that Michelangelo became apprenticed to Ghirlandaio by the time he was fourteen years old.

He made great progress. One day he corrected the drawing of another and older disciple by a few strong lines. It is wonderful to see what a difference he made. I have the very sheet of paper, which Granacci gave me and which I treasure as a relic. I showed it to Michelangelo in Rome in the year 1550. He was most interested and pleased to see it and modestly remarked that evidently he knew more as a boy than now that he was old. One day when Ghirlandaio was painting the chapel in Santa Maria Novella, he went out, and while he was gone Michelangelo drew the scaffolding, trestles, pots of paint, brushes and the apprentices at their tasks. When he returned, Domenico Ghirlandaio was amazed at the power and originality of the lad's work. "This boy knows more than I do!" he exclaimed.

But it was no wonder that Michelangelo was so able. He studied continually. He copied a copper engraving by the German Martin Schongauer. The subject was Saint Anthony tormented by devils. First he drew it in pen and ink and then he painted it. He studied actual fish scales to make the devil's scales more real. He also copied drawings of the old masters so perfectly that his copies could not be distinguished from the originals, since he smoked and tinted the paper to give it the appearance of age. He was often able to keep the originals and return his copies in their stead. He did this only because of his admiration for the old masters.

Lorenzo the Magnificent at about this time engaged the sculptor Bertoldo (once the pupil of Donatello), not so much to be curator of his great collection of antiquities in the Medici gardens, as to form a school for sculptors. It is true that Bertoldo was old and could no longer work, but he was an excellent craftsman, especially in bronze. Lorenzo was concerned because there were no sculptors comparable to the many able painters of the day. He asked Ghirlandaio to recommend and bring to the school any promising young sculptors.

Michelangelo and Granacci, among others, were sent to the Medici gardens. Torrigiano was already there working on some terra-cotta figures in high relief. Michelangelo, with great enthusiasm, tried his hand at it, and was so successful that he was given a piece of marble to work on. He began to copy the head of a marble faun, a Roman work. He changed it, opening the mouth wider to show all the teeth.

The Magnifico [Lorenzo] was delighted with it. He said that he did not think a faun as old as that would have such a perfect set of teeth. Michelangelo, in his simplicity, took him seriously and set to work again. He broke out a tooth and even filed down the gum to make it look shrunken. Lorenzo was much amused.

Lorenzo sent for Lodovico, Michelangelo's father, and formally arranged to receive Michelangelo into his princely household. The lad was then fifteen or sixteen. He stayed there four years, until the death of Lorenzo, receiving for himself an allowance of money and a purple cloak to wear, while his father, Lodovico, was made an official of the customs.

At this time Michelangelo carved a relief of the Battle of Hercules and the Centaurs. It is incredible that so young a man could have made anything so beautiful. He also did a plaque of the Virgin in very low relief so exactly in Donatello's manner that it really looks like a Donatello, except that it is more graceful and better designed. Michelangelo made the most of the unusual opportunity for study which the Medici collection afforded. He also studied Masaccio's frescoes in the church of the Carmine. Here in a brawl, the jeering Torrigiano gave him that blow on the nose which disfigured him for life.

In Rome Michelangelo made such great progress in both conception and facility of execution that even the uncultivated were impressed and saw that his work was beyond comparison with any other. The cardinal of St. Denis, a Frenchman, wished to leave a memorial of himself in Rome and one done by the hand of this most famous artist. He arranged to have Michelangelo carve a Pietà. No sculptor, no matter how distinguished an artist, could add a single grace or improve this marble masterpiece in any way either in elegance or strength. In the body of the dead Christ, to say nothing of the admirable draperies, is shown the absolute perfection of research in anatomy; every vein, every muscle, every nerve is perfectly rendered as it appears in death. Besides, there is the beauty of the face, the exquisite expression. It is a marvel that the hand of an artist, in so short a time, can transform shapeless stone into a perfection of beauty seldom achieved by nature in the flesh. The love and care which Michelangelo lavished upon this group were such that he carved his name upon it, on the ribbon that crosses the Virgin's bosom. This is the only work he ever signed. Michelangelo had happened to find a large group of strangers from Lombardy looking at the Pietà one day. They were admiring it and one said that the artist was "Our Hunchback of Milan." Michelangelo came back that night with a lantern and carved Michelangelo Buonarroti where all could see. He gained great fame from this work. I have heard dull-witted folk object that the Virgin is too young. They have not been able to understand Michelangelo's ideal conception of the nature of the Madonna's virginity.

Michelangelo now received letters from friends in Florence telling him that, if he came back, he might have the big piece of marble that Pier Soderini, then gonfaloniere[2] of the city, had talked of giving to Leonardo da Vinci, but was now proposing to present to Andrea Sansovino, an excellent sculptor, who was making every effort to get it. Few people were courageous enough to attempt to carve this eighteen-foot block of stone, which had remained in the workshop of Santa Maria del Fiore ever since a certain Maestro Simone da Fiesole had marred it thirty-five years before.

No sooner had Michelangelo arrived in Florence than he set about securing the stone. He begged it of Soderini and received it as a worthless thing. He measured the mass and accommodated his design to the injury that had been done to it. He made a little model in wax of David, sling in hand. Then he built a boarding about the marble which hid it entirely from view. He let no one look at it until he had finished it.

The problem of moving the statue [the David] from Santa Maria del Fiore to the Piazza de' Signori now confronted him, but Giuliano da Sangallo and his brother Antonio made a stout framework of wood about it and suspended the figure by means of a clever slipknot that became tighter under tension. They moved it forward, gradually, by means of beams and windlasses.

Soderini was very pleased with it when it was in place. He watched Michelangelo retouch it and said he thought the nose too short. Michelangelo saw that Soderini was badly placed to view the head, but, to satisfy him, he took his chisel and a little loose marble dust in his hand and climbed the scaffolding. As he tapped lightly on the chisel, he let the marble dust drift down. "I like it better now," said Soderini, "you have given it life." Michelangelo came down, not without compassion for those who wish to appear good judges in matters about which they know nothing.

Then Michelangelo showed the statue. And we may say that it surpasses all others, both ancient and modern. Not even the treasures of Rome—the Nile and the Tiber in the Belvedere, or the Giants of Monte Cavallo—can compare with it. The whole form is divine. The outline of the legs is most beautiful. The connection of each limb to the body is faultless. Never since has a statue been produced with so fine an attitude, so perfect a grace, such beauty of hand, of foot, of brow.

He finished four statues and began eight others of the whole monument so magnificently planned.[3] The tomb was to stand clear of the wall, a rectangle eighteen by twenty-three feet. The lower part was to be composed of a series of alternating niches and figures to support the cornices. In the niches were to be bound captives, some to symbolize provinces brought by Julius II to obedience to the Apostolic Church, others to represent the Fine Arts and Liberal Sciences languishing because of the death of their great patron the Pope. The feet of these figures were to rest upon the foundation of the base. The second stage was to have four large figures: Active Life and Contemplative life, Saint Paul and Moses. Above, the mass was to diminish gradually. There was to be a frieze in bronze, with figures of angels and other ornaments. Over all were to be two figures, one of heaven, smiling to receive the Pope, the other of Cybele, or the earth, weeping at his loss. It was planned in such a way that the spectator could walk between the niches to reach the central part. This resembled a temple and was designed to receive the dead body of the Pope. Finally, there were to be added forty statues in marble, to say nothing of the ornaments, cornices and architectural decorations.

Michelangelo sent some of the marble to Florence so he could work there in the summer and escape the malaria of Rome. In fact, he finished one whole side of the monument in Florence. In Rome he finished two statues of the Captive Arts [the Slaves] and better work has never been seen.

The Moses, ten feet high, was also completed. No modern work will ever approach it in beauty, no, nor ancient either. Seated in imposing dignity, the lawgiver rests one arm upon the tablet. With his other hand he restrains his flowing beard that descends so softly, hair by separate hair, as though the chisel had become a pencil. The countenance, sacred and mighty, is of the most sublime beauty. Dazzling in splendor, the lawgiver radiates his divinity. The draperies are beautifully handled and turned at the edges. The anatomical development, the muscles, and the veins of the hands are exhibited to the utmost perfection. The same may be said of the legs and feet. This Moses seems indeed the friend of God. Nay, Jews are to be seen every Saturday (which is their Sabbath), hurrying like flights of swallows, men and women, to visit and worship at this figure, as though it were something divine.

Michelangelo set up one portion of the tomb; that is the shorter sides of it. While he was doing this, more of his marble arrived from Carrara. Because Michelangelo found His Holiness engaged with important news just received from Bologna, he advanced the money out of his own pocket. A few days later he sought an audience with the Pope but was told to have patience by a groom of the chambers who added that he had orders not to admit him. A bishop who stood near observed that possibly the groom was unacquainted with the person whom he refused to admit. The groom replied that he knew him only too well. "I, however," he added, "am here to do as my superiors command, and to obey the orders of the Pope." Displeased with this reply, the master left, bidding the attendant tell His Holiness, when next he should inquire for Michelangelo that he had gone elsewhere. He went at once to his dwelling, where he left instructions that all his belongings should be sold to the Jews. He took horses that very night and left Rome.

Bramante, who was the friend and kinsman of Raphael and hostile to Michelangelo, influenced the mind of the Pope to drop the work on the tomb and to employ Michelangelo instead on the painting of the chapel of Pope Sixtus [Sistine Chapel] in the Vatican. Bramante told the pontiff it was an invitation to death to build a tomb while one lived. Bramante and Michelangelo's other rivals hoped to thwart Michelangelo in his sculpture, in which he was perfect, and compel him to paint in fresco, in which they expected him to prove himself inferior to Raphael. Or, should he succeed at painting, it was almost certain that he would be so enraged as to secure the success of their main purpose, which was to be rid of him.

Michelangelo returned to Rome, therefore, and found the Pope no longer disposed to have the tomb finished. He was asked instead to paint the ceiling of the chapel, a great and difficult labor. Our artist, aware of his own inexperience, excused himself from the undertaking. He proposed that the work be given to Raphael. The more he refused, the more the impetuous Pope insisted. A quarrel threatened. Michelangelo saw that the Pope was determined, so he resolved to accept the task. His Holiness ordered Bramante to prepare the scaffolding. This he did by suspending the ropes through perforations in the ceiling. Michelangelo asked how the holes were going to be filled in when the painting was done. Bramante replied that they could think about it when the time came. Michelangelo saw that the architect was either incapable or unfriendly, and he went straight to the Pope to say that the scaffolding would not do and that Bramante did not know how to construct one. Julius, in the presence of Bramante, replied that Michelangelo might make it his own way. This he did by the use of a method that did not injure the walls, and which has since been pursued by Bramante and others. Michelangelo gave the ropes that were taken from Bramante's scaffolding to a poor carpenter, who sold them for a sum that made up his daughter's dowry.

When it was half done, Pope Julius, who had gone more than once to see the work, mounting ladders with Michelangelo's assistance, insisted on having a public showing. Hasty and impatient, he would not wait for the finishing touches. In fact, when all Rome came hurrying to see the chapel, the Pope was the first to enter. He hardly waited for the dust from the removal of the scaffolding to settle. Then it was that Raphael of Urbino, who was very prompt in imitation, instantly changed his style and painted the Prophets and the Sibyls in the church of Santa Maria della Pace. Bramante tried to make the Pope give the second half of the chapel to Raphael. Hearing of this, Michelangelo complained of Bramante to the Pope. He spared no pains to point out faults in Bramante's life as well as errors in his work. Julius commanded that Michelangelo should continue the work. He completed it in twenty months, without even so much help as a man to grind his colors. It is true that Michelangelo sometimes complained that the Pope hurried him constantly by asking when it would be finished. Once Michelangelo answered, "It will be done when I believe I have satisfied art." "And we command," rejoined the pontiff, "that you satisfy our wish to have it done quickly," adding that, if it were not at once completed, he would have Michelangelo thrown from the scaffolding.

When he heard this, our artist, who feared the Pope's fury, and with good cause, instantly removed the scaffolding without retouching the painting a secco [on dry plaster], as the older masters had done. He had wanted very much to add some gold and ultramarine to the draperies to enrich the whole. The Pope, too, heard from all who praised the chapel highly that these things were still wanting and would fain have had Michelangelo do it. But Michelangelo knew it would have been too great a labor to put up the scaffolding, so the pictures remained as they were. The Pope, who saw Michelangelo often, would sometimes say, "Let the chapel be enriched with bright colors and gold, it looks poor." Then Michelangelo would answer, "Holy Father, these were poor folk and holy men, besides, who despised riches and ornament."

For this work Michelangelo was paid three thousand crowns by the Pope. He may have spent twenty-five for colors. He worked under great personal inconvenience, constantly looking upward, so that he seriously injured his eyes. For months afterward he could read a letter only when he held it above his head.

Michelangelo used no perspective, nor any one fixed point of sight, but was satisfied to paint each division with perfection of design. Truly this chapel has been, and is, the very light of our art. . . . He boldly departed from the accepted rules. The unfortunate result has been that other artists have been encouraged to an injudicious imitation outside the wholesome rules of ornamentation. Artists, however, owe a great deal to Michelangelo, who freed them from the beaten path of convention.

When it was three quarters done, Pope Paul[4] went to see it. Messer Biagio da Cesena, the master of ceremonies, when asked to give his opinion, said that he thought it very improper to have so many nude forms, shameless in their nakedness, in that sacred place. He added that such pictures were suited to a bath or a wineshop. Messer Biagio had no sooner left than our artist drew his portrait from memory, with a serpent wound around him surrounded by devils in hell. Nor could Messer Biagio persuade the Pope to have the portrait removed.

This great work may be described in the words of Dante, "Dead are the dead, the living seem to live." Michelangelo surpassed himself. The seated figure of Our Lord, terrible in his anger, turns toward the condemned, thundering anathema. Our Lady cowers in her mantle at the sight of that destruction. In a word, we have here the true Last Judgment, the real Condemnation, the effectual Resurrection. Those who thought they knew art are overcome by this work. They gaze upon the evidence of power in these contours and they tremble with fear as though some great spirit had possessed himself of the art of design. The more they examine this work, the more they are bewildered at the thought of a comparison of other paintings with this paragon.

Fortunate is he, and happy are his memories, who has seen this wonder. Thrice blessed art thou, O Paul, under whose protection was sheltered his renown! A great happiness has been his birth for all artists, since Michelangelo has solved all the difficulties that previously obscured painting, sculpture, and architecture.

About a year before his death, Vasari secretly prevailed upon Duke Cosimo to use his influence with the Pope to the end that, since Michelangelo was now much debilitated, His Holiness should keep a watch over him, have him visited daily and take measures that, in case of any sudden accident such as may easily happen to the very old, the plans for Saint Peter's, or for the sacristy, the library, or the facade of San Lorenzo might not he lost, as so frequently happens.

In Lent[6] of this year, Leonardo, Michelangelo's nephew, resolved to go to Rome. Perhaps he sensed that his kinsman was near the end of his life. Michelangelo was already suffering from a slow fever and he had his doctor, Messer Federigo Donato, write Leonardo to hasten his coming. But the malady increased, in spite of the care of those around him. Still in perfect self-possession, the master at length made his will in three clauses. He left his soul to God, his body to the earth, and his goods to his nearest relatives. He recommended his attendants to think upon the sufferings of Christ, and departed to a better life on February 17, 1564.

But now, to conclude, I will only add, that Michelangelo had an excellent constitution, a spare form, and strong nerves. He was not robust as a child, and as a man he suffered two serious attacks of illness, but he could endure much fatigue. In his latter years he wore stockings of dogskin for months together, and when he took them off the skin of the leg sometimes came with them. His face was round, the brow square and ample, with seven direct lines upon it. The temples projected much beyond the ears, which were somewhat large and stood a little off from the cheeks. His nose had been flattened by the blow of Torrigiano. His eyes were rather small, dark, with blue and yellowish points. The eyebrows had few hairs. The lips were thin and the lower slightly projected. The chin was well formed, and the beard and hair were black mingled with gray.

This master, as I said at the beginning, was certainly sent by God as an example of what an artist could be. I, who can thank God for unusual happiness, count it among the greatest of my blessings that I was born while Michelangelo still lived, was found worthy to have him for my master, and was accepted as his trusted friend. . . .

NOTES

[1] Marks which appear on the body, resembling the crucifixion wounds of Jesus.

[2] The chief magistrate.

[3] The grand tomb of Pope Julius II.

[4] Michelangelo continued work on the Sistine Chapel under a new pope, Paul III.

[5] I.e., Michelangelo.

[6] The forty weekdays before Easter, observed as a time of penitence.

A Letter to Ser Giovan Francesco Fattucci
from Michelangelo Buonarotti

Messer Giovan Francesco—You ask me in one of your letters how my affairs stand regarding Pope Julius.[1] I assure you that if damages could be claimed I should expect rather to be the creditor than the debtor. Because when he sent for me from Florence, which was, I believe, in the second year of his pontificate, I had undertaken to execute half the Sala del Consiglio of Florence, that is to say, to paint it, for which I was getting three thousand ducats; and I had already done the cartoon,[2] as is known to all Florence, so that the money seemed to me half earned. And of the twelve Apostles that I also had to execute for Santa Maria del Fiore,[3] one was blocked out, as can still be seen, and I had already transported the greater part of the marble. But when Pope Julius took me away from here I got nothing either for the one or for the other.

Then when I was in Rome with the said Pope, and when he had given me a commission for his Tomb, into which a thousand ducats' worth of marbles were to go, he had the money paid to me and sent me to Carrara to get them. I remained there eight months to have the marbles blocked out and I transported nearly all of them to the Piazza of St. Peter, but some of them remained at Ripa. Then, after I had completed the payment for the freight for the said marbles, I had no money left from what I had received for the said work, but I furnished the house I had in the Piazza of St. Peter with beds and household goods out of my own money, in anticipation of the Tomb, and I brought assistants from Florence, some of whom are still living, to work on it, and I paid them in advance out of my own money. At this point Pope Julius changed his mind and no longer wanted to go on with it. But I, not knowing this, went to ask him for money and was turned away from the audience chamber. Enraged at this, I immediately left Rome, and what I had in the house went to pieces and the said marbles, that I had transported, remained in the Piazza of St. Peter until the election of Pope Leo, and in one way and another they came to grief. Among other things which I can prove, two pieces of four and a half braccia, which had cost me over fifty gold ducats, were stolen from me by Agottino Chigi;[4] these could be recovered, because there are witnesses. But to return to the marbles, from the time that I went for them and stayed in Carrara, until I was turned away from the Palace, more than a year went by and during that time I never had anything and it cost me several tens of ducats.

Then the first time that Pope Julius went to Bologna I was forced to go there, with a rope round my neck, to ask his pardon, whereupon he gave me his figure to do in bronze, which was about seven *braccia*[5] in height, seated. When he asked me what it would cost, I replied that I believed it could be cast for about a thousand ducats; but that it was not my trade and that I did not want to be obliged to do it. He replied, 'Set to work and cast it over and over again till it succeeds, and we will give you enough to content you.' To be brief, it was cast twice, and at the end of the two years I had stayed there I found myself four and a half ducats to the good. And from that time I never had anything more. But all the expenses I had in the said two years were included in the thousand ducats for which I had said it could be cast, and these were paid me in installments by Messer Antonio Maria da Legnia[me], a Bolognese.

When I had set up the figure on the facade of San Petronio and returned to Rome, Pope Julius still did not want me to do the Tomb, and set me to paint the vault of Sixtus[6] and we made a bargain for three thousand ducats. The first design for the said work was for twelve Apostles in the lunettes and the usual ornamentations to fill the remaining area.

After the work was begun it seemed to me that it would turn out a poor affair, and I told the Pope that if the Apostles alone were put there it seemed to me that it would turn out a poor affair. He asked me why. I said, 'because they themselves were poor.' Then he gave me a new commission to do what I liked, and said he would content me and that I should paint down to the Histories below. Meanwhile, when the vault was nearly finished the Pope returned to Bologna; whereupon I went there twice for money that was owed me, but effected nothing and wasted all that time until he returned to Rome. When I returned to Rome I began to do the cartoons for the said work, that is for the ends and the sides round the said chapel of Sixtus, in the expectation of having the money to finish the work. I was never able to obtain anything; but one day when I was complaining to Messer Bernardo da Bibbiera and to Attalante that I couldn't remain in Rome any longer but must go with God, Messer Bernardo told Attalante that he would remind him that he intended to have money paid to me in any case. And he had two thousand ducats of the Camera paid to me, which, together with the first thousand for the marbles, they are putting to my account for the Tomb. But I reckoned that I was owed more for the time I had lost and the works I had done. And from the said money, as Messer Bernardo and Atralante had saved my life, I gave the former a hundred ducats and the latter fifty.

Then came the death of Pope Julius and at the beginning of Leo, as Aginensis wished to increase the size of his Tomb, that is, to execute a larger work than the one I had first designed, a new contract was drawn up. And when I did not wish them to put to the account the three thousand ducats I had received, and showed that I was owed much more, Aginensis called me an impostor.

[*Unsigned*]

NOTES

[1] Pope Julius II.

[2] A preliminary sketch.

[3] A church in Rome.

[4] A very wealthy Sienese banker who lived in Rome.

[5] The length of an arm.

[6] The Sistine Chapel.

BENVENUTO CELLINI

1500–1571

What is an artist? What is the relationship between the artist and society? The artist and the work of art? The sculptor and goldsmith Benvenuto Cellini, a central figure in the world of Renaissance art, engages these questions in his passionate and intense *Autobiography*. Cellini worked as an artist for many important patrons, including the renowned Florentine Cosimo de' Medici, who commissioned Cellini's most famous statue, *Perseus with the Head of Medusa*. Cellini comments frankly on his feelings for other prominent artists of the period. In his writing, we can experience his admiration for, and awe, of Michelangelo and Leonardo, as well as his utter disdain for, and adversarial relationship with, most other artists.

The *Autobiography* was composed between 1558 and 1562, and was not published until 1728. It is notable for the expressions of a creative and powerful mind and for its place as a document of one man's lived experience amidst the various cultural centers of the Continental Renaissance: Florence, Rome, Siena, Fountainbleau and Paris.

Cellini's *Autobiography* is full of drama, intrigue, tragedy and violence but it also serves as the ultimate expression of the artist as a "creator." In the selection included here, Cellini explicitly discusses his role as a creator of art, but implicitly reveals the extent to which he is also constructing his own identity as an artist. While reading his autobiography, think about Cellini's possible motives for writing the story of his life. In what ways can you compare his project to Montaigne's? What picture, in words, does Cellini paint of the Renaissance art world? How might his ideas be compared to the painting Las Meninas by Diego Velasquez in Chapter 23 of *The Humanistic Tradition*?

from *Autobiography*

All men of whatsoever quality they be, who have done anything of excellence, or which may properly resemble excellence, ought, if they are persons of truth and honesty, to describe their life with their own hand but they ought not to attempt so fine an enterprise till they have passed the age of forty. This duty occurs to my own mind now that I am travelling beyond the term of fifty-eight years and am in Florence, the city of my birth. Many untoward things can I remember, such as happen to all who live upon our earth; and from those adversities I am now more than at any previous period of my career—nay, it seems to me that I enjoy greater content of soul and health of body than ever I did in bygone years. I can also bring to mind some pleasant goods and some inestimable evils, which, when I turn my thoughts backward, strike terror in me, astonishment that I should have reached this age of fifty-eight, wherein, thanks be to God, I am still travelling prosperously forward.

. . . and when he [Piero Torrigiani] saw my drawings and the things which I was making, he said: "I have come to Florence to enlist as many young men as I can; for I have undertaken to execute a great work for my king, and want some of my own Florentines to help me. Now your method of working and your designs are worthy rather of a sculptor than a goldsmith; and since I have to turn out a great piece of bronze, I will at the same time turn you into a rich and able artist."

In course of conversation he happened to mention Michel Agnolo Buonarroti, led thereto by a drawing I had made from a cartoon of that divinest painter.[1] This cartoon was the first masterpiece which Michel Agnolo exhibited, in proof of his stupendous talents. He produced it in competition with another painter, Lionardo da Vinci, who made a cartoon; and both were intended for the council-hall in the palace of the Signory. They represented the taking of Pisa by the Florentines; and our admirable Lionardo had chosen to depict a battle of horses, with the capture of some standards, in as divine a style as could possibly be imagined. Michel Agnolo in his cartoon portrayed a number of foot-soldiers, who, the season being summer, had gone to bathe in Arno. He drew them at the very moment the alarm is sounded, and the men all naked run to arms; so splendid in their action that nothing survives ancient or of modern art which touches the same lofty point of excellence; and as I have already said, the design of great Lionardo was itself most admirably beautiful. These two cartoons stood, one in the palace of the Medici, the other in the hall of the Pope. So long as they remained intact, they were the school of the world. Though the divine Michel Agnolo in later life finished that great chapel of Pope Julius,[2] he never rose half-way to the same pitch of power; his genius never afterwards attained to the force of those first studies.

Now let us return to Piero Torrigiani, who, with my drawing in his hand, spoke as follows: "This Buonarroti and I used, when we were boys, to go into the Church of the Carmine, to learn drawing from the chapel of Masaccio. It was Buonarroti's habit to banter all who were drawing there; and one day, among others, when he was annoying me, I got more angry than usual, and clenching my fist, gave him such a blow on the nose, that I felt bone and cartilage go down like biscuit beneath my knuckles; and this mark of mine he will carry with him to the grave."[3] These words begat in me such hatred of the man, since I was always gazing at the masterpieces of the divine Michel Agnolo, that although I felt a wish to go with him, I now could never bear the sight of him

During that time I went to draw,[4] sometimes in Michel Agnolo's chapel, and sometimes in the house of Agostino Chigi of Siena, which contained many incomparable paintings by the hand of that great master Raffaello. This I did on feast-days, because the house was then inhabited by Messer Gismondo, Agostino's brother. They plumed themselves exceedingly when they saw young men of my sort coming to study in their palaces. Gismondo's wife, noticing my frequent presence in that house—she was a lady as courteous as could be, and of surpassing beauty—came up to me one day, looked at my drawings, and asked me if I was a sculptor or a painter; to whom I said I was a goldsmith. She remarked that I drew too well for a goldsmith; and having made one of her waiting-maids bring a lily of the finest diamonds set in gold, she showed it to me, and bade me value it. I valued it at 800 crowns. Then she said that I had very nearly hit the mark, and asked me whether I felt capable of setting the stones really well. I said that I should much like to do so, and began before her eyes to make a little sketch for it, working all the better because of the pleasure I took in conversing with so lovely and agreeable a gentlewoman. When the sketch was finished, another Roman lady of great beauty joined us; she had been above, and now descending to the ground-floor, asked Madonna Porzia what she was doing there. She answered with a smile: "I am amusing myself by watching this worthy young man at his drawing; he is as good as he is handsome." I had by this time acquired a trifle of assurance, mixed, however, with some honest bashfulness; so I blushed and said: "Such as I am, lady, I shall ever be most ready to serve you." The gentlewoman, also slightly blushing, said: "You know well that I want you to serve me;" and reaching me the lily, told me to take it away; and gave me besides twenty golden crowns which she had in her bag, and added: "Set me the jewel after the fashion you have sketched, and keep for me the old gold in which it is now set." On this the Roman lady observed: "If I were in that young man's body, I should go off without asking leave." Madonna Porzia replied that virtues rarely are at home with vices, and that if I did such a thing, I should strongly belie my good looks of an honest man. Then turning round, she took the Roman lady's hand, and with a pleasant smile said: "Farewell, Benvenuto." I stayed on a short while at the drawing I was making which was a copy of a Jove by Raffaello. When I finished it and left the house, I set myself to making a little model of wax, in order to show how the jewel would look when it was completed. This I took to Madonna Porzia, whom I found with the same Roman lady. Both of them were highly satisfied with my work and treated me so kindly that, being somewhat emboldened, I promised the jewel should be twice as good as the model. Accordingly I set hand to it, and in twelve days I finished it in the form of a fleur-de-lys, as I have said above, ornamenting it with little masks, children, and animals, exquisitely enamelled, whereby the diamonds which formed the lily were more than doubled in effect.

While I was working at this piece, Lucagnolo,[5] of whose ability I have before spoken, showed considerable discontent, telling me over and over again that I might acquire far more profit and honour by helping him to execute large plate as I had done at first. I made him answer that, whenever I chose, I should always be capable of working at great silver pieces; but that things like that on which I was now engaged were not commissioned every day; and beside their bringing no less honour than large silver plate, there was also more profit to be made by them. He laughed me in the face, and said: "Wait and see, Benvenuto; for by the time that you have finished that work of yours, I will make haste to have finished this vase, which I took in hand when you did the jewel; and then experience shall teach you what profit I shall get from my vase, and what you will get from your ornament." I answered that I was very glad indeed to enter into such a competition with so good a craftsman as he was, because the end would show which of us was mistaken. Accordingly both the one and the other of us, with a scornful smile upon our lips, bent our heads in grim earnest to the work, which both were now desirous of accomplishing so that after about ten days, each had finished his undertaking with great delicacy and artistic skill.

Lucagnolo's was a huge silver piece, used at the table of Pope Clement, into which he flung away bits of bone and the rind of divers fruits, while eating; an object of ostentation rather than necessity. The vase was adorned with two fine handles, together with many masks, both small and great; and masses of lovely foliage, in as exquisite a style of elegance as could be imagined; on seeing which I said it was the most beautiful vase that ever I set eyes on. Thinking he had convinced me, Lucagnolo replied: "Your work seems to me no less beautiful, but we shall soon perceive the difference between the two." So he took his vase and carried it to the Pope, who was very well pleased with it, and ordered at once that he should be paid at the ordinary rate of such large plate. Meanwhile I carried mine to Madonna Porzia, who looked at it with astonishment, and told me I had far surpassed my promise. Then she bade me ask for my reward whatever I liked; for it seemed to her my desert was so great that if I craved a castle she could hardly recompense me; but since that was not in her hands to bestow, she added laughing that I must beg what lay within her power. I answered that the greatest reward I could desire for my labour was to have satisfied her ladyship. Then, smiling in my turn, and bowing to her, I took my leave, saying I wanted no reward but that. She turned to the Roman lady and said: "You see that the qualities we discerned in him are companied by virtues, and not vices." They both expressed their admiration, and then Madonna Porzia continued: "Friend Benvenuto, have you never heard it said that when the poor give to the rich, the devil laughs?" I replied: "Quite true! and yet, in the midst of all his troubles, I should like this time to see him laugh;" and as I took my leave, she said that this time she had no will to bestow on him that favour.

When I came back to the shop, Lucagnolo had the money for his vase in a paper packet; and on my arrival he cried out: "Come and compare the price of your jewel with the price of my plate." I said that he must leave things as they were till the next day, because I hoped that even as my work in its kind was not less excellent than his, so I should be able to show him quite an equal price for it.

On the day following, Madonna Porzia sent a major-domo of hers to my shop, who called me out, and putting into my hands a paper packet full of money from his lady, told me that she did not choose the devil should have his whole laugh out: by which she hinted that the money sent me was not the entire payment merited by my industry, and other messages were added worthy of so courteous a lady. Lucagnolo, who was burning to compare his packet with mine, burst into the shop; then in the presence of twelve journeymen and some neighbours, eager to behold the result of this competition, he seized his packet, scornfully exclaiming "Ou! Ou!" three or four times, while he poured his money on the counter with a great noise. They were twenty-five crowns in giulios; and he fancied that mine would be four or five crowns [di moneta.][6] I for my part, stunned and stifled by his cries, and by the looks and smiles of the bystanders, first peeped into my packet; then, after seeing that it contained nothing but gold, I retired to one end of the counter, and, keeping my eyes lowered and making no noise at all, I lifted it with both hands suddenly above my head, and emptied it like a mill hopper. My coin was twice as much as his; which caused the onlookers, who had fixed their eyes on me with some derision, to turn round suddenly to him and say: "Lucagnolo, Benvenuto's pieces, being all of gold and twice as many as yours, make a far finer effect." I thought for certain that, what with jealousy and what with shame, Lucagnolo would have fallen dead upon the spot; and though he took the third part of my gain, since I was a journeyman (for such is the custom of the trade, two-thirds fall to the workman and one-third to the masters of the shop), yet inconsiderate envy had more power in him than avarice: it ought indeed to have worked quite the other way, he being a peasant's son from Iesi. He cursed his art and those who taught it him, vowing that thenceforth he would never work at large plate, but give his whole attention to those brothel gewgaws, since they were so well paid. Equally enraged on my side, I answered that every bird sang its own note; that he talked after the fashion of the hovels he came from; but that I dared swear that I should succeed with ease in making his lubberly lumber, while he would never be successful in my brothel gewgaws. Thus I flung off in a passion, telling him that I would soon show him that I spoke truth. The bystanders openly declared against him, holding him for a lout as indeed he was, and me for a man, as I had proved myself. . . .

Messer Durante of Brescia[7], whom I have previously mentioned, engaged the soldier (formerly druggist of Prato) to administer some deadly liquor in my food; the poison was to work slowly, producing its effect at the end of four or five months. They resolved on mixing pounded diamond with my victuals. Now the diamond is not a poison in any true sense of the word, but its incomparable hardness enables it, unlike ordinary stones, to retain very acute angles. When every other stone is pounded, that extreme sharpness of edge is lost; their fragments becoming blunt and rounded. The diamond alone preserves its trenchant qualities; wherefore, if it chances to enter the stomach together with food, the peristaltic motion needful to digestion brings it into contact with the coats of the stomach and the bowels, where it sticks, and by the action of fresh food forcing it further inwards, after some time perforates the organs. This eventually causes death. Any other sort of stone or glass mingled with the food has not the power to attach itself, but passes onward with the victuals. Now Messer Durante entrusted a diamond of trifling value to one of the guards; and it is said that a certain Lione, a goldsmith of Arezzo, my great enemy, was commissioned to pound it. The man happened to be very poor, and the diamond was worth perhaps some scores of crowns. He told the guard that the dust he gave him back was the diamond in question properly ground down. The morning when I took it, they mixed it with all I had to eat; it was a Friday, and I had it in salad, sauce, and pottage. That morning I ate heartily, for I had fasted on the previous evening; and this day was a festival. It is true that I felt the victuals scrunch beneath my teeth; but I was not thinking about knaveries of this sort. When I had finished, some scraps of salad remained upon my plate and certain very fine and glittering splinters caught my eye among these remnants. I collected them, and took them to the window, which let a flood of light into the room; and while I was examining them, I remembered that the food I ate that morning had scrunched more than usual. On applying my senses strictly to the matter, the verdict of my eyesight was that they were certainly fragments of pounded diamond. Upon this I gave myself up without doubt as dead, and in my sorrow had recourse with pious heart to holy prayers. I had resolved the question, and thought that I was doomed. For the space of a whole hour I prayed fervently to God, returning thanks to Him for so merciful a death. Since my stars had sentenced me to die, I thought it no bad bargain to escape from life so easily. I was resigned, and blessed the world and all the years which I had passed in it. Now I was returning to a better kingdom with the grace of God, the which I thought I had most certainly acquired.

While I stood revolving these thoughts in my mind, I held in my hand some flimsy particles of the reputed diamond, which of a truth I firmly believed to be such. Now hope is immortal in the human breast; therefore I felt myself, as it were, lured onward by a gleam of idle expectation. Accordingly, I took up a little knife and a few of those particles, and placed them on an iron bar of my prison. Then I brought the knife's point with a slow strong grinding pressure to bear upon the stone, and felt it crumble. Examining the substance with my eyes, I saw that it was so. In a moment new hope took possession of my soul, and I exclaimed: "Here I do not find my true foe, Messer Durante, but a piece of bad soft stone, which cannot do me any harm whatever!" Previously I had been resolved to remain quiet and to die in peace; now I revolved other plans; but first I rendered thanks to God and blessed poverty; for though poverty is oftentimes the cause of bringing men to death, on this occasion it had been the very cause of my salvation. I mean in this way: Messer Durante, my enemy, or whoever it was, gave a diamond to Lione to pound for me of the worth of more than a hundred crowns; poverty induced him to keep this for himself, and to pound for me a greenish beryl of the value of two carlins, thinking perhaps, because it also was a stone, that it would work the same effect as the diamond.

The first piece I cast in bronze was that great bust, the portrait of his Excellency,[8] which I had modelled in the goldsmith's workroom while suffering from those pains in my back. It gave much pleasure when it was completed, though my sole object in making it was to obtain experience of clays suitable for bronze-casting. I was of course aware that the admirable sculptor Donatello had cast his bronzes with the clay of Florence; yet it seemed to me that he had met with enormous difficulties in their execution. As I thought that this was due to some fault in the earth, I wanted to make these first experiments before I undertook my Perseus. From them I learned that the clay was good enough, but had not been well understood by Donatello, inasmuch as I could see that his pieces had been cast with the very greatest trouble. Accordingly, as I have described above, I prepared the earth by artificial methods, and found it serve me well, and with it I cast the bust; but since I had not yet constructed my own furnace, I employed that of Maestro Zanobi di Pagno, a bellfounder.

When I saw that this bust came out sharp and clean, I set at once to construct a little furnace in the workshop erected for me by the Duke, after my own plans and design, in the house which the Duke had given me. No sooner was the furnace ready than I went to work with all diligence upon the casting of Medusa, that is, the woman twisted in a heap beneath the feet of Perseus. It was an extremely difficult task, and I was anxious to observe all the niceties of art which I had learned, so as not to lapse into some error. The first cast I took in my furnace succeeded in the superlative degree, and was so clean that my friends thought I should not need to retouch it. It is true that certain Germans and Frenchmen, who vaunt the possession of marvelous secrets, pretend that they can cast bronzes without retouching them; but this is really nonsense, because the bronze, when it has first been cast, ought to be worked over and beaten in with hammers and chisels, according to the manner of the ancients and also to that of the moderns—I mean such moderns as have known how to work in bronze.

The result of this casting greatly pleased his Excellency, who often came to my house to inspect it, encouraging me by the interest he showed to do my best. The furious envy of Bandinello,[9] however, who kept always whispering in the Duke's ears, had such effect that he made him believe my first successes with a single figure or two proved nothing; I should never be able to put the whole large piece together, since I was new to the craft, and his Excellency ought to take good heed he did not throw his money away. These insinuations operated so efficiently upon the Duke's illustrious ears, that part of my allowance for workpeople was drawn. I felt compelled to complain pretty sharply to his Excellency; and having gone to wait on him one morning in the Via de' Servi, I spoke as follows: "My lord. I do not now receive the monies necessary for my task, which makes me fear that your Excellency has lost confidence in me. Once more then I tell you that I feel quite able to execute this statue three times better than the model, as I have before engaged my word."

Having succeeded so well with the cast of the Medusa, I had great hope of bringing my Perseus through; for I had laid the wax on, and felt confident that it would come out in bronze as perfectly as the Medusa. The waxen model produced so fine an effect, that when the Duke saw it and was struck with its beauty—whether somebody had persuaded him it could not be carried out with the same finish in metal, or whether he thought so for himself—he came to visit me more frequently than usual, and on one occasion said: "Benvenuto, this figure cannot succeed in bronze; the laws of art do not admit of it." These words of his Excellency stung me so sharply that I answered: "My lord, I know how very little confidence you have in me; and I believe the reason of this is that your most illustrious Excellency lends too ready an ear to my calumniators, or else indeed that you do not understand my art." He hardly let me close the sentence when he broke in: "I profess myself a connoisseur, and understand it very well indeed." I replied: " Yes, like a prince, not like an artist; for if your Excellency understood my trade as well as you imagine, you would trust me on the proofs I have already given. These are, first, the colossal bronze bust of your Excellency, which is now in Elba; secondly, the restoration of the Ganymede in marble, which offered so many difficulties and cost me so much trouble, that I would rather have made the whole statue new from the beginning; thirdly, the Medusa, cast by me in bronze, here now before your Excellency's eyes, the execution of which was a greater triumph of strength and skill than any of my predecessors in this fiendish art yet achieved. Look you, my lord! I constructed that furnace anew on principles quite different from those of other founders; in addition to many technical improvements and ingenious devices, I supplied it with two issues for the metal, because this difficult and twisted figure could not otherwise have come out perfect. It is only owing to my intelligent insight into means and appliances that the statue turned out as it did; a triumph judged impossible by all practitioners of this art. I should like you furthermore to be aware, my lord, for certain, that the sole reason why I succeeded with all those great arduous works in France under his most admirable Majesty King Francis, was the high courage which that good monarch put into my heart by the liberal allowances he made me, and the multitude of workpeople he left at my disposal. I could have as many as I asked for, and employed at times above forty, all chosen by myself. These were the causes of my having there produced so many masterpieces in so short a space of time. Now then, my lord, put trust in me; supply me with the aid I need. I am confident of being able to complete a work which will delight your soul. But if your Excellency goes on disheartening me, and does not advance me the assistance which is absolutely required, neither I nor any man alive upon this earth can hope to achieve the slightest thing of value."

It was as much as the Duke could do to stand by and listen to my pleadings. He kept turning first this way and then that; while I, in despair, poor wretched I, was calling up remembrance of the noble state I held in France, to the great sorrow of my soul. All at once he cried: "Come, tell me, Benvenuto, how is it possible that yonder splendid head of Medusa, so high up there in the grasp of Perseus, should ever come out perfect?" I replied upon the instant: Look you now, my lord! If your Excellency possessed that knowledge of the craft which you affirm you have, you would not fear one moment for the splendid head you speak of. There is good reason, on the other hand, to feel uneasy about this right foot, so far below and at a distance from the rest." When he heard these words, the Duke turned, half in anger, to some gentlemen in waiting, and exclaimed: "I verily believe that this Benvenuto prides himself on contradicting everything one says." Then he faced round to me with a touch of mockery, upon which his attendants did the like, and began to speak as follows: "I will listen patiently to any argument you can possibly produce in explanation of your statement, which may convince me of its probability." I said in answer: "I will adduce so sound an argument that your Excellency shall perceive the full force of it." So I began: "You must know, my lord, that the nature of fire is to ascend, and therefore I promise you that Medusa's head will come out famously; but since it is not in the nature of fire to descend, and I must force it downwards six cubits by artificial means, I assure your Excellency upon this most convincing ground of proof that the foot cannot possibly come out. It will, however, be quite easy for me to restore it." "Why, then," said the Duke, "did you not devise it so that the foot should come out as well as you affirm the head will?" I answered: "I must have made a much larger furnace, with a conduit as thick as my leg; and so I might have forced the molten metal by its own weight to descend so far. Now, my pipe, which runs six cubits to the statue's foot, as I have said, is not thicker than two fingers. However, it was not worth the trouble and expense to make a larger; for I shall easily be able to mend what is lacking. But when my mould is more than half full, as I expect, from this middle point upwards, the fire ascending by its natural property, then the heads of Perseus and Medusa will come out admirably; you may be quite sure of it." After I had thus expounded these convincing arguments, together with many more of the same kind, which it would be tedious to set down here, the Duke shook his head and departed without further ceremony.

Abandoned thus to my own resources, I took new courage, and banished the sad thoughts which kept recurring to my mind, making me often weep bitter tears of repentance for having left France; for though I did so only to revisit Florence, my sweet birthplace, in order that I might charitably succour my six nieces, this good action, as I well perceived, had been the beginning of my great misfortune. Nevertheless, I felt convinced that when my Perseus was accomplished, all these trials would be turned to high felicity and glorious well-being.

Accordingly I strengthened my heart, and with all the forces of my body and my purse, employing what little money still remained to me, I set to work. First I provided myself with several loads of pinewood from the forests of Serristori, in the neighbourhood of Montelupo. While these were on their way, I clothed my Perseus with the clay which I had prepared many months beforehand, in order that it might be duly seasoned. After making its clay tunic (for that is the term used in this art) and properly arming it and fencing it with iron girders, I began to draw the wax out by means of a slow fire. This melted and issued through numerous air-vents I had made; for the more there are of these, the better will the mould fill. When I had finished drawing off the wax, I constructed a funnel-shaped furnace all round the model of my Perseus. It was built of bricks, so interlaced, the one above the other, that numerous apertures were left for the fire to exhale at. Then I began to lay on wood by degrees, and kept it burning two whole days and nights. At length, when all the wax was gone, and the mould was well baked, I set to work at digging the pit in which to sink it. This I performed with scrupulous regard to all the rules of art.

When I had finished that part of my work, I raised the mould by windlasses and stout ropes to a perpendicular position, and suspending it with the greatest care one cubit above the level of the furnace, so that it hung exactly above the middle of the pit, I next lowered it gently down into the very bottom of the furnace, and had it placed with every possible precaution for its safety. When this delicate operation was accomplished, I began to bank it up with the earth I had excavated; and, ever as the earth grew higher, I introduced its proper air-vents, which were little tubes of earthenware, such as folk use for drains and such-like purposes. At length, I felt sure that it was admirably fixed, and that the filling-in of the pit and the placing of the air-vents had been properly performed. I also could see that my workpeople understood my method, which differed very considerably from that of all the other masters in the trade. Feeling confident, then, that I could rely upon them, I next turned to my furnace, which I had filled with numerous pigs of copper and other bronze stuff. The pieces were piled according to the laws of art, that is to say, so resting one upon the other that the flames could play freely through them, in order that the metal might heat and liquefy the sooner. At last I called out heartily to set the furnace going. The logs of pine were heaped in, and, what with the unctuous resin of the wood and the good draught given, my furnace worked so well that I was obliged to rush from side to side to keep it going. The labour was more than I could stand; yet I forced myself to strain every nerve and muscle. To increase my anxieties, the workshop took fire, and we were afraid lest the roof should fall upon our heads; while, from the garden, such a storm of wind and rain kept blowing in, that it perceptibly cooled the furnace.

Battling thus with all these untoward circumstances for several hours, and exerting myself beyond even the measure of my powerful constitution, I could at last bear up no longer, and a sudden fever, of the utmost possible intensity, attacked me. I felt absolutely obliged to go and fling myself upon my bed. Sorely against my will having to drag myself from the spot, I turned to my assistants, about ten or more in all, what with master-founders, hand-workers, country-fellows, and my own special journeymen, among whom was Bernardino Mannellini of Mugello, my apprentice through several years. To him in particular I spoke: "Look, my dear Bernardino, that you observe the rules which I have taught you; do your best with all despatch, for the metal will soon be fused. You cannot go wrong; these honest men will get the channels ready; you will easily be able to drive back the two plugs with this pair of iron crooks; and I am sure that my mould will fill miraculously. I feel more ill than I ever did in all my life, and verily believe that it will kill me before a few hours are over." Thus, with despair at heart, I left them, and betook myself to bed.

No sooner had I got to bed, than I ordered my serving maids to carry food and wine for all the men into the work shop; at the same time I cried: "I shall not be alive tomorrow." They tried to encourage me, arguing that my illness would pass over, since it came from excessive fatigue. In this way I spent two hours battling with the fever, which steadily increased, and calling out continually: "I feel that I am dying." My housekeeper, who was named Mona Fiore da Castel del Rio, a very notable manager and no less warm-hearted, kept chiding me for my discouragement; but, on the other hand, she paid me every kind attention which was possible. However, the sight of my physical pain and moral dejection so affected her, that, in spite of that brave heart of hers, she could not refrain from shedding tears; and yet, so far as she was able, she took good care I should not see them. While I was thus terribly afflicted, I beheld the figure of a capital S. He raised a lamentable, doleful voice, like one who announces their last hour to men condemned to die upon the scaffold, and spoke these words: "O Benvenuto! your statue is spoiled, and there is no hope whatever of saving it." No sooner had I heard the shriek of that wretch than I gave a howl which might have been heard from the sphere of flame. Jumping from my bed, I seized my clothes and began to dress. The maids, and my lads, and every one who came around to help me, got kicks or blows of the fist, while I kept crying out in lamentation: "Ah! Traitors! enviers! This is an act of treason, done by malice prepense! But I swear by God that I will sift it to the bottom, and before I die will leave such witness to the world of what I can do as shall make a score of mortals marvel."

When I had got my clothes on, I strode with soul bent on mischief toward the workshop; there I beheld the men, whom I had left erewhile in such high spirits, standing stupefied and downcast. I began at once and spoke: "Up with you! Attend to me! Since you have not been able or willing to obey the directions I gave you, obey me now that I am with you to conduct my work in person. Let no one contradict me, for in cases like this we need the aid of hand and hearing, not of advice." When I had uttered these words, a certain Maestro Alessandro Lastricati broke silence and said: "Look you, Benvenuto, you are going to attempt an enterprise which the laws of art do not sanction, and which cannot succeed." I turned upon him with such fury and so full of mischief, that he and all the rest of them exclaimed with one voice: "On then! Give orders! We will obey your least commands, so long as life is left in us." I believe they spoke thus feelingly because they thought I must fall shortly dead upon the ground. I went immediately to inspect the furnace, and found that the metal was all curdled; an accident which we express by "being caked." I told two of the hands to cross the road, and fetch from the house of the butcher Capretta a load of young oak-wood, which had lain dry for above a year; this wood had been previously offered me by Madame Ginevra, wife of the said Capretta. So soon as the first armfuls arrived, I began to fill the grate beneath the furnace. Now oak-wood of that kind heats more powerfully than any other sort of tree; and for this reason, where a slow fire is wanted, as in the case of gun-foundry, alder or pine is preferred. Accordingly, when the logs took fire, oh! how the cake began to stir beneath that awful heat, to glow and sparkle in a blaze! At the same time I kept stirring up the channels, and sent men upon the roof to stop the conflagration, which had gathered force from the increased combustion in the furnace; also I caused boards, carpets, and other hangings to be set up against the garden; in order to protect us from the violence of the rain.

When I had thus provided against these several disasters, I roared out first to one man and then to another: "Bring this thing here! Take that thing there!" At this crisis, when the whole gang saw the cake was on the point of melting, they did my bidding, each fellow working with the strength of three. I then ordered half a pig of pewter to be brought, which weighed about sixty pounds, and flung it into the middle of the cake inside the furnace. By this means, and by piling on wood and stirring now with pokers and now with iron rods, the curdled mass rapidly began to liquefy. Then, knowing I had brought the dead to life again, against the firm opinion of those ignoramuses, I felt such vigour fill my veins, that all those pains of fever, all those fears of death, were quite forgotten.

All of a sudden an explosion took place, attended by a tremendous flash of flame, as though a thunderbolt had formed and been discharged amongst us. Unwonted appalling terror astonied every one, and me more even than the rest. When the din was over and the dazzling light extinguished, we began to look each other in the face. Then I discovered that the cap of the furnace had blown up, and the bronze was bubbling over from its source beneath. So I had the mouths of my mould immediately opened, and the same time drove in the two plugs which kept back the molten metal. But I noticed that it did not flow as rapidly as usual, the reason being probably that the fierce heat of the fire we kindled had consumed its base alloy. Accordingly I sent for all my pewter platters, porringers, and dishes, to the number of some two hundred pieces, and had a portion of them cast, one by one, into the channels, the rest into the furnace. This expedient succeeded, and every one could perceive that my bronze was in most perfect liquefaction, and my mould was filling; whereupon they all with heartiness and happy cheer assisted and obeyed my bidding, while I, now here, now there, gave orders, helped with my own hands and cried aloud: "O God! Thou that by Thy immeasurable power didst rise from the dead, and in Thy glory didst ascend to heaven!" . . . even thus in a moment my mould was filled; and seeing my work finished, I fell upon my knees, and with all my heart gave thanks to God.

After all was over, I turned to a plate of salad on a bench there, and ate with hearty appetite, and drank together with the whole crew. Afterwards I retired to bed, healthy and happy, for it was now two hours before morning, and slept as sweetly as though I had never felt a touch of illness. My good housekeeper, without my giving any orders, had prepared a fat capon for my repast. So that, when I rose, about the hour for breaking fast, she presented herself a smiling countenance, and said: Oh! is that the man who felt that he was dying? Upon my word, I think the blows and kicks you dealt us last night, when you were so enraged and had that demon in your body as it seemed, must have frightened away your mortal fever! The fever feared that it might catch it too, as we did!" All my poor household, relieved in like measure from anxiety and overwhelming labour, went at once to buy earthen vessels in order to replace the pewter I had cast away. Then we dined together joyfully; nay, I cannot remember a day in my whole life when I dined with greater gladness or a better appetite.

After our meal I received visits from the several men who had assisted me. They exchanged congratulations, and thanked God for our success, saying they had learned and seen things done which other masters judged impossible. I too grew somewhat glorious; and deeming I had shown myself a man of talent, indulged a boastful humour. So I thrust my hand into my purse, and paid them all to their full satisfaction.

That evil fellow, my mortal foe, Messer Pier Franceso Ricci, majordomo of the Duke, took great pains to find out how the affair had gone. In answer to his questions, the two men whom I suspected of having caked my metal for me said I was no man, but of a certainty some powerful devil, since I had accomplished what no craft of the art could do; indeed they did not believe a mere ordinary fiend could work such miracles as I in other ways had shown. They exaggerated the whole affair so much, possibly in order to excuse their own part in it, that the majordomo wrote an account to the Duke, who was then in Pisa, far more marvellous and full of thrilling incidents than what they had narrated.

After I had let my statue cool for two whole days, I began to uncover it by slow degrees. The first thing I found was that the head of Medusa had come out most admirably, thanks to the air-vents; for, as I had told the Duke, it is the nature of fire to ascend. Upon advancing farther, I discovered that the other head, that, namely, of Perseus, had succeeded no less admirably; and this astonished me far more, because it is at a considerably lower level than that of the Medusa. Now the mouths of the mould were placed above the head of Perseus and behind his shoulders; and I found that all the bronze my furnace contained had been exhausted in the head of this figure. It was a miracle to observe that not one fragment remained in the orifice of the channel, and that nothing was wanting to the statue. In my great astonishment I seemed to see in this the hand of God arranging and controlling all.

I went on uncovering the statue with success, and ascertained that everything had come out in perfect order, until I reached the foot of the right leg on which the statue rests. There the heel itself was formed, and going farther, I found the foot apparently complete. This gave me great joy on the one side, but was half unwelcome to me on the other, merely because I had told the Duke that it could not come out. However, when I reached the end, it appeared that the toes and a little piece above them were unfinished, so that about half the foot was wanting. Although I knew that this would add a trifle to my labour, I was very well pleased, because I could now prove to the Duke how well I understood my business. It is true that far more of the foot than I expected had been perfectly formed; the reason of this was that, from causes I have recently described, the bronze was hotter than our rules of art prescribe; also that I had been obliged to supplement the alloy with my pewter cups and platters, which no one else, I think, had ever done before.

Having now ascertained how successfully my work had been accomplished, I lost no time in hurrying to Pisa, where I found the Duke. He gave me a most gracious reception, as did also the Duchess; and although the majordomo had informed them of the whole proceedings, their Excellencies deemed my performance far more stupendous and astonishing when they heard the tale from my own mouth. When I arrived at the foot of Perseus, and said it had not come out perfect, just as I previously warned his Excellency, I saw an expression of wonder pass over his face, while he related to the Duchess how I had predicted this beforehand, observing the princes to be so well disposed towards me, I begged leave from the Duke to go to Rome. He granted it in most obliging terms, and bade me return as soon as possible to complete his Perseus; giving me letters of recommendation meanwhile to his ambassador, Averardo Serristori.

NOTES

[1]A preliminary sketch.

[2]The Sistine Chapel in the Vatican.

[3]Profile portraits of Michelangelo show the bridge of his nose bent, as if it had been broken.

[4]Cellini is now in Rome.

[5]Master of the shop for which Cellini is a journeyman.

[6]Silver coinage *di moneta* was worth ten times coinage *di giuli*. Cellini was paid in golden crowns, which had a much higher value.

[7]Cellini, who has been imprisoned by the Pope—though in commodious quarters—fears the enmity of Messer Durante.

[8]Cosimo de' Medici, Duke of Florence.

[9]A rival artist.

John Calvin

1509-1564

The son of a lawyer and notary in the northern French town of Noyon, John Calvin was sent to the University of Paris at the age of fourteen. While preparing for the priesthood, he came into contact with the humanist and Greek scholar Guillaume Bude and with the important literary figure François Rabelais. After receiving his M.A. at the age of 18, Calvin turned to the study of law at Orleans. He completed all the requirements for his license to practice law, but instead he returned to Paris in 1531 in order to continue his classical studies. It was during this time that Calvin underwent a conversion to Protestantism, and in 1533 he was forced to flee Paris. Settling first at Strasbourg, then at Basel, and finally in Geneva, Calvin published the first edition of his greatest work, *The Institutes of the Christian Religion*, in 1536. He continued to expand this influential theological text throughout the course of his remaining life. From 1541 until his death 23 years later, Calvin was the dominant religious and political personality in Geneva.

Calvin's study of the ancient Stoics brought him into contact with the powerful notion of divine providence. In *The Institutes*, it is the sublime majesty and infinite power of God, not His benevolence as defined by sinful humans, which stands at the center of the Christian story. Developing ideas expressed first by St. Augustine of Hippo and much later by Martin Luther, Calvin insisted that God exercised His divine prerogative in foreordaining some humans for eternal salvation and others for damnation.

In addition to its theological implications, some of which are treated in this selection, the concept of predestination exercised an enormous influence on subsequent social, political, and economic thought, both in Europe and in America. Where Lutheranism was socially conservative and deferential to existing political authority, Calvinism was an activist force committed to reforming all compartments of life. In reading this selection, consider how the emphasis on predestination might come into conflict with Christianity's centuries-old concern with free will and moral accountability. How might the idea of predestination condition social attitudes towards poverty and personal misfortune? Does the Calvinist view of God overlook qualities long thought to be at the heart of the Gospel message? How can we reconcile Calvin the humanist scholar with Calvin the Protestant reformer?

from *Institutes of the Christian Religion*

BOOK II. *Chapter II. Section 3.*

It is impossible for us to think of our first original, for the end for which we were created, without being urged to meditate on immortality, and to seek the kingdom of God. But such meditation, so far from raising our spirits, rather casts them down, and makes us humble. For what is our original? One from which we have fallen. What the end of our creation? One from which we have altogether strayed, so that, weary of our miserable lot, we groan, and groaning sigh for a dignity now lost. When we say that man should see nothing in himself which can raise his spirits, our meaning is, that he possesses nothing on which he can proudly plume himself. Hence, in considering the knowledge which man ought to have of himself, it seems proper to divide thus, first, to consider the end for which he was created, and the qualities—by no means contemptible qualities—with which he was endued, thus urging him to meditate on divine worship and the future life; and, secondly, to consider his faculties, or rather want of faculties—a want which, when perceived, will annihilate all his confidence, and cover him with confusion. The tendency of the former view is to teach him what his duty is, of the latter, to make him aware how far he is able to perform it. We shall treat of both in their proper order.

BOOK II. *Chapter II. Section 4.*

As the act which God punished so severely must have been not a trivial fault but a heinous crime, it will be necessary to attend to the peculiar nature of the sin which produced Adam's fall, and provoked God to inflict such fearful vengeance on the whole human race. The common idea of sensual intemperance is childish. The sum and substance of all virtues could not consist in abstinence from a single fruit amid a general abundance of every delicacy that could be desired, the earth, with happy fertility, yielding not only abundance, but also endless variety. We must, therefore, look deeper than sensual intemperance. The prohibition to touch the tree of the knowledge of good and evil was a trial of obedience, that Adam, by observing it, might prove his willing submission to the command of God. For the very term shows the end of the precept to have been to keep him contented with his lot, and not allow him arrogantly to aspire beyond it. The promise, which gave him hope of eternal life as long as he should eat of the tree of life, and, on the other hand, the fearful denunciation of death the moment he should taste of the tree of the knowledge of good and evil, were meant to prove and exercise his faith. Hence it is not difficult to infer in what way Adam provoked the wrath of God. Augustine, indeed, is not far from the mark, when he says (in Psal. xix.), that pride was the beginning of all evil, because, had not man's ambition carried him higher than he was permitted he might have continued in his first estate. A further definition, however, must be derived from the kind of temptation which Moses describes. When, by the subtlety of the devil, the woman faithlessly abandoned the command of God, her fall obviously had its origin in disobedience. This Paul confirms, when he says, that, by the disobedience of one man, all were destroyed. At the same time, it is to be observed, that the first man revolted against the authority of God, not only in allowing himself to be ensnared by the wiles of the devil, but also by despising the truth, and turning aside to lies. Assuredly, when the word of God is despised, all reverence for Him is gone. His majesty cannot be duly honored among us, nor his worship maintained in its integrity, unless we hang as it were upon his lips. Hence infidelity was at the root of the revolt. From infidelity, again, sprang ambition and pride, together with ingratitude; because Adam, by longing for more than was allotted him, manifested contempt for the great liberality with which God had enriched him. It was surely monstrous impiety that a son of earth should deem it little to have been made in the likeness, unless he were also made the equal of God. If the apostacy by which man withdraws from the authority of his Maker, nay, petulantly shakes off his allegiance to him, is a foul and execrable crime, it is in vain to extenuate the sin of Adam. Nor was it simple apostacy. It was accompanied with foul insult to God, the guilty pair assenting to Satan's calumnies when he charged God with malice, envy, and falsehood. In fine, infidelity opened the door to ambition, and ambition was the parent of rebellion, man casting off the fear of God, and giving free vent to his lust. Hence, Bernard truly says, that, in the present day, a door of salvation is opened to us when we receive the gospel with our ears, just as by the same entrance, when thrown open to Satan, death was admitted. Never would Adam have dared to show any repugnance to the command of God if he had not been incredulous as to his word. The strongest curb to keep all his affections under due restraint, would have been the belief that nothing was better than to cultivate righteousness by obeying the commands of God, and that the highest possible felicity was to be loved by him. Man, therefore, when carried away by the blasphemies of Satan, did his very utmost to annihilate the whole glory of God.

BOOK II. *Chapter II. Section 12*

I feel pleased with the well-known saying which has been borrowed from the writings of Augustine, that man's natural gifts were corrupted by sin, and his supernatural gifts withdrawn; meaning by supernatural gifts the light of faith and righteousness, which would have been sufficient for the attainment of heavenly life and everlasting felicity. Man, when he withdrew his allegiance to God, was deprived of the spiritual gifts by which he had been raised to the hope of eternal salvation. Hence it follows, that he is now an exile from the kingdom of God, so that all things which pertain to the blessed life of the soul are extinguished in him until he recover them by the grace of regeneration. Among these are faith, love to God, charity towards our neighbor, the study of righteousness and holiness. All these, when restored to us by Christ, are to be regarded as adventitious and above nature. If so, we infer that they were previously abolished. On the other hand, soundness of mind and integrity of heart were, at the same time, withdrawn, and it is this which constitutes the corruption of natural gifts. For although there is still some residue of intelligence and judgment as well as will, we cannot call a mind sound and entire which is both weak and immersed in darkness. As to the will, its depravity is but too well known. Therefore, since reason, by which man discerns between good and evil, and by which he understands and judges, is a natural gift, it could not be entirely destroyed; but being partly weakened and partly corrupted, a shapeless ruin is all that remains. In this sense it is said (John 1: 5), that "the light shineth in darkness, and the darkness comprehended it not;" these words clearly expressing both points—viz., that in the perverted and degenerate nature of man there are still some sparks which show that he is a rational animal, and differs from the brutes, inasmuch as he is endued with intelligence, and yet, that this light is so smothered by clouds of darkness, that it cannot shine forth to any good effect. In like manner, the will, because inseparable from the nature of man, did not perish, but was so enslaved by depraved lusts as to be incapable of one righteous desire. The definition now given is complete, but there are several points which require to be explained. Therefore, proceeding agreeably to that primary distinction (Book I. c. xv, sec. 7 and 8), by which we divided the soul into intellect and will, we will now inquire into the power of the intellect.

Chapter XXI: Eternal Election, Or God's Predestination of Some Salvation, And of Others to Destruction

BOOK III. *Chapter XXI. Section 1.*

The covenant of life not being equally preached to all, and among those to whom it is preached not always finding the same reception, this diversity discovers the wonderful depth of the Divine judgment. Nor is it to be doubted that this variety also follows, subject to the decision of God's eternal election. If it be evidently the result of the Divine will, that salvation is freely offered to some, and others are prevented from attaining it—this immediately gives rise to important and difficult questions, which are incapable of any other explication, than by the establishment of pious minds in what ought to be received concerning election and predestination—a question, in the opinion of many, full of perplexity; for they consider nothing more unreasonable, than that, of the common mass of mankind, some should be predestinated to salvation, and others to destruction. But how unreasonably they perplex themselves will afterwards appear from the sequel of our discourse. Besides, the very obscurity which excited such dread, not only displays the utility of this doctrine, but shows it to be productive of the most delightful benefit. We shall never be clearly convinced as we ought to be, that our salvation flows from the fountain of God's free mercy, till we are acquainted with his eternal election, which illustrates the grace of God by this comparison, that he adopts not all promiscuously to the hope of salvation, but gives to some what he refuses to others. Ignorance of this principle evidently detracts from the Divine glory, and diminishes real humility. But according to Paul, what is so necessary to be known, never can be known, unless God, without any regard to works, chooses those whom he has decreed. "At this present time also, there is a remnant according to the election of grace. And if by grace, then it is not more of works; otherwise, grace is not more grace. But if it be of works, then it is no more grace; otherwise, work is no more work." If we need to be recalled to the origin of election, to prove that we obtain salvation from no other source than the mere goodness of God, they who desire to extinguish this principle, do all they can to obscure what ought to be magnificently and loudly celebrated, and to pluck up humility by the roots. In ascribing the salvation of the remnant of the people to the election of grace, Paul clearly testifies, that it is then only known that God saves whom he will of his mere good pleasure, and does not dispense a reward to which there can be no claim. They who shut the gates to prevent any one from presuming to approach and taste this doctrine, do no less injury to man than to God; for nothing else will be sufficient to produce in us suitable humility, or to impress us with a due sense of our great obligations to God. Nor is there any other basis for solid confidence, even according to the authority of Christ, who, to deliver us from all fear, and render us invincible amidst so many dangers, snares, and deadly conflicts, promises to preserve in safety all whom the Father has committed to his care. Whence we infer, that they who know not themselves to be God's peculiar people will be tortured with continual anxiety; and therefore, that the interest of all believers, as well as their own, is very badly consulted by those who, blind to the three advantages we have remarked, would wholly remove the foundation of our salvation. And hence the Church rises to our view, which otherwise, as Bernard justly observes, could neither be discovered nor recognized among creatures, being in two respects wonderfully concealed in the bosom of a blessed predestination, and in the mass of a miserable damnation. But before I enter on the subject itself, I must address some preliminary observations to two sorts of persons. The discussion of predestination—a subject of itself rather intricate—is made very perplexed, and therefore dangerous, by human curiosity, which no barriers can restrain from wandering into forbidden labyrinths, and soaring beyond its sphere, as if determined to leave none of the Divine secrets unscrutinized or unexplored. As we see multitudes every where guilty of this arrogance and presumption, and among them some who are not censurable in other respects, it is proper to admonish them of the bounds of their duty on this subject. First, then, let them remember that when they inquire into predestination, they penetrate the inmost recesses of Divine wisdom, where the careless and confident intruder will obtain no satisfaction to his curiosity, but will enter a labyrinth from which he will find no way to depart. For it is unreasonable that man should scrutinize with impunity those things which the Lord has determined to be hidden in himself; and investigate, even from eternity, that sublimity of wisdom which God would have us to adore and not comprehend, to promote our admiration of his glory. The secrets of his will which he determined to reveal to us, he discovers in his word; and these are all that he foresaw would concern us or conduce to our advantage.

BOOK III. *Chapter XXI. Section 2.*

"We are come into the way of faith," says Augustine; "let us constantly pursue it. It conducts into the king's palace, in which are hidden all the treasures of wisdom and knowledge. For the Lord Christ himself envied not his great and most select disciples when he said, 'I have many things to say unto you, but ye cannot bear them now.' We must walk, we must improve, we must grow, that our hearts may be able to understand those things of which we are at present incapable. If the last day finds us improving, we shall then learn what we never could learn in the present state." If we only consider that the word of the Lord is the only way to lead us to an investigation of all that ought to be believed concerning him, and the only light to enlighten us to behold all that ought to be seen of him, this consideration will easily restrain and preserve us from all presumption. For we shall know that when we have exceeded the limits of the word, we shall get into a devious and darksome course, in which errors, slips, and falls will often be inevitable. Let us, then, in the first place, bear in mind, that to desire any other knowledge of predestination that what is unfolded in the word of God, indicates as great folly, as a wish to walk through unpassable roads, or to see in the dark. Nor let us be ashamed to be ignorant of some things relative to a subject in which there is a kind of learned ignorance. Rather let us abstain with cheerfulness from the pursuit of that knowledge, the affectation of which is foolish, dangerous, and even fatal. But if we are stimulated by the wantonness of intellect, we must oppose it with a reflection calculated to repress it, that as "it is not good to eat much honey, so for men to search their own glory, is not glory." For there is sufficient to deter us from that presumption, which can only precipitate us into ruin.

BOOK III. *Chapter 21. Section 5.*

Predestination, by which God adopts some to the hope of life, and adjudges others to eternal death, no one, desirous of the credit of piety, dares absolutely to deny. But it is involved in many cavils, especially by those who make foreknowledge the cause of it. We maintain, that both belong to God; but it is preposterous to represent one as dependent on the other. When we attribute foreknowledge to God, we mean that all things have ever been, and perpetually remain, before his eyes, so that to his knowledge nothing is future or past, but all things are present; and present in such a manner, that he does not merely conceive of them from ideas formed in his mind, as things remembered by us appear present to our minds, but really beholds and sees them as if actually placed before him. And this foreknowledge extends to the whole world, and to all the creatures. Predestination we call the eternal decree of God, by which he has determined in himself, what he would have to become of every individual of mankind. For they are not all created with a similar destiny; but eternal life is foreordained for some, and eternal damnation for others. Every man, therefore, being created for one or the other of these ends, we say, he is predestinated either to life or to death. This God has not only testified in particular persons, but has given a specimen of it in the whole posterity of Abraham, which should evidently show the future condition of every nation to depend upon his decision. "When the Most High divided the nations, when he separated the sons of Adam, the Lord's portion was his people; Jacob was the lot of his inheritance." The separation is before the eyes of all: in the person of Abraham, as in the dry trunk of a tree, one people is peculiarly chosen to the rejection of others: no reason for this appears, except that Moses, to deprive their posterity of all occasion of glorying, teaches them that their exaltation is wholly from God's gratuitous love. He assigns this reason for their deliverance, that "he loved their fathers, and chose their seed after them." More fully in another chapter: "The Lord did not set his love upon you, nor choose you, because you were more in number than any people; but because the Lord loved you." He frequently repeats the same admonition: "Behold, the heaven is the Lord's thy God, the earth also, with all that therein is. Only the Lord had a delight in thy fathers to love them, and he chose their seed after them." In another place, sanctification is enjoined upon them, because they were chosen to be a peculiar people. And again, elsewhere, love is asserted to be the cause of their protection. It is declared by the united voice of the faithful, "He hath chosen our inheritance for us, the excellency Jacob, whom he loved." For the gifts conferred on them by God, they all ascribe to gratuitous love, not only from a consciousness that these were not obtained by any merit of theirs, but from a conviction, that the holy patriarch himself was not endued with such excellence as to acquire the privilege of so great an honour for himself and his posterity.

Chapter VI: The Life of A Christian. Scriptural Arguments and Exhortations to It

BOOK III. *Chapter VI. Section 1.*

We have said that the end of regeneration is, that the life of believers may exhibit a symmetry and agreement between the righteousness of God and their obedience; and that thus they may confirm the adoption by which they are accepted as his children. But though the law of God contains in it that newness of life by which his image is restored in us, yet since our tardiness needs much stimulation and assistance, it will be useful to collect from various places of Scripture a rule for the reformation of the life, that they who cordially repent may not be bewildered in their pursuits. Now, when I undertake the regulation of a Christian's life, I know that I am entering on an argument various and copious, and the magnitude of which might fill a large volume, if I designed a complete discussion of every part of it. For we see to what great prolixity the fathers have extended the exhortations composed by them only on single virtues; and that without any excessive loquacity; for, whatever virtue it is intended to recommend in an oration, the copiousness of the matter naturally produces such a diffusiveness of style, that unless you have spoken largely, you seem not to have done justice to the subject. But my design is not to extend the plan of life, which I am now about to deliver, so far as particularly to discourse on each distinct virtue, and expatiate into exhortations. These things may be sought in the writings of others, especially in the homilies of the fathers. It will be sufficient for me if I point out a method by which a pious man may he conducted to the right end in the regulation of his life, and briefly assign a universal rule, which he may properly estimate his duties. There will, perhaps at some future period be a suitable opportunity for declamations; or I shall leave to others an office for which I am not calculated. I am naturally fond of brevity; and, perhaps, were I desirous of speaking in a more copious manner, I should not succeed. And if a more prolix method of teaching were most acceptable, yet I should scarcely be inclined to make the trial. The plan of the present work, however, requires me to treat a simple doctrine with all possible brevity. As the philosophers have certain principles of rectitude and honour, whence they deduce particular duties and the whole circle of virtues, so the Scripture is not without its order in this respect, but maintains an economy superlatively beautiful, and far more certain, than all the systems of the philosophers. There is only this difference—that, the philosophers being ambitious men, they have sedulously affected an exquisite perspicuity of method, in order to make an ostentatious display of their ingenious dexterity. But the Spirit, whose teaching is void of affectation, has not so exactly or perpetually served a methodical plan; which, nevertheless, by using it in some places, he sufficiently indicates ought not to be neglected by us.

BOOK III. *Chapter VI. Section 2.*

This Scripture plan, of which we are now treating, consists chiefly in these two things—the first, that a love of righteousness to which we have otherwise no natural propensity, be instilled and introduced into our hearts; the second that a rule be prescribed to us, to prevent our taking any devious steps in the race of righteousness. Now, in the recommendation of righteousness, it uses a great number of very excellent arguments, many of which we have before noticed on different occasions, and some we shall briefly touch on in this place. With what better foundation can it begin, than when it admonishes us that we ought to be holy, because our God is holy? For when we were dispersed like scattered sheep, and lost in the labyrinth of the world, he gathered us together again, that he might associate us to himself. When we hear any mention of our union with God, we should remember that holiness must be the bond of it; not that we attain communion with him by the merit of holiness, (since it is rather necessary for us, in the first place, to adhere to him, in order that, being endued with his holiness, we may follow whither he calls;) but because it is a peculiar property of his glory not to have any intercourse with iniquity and uncleanness. Wherefore also it teaches, that this is the end of our vocation, which it is requisite for us always to keep in view, if we desire to correspond to the design of God in calling us. For to what purpose was it that we were delivered from the iniquity and pollution of the world, in which we had been immerged, if we permit ourselves to wallow in them as long as we live? Besides, it also admonishes us that, to be numbered among the people of God, we must inhabit the holy city of Jerusalem; which, he having consecrated it to himself, cannot without impiety be profaned by impure inhabitants. Whence these expressions: "He shall abide in the tabernacle of the Lord, that walketh uprightly and worketh righteousness," and etc., because it is very unbecoming the sanctuary which he inhabits, to be rendered as filthy as a stable.

BOOK III. *Chapter VI. Section 3.*

And as a further incitement to us, it shows, that as God the father has reconciled us to himself in Christ, so he has exhibited to us in him a pattern, to which it is his will that we should be conformed. Now, let those who are of opinion that the philosophers have the only just and orderly systems of moral philosophy, show me, in any of their works, a more excellent economy than that which I have stated. When they intend to exhort us to the sublimest virtue, they advance no argument but that we ought to live agreeably to nature; but the Scripture deduces its exhortation from the true source, when it not only enjoins us to refer our life to God the author of it, to whom it belongs, but, after having taught us, that we are degenerated from the original state in which we were created, adds, that Christ, by whom we have been reconciled to God, is proposed to us as an example, whose character we should exhibit in our lives. What can be required more efficacious than this one consideration? Indeed, what can be required besides? For if the Lord has adopted us as his sons on this condition,—that we exhibit in our life an imitation of Christ the bond of our adoption,—unless we addict and devote ourselves to righteousness, we not only most perfidiously revolt from our Creator, but also abjure him as our Saviour. The Scripture derives matter of exhortation from all the blessings of God which it recounts to us, and from all the parts of our salvation. It argues, that since God has discovered himself as a Father to us, we must be convicted of the basest ingratitude, unless we, on out part, manifest ourselves to be his children; that since Christ has purified us in the layer of his blood, and has communicated this purification by baptism, it does not become us to be defiled with fresh pollution; that since he has united us to his body, we should, as his members, solicitously beware lest we asperse ourselves with any blemish or disgrace; that since he who is our Head has ascended to heaven, we ought to divest ourselves of all terrestrial affection, and aspire thither with all our soul; that since the Holy Spirit has dedicated us as temples to God, we should use our utmost exertions, that the glory of God may be displayed by us; and ought not to allow ourselves to be profaned with the pollution of sin; that since both our soul and our body are destined to heavenly incorruption and a never-fading crown, we ought to exert our most strenuous efforts to preserve them pure and uncorrupt till the day of the Lord. These I say, are the best foundations for the proper regulation of the life, such as we cannot find in the philosophers; who, in the recommendation of virtue, never rise above the natural dignity of man.

Louise Labé

1520–1566

Louise Labé's writings, and the author herself, have enjoyed a recent popularity among students and scholars of Renaissance women writers. Little is known of her life. She was born into a family of successful merchants. She lived in Lyons, which in the early 1500s was, like Paris, a thriving cultural center.

While we don't know many factual details of Labé's life, we do have an interesting record of her legend. There seems to have been a heated contemporary debate over her personal integrity; was she a scandalous, promiscuous woman who transgressed social and sexual boundaries or was she a virtuous, learned artist? Of course, the connection in women between a loquacious tongue and a lascivious body was a common strategy employed to encourage women to remain outside of the public sphere. Labé's only published material, entitled *Oeuvres* (1555), met with success since a second edition was published a year later, and a pirated version appeared shortly thereafter.

The dedicatory letter included here illustrates the sixteenth-century quarrels over women. In the letter she appeals to women to establish their right to read and write. How can you read Labé's epistle as an extension of Marie de France's argument of using one's gifts? The sonnets represent Labé's most frequently studied material and demonstrate her insertion into the humanist program as well as her divergence from it. Her use of the sonnet form is at once conventional and new. As you read the poems look for such commonplace traits as the expression of unrequited love, the cold and distant lover, the veiled autobiographical plot and the expression of frustration and desire. Does Labé's poetry seem "gendered" in any way? How might you compare her sonnets to Petrarch's or Shakespeare's?

from *Oeuvres*

T[o] M[ademoiselle] C[le'mence] d[e] B[ourges, of] L[yons]

Now that the time has come, Mademoiselle, that men's harsh laws no longer prevent women from devoting themselves to the arts and sciences, it seems to me that those who have the opportunity ought to study them, using the rightful freedom that members of our sex have so ardently desired in the past. In this way we can show men the wrong they have done us by preventing our getting the benefit and recognition that we could have derived from such study. If any one of us reaches the point where she can set down her thoughts in writing, she ought to do so carefully, not shunning the recognition, but rather adorning herself with it instead of with chains, rings, and sumptuous clothes. These things cannot really be considered ours. They are only thought to be ours because we use them. But the honor that our knowledge brings us will be entirely our own. Neither a robber's craft, nor an enemy's force, nor the passage of time can take them away from us.

Had I been blessed with a mind capable of understanding whatever it wanted to, I would set a good example rather than admonishing others. Since I spent part of my youth training myself in music, however, and since I found the time that remained too short for my unsophisticated mind, and since I cannot, by myself, satisfy my desire to see our sex surpass or equal men, not only in beauty, but in knowledge and virtue, I can only urge noble women to raise their minds somewhat above their distaffs and spindles, and to devote themselves to showing the world that our not being fit for command does not mean that we should be looked down upon as partners either in domestic or in public affairs by those who govern and are in a position of authority. Such study will contribute not only to the reputation of our sex, but to the general good, for men will put more effort into all branches of learning, because they would be ashamed to be surpassed by women over whom they have always claimed superiority in almost everything.

We ought, therefore, to encourage each other in such a laudable undertaking. You yourself should spare no effort and should not dismiss it from your mind—already graced with so many diverse accomplishments. You should devote your youth and the means with which fortune has favored you to acquiring the recognition that letters and learning usually bestow on their followers. There is something else besides the recognition and reputation to recommend the study of letters: the pleasure that it normally brings should encourage every one of us to pursue it. Such pleasure is different from other pastimes, for when someone has had enough of them, he can boast only of having put in his time. Study, on the other hand, gives an inner satisfaction that lasts much longer.

We enjoy the past, and it is more useful than the present. Pleasures involving the senses are immediately lost, never to return, and sometimes our memory of them is as distressing as the acts were delightful. It is even truer of other pleasures: whatever our memories of them are, they cannot recapture the mood of the moment. No matter how vivid an image is etched in our minds, we know perfectly well that it is only a shadow—misleading and deceiving us. However, if we have put our thoughts down in writing, then even if we are preoccupied and distracted by any number of things, we can relive the situation and mood that prevailed at that time by re-reading what we wrote.

Then our satisfaction is two-fold, for we renew the pleasure that we once found either in the subject that we were describing or in the understanding of the fields of knowledge that we were pursuing at the time; and, in addition, being able to judge our original opinions brings a special satisfaction of its own. The two advantages ought to encourage you to take up writing. You may be sure that the first cannot fail to be associated with your writings, as it does all of your other actions and your way life. As for the second, it will depend on you and on the pleasure you get from the subjects on which you write.

As for myself, both when I first wrote these juvenilia and more recently when I came to look them over again, I was looking only for a respectable pastime and a way to keep busy. I never intended anyone else to see them. But since some my friends have managed to read them without my knowledge, and since (how readily we believe those who praise us) they have led me to believe that they should be published; I did not dare refuse outright, but I did threaten to make them responsible for half of the shame that might ensue.

Since women hesitate to appear in public alone, I have chosen you to be my guide, by dedicating this little book to you. I do so only to assure you of the good will that I have so long felt toward you and to encourage you, when you have seen my own rough, poorly-constructed work, to bring out one of your own, better polished and more beautiful.

God keep you in good health.

Lyons, July 24, 1555

Your humble friend, Louise Labé

SONNETS

VII

All that lives is under death's control
When from the body the subtle soul departs;
I am the body, you the better part;
Where are you, then, my well-beloved soul?

Leave me not so long as in a swoon;
To save me later, you would come too late;
Abandon not your body to this fate,
But its more worthy half give back, and soon.

And grant, my love, that I need fear from you
No danger when love's meetings we renew.
Accepting them, not with severity,
Not stiffly, but with such a kindly grace
As will gently give me back your lovely face
That has been cruel but smiles once more on me.

VIII

I live, I die, I drown, and yet I burn;
I'm far too hot while it is bitter cold.
My life is too relaxed and too controlled;
Great cares I have, and then some joys return.

Both tears and laughter have me in their power;
And in the midst of pleasure, grief is sure.
Well-being leaves and ever shall endure.
I wither at the moment that I flower.

Love leads me thus on an ever-changing way;
And when I think I suffer increased pain,
I suddenly shall find my sorrow gone.

Then, when I think joy cannot be withdrawn,
I have the happiness for which I pray,
He thrusts me back in my first grief again.

XVIII

Kiss me. Again. More kisses I desire.
Give me one your sweetness to express.
Give me the most passionate you possess.
Four I'll return, and hotter than the fire.

There, did they burn? I'll change that hurt to pleasure
By giving you ten others—all quite light.
Thus, as we mingle our kisses with delight,
Let us enjoy each other at our leisure.

This to teach one a double life shall give.
Each by himself and in his love shall live.
Allow my love this mad and foolish thought:

I'm always sad when living so discreetly,
And never find my happiness completely,
Unless a sally from my self I've sought.

ELIZABETH I, QUEEN OF ENGLAND

1533-1603

Elizabeth Tudor, daughter of King Henry the VIII of England and his second wife Anne Boleyn, ascended the throne in 1558 and ruled England for nearly fifty years. During that period, England and the rest of Western Europe underwent tremendous social, spiritual and political change. Hers was the age of "discovery," of the Protestant Reformation, of the growth of London into a mercantile city with newly emerging social classes. Her rule during these turbulent times was remarkable for a number of reasons, the most obvious being that she was a woman who governed a culture still medieval in its ideas about women's location on the "great chain of being."

As a ruler, and as an aristocratic woman who had the rare opportunity of receiving a humanist education, Elizabeth was well aware of these ideas and worked to alleviate the anxieties and tensions brought about by her presence on the throne. One of her strategies for quelling the fears of her subjects revolved around the medieval doctrine, also used by her father, that the monarch had two bodies: a body natural and a body politic. Scholars refer to this term as "the King's two bodies," which, when applied to Elizabeth, is called—predictably—"the Queen's two bodies." In this scheme, Elizabeth makes a distinction between her frail, womanly "body natural" and her strong, spiritually gender-free "body politic." When addressing her people or her parliament on important issues of state, she frequently employed this notion and we can see it at work in the rhetoric of her speeches.

Elizabeth's accomplishments as a writer have only recently been the subject of scholarly attention. She translated Marguerite de Naravrre's *Mirror of the Sinful Soul* (ca. 1544), wrote occasional poetry, a complete book of original prayers and other translations of religious works. By far, the works which have interested scholars most have been her political letters and speeches. These works are significant not only as an illustration of her rhetorical skills, but as documents that reveal how an individual in power shapes herself and creates a distinct political persona.

The following selections of Elizabeth's public speaking reflect the Queen in moments when the political and the personal intersect. One complication when studying Elizabeth's speeches is that many different versions survive and each seems to reflect a slight shift in emphasis for a particular audience (or a particular political agenda). For this reason, we offer two versions of the Marriage speeches of 1559, which reflect how the Queen, shortly after she came to the throne, responded to a parliamentary delegation who urged her to marry early. The first speech was published in William Camden's *The History of the most renowned and victorious princess Elizabeth* (the English translation was published in 1688); the second in Simond D'Ewes's *A compleat journal of the votes, speeches, and debates both of the House of Lords and of the House of Commons* (published in 1693). The speeches can be compared on a number of levels: the first speech was informal and spontaneous; the second, cautious and evasive. Both speeches showcase Elizabeth's skill as a speaker and as a politician. The other selections, "The Tilbury Speech" and "The Golden Speech" of 1601, demonstrate the Queen's keen political savvy and her astute ability simultaneously to emphasize and diminish her sex.

How do the various strategies discussed above work in these readings? What might the speeches reveal about Renaissance notions of the individual? Of public versus private? Man versus woman? Of the relationship between a ruler and her subjects? Would Machiavelli have approved of Elizabeth as a "prince"? Why or why not?

The Public Speeches

MARRIAGE SPEECH
or
The History
of the
Most Renowned and Victorious
Princess
Elizabeth,
Late Queen of England
Containing All the Most Important and Remarkable Passages
of State, both at Home and Abroad
(so far as they were linked with English Affairs)
during her
Long and Prosperous Reign
Written by William Camden,
Clarenceux King at Arms.

When the Assembly of Parliament was now to be dissolved, they all thought good that the Third Estate, or Lower House, should advise the Queen to marry betimes: yet would not the Temporal Lords join with them, lest any of them might seem to propound it in hope to prefer himself. Thomas Gargrave therefore, Speaker of the Lower House, with some few selected men, after leave obtained, came unto the Queen, and making his excuse by his office, the queen's courtesy, and the weightiness of the matter, went forward to this purpose:

"There is nothing which with more ardent affection we beg of God in our daily prayers, than that our happiness hitherto received by your most gracious government may be perpetuated to the English nation unto all eternity; whilst in our mind and cogitation we cast many ways how this may be effected, we can find none at all, unless your Majesty should either reign for ever, (which to hope for is not lawful;) or else by marriage bring forth children, heirs both of their mother's virtue and empire, (which God Almighty grant). This is the single, the only, the all-comprehending prayer of all Englishmen. All other men, of what place and degree soever, but especially princes, must have a care, that though themselves be mortal, yet the Commonwealth may continue immortal. This immortality may your Majesty give to the English, if (as your humane nature, age, beauty and fortune do require), you will take some man to your husband, who may be a comfort and help unto you, and a consort in prosperity and adversity. For (questionless) more availeth the help of one only husband for the effecting of matters, than the joint industry of many men. Nothing can be more contrary to the public respects, than that such a princess, in whose marriage is comprehended the safety and peace of the Commonwealth, should live unmarried, and as it were a vestal virgin. A kingdom received from ancestors is to be left to children, who will be both an ornament and strength to the realm. The kings of England have never been more careful of any thing, than that the royal family might not fail of issue. Hence it was, that within our fresh memory Henry the VII your grandfather, provided his sons Arthur and Henry of marriage even in their tender years. Hence it was that your father sought to procure Mary Queen of Scots to be a wife for his young son Prince Edward, then scarce eight years old: and very lately your sister, Queen Mary, being well in years, married Philip of Spain. If lack of children use to be inflicted by God as a great punishment as well upon royal as private families; what and how great a sin may it be, if the prince voluntarily pluck it upon himself, whereby an infinite heap of miseries must needs overwhelm the Commonwealth with all calamities which the mind even dreadeth to remember? Which that it may not come to pass, not only we few that are here to present, but even all England, yea all English men, do prostrate our selves at your feet, and with humble voice and frequent sighs do from the bottom of our hearts most submissively pray and beseech you."

These things spake he eloquently and more amply. She answered briefly:

"In a matter most unpleasing, most pleasing to me is the apparent good will of you and my people, as proceeding from a very good mind towards me and the Commonwealth. Concerning marriage, which ye so earnestly move me to, I have been long since persuaded, that I was sent into this world by God to think and do those things chiefly which may tend to his glory. Hereupon have I chosen that kind of life which is most free from the troublesome cares of this world, that I might attend the service of God alone. From which if either the tendred marriages of most potent princes, or the danger of death intended against me, could have removed me, I had long agone enjoyed the honor of an husband. And these things have I thought upon when I was a private person. But now that the public care of governing the kingdom is laid upon me, to draw upon me also the cares of marriage may seem a point of inconsiderate folly. Yea, to satisfy you, I have already joined myself in marriage to an husband, namely, the kingdom of England. And behold" (said she which I marvel ye have forgotten) "the pledge of this my wedlock and marriage with my kingdom."

(And therewith she drew the ring from her finger, and showed it, wherewith at her coronation she had in a set form of words solemnly given herself in marriage to her Kingdom.) Here having made a pause:

"And do not" (saith she) "upbraid me with miserable lack of children: for every one of you, and as many as are Englishmen, are children and kinsmen to me; of whom if God deprive me not, (which God forbid) I cannot without injury be accounted barren. But I commend you that ye have not appointed me an husband, for that were most unworthy the majesty of an absolute princess, and unbeseeming your wisdom, which are subjects born. Nevertheless if it please God that I enter into another course of life, I promise you I will do nothing which may be prejudicial to the Commonwealth, but will take such a husband, as near as may be, as will have as great a care of the Commonwealth as myself. But if I continue in this kind of life I have begun, I doubt not but God will so direct mine own and your counsels, that ye shall not need to doubt of a successor which may be more beneficial to the Commonwealth than he which may be born of me, considering that the issue of the best princes many times degenerateth. And to me it shall be a full satisfaction, both for the memorial of my name, and for my glory also, if when I shall let my last breath, it be engraven upon my marble tomb, 'Here lieth Elizabeth, which reigned a virgin, and died a virgin'."

Marriage Speech

Journals of all the Parliaments
During the Reign of
Queen Elizabeth
both of the
House of Lords
and
House of Commons
Collected By SIR SIMONDS D'EWES
of Stow-Hall in the County
Of Suffolk, Knight and Baronet.

It was ordered by the House, that Mr. Speaker with all the Privy-Council, and thirty other members of the same, should attend upon the Queen this afternoon, to petition her Majesty, touching her marriage, in such manner and form, as had been on Saturday last agreed upon; but whether they were admitted to her Majesties presence, doth not appear, nor can possibly be gathered out of the original journal-book of the House of Commons; neither in what manner their petition was framed, although it is plain by her Majesties answer, inserted at large, on Friday the 10th day of this instant February ensuing, that it was only general, to persuade her Majesty, for the welfare of her state and Kingdom, to be pleased to marry, without limiting the time, person or place. And howsoever, whether this aforesaid petition were delivered this afternoon or no, most likely it is, that her Majesty deferred, and took time to give an answer in so weighty a business, until the said 10th day of February aforesaid, which I do the rather gather, not only from the above-mentioned original journal-book itself, in which there is no report or mention of her Majesties speech, made unto the House by the Speaker, until in the forenoon of the said day; but also from an ancient written copy of her Majesties said answer, which I had by me, in which it is referred unto the said 10th day of February, as then uttered by her, which will also more fully appear in the passages of the said day, where it is at large set down.

Friday 10 Feb. Mr. Speaker declared the Queens Majesties answer to the message, which was read to the House by Mr. Mason, to the great honor of the Queen, and the contentation of this House; which is all that is contained in the original journal-book of the House of Commons, touching this great business of their petition, preferred to her Majesty, to induce her to marry; and therefore it shall not be amiss to leave some larger memorial thereof; for this business, having been first propounded and resolved on in the said House, on Saturday the 4th day of this instant February foregoing, and preferred to her Majesty (as it should seem) on the Monday following in the afternoon, was not answered by her Majesty until this morning, and was then also read in the said House; as appeareth by the foregoing imperfect mentioning thereof. And I am the rather induced to conceive, that her Majesty gave not her answer until this morning, to the said petition of the Commons, from a copy of the said answer, which I have by me, written by Alexander Evesham, which said answer out of the said copy (in which it is referred to this instant 10th day of February) with the title and subscription thereof, do now in the next place follow, verbatim.

Friday 10th of Feb. 1558. &c. The answer of the Queens Highness, to the petition propounded unto her, by the Lower House, concerning her marriage.

"As I have good cause, so do I give you all my hearty thanks, for the good zeal and loving care you seem to have, as well towards me, as to the whole estate of your country. Your petition I perceive consisteth of three parts, and my answer to the same shall depend of two.

And to the first part, I may say unto you, that from my years of understanding, sith I first had consideration of my self to be born a servant of Almighty God, I happily chose this kind of life, in the which I yet live: which, I assure you, for mine own part, hath hitherto best contented my self, and I trust hath been most acceptable unto God: from the which, if either ambition of high estate, offered to me in marriage, by the pleasure and appointment of my prince (whereof I have some record in this presence, as you our treasurer well know) or if eschewing the danger of mine enemies, or the avoiding of the peril of death, whose messenger, or rather a continual watchman, the princes indignation, was no little time daily before mine eyes (by whose means—although I know, or justly may suspect—yet I will not now utter, or if the whole cause were in my sister herself, I will not now burthen her therewith, because I will not charge the dead) if any of these, I say, could have drawn, or dissuaded me from this kind of life, I had not now remained in this estate, wherein you see me. But so constant have I always continued in this determination, although my youth and words may seem to some hardly to agree together, yet is it most true, that at this day I stand free from any other meaning, that either I have had in times past, or have at this present; with which trade of life I am so thoroughly acquainted, that I trust, God, who hath hitherto therein preserved and led me by the hand, will not of his goodness suffer me to go alone.

For the other part, the manner of your petition I do well like, and take it in good part, because it is simple, and containeth no limitation of place or person; if it had been otherwise, I must needs have misliked it very much, and thought it in you a very great presumption, being unfitting and altogether unmeet for you to require them, that may command; or those to appoint whose parts are to desire, or such to bind and limit, whose duties are to obey, or to take upon you to draw my love to your liking, or to frame my will to your fantasy: For a guerdon constrained, and gift freely given, can never agree together. Nevertheless, if any of you be in suspect, whensoever it may please God to incline my heart to another kind of life, you may very well assure yourselves, my meaning is not to determine any thing, wherewith the realm may or shall have just cause to be discontented. And therefore put that clean out of your heads. For I assure you (what credit my assurance may have with you, I cannot tell, but what credit it shall deserve to have, the sequel shall declare) I will never in that matter conclude any thing that shall be prejudicial to the realm. For the well, good and safety whereof, I will never shun to spend my life, and whomsoever my chance shall be to light upon, I trust he shall be such, as shall be as careful for the realm, as you; I will not say as myself, because I cannot so certainly determine of any other, but by my desire he shall be such as shall be as careful for the preservation of the realm, and you, as myself. And albeit it might please Almighty God to continue me still in this mind, to live out of the state of marriage, yet is it not to be feared but he will so work in my heart, and in your wisdom, as good provision by his help may be made, whereby the realm shall not remain destitute of an heir that may be a fit governor, and peradventure more beneficial to the realm than such off-spring as may come of me. For though I be never so careful of your well doing, and mind ever so to be, yet may my issue grow out of kind, and become perhaps ungracious, and in the end, this shall be for me sufficient, that a marble stone shall declare, that a Queen having reigned such a time, lived and died a virgin. And here I end, and take your coming to me in good part, and give unto you all my hearty thanks, more yet for your zeal and good meaning, than for your petition."

And under her Majesties answer aforesaid, was subscribed in the same hand, as followeth.

This was copied out of a printed copy, garnished with gilt letters, given to the Honorable the Lady Stafford, of her Majesties Privy Chamber, and written out by Alexander Evesham, 1590. By which subscription the authenticknes of this Copy doth sufficiently appear.

To the Troops at Tilbury, 1588

My loving people: We have been persuaded by some that are careful of our safety to take heed how we commit ourselves to armed multitudes for fear of treachery. But I assure you I do not desire to live to distrust my faithful and loving people. Let tyrants fear! I have always so behaved myself that under God I have placed my chief strength and safeguard in the loyal hearts and good will of my subjects. And therefore I am come amongst you, as you see, at this time, not for my recreation and disport; but being resolved in the midst of the heat of the battle to live or die amongst you all; to lay down for my God and for my Kingdom and for my people my honor and my blood even in the dust.

I know I have the body but of a weak and feeble woman; but I have the heart and stomach of a king, and of a king of England too, and think foul scorn that Parma or Spain or any prince of Europe should dare to invade the borders of my realm; to which, rather than any dishonor should grow by me, I myself will take up arms; I myself will be your general, judge, and rewarder of every one of your virtues in the field.

I know already, for your forwardness you have deserved rewards and crowns; and we do assure you on the word of a prince they shall be duly paid you.

In the meantime, my lieutenant-general shall be in my stead, than whom never prince commanded a more noble or worthy subject; not doubting but by your obedience to my general, by your concord in the camp, and your valor in the field, we shall shortly have a famous victory over those enemies of my God, of my kingdoms, and of my people.

The Golden Speech of 1601

Mr. Speaker: We have heard your declaration and perceive your care of our state, by falling into the consideration of a grateful acknowledgment of such benefits as you have received; and that your coming is to present thanks unto us, which I accept with no less joy than your loves can have desire to offer such a present. I do assure you that there is no prince that loveth his subjects better, or whose love can countervail our love. There is no jewel, be it of never so rich a prize, which I prefer before this jewel, I mean your love, for I do more esteem it than any treasure or riches, for that we know how to prize, but love and thanks I count inestimable. And though God has raised me high, yet this I count the glory of my crown, that I have reigned with your loves. This makes me that I do not so much rejoice that God hath made me to be a queen as to be a queen over so thankful a people. Therefore I have cause to wish nothing more than to content the subject, and that is a duty which I owe. Neither do I desire to live longer days than that I may see your prosperity, and that is my only desire. And as I am that person that still, yet under God, hath delivered you, so I trust, by the almighty power of God, that I still shall be His instrument to preserve you from envy, peril, dishonor, shame, tyranny, and oppression, partly by means of your intended helps, which we take very acceptably, because it manifests the largeness of your loves and loyalties unto your sovereign. Of myself I must say this: I never was any greedy, scraping grasper, nor a strait fast-holding prince, nor yet a waster; my heart was never set on worldly goods, but only for my subjects' good. What you do bestow on me I will not hoard up, but receive it to bestow on you again. Yea, mine own properties I count yours, to be expended for your good. Therefore render unto them, I beseech you, Mr. Speaker, such thanks as you imagine my heart yieldeth, but my tongue cannot express.

[During these words the assemblage had knelt. Because she had yet more to say and was conscious of their possible discomfort, Elizabeth invited the men to stand.]

Mr. Speaker, I would wish you and the rest to stand up, for I shall yet trouble you with longer speech.

Mr. Speaker, you give me thanks, but I doubt me I have more cause to thank you all than you me: and I charge you to thank them of the House of Commons from me, for had I not received a knowledge from you, I might have fallen into the lap of an error only for lack of true information. Since I was queen, yet never did I put my pen to any grant, but that upon pretext and semblance made unto me that it was both good and beneficial to the subjects in general, though a private profit to some of my ancient servants who had deserved well. But the contrary being found by experience, I am exceedingly beholding to such subjects as would move the same at first. And I am not so simple to suppose but that there be some of the Lower House whom these grievances never touched, and for them I think they speak out of zeal to their countries and not out of spleen or malevolent affection, as being parties grieved. And I take it exceeding grateful from them because it gives us to know that no respects or interests had moved them, other than the minds they bear to suffer no diminution of our honor and our subjects' love unto us. The zeal of which affection, tending to ease my people and knit their hearts unto me, I embrace with a princely care. Far above all earthly treasure I esteem my people's love, more than which I desire not to merit. That my grants should be grievous to my people and oppressions to be privileged under color of our patents, our kingly dignity shall not suffer it. Yea, when I heard it, I could give no rest to my thoughts until I had reformed it. Shall they think to escape unpunished that have thus oppressed you and have been respectless of their duty and regardless of our honor? No. Mr. Speaker, I assure you, were it more for conscience sake than for any glory or increase of love that I desire these errors, troubles, vexations, and oppressions done by these varlets and lewd persons, not worthy the name of subjects, should not escape without condign punishment. But I perceive they dealt with me like physicians who, ministering a drug, make it more acceptable by giving it a good aromatical savour, or when they give pills, do gild them all over. I have ever used to set the last judgment day before mine eyes and so to rule as I shall be judged to answer before a higher Judge. To whose judgment seat I do appeal that never thought was cherished in my heart that tended not to my people's good. And if my kingly bounty have been abused and my grants turned to the hurt of my people, contrary to my will and meaning, or if any in authority under me have neglected or perverted what I have committed to them, I hope God will not lay their culps and offences to my charge. And though there were danger in repealing our grants, yet what danger would not I rather incur for your own good, than I would suffer them still to continue? I know the title of a king is a glorious title, but assure yourself that the shining glory of princely authority hath not so dazzled the eyes of our understanding but that we well know and remember that we also are to yield an account of our actions before the Great Judge. To be a king and wear a crown is more glorious to them that see it than it is pleasure to them that bear it. For myself, I was never so much enticed with the glorious name of a king or royal authority of a queen as delighted that God hath made me this instrument to maintain His truth and glory, and to defend this kingdom, as I said, from peril, dishonor, tyranny, and oppression. There will never queen sit in my seat with more zeal to my country or care to my subjects, and that will sooner with willingness yield and venture her life for your good and safety than myself. And though you have had and may have many princes more mighty and wise sitting in this seat, yet you never had or shall have any that will be more careful and loving. Should I ascribe anything to myself and my sexly weakness, I were not worthy to live then, and of all most unworthy of the mercies I have had from God, Who hath ever yet given me a heart which never yet feared foreign or home enemies. I speak it to give God the praise as a testimony before you, and not to attribute anything unto myself. For I, O Lord, what am I, whom practices and perils past should not fear! O what can I do that I should speak for any glory! God forbid. This, Mr. Speaker, I pray you deliver unto the House, to whom heartily recommend me. And so I commit you all to your best fortunes and further counsels. And I pray you, Mr. Comptroller, Mr. Secretary, and you of my council, that before these gentlemen depart into their countries, you bring them all to kiss my hand.

Philippe Duplessis Mornay

1549-1623

The second half of the sixteenth century in France was a time of violent religious strife and political instability. At the height of the chaos, the young King Charles IX, perhaps influenced by his mother Catherine de' Medici, ordered an attack on the minority Protestant population (known as Huguenots) of Paris. Upwards of 10,000 Huguenots were murdered in what was later referred to as the "St. Bartholomew's Day Massacre" of 1572, and the killing soon spread into the countryside. In the face of such terror, where the very survival of French Protestantism lay in the balance, powerful theories of resistance were put forward in order to counter the prerogative claims of the monarch.

A Defense of Liberty against Tyrants (1579) is perhaps the most important of these resistance theories. Although scholars still debate its authorship, the most likely candidate is the Philippe Duplessis Mornay, a nobleman and adviser to the Protestant leader Henry of Navarre. Originally published in Latin but quickly translated into French in 1581, the *Defense* appeared in English in 1648, one year before the execution of King Charles I by his own Calvinist subjects (referred to derisively as Puritans). Mornay's demand that "Kings and magistrates who have received the sword from the people as a whole, should make sure that the general body of the Church is rightly governed" certainly resonated in both French and English Calvinist communities.

More importantly, the book sought to outline two essential contracts around which the lives of all persons are regulated, the first between God and the people, and a second between the temporal ruler and his subjects. For Mornay, it was the first contract which took precedence; thus, the magistrate who willfully and consistently violated his or her trust forfeited any claim to his subjects's obedience. In reading this selection, recall our Humanities 214 theme on the relationship between the individual and society. Is civil society or government the product of divine will, or is it simply a human artifact or creation, capable of amendment when necessary? While *A Defense of Liberty against Tyrants* may advocate resistance to unjust authority, is justice defined in categories that we would find comfortable?

from *Vindiciae contra Tyrannos*
[A Defense of Liberty against Tyrants]

The First Question
WHETHER SUBJECTS BE BOUND, OR OUGHT, TO OBEY PRINCES IF THEY COMMAND ANYTHING AGAINST THE LAW OF GOD?

At first sight this question may appear to be altogether superfluous and pointless, since it seems to call into doubt—as if there were still room for argument—what is assuredly the most certain axiom held by Christians, proven by so many testimonies in Holy Scripture, by so many examples from different ages and so many pyres of pious martyrs. For whence, you may say have arisen so many great tribulations of the pious, if not from this single cause: that they have always considered that God should be obeyed simply and absolutely, but kings only in so far as they command nothing against the law of God? Why otherwise the opinion of the apostles, that God should be obeyed rather than men? Again, since the sole will of the one God is forever just, but that of others can frequently be unjust, who may doubt that the former alone should be obeyed without any reservation, but the latter always with some reservation?

But clearly today many princes exist who, although professing the name of Christ, boldly arrogate to themselves immense power which is not derived from God; and there are many obsequious flatterers who worship them as they were earthly gods. And there are even many who, either possessed by fear or constrained by some other force, consider—or wish to appear to consider—that princes are not to be denied subservience in anything. Moreover, it seems to be a defect of our times that nothing is so stable that may not be uprooted, nothing so certain that it may not be disputed, nothing so sacrosanct that it may not be violated. Indeed, I fear that to anyone assessing the matter carefully, this question will not only appear as far from pointless, but, in our age above all, as manifestly necessary. Certainly for myself, when I consider the cause of so many great calamities which have been rending the Christian world for several years, that statement of the prophet Hosea springs to mind: 'the princes of Judah were like those who break the bounds [*terminus*]: therefore I will pour my anger over them like water. Indeed, Ephraim is crushed in judgement because he followed impious commands.' Here you have the sin of princes and of the people in a single word. For those princes who are not content with that jurisdiction which Almighty God has bestowed upon them, break the bounds, and attempt to usurp by force that supreme jurisdiction which He has retained for Himself over all. It is not, I say, enough for them to use the goods and bodies of their subjects in accordance with their own whim and pleasure, unless they also arrogate to themselves the souls of the wretched, which are the absolute preserve [*peculium*] of Christ. Nor are they content with the earth, but they even advance daringly on heaven itself and try to seize it with scaling ladders. Evidently, as the poet Ovid says:

By every lawful means they try
to win the heavens. Quirinus,
Liber, Alcides, and now Caesar have their temples.

But the people follows impious commands by assenting or toadying to whatever has been ordered contrary to the law of God; by, as it were, burning incense as if to the gods; by not repelling those who aspire to the throne of God when it could do so; and by failing to withhold from Caesar those things which are properly God's. Indeed, there is no-one who does not see this. If anyone does not obey a prince who commands impiety, he is straightaway deemed a rebel and traitor, guilty of high treason [*Maiestatis reus*]. These charges were laid against Christ, His apostles, and all the early Christians. If anyone, following the example of Ezra or Nehemiah, prepares to construct the temple of the Lord, he is aspiring to the kingdom, attempting to bring about revolution [*res novas molitur*], and undermining the commonwealth. For you may hear innumerable flatterers immediately clamouring to kings that if the temple is once restored, it's all up with the kingdom: you can no longer expect tribute and taxes from these men. But what sort of madness is this? In the last resort, those commonwealths are considered stable which have the temple of God located in their midst, and which are themselves the temple of God. Those princes rule truly who rule with God, since they all rule wholly through Him. On the other hand, what κακοξηλια [unhappy rivalry] on the part of men has considered the commonwealth not well constituted unless the temple had been razed; or a kingdom insecure and unstable, unless Almighty God had been cast out, if that were possible? From this result so many Giant-like ventures and similar downfalls of Giants; the many deaths of princes and the manifold destruction of nations. But if these sycophants knew the difference between God and Caesar, between the King of kings and a king, between the Lord [*dominus*] and a vassal [*vassalus*], what He requires from His subjects by way of tribute, and what He allows them over their subjects; then without doubt so many princes would not attempt to disturb the kingdom of God, nor would they be deposed from their own kingdoms by the just anger of God's judgement and vengeance. Nor, in addition, would the people suffer so many calamities, depredations, and ravages. So it is advantageous for princes to know the extent to which they ought to command, and for subjects to understand how far they should obey; lest the former, by usurping another's jurisdiction, or the latter, by complying with anyone administering justice outside his jurisdiction, should each incur punishment. This is the goal of the present question, of which, above all, we make Holy Scripture the judge.

The question is whether subjects are bound to obey kings if they command something contrary to the law of God—that is, whether God or a king should be obeyed the more? When it has been settled in the case of a king, whose power is considered to be the fullest, the same approach will apply to other magistrates. In the first place, the Holy Scriptures teach that God rules by His own authority, but kings as if by sufferance of another [*precario*]: God by Himself, and kings through God: that God exercises His own jurisdiction, but kings only a delegated one. It follows, therefore, from Wisdom ch. 6, Proverbs ch. 8, and Job ch. 12 etc., that God's jurisdiction is immeasurable, whilst that of kings is measured; that God's sway [*potentia*] is infinite, whilst that of kings is limited; that the kingdom of God is not circumscribed by any frontiers [*limites*], whilst on the contrary those of kings are restricted to specific regions and bounded by certain boundaries [*cancelli*]. Furthermore, God created heaven and earth out of nothing, so by right He is truly the lord [*dominus*] and proprietor [*proprietarius*] of heaven and earth. But those who inhabit the earth are, as it were, his tenants and copyholders [*coloni & emphyteutae*]; those who have jurisdiction on earth and preside over others for any reason, are beneficiaries and vassals [*beneficiarii & clientes*] of God and are bound to receive and acknowledge investiture from Him. In short, God is the only proprietor and the only lord: all men, of whatever rank they may ultimately be, are in every respect his tenants [*coloni*], bailiffs, officers, and vassals. The more ample the proceeds they receive, the larger the dues they owe; the greater the authority they attain, the more strictly are they bound to render an account [*rationem reddere*]; the more distinguished the honour they gain, the heavier the burdens for which they are liable.

The Second Question
WHETHER PRIVATE PERSONS MAY RESIST WITH ARMS

It now remains for us to consider individuals [*singuli*], who are described as private. In the first place, individuals are not bound by the covenant between God and the whole people that it should be the people of God. For what is owed to a corporation [*universitas*] is not owed to individuals, just as what a corporation owes is not owed by individuals. Further, they are not bound by office, for each one is bound to serve God in that function to which he is called. But private individuals have no power, fill no magistracy, hold no command nor any right of the sword [*ius gladius*]. Therefore, since God has not handed the sword to private individuals, so he does not demand use of the sword from them. To private individuals it is said: 'Put your sword in its sheath'; but to magistrates: 'You do not bear the sword in vain.' The former are at fault if they draw it, the latter are guilty of serious negligence if they do not draw it when the need arises. 'So what?', you may ask; 'Surely individuals have a covenant with God, just like all together as a whole [*universi*], the commoners as well as magistrates? Otherwise, what is the purpose of circumcision, of baptism, and of so many repeated citations of the sacred covenant throughout Scripture?' This is absolutely right, but the issue is much more complicated. All subjects of a just prince, whatever their rank may be, are in the final analysis wholly bound to obey him; but some, as magistrates, are bound by a certain particular obligation also to take care that others obey. In the same way all men are in general bound to serve the interests of God; but some accept a heavier burden together with higher rank, so that, if they neglect it, they are in some way liable for the faults of others. Kings, all together as a whole [*universi*], and those magistrates who hold the sword from all together as a whole, ought to ensure that the body [*corpus*] of the church is properly governed; individuals need only ensure that they are members [*membra*] of this church. The former should take care that the temple of the Lord should not be defiled or collapse, but that it should be secure against all internal corruption and external attack; the latter that their own body, which is the temple of God, should not be impure, so that God's spirit might dwell in it. 'Whoever shall destroy the Lord's temple, which is you', says Paul, 'God shall also destroy him.' For this reason the sword—with which they are girded openly—is entrusted to the former. To the latter is committed only the sword of the spirit (that is, the word of the Lord) with which Paul girds all Christians against the onslaught of the devil.

What, then, may individuals do, if the king wishes to drive them into impious rites? If the nobles, who hold authority from the whole people, or at least its magistrates, should interpose themselves, should not individuals obey them and comply with them, and assist the pious endeavours of the pious with every effort and with all zeal, as if they were fighting for God Himself? Amongst others, they have the example of the captains of hundreds and soldiers who eagerly obeyed the princes of Judah vindicating, at the instigation of Jehoiada, the church from idolatry and the kingdom from the tyranny of Queen Athaliah. But if the nobles and magistrates applaud a raging king, or at least do not resist him, Christ's counsel is ready to hand: that they should retire to another city. They have the example of the pious men from the ten tribes of Israel: after the true worship of God had been suppressed by Jeroboam, with all together as a whole [*universi*] conniving, they withdrew to the king of Judah, around whom the worship of God persisted. If the opportunity to flee to another has not been granted, they should renounce life rather than God, and be crucified themselves rather than crucify Christ anew, as the apostle says. 'Do not fear', says our Lord, 'those who can only kill the body.' This we have been taught by His example, and those of the apostles and innumerable pious martyrs.

Will it therefore be unlawful for any private individual to resist with arms? What, then, should we determine concerning Moses, who led Israel away despite the wishes of King Pharaoh? Or what should we conclude about Ehud who killed King Eglon of Moab at the end of the eighteenth year of the king's reign, when the kingdom could have seemed to have been acquired by long possession [*usucaptum*], and freed Israel from the yoke of the Moabites? Or, lastly, what should we decide with regard to Jehu who killed King Joram against whom he was fighting, extirpated the line of Ahab, and put to death all the followers of Baal? Were not all these private individuals? Certainly if you consider them all in themselves, you can say that they were private individuals, because they were not constituted ordinarily. But since we know that they were called extraordinarily, and that, as it were, God manifestly girded them with His sword, not only do we not consider them private individuals, but we deem them to be more powerful than any ordinary magistrate. Moses' calling was sanctioned both by the express word of God and by manifest signs. Ehud was said to be raised up by God in order to save Israel by killing the tyrant. Jehu was anointed at the command of the prophet Elisha in order to wipe out the line of Ahab, although certain leading men acclaimed him as king before he embarked on the task. The same may be shown concerning other examples which can be adduced from Holy Scripture.

But when God has neither spoken with his own mouth nor, extraordinarily, through the prophets, we should be especially sober and circumspect in this matter. For if anyone lays claim to that authority for himself, as though he were inspired by the divine spirit, he should certainly make sure that he is not puffed up with pride, that he is not God to himself, that he does not derive that great spirit for himself from within himself, and that he does not, therefore, conceive a vanity and beget a lie. But the people should also beware lest in desiring to be a soldier under Christ's ensign, it fights to its own great harm—perhaps for some Theudas the Galilean or Bar Kochba (as happened not long ago in Germany with the followers of Thomas Müntzer). Yet for all that, I do not say that the very same God who has visited Pharaohs and Ahabs upon us in this our age, may not also raise up a few extraordinary liberators from time to time. Certainly none of His justice and mercy ever passes into abeyance. But clearly if those external signs are less in evidence, it is necessary that we should at least recognise these interior ones by their effects: a mind empty of all ambition, authentic and earnest zeal, and finally conscience and knowledge, so as to prevent him being led on by error to foreign gods, or becoming over-excited by the frenzy of ambition to serve himself rather than the true God.

The Third Question

WHETHER, AND TO WHAT EXTENT, IT MAY BE LAWFUL TO RESIST A PRINCE WHO IS OPPRESSING OR RUINING THE COMMONWEALTH; ALSO BY WHOM, HOW, AND BY WHAT RIGHT IT MAY BE ALLOWED.

Because we are here concerned with the legitimate authority of a prince, I have not the shadow of a doubt that this question will be hateful to tyrants and evil princes. For they think that whatever they desire is permitted to them. It is not surprising if they can in no way endure the voice of reason and law. But I hope that it will be acceptable at least to good princes, who know that a magistrate—whatever authority he may possess—is nothing other than the living law. Nor indeed if anything be said harshly against tyrants, will it do any damage to good princes, as if it had any relevance to them at all. Tyrants and kings, unjust and just princes, are diametrically opposed. Thus it is so far from being the case that what is said against tyrants should detract in any way from kings, that on the contrary the more it does detract from the former, the more glory accrues to the latter; nor can the former be denounced without the latter being praised. I am indifferent to whatever the former may feel. I do not write for them, but against them. I can scarcely doubt that the latter will consent, for they ought to hate tyrants and iniquitous princes no less than shepherds hate wolves, doctors hate poisoners, and prophets hate false prophets. For that hatred which nature imprints in dogs against wild animals, reason must necessarily engender universally in kings against tyrants; for as the latter live by spoil, the former are born and granted for its repression. Perhaps flatterers of tyrants will frown, if they have the gall, but it would be more fitting that they blushed. I know that friends of kings will not simply assent and nod approval; they will also not be afraid to lend their support. Therefore, as he who reads this is moved to applause or to anger, so he will realise what his own attitude is. And so let us tackle the issue.

KINGS ARE MADE BY THE PEOPLE

We have demonstrated above that God institutes kings, gives kingdoms to them, and elects them. We now say that the people constitutes kings, confers kingdoms, and approves the election by its vote [*suffragio*]. Indeed, God willed that it should be done in this way, so that whatever authority and power they have, should be received from the people after Him; and that thus they would apply all their care, thought, and effort to the welfare of the people [*utilitas populi*]. Nor would they consider themselves to preside over other men by some excellence of nature, as men do with sheep or cattle. Rather, they should remember that they are born entirely by the same lot as other men, and that they are elevated from the ground to their position by the votes and, as it were, on the shoulders of the people, in order that the burdens of the commonwealth should henceforth, for the most part, rest on their shoulders.

Since absolutely no-one is born a king in himself, and no-one can rule without a people. But, on the contrary, a people can exist of itself and is prior in time to a king. It is definitely established that all kings were first constituted by the people. Even if in certain regions the free operation of election may seem to have fallen into abeyance because sons or descendants, by imitating the virtue of their fathers, appear to make the kingdom hereditary, as it were, to themselves, nevertheless in all well-constituted kingdoms this custom has always persisted: that children do not succeed to the dead before they are constituted as if anew by the people. Nor are they born to their fathers as heirs, but they are only considered at last to be kings when they receive investiture of the kingdom, as if through the sceptre and diadem, from those who represent the people's majesty. In Christian kingdoms, which are nowadays said to descend by succession, there persist particularly obvious vestiges of this very practice.

For the kings of France, Spain, England, and others, are accustomed to be inaugurated, and, as it were, put in possession of the kingdom, by the estates [*ordines*] of the realm—the peers, patricians, and magnates—who represent the corporation of the people. Similarly the emperors of Germany are inaugurated by the electors, and the kings of Poland by the *wojewodas* or palatines, where election determines their whole right. Regal honour is not accorded to the former in the cities of the kingdom before they have been properly inaugurated; so much so that at one time regnal dates were only calculated from the day of inauguration, which practice was strictly followed in Gaul. But lest we should be deceived by a continuous series of several successions in these very kingdoms, the estates of the realm have often preferred the agnate to the son, and the second- to the first-born. Thus in France, Louis was preferred to his brother Robert, count of Dreux; and likewise Henry, the second-born brother, to Robert Capet, the nephew; and similarly in other cases. What is more, that same kingdom has been transferred from dynasty to dynasty by the authority of the people even when legitimate heirs survived—from the Merovingians to the Carolingians, and from the Carolingians to the Capetians. And similar things have been done in other kingdoms, as is agreed by the most reliable historians. But not to stray from France, which has always been considered a model for other kingdoms—in which, I say, succession appears to have obtained to the fullest extent—we read of the election of Pharamond in the year 419, of Pippin in 751, and of Pippin's sons Charlemagne and Carloman in 768, without any regard to the father. When Carloman eventually died in 771, Charlemagne did not immediately acquire his brother's portion, as usually happens with inheritances, but only did so by determination of the people and the public council. Louis the Pious was elected in 812 by the same authority, although he was the son of Charlemagne. In the testament of this Charles, which survives in Nauclerus, he asked the people to elect whomsoever it wished from amongst his grandsons through a public council of the kingdom, and he commanded the uncles to acquiesce in the people's decision. On this basis, Charles the Bald, the grandson [of Charlemagne] by Judith and Louis the Pious, claimed to be king-elect, according to the historian Aimon. To summarise: all kings were wholly elected from the beginning. Those who today seem to come to the kingdom by succession must first be constituted by the people. Finally, although it has been the custom in some regions for the people to choose its kings for itself from a certain lineage on account of some outstanding merits, it chooses the stem and not the offshoot. Its choice is not such that if degeneration occur, it may not elect another. The offspring of that stem are not so much born, as made, kings; they are held to be not so much kings, as candidates for kingship.

THE PEOPLE IS MORE POWERFUL THAN THE KING

So, as kings are constituted by the people, it seems definitely to follow that the whole people [*Populus universus*] is more powerful than the king. For such is the force of the word: one who is constituted by another is held to be lesser; and one who receives his authority from another is inferior to his appointer. Potiphar, the Egyptian, set Joseph over his household; Nebuchadnezzar set Daniel over the province of Babylon; and Darius set one hundred and twenty governors over the kingdom. Assuredly, masters [*domini*] are said to constitute their servants [*servi*], and kings their ministers. In the same way the people constitutes the king, as a minister of the commonwealth. Good kings have not disdained this title, and even bad ones have affected it: so much so that for many centuries none of the Roman emperors wanted to be called lord [*dominus*]—except for overt tyrants like Nero, Domitian, and Caligula.

It is established, then, that kings were instituted on account of the people. For you cannot say that all men together as a whole [*universi*] were created for the sake of more or less a hundred simple men—for the most part far worse than and inferior to the rest—rather than the latter for the sake of the former. For reason requires that he be considered the greater, for whose sake another is raised up. Thus for the sake of a ship, its master [*dominus*] appoints a pilot, who sits at the helm lest she break up on a rock or fail to hold her course. Indeed, he who is engaged in this occupation is obeyed by the others, and even the master himself submits. Yet he is still a servant [*servus*] of the ship, like any common deck-hand; he does not differ so much from a deck hand in *genus*, but in *species*. In a commonwealth, which is often compared to a ship, the king is in the position of pilot, and the people in that of master [*loco domini*]. So while the former takes care of public safety, the people obeys and submits to him. However, he is—or ought to be considered to be—no less a servant [*servus*] of the commonwealth than any judge or tribune. He differs from these in no other respect than that he is bound to carry greater burdens, and to meet more dangers. Consequently, whatever a king gains either by war or when he annexes neighbouring territory by right of war; or whatever he gains by jurisdiction, as when returns are made to the fisc; he acquires not for himself, but for the kingdom—for the people, I say, which constitutes the kingdom—just like a servant [*servus*] for his master [*dominus*]. Nor can any binding agreement be contracted with him except by authority of the people.

Consequently innumerable peoples live without a king, but you cannot conceive of a king without a people. For that reason certain men do not attain royal dignity just because they differ from others in species, and because they ought to be in charge over these by a certain natural superiority, like shepherds with sheep. Rather they are raised from the same substance [*massa*], and the people elevates them to that position [*gradus*], so that if they have any authority and power, they should hold it as something received, and as possessed by a sort of precarious grant. This is shown very clearly by the ancient ritual of the Franks, who proclaimed a king by raising him on a shield. Why, I ask, are kings said to have innumerable eyes and ears, far-reaching hands and very swift feet? Is it because they are like Argos, Geryonus, Midas, and those others told of in legend? Not at all. Rather, it is clearly because the whole people, whose concern this is, lends its eyes, its ears, its strength and faculties to the king for the use of the commonwealth. If the people deserts the king, he who once seemed sharp-eyed and sharp-eared, mighty and active, will begin to go blind and deaf, and will suddenly fall down. He who once triumphed in splendour, will in an instant become vile to all. He who was once graced with almost divine honours, will be forced to become a schoolmaster at Corinth. Undermine only the pedestal of that Gigantic mass, and, like the Rhodian Colossus, it must collapse and shatter to smithereens. So since the king exists through the people and on account of the people, he cannot remain standing without the people. Who would find it strange, then, if we conclude that the people is more powerful than the king?

WHAT THE PURPOSE OF KINGS IS

Now since kings are constituted by the people, and certain partners in rule, as it were [*quasi imperii consortes*], who are inferior to the king individually; [*singuli*], but his superiors all together as a whole [*universi*], are joined them to restrain them within their office; it follows that we should look why they were first constituted and in what, primarily, their office consists. For something is only considered just and good when it achieves that end for which it was instituted. In the first place, it is clear that men are free by nature, impatient of servitude, and are born more to command than to obey. They would not willingly have elected the command of another, and renounce the law, as it were, of their own nature, in order to hear another's law, except for the sake of some great advantage [*non nisi magnae cuiusdam utilitatis causa imperium alienum ultro elegisse, & suae quasi naturae legi, ut alienum ferrent renunciasse*]. For as Æsop says, the horse which was formerly accustomed to wander freely, would not have tolerated any bridle or rider except in the hope of defeating the hull. So let us not suppose that kings were elected in order to divert the goods produced by the sweat of many to their own [private] use: for each man loves and pursues his own interests; nor were they elected in order to abuse public power [*potentia*] for the sake of their own desires: for normally men pursue the more powerful with hatred or envy. But clearly, they should defend individuals from each other [*singulos a mutuis*] and all together as a whole [*universos*] from external attack, either by exercising jurisdiction [*iure dicundo*] or by repelling force with force. 'For this reason', says Augustine, 'those who are concerned [*consulunt*] for the welfare of others are said to command [*imperare*], as a man does his wife and parents do children; and those who are the object of concern are considered to obey. And yet those who command in this way really serve those whom they are said to command; because', he says, 'they do not command out of desire for domination [*dominandi*] but out of a duty to show concern; not with the arrogance of ruling, but with compassion in providing'.

So to command is nothing other than to show concern: the one purpose of command is the people's welfare. The only office of emperors and kings is to show concern for the people. For royal dignity is not really an honour, but a burden; not an immunity, but a function; not a dispensation, but a vocation; not licence, but public service. It was so touched with honour because, in those primordial times, scarcely anyone would have wanted to taste these inconveniences unless they were enwrapped, as it were, in honour; so much so that nothing is truer than what a certain person [*ille*] used to say: that if everyone knew how much trouble was entwined around the royal diadem, you would find no-one who, even on coming across it in the street, would want to place it on his head. So when [the distinction between] 'MINE' and 'THINE' entered the world, and conflicts arose about the ownership [*dominium*] of things between citizens, and soon even wars arose between neighbouring countries concerning their frontiers [*fines*], the people began to resort to one person who would justly and vigorously see to it both that the poorer should not suffer violence from the rich, and that everyone together as a whole [*universi*] should not do so from their neighbours. And so, as struggles and wars posed an increasing threat, so also he whose vigour and commitment were high in the opinion of all was elected. Thus at one time kings were created to exercise jurisdiction at home and to lead the army abroad. Not only did they repel enemy invasions, depopulation of the countryside, and other calamities of the body; even more they excluded disgrace, wickedness, and vice from the commonwealth, or repressed them: the former was achieved by war and the latter by law [*iure*] Indeed, this is quite plain from all sacred and secular writers.

WHO TYRANTS ARE

Since we have described the king hitherto, we will now describe the tyrant in a little more detail. We have said that the king is one who has been granted the kingdom either by lineage or by election, has had it ceremonially entrusted to him, and who also rules and governs it legitimately. Since a tyrant is clearly the opposite of a king, it follows that he must be one who has either usurped command by force and deception, or one who rules the kingdom granted freely and voluntarily to him contrary to what is right and proper [*contra ius et fas*], and obstinately administers it contrary to the laws and contracts [*pacta*] to which he has solemnly bound himself. Both these definitions can even apply to one and the same man. The former is commonly called a tyrant without title, and the latter a tyrant by practice.

But it can happen that someone who has occupied a kingdom by force rules it justly, and one to whom it is granted by right, does so unjustly. And clearly, since kingship is more a right than an inheritance, more a performance than a possession, he who performs his function [*munus*] badly seems more worthy of the name tyrant than he who has not received his function in the proper fashion [*rite*]. Thus a pope who enters office wrongly is said to be an intruder, and one who governs badly is called an abuser. Pythagoras used to say, "ξενοζ ανηρ δικαιοζ ον μονον πολιτον, αλλα και σνγγενουζ διαφερει ['Any just foreigner excels not only a citizen, but also a relative']. So it is lawful for us to say that a prince who is not properly [*rite*] constituted, but who is just, greatly excels one who has been properly inaugurated, but who governs unjustly. For since kings are instituted to nourish, judge, and care for the people, I obviously prefer for a thief to succour me, than for a pastor to devour me; for a robber to judge me, than for a judge to do me violence; I would rather be cured by a quack, than poisoned to death by a properly qualified doctor; I would prefer a false tutor who administered my goods well, to a legitimate one who squandered them. Then, no matter how much ambition may tempt him, he could be seen—in a certain way—to have used force at first in order to exercise justice afterwards—like Cyrus, Alexander, and the Romans, who conceded full autonomy, immunities, and privileges to those they had defeated. But the tyrant by practice is seen to vaunt his right to such an extent that he rules unjustly—as not only the princes of Muscovy and Turkey, but also many Christian ones do nowadays. Thus the deeds of tyrants without title grow in strength with the passage of time; but the deeds of those by practice become more and more degenerate the older they get. 'But if', says Augustine, 'those kingdoms in which justice has no place are only large robber bands', then both types of tyrant are definitely equals in this respect, because each is a thief and a robber, and each is an unjust possessor. For the thief who seizes another's belongings against the will of the owner is clearly no less an unjust possessor than he who ill-uses something granted to him. But he who seizes something in order to destroy it commits a far worse outrage than one who does so in order to preserve it; just as the offence of one who governs unjustly, supported by an empty title, is more heinous than one who is utterly destitute of any title, and yet governs justly the kingdom annexed by force.

JAMES VI AND I

1566-1625

Born in 1566, James Stuart was the son of Mary Queen of Scots and Henry Stuart, Lord Darnley. Within the next year his mother was forced to abdicate and the infant James was crowned King of Scotland. After a long and turbulent regency, James assumed control of the government and reigned successfully until he inherited the English crown at the death of Elizabeth I in 1603. Before becoming King of England, however, James published two books on the topic of royal government and the proper relationship between monarch and subject. Written for a Scottish audience, *The True Law of Free Monarchy* (1598) is the more significant of these two works, both in terms of its reflection of continental trends in early modern political thought, and with respect to its influence on subsequent theorists such as Thomas Hobbes in England and Bishop Bossuet in France.

King James I was perhaps the most moderate and responsible of those late Renaissance figures who supported the idea of divine-right and absolute monarchy. Even the English philosopher John Locke, whose name is always associated with opposition to absolutist theory, spoke approvingly of James, "that learned King who well understood the notions of things." Today the term absolutism often is loosely, and mistakenly, associated with tyrannical or despotic government. Building on the work of his contemporary Jean Bodin in France, James did not stress the unlimited and arbitrary power of kings, but merely the need for an uncontested source of sovereign authority in every territorial state, an authority unlimited in its jurisdiction and perpetual in its exercise of power. During the seventeenth century, absolutism was associated most often with efficiency in government, with the well-being of the collective community, and with the security of state against foreign aggression.

The True Law of Free Monarchy utilizes theological arguments drawn from Scripture, historical arguments based on a widely shared understanding of the Scottish constitutional system, and patriarchal notions which equate the head of state with the male head of family, in order to enhance the power of the personal monarch. In reading this selection, what limits does James place upon himself, and by implication upon all other legitimate monarchs, in the exercise of his God-given office? Under what conditions, if any, can subjects resist their king? How does James link religious precepts with political practice? Have we now reached a point in the Western experience where religion and politics are separate concerns?

The True Law of Free Monarchies
or
The Reciprock and Mutual Duetie
Betwixt a Free King, and His naturall Subjects

As there is not a thing so necessarie to be knowne by the people of any land, next the knowledge of their God, as the right knowledge of their alleageance, according to the forme of governement established among them, especially in a *Monarchie* (which forme of government, as resembling the Divinitie, approcheth nearest to perfection, as all the learned and wise men from the beginning have agreed upon; Unitie being the perfection of all things), So hath the ignorance, and (which is worse) the seduced opinion of the multitude blinded by them, who thinke themselves able to teach and instruct the ignorants, procured the wracke and overthrow of sundry flourishing Commonwealths; and heaped heavy calamaties, threatning utter destruction upon others. And the smiling successe, that unlawfull rebellions have oftentimes had against Princes in aages past (such hath bene the misery, and iniquitie of the time) hath by way of practise strengthened many in their errour: albeit there cannot be a more deceiveable argument; then to judge ay the justnesse of the cause by the event thereof; as hereafter shalbe proved more at length. And among others, no Commonwealth, that ever hath bene since the beginning, hath had greater need of the trew knowledge of this ground, then this our so long disordered, and distracted Common-wealth hath: the misknowledge hereof being the onely spring, from whence have flowed so many endlesse calamaties, miseries, and confusions, as is better felt by many, then the cause thereof well knowne, and deepely considered. The naturall zeale therefore, that I beare to this my native countrie, with the great pittie I have to see the so-long disturbance thereof for lacke of the trew knowledge of this ground (as I have said before) hath compelled me at last to breake silence, to discharge my conscience to you my deare country men herein, that knowing the ground from whence these your many endlesse troubles have proceeded, as well as ye have already too-long tasted the bitter fruites thereof, ye may by knowledge, and eschewing of the cause escape, and divert the lamentable effects that ever necessarily follow thereupon. I have chosen then onely to set downe in this short Treatise, the trew grounds of the mutuall duetie, and alleageance betwixt a free and absolute *Monarche*, and his people; not to trouble your patience with answering the contrary propositions, which some have not bene ashamed to set downe in writ, to the poysoning of infinite number of simple soules, and their owne perpetuall, and will deserved infamie: For by answering them, I could not have eschewed whiles[1] to pick, and byte wel saltly their persons; which would rather have bred contentiousnesse among the readers (as they had liked or misliked) then sound instruction of the trewth: Which I protest to him that is the searcher of all hearts, is the onely marke that I shoot at herein.

First then, I will set downe the trew grounds, whereupon I am to build, out of the Scriptures, since *Monarchie* is the trew paterne of Divinitie, as I have already said: next, from the fundamental Lawes of our owne Kingdome, which nearest must concerne us: thirdly, from the law of Nature, by divers similitudes drawne out of the same: and will conclude syne[2] by answering the most waighty and appearing incommodities that can be objected.

The Princes duetie to his Subjects is so clearely set downe in many places of the Scriptures, and so openly confessed by all the good Princes, according to their oath in their Coronation, as not needing to be long therein, I shall as shortly as I can runne through it.

Kings are called Gods by the propheticall King *David*, because they sit upon GOD his Throne in the earth, and have the count of their administration to give unto him. Their office is, "To minister Justice and Judgement to the people," as the same *David* saith: "To advance the good, and punish the evill," as he likewise saith: "To establish good Lawes to his people, and procure obedience to the same," as divers good Kings of *Judah* did: "To procure the peace of the people," as the same *David* saith: "To decide all controversies that can arise among them," as *Salomon* did: "To be the minister of God for the weale of them that doe well, and as the minister of God, to take vengeance upon them that doe evill," as S. *Paul* saith. And finally, "As a good pastour, to goe out and in before his people: as is said in the first of *Samuel*: "That through the Princes prosperitie, the peoples peace may be procured," as *Jeremie* saith.

And therefore in the Coronation of our owne Kings, as well as of every Christian *Monarche*, they give their Oath, first to maintaine the Religion presently professed within their countrie, according to their lawes, whereby it is established, and to punish all those that should presse to alter, or disturbe the profession thereof; And next to maintaine all the lowable and good Lawes made by their predecessours: to see them put in execution, and the breakers and violaters thereof, to be punished, according to the tenour of the same: And lastly, to maintaine the whole countrey, and every state therein, in all their ancient Priveledges and Liberties, as well against all forreine enemies, as among themselves: And shortly to procure the weale and flourishing of his people, not onely in maintaining and putting to execution the olde lowable lawes of the countrey, and by establishing of new (as necessitie and evill maners will require) but by all other meanes possible to fore-see and prevent all dangers, that are likely to fall upon them, and to maintaine concord, wealth, and civilitie among them, as a loving Father, and careful watchman, caring for them more then for himselfe, knowing himselfe to be ordained for them, and they not for him; and therefore countable to that great God, who placed him as the lieutenant over them, upon the perill of his soule to procure the weale of both soules and bodies, as farre as in him lieth, of all them that are committed to his charge. And this oath in the Coronation is the clearest, civill, and fundamental Law, whereby the Kings office is properly defined.

By the Law of Nature the King become a naturall Father to all his Leiges at his Coronation: And as the Father of his fatherly duty is bound to care for the nourishing, education, and vertuous government of his children; even so is the king bound to care for all his subjects. As all the toile and paine that the father can take for his children, will be thought light and well bestowed by him, so that the effect thereof redound to their profite and weale; so ought the Prince to doe towards his people.

As the kindly father ought to foresee all inconvenients and dangers that may arise towards his children, and though with the hazard of his owne person presse to prevent the same; so ought the King towards his people. As the fathers wrath and correction upon any of his children that offendeth, ought to be by a fatherly chastisement seasoned with pitie, as long as there is any hope of amendment in them; so ought the King towards any of his Lieges that offend in that measure. And shortly, as the Fathers chiefe joy ought to be in procuring his childrens welfare, rejoycing at their weale, sorrowing and pitying their evill, to hazard for their safetie, travell for their rest, wake for their sleepe; and in a word, to thinke that his earthly felicitie and life standeth and liveth more in them nor in himselfe; so ought a good Prince thinke of his people.

Preces, & Lachrymæ sunt arma Ecclesiæ.[3]

Now as for the describing the allegiance, that the lieges owe to their native King, out of the fundamentall and civill Lawe, especially of this countrey, as I promised, the ground must first be set downe of the first maner of establishing the Lawes and forme of governement among us; that the ground being first right laide, we may thereafter build rightly thereupon. Although it be trew (according to the affirmation of those that pryde themselves to be the scourges of Tyrants) that in the first beginning of Kings rising among Gentiles, in the time of the first aage, divers commonwealths and societies of men choosed out one among themselves, who for his vertues and valour, being more eminent that the rest, was chosen out by them, and set up in that roome, to maintaine the weakest in their right, to throw downe oppressours, and to foster and continue the societie among men; which could not otherwise, but by vertue of that unitie be wel done: yet these examples are nothing pertinent to us; because our Kingdome and divers other Monarchies are not in that case, but had their beginning in a farre contrary fashion.

For as our Chronicles beare witnesse, this Ile, and especially our part of it, being scantly inhabited, but by very few, and they as barbarous and scant of civilitie, as number, there comes our first King *Fergus*, with a great number with him, out of *Ireland*, which was long inhabited before us, and making himselfe master of the countrey, by his owne friendship, and force, as well of the *Ireland-men* that came with him, as of the countrey-men that willingly fell to him, hee made himselfe King and Lord, as well of the whole landes, as of the whole inhabitants within the same. Thereafter he and his successours, a long while after their being Kinges, made and established their lawes from time to time, and as the occasion required. So the trewth is directly contrarie in our state to the false affirmation of such seditious writers, as would perswade us, that the Lawes and state of our countrey were established before the admitting of a king: where by the contrarie ye see it plainely prooved, that a wise king coming in among barbares,[4] first established the estate and forme of governement, and thereafter made lawes by himselfe, and his successours according thereto.

The kings therefore in *Scotland* where before any estates or rankes of men within the same, before any Parlaiments were holden, or lawes made: and by them was the land distributed (which at the first was whole theirs) states erected and decerned, and formes of governement devised and established: And so it followes of necessitie, that the kings were the authors and makers of the Lawes, and not the Lawes of the kings. And to proove this my assertion more clearly, it is evident by the rolles of our Chancellery (which containe our eldest and fundamentall Lawes) that the King is *Dominus omnium bonorum*,[5] and *Dominus directus totius Dominii*,[6] the whole subjects being but his vassals, and from him holding all their lands as their over-lord, who according to good services done unto him, chaungeth their holdings from tacke[7] to few, from ward[8] to blanch,[9] erecteth new Baronies, and uniteth olde, without advice or authoritie of either Parliament or any other subalterin judiciall seate: So as if wrong might bee admitted in play (albeit I grant wrong should be wrong in all persons) the King might have a better colour for his pleasure, without further reason, to take the land from his lieges, as over-lord of the whole, and doe with it as pleaseth him, since all that they hold is of him, then, as foolish writers say, the people might unmake the king, and put an other in his roome: But either of them as unlawful, and against the ordinance of God, ought to be alike odious to be thought, much lesse put in practise.

And according to these fundamentall Lawes already alledged, we daily see that in the Parliament (which is nothing else but the head Court of the king and his vassals) the lawes are but craved by his subjects, and onely made by him at their rogation,[10] and with their advice: For albeit the king make daily statutes and ordinances, enjoyning such paines thereto as hee thinkes meet, without any advice of Parliament or estates; yet it lies in the power of no Parliament, to make any kinde of Lawe of Statute, without his Scepter be to it, for giving it the force of a Law: And although divers changes have beene in other countries of the blood Royall, and kingly house, the kingdome being reft by conquest from one to another, as in our nieghbour countrey *England*, (which was never in ours) yet the same ground of the kings right over all the land, and subjects thereof remaineth alike in all other free Monarchies, as well as in this: For when the Bastard of *Normandie* came into *England*, and made himselfe king, was it not by force, and with a mighty army? Where he gave the Law, and tooke none, changed the Lawes, inverted the order of governement, set downe the strangers his followers in many of the old possessours roomes, as at this day well appeareth a great part of the Gentlemen in *England*, beeing come of the *Norman* blood, and their old Lawes, which to this day are ruled by, are written in his language, and not in theirs: And yet his successours have with great happinesse enjoyed the Crowne to this day; Whereof the like was also done by all them that conquested them before.

And for conclusion of this point, that the king is over-lord over the whole lands, it is likewise daily proved by the Law of our hoordes, of want of Heires, and of Bastardies: For if a hoord be found under the earth, because it is no more in the keeping or use of any person, it of the law pertains to the king. If a person, inheritour of any lands or goods, dye without any sort of heires, all his landes and goods returne to the king. And if a bastard die unrehabled without heires of his bodie (which rehabling onely lyes in the kings hands) all that hee hath likewise returnes to the king. And as ye see it manifest, that the King is over-Lord if the whole land: so is he Master over every person that inhabiteth the same, having power over the life and death of every one of them: For although a just Prince will not take the life of any of his subjects without a cleare law; yet the same lawes whereby he taketh them, are made by himselfe, or his predecessours; and so the power flowes alwaies from him selfe; as by daily experience we see, good and just Princes will from time to time make new laws and statutes, adjoyning the penalties to the breakers thereof, which before the law was made, had beene no crime to the subject to have committed. Not that I deny the old definition of a King, and of a law; which makes the king to bee a speaking law, and the Law a dumbe king: for certainely a king will not onely delight to rule his subjects by the lawe, but even will conforme himselfe in his owne actions thereunto, alwaies keeping that ground, that the health of the common-wealth be his chiefe lawe: And where he sees the lawe doubtsome or rigorous, hee may interpret or mitigate the same, lest otherwise *Summum ius*[11] bee *summa iniuria*:[12] And therefore generall lawes, made publickly in Parliament, may upon knowen respects to the King by his authoritie bee mitigated, and suspended upon causes onely knowen to him.

As likewise, although I have said, a good king will frame all his actions to be according to the Law; yet is hee not bound thereto but of his good will, and for good example-giving to his subjects: For as in the law of abstaining from eating of flesh in *Lenton*, the king will, for examples sake, make his owne house to observe the Law; yet no man will thinke he needs to take a licence to eate flesh. And although by our Lawes, the bearing and wearing of hag-buts,[13] and pistolets be forbidden, yet no man can find any fault in the King, for causing his traine use them in any raide upon the Borderers, or other malefactours or rebellious subjects. So as I have alreadie said, a good King, although hee be above the Law, will subject and frame his actions thereto, for examples sake to his subjects, and of his owne free-will, but not as subject or bound thereto.

Since I have so clearley prooved then out of the fundamentall lawes and practise of this country, what right & power a king hath over his land and subjects, it is easie to be understood, what allegeance & obedience his lieges owe unto him; I meane alwaies of such free Monarchies as our king is, and not of elective kings, and much lesse of such sort of governors, as the dukes of *Venice* are, whose Aristocratick and limited government, is nothing like to free Monarchies; although the malice of some writers hath not beene ashamed to mis-know any difference to be betwixt them. And if it be not lawfull to any particular Lordes tenants or vassals, upon whatsoever pretext, to controll and displace their Master, and over-lord (as is clearer nor the Sunne by all Lawes of the world) how much lesse may the subjects and vassals of the great over-lord the KING controll or displace him? And since in all inferiour judgements in the land, the people may not upon any respects displace their Magistrates, although but subaltern: for the people of a borough, cannot displace their Provost before the time of their election: nor in Ecclesiasticall policie the flocke can upon any pretence displace the Pastor, nor judge of him: yea even the poore Schoolemaster cannot be displaced by his schollers: If these, I say (whereof some are but inferiour, subaltern, and temporall Magistrates, and none of them equall in any dignitie of a King) cannot be displaced for any occasion or pretext by them that are ruled by them: how much lesse is it lawfull upon any pretext to controll or displace the great Provost, and great Schoole-master of the whole land: except by inverting the order of all Law and reason, the commanded may be made to command the commander, the judge to judge their judge, and they that are governed, to governe their time about their Lord and governer.

And the agreement of the Law of nature in this our ground with the Lawes and constitutions of God, and man, already alledged, will by two similitudes easily appeare. The King towards his people is rightly compared to a father of children, and to head of a body composed of divers members: For as fathers, the good Princes, and Magistrates of the people of God acknowledged themselves to their subjects. And for all other well ruled Common-wealths, the stile of *Pater patriae*[14] was ever, and is commonly used to Kings. And the proper office of a King towards his Subjects, agrees very wel with the office of the head towards the body, and all members thereof: For from the head, being the seate of Judgement, proceedeth the care and foresight of guiding, and preventing all evill that may come to the body or any part thereof. The head cares for the body, so doeth the King for his people. As the discourse and direction flowes from the head, and the execution according thereunto belongs to the rest of the members, every one according to their office: so is it betwixt a wise Prince, and his people. As the judgement coming from the head may not onely imploy the members, every one in their owne office as long as they are able for it; but likewise in case any of then be affected with any infirmitie must care and provide for their remedy, in-case it be curable, and if otherwise, gar cut them off for feare of infecting of the rest: even so is it betwixt the Prince, and his people. And as there is ever hope of curing any diseased member by the direction of the head, as long as it is whole; but by the contrary, if it be troubled, all the members are partakers of that paine, so is it betwixt the Prince and his people.

And now first for the fathers part (whose naturall love to his children I described in the first part of this my discourse, speaking of the dutie that Kings owe to their Subjects) consider, I pray you what duetie his children owe to him, & whether upon any pretext whatsoever, it wil not be thought monstrous and unnaturall to his sons, to rise up against him, to control him at their appetite, and when they thinke good to sley him, or cut him off, and adopt to themselves any other they please in his roome: Or can any pretence of wickedness or rigor on his part be a just excuse for his children to put hand into him? And although wee see by the course of nature, that love useth to descend more then to ascend, in case it were trew, that the father hated and wronged the children never so much, will any man, endued with the least sponke[15] of reason, thinke it lawfull for them to meet him with the line? Yea, suppose the father were furiously following his sonnes with a drawen sword, is it lawfull for them to turne and strike againe, or make any resistance but by flight? I thinkle surely, if there were no more but the example of bruit beasts & unreasonable creatures, it may serve well enough to qualifie and prove this my argument. We reade often the pietie that the Storkes have to their olde and decayed parents: And generally wee know, that there are many sorts of beasts and fowles, that with violence and many bloody strokes will beat and banish their yong ones from them, how soone they perceive them to be able to fend themselves; but wee never read or heard of any resistance on their part, except among the vipers; which prooves such persons, as ought to be reasonable creatures, and yet unnaturally follow this example, to be endued with their viperous nature.

NOTES

[1]sometimes
[2]directly
[3]prayers and tears are the weapons/arms of the church
[4]barbarians
[5]Lord of all good things
[6]Lord directs the entire kingdom
[7]rent
[8]guardianship
[9]check out of
[10]supplication
[11]highest right
[12]most serious injury/harm
[13]an early portable fire-arm
[14]father of the father land
[15]spa

Michel Eyquem de Montaigne

1533-1592

Translated into English by John Florio in 1603, Montaigne's *Essays* had profound effects on many English writers, such as Francis Bacon and William Shakespeare. Montaigne was a scholar, lawyer and skeptical philosopher who created a new prose form when he endeavored to record his response to and reflections on his experiences in life.

The *Essays* have often been described as an extended autobiography. In this three-book collection of chapters, Montaigne makes a number of attempts or trials—*essais*—to explore his response to different subjects and situations. His aim is to present a portrait of himself for his friends and relatives; in doing so, he believes that he can offer the world an example of "the essential man," not as a static being, but as one who retains a central identity amidst a fluctuating world.

Montaigne's famous question, *Que scais je*? ("What do I know?") reveals his characteristic skepticism as well as his attitudes toward the nature of truth. Through his forays into the rigorous questioning of established beliefs, Montaigne's essays reveal his understanding that truth as we know it depends wholly on the inquirer's perspective. His French follower, René Descartes (1596-1650), would carry Montaigne's inquiries even farther by wondering if it is possible to be certain of anything.

In the first two selections, "On Cannibals" and "On the Custom of Wearing Clothes," how does Montaigne introduce the concept of cultural relativism? Why might this idea be gaining importance in 16th-century Western Europe? How does Montaigne characterize the native peoples? In what ways might he be invoking the idea of the "noble savage"? How are Montaigne's ideas at work in William Shakespeare's play *Othello*? How can the last selection, "On Experience," be read as a doctrine of epistemology? How does it compare to the other methods of "coming to know" which we have encountered in Humanities 124 and 214? How is Montaigne's idea of experience profoundly different from Hildegard of Bingen's and Margery Kempe's? From Aquinas's? In what ways can Sei Shonagon's "project" be compared to Montaigne's?

Essays

Of Cannibals

When King Pyrrhus passed over into Italy, after he had reconnoitered the formation of the army that the Romans were sending to meet him, he said: "I do not know what barbarians these are" (for so the Greeks called all foreign nations), "but the formation of this army that I see is not at all barbarous." The Greeks said as much of the army that Flamininus brought into their country, and so did Philip, seeing from a knoll the order and distribution of the Roman camp, in his kingdom, under Publius Sulpicius Galba. Thus we should beware of clinging to vulgar opinions, and judge things by reason's way, not by popular say.

I had with me for a long time a man who had lived for ten or twelve years in that other world which has been discovered in our century, in the place where Villegaignon landed, and which he called Antarctic France. This discovery of a boundless country seems worthy of consideration. I don't know if I can guarantee that some other such discovery will not be made in the future, so many personages greater than ourselves having been mistaken about this one. I am afraid we have eyes bigger than our stomachs, and more curiosity than capacity. We embrace everything, but we clasp only wind.

Plato brings in Solon, telling how he had learned from the priests of the city of Saïs in Egypt that in days of old, before the Flood, there was a great island named Atlantis, right at the mouth of the Strait of Gibraltar, which contained more land than Africa and Asia put together, and that the kings of that country, who not only possessed that island but had stretched out so far on the mainland that they held the breadth of Africa as far as Egypt, and the length of Europe as far as Tuscany, undertook to step over into Asia and subjugate all the nations that border on the Mediterranean, as far as the Black Sea; and for this purpose crossed the Spains, Gaul, Italy, as far as Greece, where the Athenians checked them; but that some time after, both the Athenians and themselves and their island were swallowed up by the Flood.

It is quite likely that that extreme devastation of waters made amazing changes in the habitations of the earth, as people maintain that the sea cut off Sicily from Italy—

> 'Tis said an earthquake once asunder tore
> These lands with dreadful havoc, which before
> Formed but one land, one coast
>
> Virgil[1]

—Cyprus from Syria, the island of Euboea from the mainland of Boeotia; and elsewhere joined lands that were divided, filling the channels between them with sand and mud:

A sterile marsh, long fit for rowing, now
Feeds neighbor towns, and feels the heavy plow.
Horace

But there is no great likelihood that that island was the new world which we have just discovered; for it almost touched Spain, and it would be an incredible result of a flood to have forced it away as far as it is, more than twelve hundred leagues; besides, the travels of the moderns have already almost revealed that it is not an island, but a mainland connected with the East Indies on one side, and elsewhere with the lands under the two poles; or, if it is separated from them, it is by so narrow a strait and interval that it does not deserve to be called an island on that account.

It seems that there are movements, some natural, others feverish, in these great bodies, just as in our own. When I consider the inroads that my river, the Dordogne, is making in my lifetime into the right bank in its descent, and that in twenty years it has gained so much ground and stolen away the foundations of several buildings, I clearly see that this is an extraordinary disturbance; for if it had always gone at this rate, or was to do so in the future, the face of the world would be turned topsy-turvy. But rivers are subject to changes: now they overflow in one direction, now in another, now they keep to their course. I am not speaking of the sudden inundations whose causes are manifest. In Médoc, along the seashore, my brother, the sieur d'Arsac, can see an estate of his buried under the sands that the sea spews forth; the tops of some buildings are still visible; his farms and domains have changed into very thin pasturage. The inhabitants say that for some time the sea has been pushing toward them so hard that they have lost four leagues of land. These sands are its harbingers; and we see great dunes of moving sand that march half a league ahead of it and keep conquering land.

The other testimony of antiquity with which some would connect this discovery is in Aristotle, at least if that little book *Of Unheard-of Wonders* is by him. He there relates that certain Carthaginians, after setting out upon the Atlantic Ocean from the Strait of Gibraltar and sailing a long time, at last discovered a great fertile island, all clothed in woods and watered by great deep rivers, far remote from any mainland; and that they, and others since, attracted by the goodness and fertility of the soil, went there with their wives and children, and began to settle there. The lords of Carthage, seeing that their country was gradually becoming depopulated, expressly forbade anyone to go there any more, on pain of death, and drove out these new inhabitants, fearing, it is said, that in course of time they might come to multiply so greatly as to supplant their former masters and ruin their state. This story of Aristotle does not fit our new lands any better than the other.

This man I had was a simple, crude fellow—a character fit to bear true witness; for clever people observe more things and more curiously, but they interpret them; and to lend weight and conviction to their interpretation, they cannot help altering history a little. They never show you things as they are, but bend and disguise them according to the way they have seen them; and to give credence to their judgment and attract you to it, they are prone to add something to their matter, to stretch it out and amplify it. We need a man either very honest, or so simple that he has not the stuff to build up false inventions and give them plausibility; and wedded to no theory. Such was my man; and besides this, he at various times brought sailors and merchants, whom he had known on that trip, to see me. So I content myself with his information, without inquiring what the cosmographers say about it.

We ought to have topographers who would give us an exact account of the places where they have been. But because they have over us the advantage of having seen Palestine, they want to enjoy the privilege of telling us news about all the rest of the world. I would like everyone to write what he knows, and as much as he knows, not only in this, but in all other subjects; for a man may have some special knowledge and experience of the nature of a river or a fountain, who in other matters knows only what everybody knows. However, to circulate this little scrap of knowledge, he will undertake to write the whole of physics. From this vice spring many great abuses.

Now to return to my subject, I think there is nothing barbarous and savage in that nation, from what I have been told, except that each man calls barbarism whatever is not his own practice; for indeed it seems we have no other test of truth and reason than the example and pattern of the opinions and customs of the country we live in. *There* is always the perfect religion, perfect government, the perfect and accomplished manners in all things. Those people are wild, just as we call wild the fruits that Nature has produced by herself and in her normal course; whereas really it is those that we have changed artificially and led astray from the common order, that we should rather call wild. The former retain alive and vigorous their genuine, their most useful and natural, virtues and properties, which we have debased in the latter in adapting them to gratify our corrupted taste. And yet for all that, the savor and delicacy of some uncultivated fruits of those countries is quite as excellent, even to our taste, as that of our own. It is not reasonable that art should win the place of honor over our great and powerful mother Nature. We have so overloaded the beauty and richness of her works by our inventions that we have quite smothered her. Yet wherever her purity shines forth, she wonderfully puts to shame our vain and frivolous attempts

> Ivy comes readier without our care;
> In lonely caves the arbutus grows more fair;
> No art with artless bird song can compare.
>
> Propertius

All our efforts cannot even succeed in reproducing the nest of the tiniest little bird, its contexture, its beauty and convenience; or even the web of the puny spider. All things, says Plato, are produced by nature, by fortune, or by art; the greatest and most beautiful by one or the other of the first two, the least and most imperfect by the last.

These nations, then, seem to me barbarous in this sense, that they have been fashioned very little by the human mind, and are still very close to their original naturalness. The laws of nature still rule them, very little corrupted by ours, and they are in such a state of purity that I am sometimes vexed that they were unknown earlier, in the days when there were men able to judge them better than we. I am sorry that Lycurgus and Plato did not know of them; for it seems to me that what we actually see in these nations surpasses not only all the pictures in which poets have idealized the golden age and all their inventions in imagining a happy state of man, but also the conceptions and the very desire of philosophy. They could not imagine a naturalness so pure and simple as we see by experience; nor could they believe that our society could be maintained with so little artifice and human solder. This is a nation, I should say to Plato, in which there is no sort of traffic, no knowledge of letters, no science of numbers, no name for a magistrate or for political superiority, no custom of servitude, no riches or poverty, no contracts, no successions, no partitions, no occupations but leisure ones, no care for any but common kinship, no clothes, no agriculture, no metal, no use of wine or wheat. The very words that signify lying, treachery, dissimulation, avarice, envy, belittling, pardon—unheard of. How far from this perfection would he find the republic that he imagined:

Men fresh sprung from the gods [Seneca].

These manners nature first ordained.
Virgil

For the rest, they live in a country with a very pleasant and temperate climate, so that according to my witnesses it is rare to see a sick man there; and they have assured me that they never saw one palsied, bleary-eyed, toothless, or bent with age. They are settled along the sea and shut in on the land side by great high mountains, with a stretch about a hundred leagues wide in between. They have a great abundance of fish and flesh which bear no resemblance to ours, and they eat them with no other artifice than cooking. The first man who rode a horse there, though he had had dealings with them on several other trips, so horrified them in this posture that they shot him dead with arrows before they could recognize him.

Their buildings are very long, with a capacity of two or three hundred souls; they are covered with the bark of great trees, the strips reaching to the ground at one end and supporting and leaning on one another at the top, in the manner of some of our barns, whose covering hangs down to the ground and acts as a side. They have wood so hard that they cut with it and make of it their swords and grills to cook their food. Their beds are of a cotton weave, hung from the roof like those in our ships, each man having his own; for the wives sleep apart from their husbands.

They get up with the sun, and eat immediately upon rising, to last them through the day; for they take no other meal than that one. Like some other Eastern peoples, of whom Suidas tells us, who drank apart from meals, they do not drink then; but they drink several times a day, and to capacity. Their drink is made of some root, and is of the color of our claret wines. They drink it only lukewarm. This beverage keeps only two or three days; it has a slightly sharp taste, is not at all heady, is good for the stomach, and has a laxative effect upon those who are not used to it; it is a very pleasant drink for anyone who is accustomed to it. In place of bread they use a certain white substance like preserved coriander. I have tried it; it tastes sweet and a little flat.

The whole day is spent in dancing. The younger men go to hunt animals with bows. Some of the women busy themselves meanwhile with warming their drink, which is their chief duty. Some one of the old men, in the morning before they begin to eat, preaches to the whole barnful in common, walking from one end to the other, and repeating one single sentence several times until he has completed the circuit (for the buildings are fully a hundred paces long). He recommends to them only two things: valor against the enemy and love for their wives. And they never fail to point out this obligation, as their refrain, that it is their wives who keep their drink warm and seasoned.

There may be seen in several places, including my own house, specimens of their beds, of their ropes, of their wooden swords and the bracelets with which they cover their wrists in combats, and of the big canes open at one end, by whose sound they keep time in their dances. They are close shaven all over, and shave themselves much more cleanly than we, with nothing but a wooden or stone razor. They believe that souls are immortal, and that those who have deserved well of the gods are lodged in that part of heaven where the sun rises, and the damned in the west.

They have some sort of priests and prophets, but they rarely appear before the people, having their home in the mountains. On their arrival there is a great feast and solemn assembly of several villages—each barn, as I have described it, makes up a village, and they are about one French league from each other. The prophet speaks to them in public, exhorting them to virtue and their duty; but their whole ethical science contains only these two articles: resoluteness in war and affection for their wives. He prophesies to them things to come and the results they are to expect from their undertakings, and urges them to war or holds them back from it; but this is on the condition that when he fails to prophesy correctly, and if things turn out otherwise than he has predicted, he is cut into a thousand pieces if they catch him, and condemned as a false prophet. For this reason, the prophet who has once been mistaken is never seen again.

Divination is a gift of God; that is why its abuse should be punished as imposture. Among the Scythians, when the soothsayers failed to hit the mark, they were laid, chained hand and foot, on carts full of heather and drawn by oxen, on which they were burned. Those who handle matters subject to the control of human capacity are excusable if they do the best they can. But these others, who come and trick us with assurances of an extraordinary faculty that is beyond our ken, should they not be punished for not making good their promise, and for the temerity of their imposture?

They have their wars with the nations beyond the mountains, further inland, to which they go quite naked, with no other arms than bows or wooden swords ending in a sharp point, in the manner of the tongues of our boar spears. It is astonishing what firmness they show in their combats, which never end but in slaughter and bloodshed; for as to routs and terror, they know nothing of either.

Each man brings back as his trophy the head of the enemy he has killed, and sets it up at the entrance to his dwelling. After they have treated their prisoners well for a long time with all the hospitality they can think of, each man who has a prisoner calls a great assembly of his acquaintances. He ties a rope to one of the prisoner's arms, by the end of which he holds him, a few steps away, for fear of being hurt, and gives his dearest friend the other arm to hold in the same way; and these two, in the presence of the whole assembly, kill him with their swords. This done, they roast him and eat him in common and send some pieces to their absent friends. This is not, as people think, for nourishment, as of old the Scythians used to do; it is to betoken an extreme revenge. And the proof of this came when they saw the Portuguese, who had joined forces with their adversaries, inflict a different kind of death on them when they took them prisoner, which was to bury them up to the waist, shoot the rest of their body full of arrows, and afterward hang them. They thought that these people from the other world, being men who had sown the knowledge of many vices among their neighbors and were much greater masters than themselves in every sort of wickedness, did not adopt this sort of vengeance without some reason, and that it must be more painful than their own; so they began to give up their old method and to follow this one.

I am not sorry that we notice the barbarous horror of such acts, but I am heartily sorry that, judging their faults rightly, we should be so blind to our own. I think there is more barbarity in eating a man alive than in eating him dead; and in tearing by tortures and the rack a body still full of feeling, in roasting a man bit by bit, in having him bitten and mangled by dogs and swine (as we have not only read but seen within fresh memory, not among ancient enemies, but among neighbors and fellow citizens, and what is worse, on the pretext of piety and religion), than in roasting and eating him after he is dead.

Indeed, Chrysippus and Zeno, heads of the Stoic sect, thought there was nothing wrong in using our carcasses for any purpose in case of need, and getting nourishment from them; just as our ancestors, when besieged by Caesar in the city of Alésia, resolved to relieve their famine by eating old men, women, and other people useless for fighting.

> The Gascons once, 'tis said, their life renewed
> By eating of such food.
>
> Juvenal

And physicians do not fear to use human flesh in all sorts of ways for our health, applying it either inwardly or outwardly. But there never was any opinion so disordered as to excuse treachery, disloyalty, tyranny, and cruelty, which are our ordinary vices.

So we may well call these people barbarians, in respect to the rules of reason, but not in respect to ourselves, who surpass them in every kind of barbarity.

Their warfare is wholly noble and generous, and as excusable and beautiful as this human disease can be; its only basis among them is their rivalry in valor. They are not fighting for the conquest of new lands, for they still enjoy that natural abundance that provides them without toil and trouble with all necessary things in such profusion that they have no wish to enlarge their boundaries. They are still in that happy state of desiring only as much as their natural needs demand; any thing beyond that is superfluous to them.

They generally call those of the same age, brothers; those who are younger, children; and the old men are fathers to all the others. These leave to their heirs in common the full possession of their property, without division or any other title at all than just the one that Nature gives to her creatures in bringing them into the world.

If their neighbors cross the mountains to attack them and win a victory, the gain of the victor is glory, and the advantage of having proved the master in valor and virtue; for apart from this they have no use for the goods of the vanquished, and they return to their own country, where they lack neither anything necessary nor that great thing, the knowledge of how to enjoy their condition happily and be content with it. These men of ours do the same in their turn. They demand of their prisoners no other ransom than that they confess and acknowledge their defeat. But there is not one in a whole century who does not choose to die rather than to relax a single bit, by word or look, from the grandeur of an invincible courage; not one who would not rather be killed and eaten than so much as ask not to be. They treat them very freely, so that life may be all the dearer to them, and usually entertain them with threats of their coming death, of the torments they will have to suffer, the preparations that are being made for that purpose, the cutting up of their limbs, and the feast that will be made at their expense. All this is done for the sole purpose of extorting from their lips some weak or base word, or making them want to flee, so as to gain the advantage of having terrified them and broken down their firmness. For indeed, if you take it the right way, it is in this point alone that true victory lies:

> It is no victory
> Unless the vanquished foe admits your mastery.
>
> Claudian

The Hungarians, very bellicose fighters, did not in olden times pursue their advantage beyond putting the enemy at their mercy. For having wrung a confession from him to this effect, they let him go unharmed and unransomed, except, at most, for exacting his promise never again to take up arms against them.

We win enough advantages over our enemies that are borrowed advantages, not really our own. It is the quality of a porter, not of valor, to have sturdier arms and legs; agility is a dead and corporeal quality; it is a stroke of luck to make our enemy stumble, or dazzle his eyes by the sunlight; it is a trick of art and technique, which may be found in a worthless coward, to be an able fencer. The worth and value of a man is in his heart and his will; there lies his real honor. Valor is the strength, not of legs and arms, but of heart and soul; it consists not in the worth of our horse or our weapons, but in our own. He who falls obstinate in his courage, "if he has fallen, he fights on his knees" [Seneca]. He who relaxes none of his assurance, no matter how great the danger of imminent death; who, giving up his soul, still looks firmly and scornfully at his enemy—he is beaten not by us, but by fortune; he is killed, not conquered.

The most valiant are sometimes the most unfortunate. Thus there are triumphant defeats that rival victories. Nor did those four sister victories, the fairest that the sun ever set eyes on—Salamis, Plataea, Mycale, and Sicily—ever dare match all their combined glory against the glory of the annihilation of King Leonidas and his men at the pass of Thermopylae.

Who ever hastened with more glorious and ambitious desire to win a battle than Captain Ischolas to lose one? Who ever secured his safety more ingeniously and painstakingly than he did his destruction? He was charged to defend a certain pass in the Peloponnesus against the Arcadians. Finding himself wholly incapable of doing this, in view of the nature of the place and the inequality of the forces, he made up his mind that all who confronted the enemy would necessarily have to remain on the field. On the other hand, deeming it unworthy both of his own virtue and magnanimity and of the Lacedaemonian name to fail in his charge, he took a middle course between these two extremes, in this way. The youngest and fittest of his band he preserved for the defense and service of their country, and sent them home; and with those whose loss was less important, he determined to hold this pass, and by their death to make the enemy buy their entry as dearly as he could. And so it turned out. For he was presently surrounded on all sides by the Arcadians, and after slaughtering a large number of them, he and his men were all put to the sword. Is there a trophy dedicated to victors that would not be more due to these vanquished? The role of true victory is in fighting, not in coming off safely; and the honor of valor consists in combating, not in beating.

To return to our story. These prisoners are so far from giving in, in spite of all that is done to them, that on the contrary, during the two or three months that they are kept, they wear a gay expression; they urge their captors to hurry and put them to the test; they defy them, insult them, reproach them with their cowardice and the number of battles they have lost to the prisoners' own people.

I have a song composed by a prisoner which contains this challenge, that they should all come boldly and gather to dine off him, for they will be eating at the same time their own fathers and grandfathers, who have served to feed and nourish his body. "These muscles," he says, "this flesh and these veins are your own, poor fools that you are. You do not recognize that the substance of your ancestors' limbs is still contained in them. Savor them well; you will find in them the taste of your own flesh." An idea that certainly does not smack of barbarity. Those that paint these people dying, and who show the execution, portray the prisoner spitting in the face of his slayers and scowling at them. Indeed, to the last gasp they never stop braving and defying their enemies by word and look. Truly here are real savages by our standards; for either they must be thoroughly so, or we must be; there is an amazing distance between their character and ours.

The men there have several wives, and the higher their reputation for valor the more wives they have. It is a remarkably beautiful thing about their marriages that the same jealousy our wives have to keep us from the affection and kindness of other women, theirs have to win this for them. Being more concerned for their husbands' honor than for anything else, they strive and scheme to have as many companions as they can, since that is a sign of their husbands' valor.

Our wives will cry "Miracle!" but it is no miracle. It is a properly matrimonial virtue, but one of the highest order. In the Bible, Leah, Rachel, Sarah, and Jacob's wives gave their beautiful handmaids to their husbands; and Livia seconded the appetites of Augustus, to her own disadvantage; and Stratonice, the wife of King Deiotarus, not only lent her husband for his use a very beautiful young chambermaid in her service, but carefully brought up her children, and backed them up to succeed to their father's estates.

And lest it be thought that all this is done through a simple and servile bondage to usage and through the pressure of the authority of their ancient customs, without reasoning or judgment, and because their minds are so stupid that they cannot take any other course, I must cite some examples of their capacity. Besides the warlike song I have just quoted, I have another, a love song, which begins in this vein: "Adder, stay; stay, adder, that from the pattern of your coloring my sister may draw the fashion and the workmanship of a rich girdle that I may give to my love; so may your beauty and your pattern be forever preferred to all other serpents." This first couplet is the refrain of the song. Now I am familiar enough with poetry to be a judge of this: not only is there nothing barbarous in this fancy, but it is altogether Anacreontic. Their language, moreover, is a soft language, with an agreeable sound, somewhat like Greek in its endings.

Three of these men, ignorant of the price they will pay some day, in loss of repose and happiness, for gaining knowledge of the corruptions of this side of the ocean; ignorant also of the fact that of this intercourse will come their ruin (which I suppose is already well advanced: poor wretches, to let themselves be tricked by the desire for new things, and to have left the serenity of their own sky to come and see ours!)—three of these men were at Rouen, at the time the late King Charles IX was there. The king talked to them for a long time; they were shown our ways, our splendor, the aspect of a fine city. After that, someone asked their opinion, and wanted to know what they had found most amazing. They mentioned three things, of which I have forgotten the third, and I am very sorry for it; but I still remember two of them. They said that in the first place they thought it very strange that so many grown men, bearded, strong, and armed, who were around the king (it is likely that they were talking about the Swiss of his guard) should submit to obey a child, and that one of them was not chosen to command instead. Second (they have a way in their language of speaking of men as halves of one another), they had noticed that there were among us men full and gorged with all sorts of good things, and that their other halves were beggars at their doors, emaciated with hunger and poverty; and they thought it strange that these needy halves could endure such an injustice, and did not take the others by the throat, or set fire to their houses.

I had a very long talk with one of them; but I had an interpreter who followed my meaning so badly, and who was so hindered by his stupidity in taking in my ideas, that I could get hardly any satisfaction from the man. When I asked him what profit he gained from his superior position among his people (for he was a captain, and our sailors called him king), he told me that it was to march foremost in war. How many men followed him? He pointed to a piece of ground, to signify as many as such a space could hold; it might have been four or five thousand men. Did all his authority expire with the war? He said that this much remained, that when he visited the villages dependent on him, they made paths for him through the underbrush by which he might pass quite comfortably.

All this is not too bad—but what's the use? They don't wear breeches.

Of the Custom of Wearing Clothes

Wherever I want to turn, I have to force some barrier of custom, so carefully has it blocked all our approaches. I was wondering in this shivery season whether the fashion of going stark naked in these lately discovered nations is forced on them by the warm temperature of the air, as we say of the Indians and Moors, or whether it is the original way of mankind. Inasmuch as all things under heaven, as Holy Writ says, are subject to the same laws, men of understanding, in considerations like these (where we must distinguish natural from artificial laws), are wont to have recourse to the general order of the world, in which there can be nothing counterfeit.

Now, since everything else is furnished with the exact amount of thread and needle required to maintain its being, it is in truth incredible that we alone should be brought into the world in a defective and indigent state, in a state such that we cannot maintain ourselves without external aid. Thus I hold that, just as plants, trees, animals, all things that live, are naturally equipped with sufficient covering to defend themselves against the injury of the weather,

> And therefore everything is covered o'er
> With either hide, silk, shells, thick skin, or bark,
>
> Lucretius

so were we; but like those who by artificial light extinguish the light of day, we have extinguished our own means by borrowed means. And it is easy to see that it is custom that makes impossible for us what is not impossible in itself; for of those nations that have no knowledge of clothes, there are some situated under much the same sky as ours; and besides, our most delicate parts are those that are always kept uncovered: eyes, mouth, nose, ears; with our peasants, as with our ancestors, the chest and belly. If we had been born with natural petticoats and breeches, there can be no doubt but that Nature would have armed with a thicker skin the parts she intended to expose to the beating of the seasons, as she has done for the fingertips and the soles of the feet.

Why does this seem hard to believe? Between my way of dressing and that of a peasant of my region I find far more distance than there is between his way and that of a man dressed only in his skin.

How many men, especially in Turkey, go naked as a matter of religion!

Someone or other was asking one of our beggars whom he saw in the depth of winter as cheery in his shirt as someone muffled to the ears in sables, how he could endure it. "And you, sir," he answered, "you have your face uncovered; now, I am all face." The Italians tell this story of the duke of Florence's fool, I think it was: that on his master's inquiring how, so poorly clad, he could bear the cold which he himself had trouble bearing, the fool replied, "Follow my rule, and pile on you all the garments you have, as I do, and you won't suffer from the cold any more than I do." King Massinissa, even in his extreme old age, could not be induced to go with his head covered, however cold, stormy, or rainy it might be. This is also said of the Emperor Severus.

In the battles fought between the Egyptians and the Persians, Herodotus says it was remarked both by others and by himself that of those who remained dead on the field, the skulls of the Egyptians were incomparably harder than those of the Persians, because the latter kept their heads always covered, first with caps and then with turbans, whereas the former kept theirs shaven and bare from infancy.

And King Agesilaus observed until his decrepitude the habit of wearing the same clothing in winter as in summer. Caesar, says Suetonius, always marched at the head of his army, most of the time on foot, head bare, whether it was sunny or raining; and they say as much of Hannibal:

> Then with bare head
> He met the frenzy of the storm, the falling sky.
> Silius Italicus

A Venetian who stayed in the kingdom of Pegu a long time and has only just come back writes that the men and women there always go barefoot, even on horseback, and with the other parts of the body clothed.

And Plato gives this wonderful advice, for the health of the whole body: to give the head and feet no other covering than that which nature has provided.

The man whom the Poles chose for their king after ours, and who is in truth one of the greatest princes of our century, never wears gloves, or changes, for winter or any weather whatever, the bonnet that he wears indoors.

Whereas I cannot bear to go unbuttoned and untied, the laborers in my neighborhood would feel fettered if they were otherwise. Varro maintains that when it was ordained that we should keep our head uncovered in the presence of the gods or the magistrate, it was done more for our health, and to harden us against the attacks of the weather, than on account of reverence.

And since we are on the subject of cold, and Frenchmen, accustomed to array ourselves in varied colors (not I, for I scarcely wear anything but black or white, in imitation of my father), let us add in another connection that Captain Martin du Bellay says he saw, on the march to Luxemburg, frosts so severe that the supply of wine was cut with hatchets and axes, distributed to the soldiers by weight, and carried away in baskets. And Ovid, very close:

> Uncasked, the wines retain the shape of casks,
> And lumps are passed around instead of flasks.
> Ovid

The frosts are so bitter at the mouth of Lake Maeotis that in the same place where Mithridates' lieutenant had fought the enemy dryfooted and defeated them in the winter, he won a naval battle against them the next summer.

The Romans suffered a great disadvantage in their combat with the Carthaginians near Placentia, because they went to the charge with their blood congealed and limbs benumbed with cold, whereas Hannibal had passed out fire throughout his host to warm his soldiers, and distributed oil among each company, so that by anointing themselves they might render their sinews more supple and limber, and encrust their pores against the assault of the air and the freezing wind that was blowing.

The retreat of the Greeks from Babylon into their country is famous for the difficulties and hardships that they had to overcome. This was one: they were met by a terrible blizzard in the mountains of Armenia, and lost all knowledge of the country and the roads. Being quite simply besieged by the storm, they were a day and a night without eating or drinking, most of their animals dead, many of themselves dead, many blinded by the driving hail and the glare of the snow, many crippled in their extremities', many stiff, numb, and immobilized with cold, though still in possession of all their senses.

Alexander saw a nation in which they bury their fruit trees in winter to protect them from the frost.

On the subject of clothing, the king of Mexico changed his clothes four times a day and never put them on again, using his cast-offs for his continual liberalities and rewards; likewise neither pot, nor dish, nor any kitchen or table utensil was ever put before him twice.

Of Experience

There is no desire more natural than the desire for knowledge. We try all the ways that can lead us to it. When reason fails us, we use experience—

Experience, by example led,
By varied trials art has bred
Manilius

—which is a weaker and less dignified means. But truth is so great a thing that we must not disdain any medium that will lead us to it. Reason has so many shapes that we know not which to lay hold of; experience has no fewer. The inference that we try to draw from the resemblance of events is uncertain, because they are always dissimilar: there is no quality so universal in this aspect of things as diversity and variety.

Both the Greeks and the Latins, and we ourselves, use eggs for the most express example of similarity. However, there have been men, and notably one at Delphi, who recognized marks of difference between eggs, so that he never took one for another; and although there were many hens, he could tell which one the egg came from.

Dissimilarity necessarily intrudes into our works; no art can attain similarity. Neither Perrozet nor any other can smooth and whiten the backs of his cards so carefully that some gamesters will not distinguish them simply by seeing them slip through another man's hands. Resemblance does not make things so much alike as difference makes them unlike. Nature has committed herself to make nothing separate that was not different.

Therefore I do not much like the opinion of the man who thought by a multiplicity of laws to bridle the authority of judges, cutting up their meat for them. He did not realize that there is as much freedom and latitude in the interpretation of laws as in their creation. And those people must be jesting who think they can diminish and stop our disputes by recalling us to the express words of the Bible. For our mind finds the field no less spacious in registering the meaning of others than in presenting its own. As if there were less animosity and bitterness in commenting than in inventing!

We see how mistaken he was. For we have in France more laws than all the rest of the world together, and more than would be needed to rule all the worlds of Epicurus: "As formerly we suffered from crimes, so now we suffer from laws" [Tacitus]. And yet we have left so much room for opinion and decision to our judges, that there never was such a powerful and licentious freedom. What have our legislators gained by selecting a hundred thousand particular cases and actions, and applying a hundred thousand laws to them? This number bears no proportion to the infinite diversity of human actions. Multiplication of our imaginary cases will never equal the variety of the real examples. Add to them a hundred times as many more: and still no future event will be found to correspond so exactly to any one of all the many, many thousands of selected and recorded events that there will not remain some circumstance, some difference, that will require separate consideration in forming a judgment. There is little relation between our actions, which are in perpetual mutation, and fixed and immutable laws. The most desirable laws are those that are rarest, simplest, and most general; and I even think that it would be better to have none at all than to have them in such numbers as we have.

Nature always gives us happier laws than those we give ourselves. Witness the picture of the Golden Age of the poets; and the state in which we see nations live which have no other laws. Here are some who employ, as the only judge in their quarrels, the first traveler passing through their mountains. And these others on market day elect one of themselves who decides all their suits on the spot. What would be the danger in having our wisest men settle ours in this way, according to the circumstances and at sight, without being bound to pecedents, past or future? For every foot its own shoe. King Ferdinand, when he sent colonists to the Indies, wisely provided that no students of jurisprudence should accompany them, for fear that lawsuits might breed in this new world, this being by nature a science generating altercation and division; judging, with Plato, that lawyers and doctors are a bad provision for a country.

Why is it that our common language, so easy for any other use, becomes obscure and unintelligible in contracts and wills, and that a man who expresses himself so clearly, whatever he says or writes, finds in this field no way of speaking his mind that does not fall into doubt and contradiction? Unless it is that the princes of this art, applying themselves with particular attention to picking out solemn words and contriving artificial phrases, have so weighed every syllable, so minutely examined every sort of combination, that here they are at last entangled and embroiled in the endless number of figures and in such minute partitions that they can no longer fall under any rule or prescription or any certain interpretation. "What is broken up into dust becomes confused" [Seneca].

Who has seen children trying to divide a mass of quicksilver into a certain number of parts? The more they press it and knead it and try to constrain it to their will, the more they provoke the independence of this spirited metal; it escapes their skill and keeps dividing and scattering in little particles beyond all reckoning. This is the same; for by subdividing these subtleties they teach men to increase their doubts; they start us extending and diversifying the difficulties, they lengthen them, they scatter them. By sowing questions and cutting them up, they make the world fructify and teem with uncertainty and quarrels, as the earth is made more fertile the more it is crumbled and deeply plowed. "Learning makes difficulties" [Quintilian].

I do not know what to say about it, but it is evident from experience that so many interpretations disperse the truth and shatter it. Aristotle wrote to be understood; if he did not succeed, still less will another man, less able, and not treating his own ideas. By diluting the substance we allow it to escape and spill it all over the place; of one subject we make a thousand, and, multiplying and subdividing, fall back into Epicurus' infinity of atoms. Never did two men judge alike about the same thing, and it is impossible to find two opinions exactly alike, not only in different men, but in the same man at different times. Ordinarily I find subject for doubt in what the commentary has not deigned to touch on. I am more apt to trip on flat ground, like certain horses I know which stumble more often on a smooth road.

Who would not say that glosses increase doubts and ignorance, since there is no book to be found, whether human or divine, with which the world busies itself, whose difficulties are cleared up by interpretation? The hundredth commentator hands it on to his successor thornier and rougher than the first one had found it. When do we agree and say, "There has been enough about this book; henceforth there is nothing more to say about it"?

This is best seen in law practice. We give legal authority to numberless doctors, numberless decisions, and as many interpretations. Do we therefore find any end to the need of interpreting? Do we see any progress and advance toward tranquillity? Do we need fewer lawyers and judges than when this mass of law was still in its infancy? On the contrary, we obscure and bury the meaning; we no longer find it except hidden by so many enclosures and barriers.

Men do not know the natural infirmity of their mind: it does nothing but ferret and quest, and keeps incessantly whirling around, building up and becoming entangled in its own work, like our silkworms and is suffocated in it. "A mouse in a pitch barrel" [Erasmus]. It thinks it notices from a distance some sort of glimmer of imaginary light and truth: but while running toward it, it is crossed by so many difficulties and obstacles, and diverted by so many new quests, that it strays from the road, bewildered. Not very different from what happened to Aesop's dogs who, discovering something that looked like a dead body floating in the sea, and being unable to approach it, attempted to drink up the water and dry up the passage, and choked in the attempt. To which may be joined what a certain Crates said of the writings of Heraclitus, that they needed a good swimmer for a reader, so that the depth and weight of Heraclitus' learning should not sink him and drown him.

It is only personal weakness that makes us content with what others or we ourselves have found out in this hunt for knowledge. An abler man will not rest content with it. There is always room for a successor, yes, and for ourselves, and a road in another direction. There is no end to our researches; our end is in the other world. It is a sign of contraction of the mind when it is content, or of weariness. A spirited mind never stops within itself; it is always aspiring and going beyond its strength; it has impulses beyond its powers of achievement. If it does not advance and press forward and stand at bay and clash, it is only half alive. Its pursuits are boundless and without form; its food is wonder, the chase, ambiguity. Apollo revealed this clearly enough, always speaking to us equivocally, obscurely, and obliquely, not satisfying us, but keeping our minds interested and busy. It is an irregular, perpetual motion, without model and without aim. Its inventions excite, pursue, and produce one another.

So in a running stream one wave we see
After another roll incessantly,
And line by line, each does eternally
Pursue the other, each the other flee.
By this one, that one ever on is sped,

And this one by the other ever led;
The water still does into water go,
Still the same brook, but different waters flow.
La Boétie

It is more of a job to interpret the interpretations than to interpret the things, and there are more books about books than about any other subject: we do nothing but write glosses about each other. The world is swarming with commentaries; of authors there is a great scarcity.

Is it not the chief and most reputed learning of our times to learn to understand the learned? Is that not the common and ultimate end of all studies?

Our opinions are grafted upon one another. The first serves as a stock for the second, the second for the third. Thus we scale the ladder, step by step. And thence it happens that he who has mounted highest has often more honor than merit; for he has only mounted one speck higher on the shoulders of the next last.

How often and perhaps how stupidly have I extended my book to make it speak of itself! Stupidly, if only for this reason, that I should have remembered what I say of others who do the same: that these frequent sheep's eyes at their own work testify that their heart thrills with love for it, and that even the rough, disdainful blows with which they beat it are only the love taps and affectations of maternal fondness; in keeping with Aristotle, to whom self-appreciation and self-depreciation often spring from the same sort of arrogance. For as for my excuse, that I ought to have more liberty in this than others, precisely because I write of myself and my writings as of my other actions, because my theme turns in upon itself—I do not know whether everyone will accept it.

I have observed in Germany that Luther has left as many divisions and altercations over the uncertainty of his opinions, and more, as he raised about the Holy Scriptures.

Our disputes are purely verbal. I ask what is "nature," "pleasure," "circle," "substitution." The question is one of words, and is answered in the same way. "A stone is a body." But if you pressed on: "And what is a body?"—"Substance."—And what is substance?" and so on, you would finally drive the respondent to the end of his lexicon. We exchange one word for another word, often more unknown. I know better what is man than I know what is animal, or mortal, or rational. To satisfy one doubt, they give me three; it is the Hydra's head.

Socrates asked Meno what virtue was. "There is," said Meno, "the virtue of a man and of a woman, of a magistrate and of a private individual, of a child and of an old man." 'That's fine," exclaimed Socrates; "we were in search of one virtue, and here is a whole swarm of them."

We put one question, they give us back a hive of them. As no event and no shape is entirely like another, so none is entirely different from another. An ingenious mixture on the part of nature. If our faces were not similar, we could not distinguish man from beast; if they were not dissimilar, we could not distinguish man from man. All things hold together by some similarity; every example is lame, and the comparison that is drawn from experience is always faulty and imperfect; however, we fasten together our comparisons by some corner. Thus the laws serve, and thus adapt themselves to each of our affairs, by some roundabout, forced, and biased interpretation.

In China—a kingdom whose government and arts, without dealings with and knowledge of ours, surpass our examples in many branches of excellence, and whose history teaches me how much ampler and more varied the world is than either the ancients or we ourselves understand—the officers deputed by the prince to inspect the state of his provinces, even as they punish those who are corrupt in their office, also reward, from pure liberality, those who have conducted themselves better than the average and better than the requirements of their duty. People come before them not merely to defend themselves, but to gain by it, and not simply to be paid, but also to receive presents.

No judge has yet, thank God, spoken to me as a judge in any cause whatever, my own or another man's, criminal or civil. No prison has received me, not even for a visit. Imagination makes the sight of one, even from the outside, unpleasant to me. I am so sick for freedom, that if anyone should forbid me access to some corner of the Indies, I should live distinctly less comfortably. And as long as I find earth or air open elsewhere, I shall not lurk in any place where I have to hide. Lord, how ill could I endure the condition in which I see so many people, nailed down to one section of this kingdom, deprived of the right to enter the principal towns and the courts and to use the public roads, for having quarreled with our laws! If those that I serve threatened even the tip of my finger, I should instantly go and find others, wherever it might be. All my little prudence in these civil wars in which we are now involved is employed to keep them from interrupting my freedom of coming and going.

Now laws remain in credit not because they are just, but because they are laws. That is the mystic foundation of their authority; they have no other. And that is a good thing for them. They are often made by fools, more often by people who, in their hatred of equality, are wanting in equity; but always by men, vain and irresolute authors.

There is nothing so grossly and widely and ordinarily faulty as the laws. Whoever obeys them because they are just, does not obey them for just the reason he should. Our French laws, by their irregularity and lack of form, rather lend a hand to the disorder and corruption that is seen in their administration and execution. Their commands are so confused and inconsistent that they are some excuse for both disobedience and faulty interpretation, administration, and observance.

Then whatever may be the fruit we can reap from experience, what we derive from foreign examples will hardly be much use for our education, if we make such little profit from the experience we have of ourselves, which is more familiar to us, and certainly sufficient to inform us of what we need.

I study myself more than any other subject. That is my metaphysics, that is my physics.

By what art God our home, the world, controls;
Whence the moon rises, where she sets, how rolls
Her horns together monthly, and again
Grows full; whence come the winds that rule the main;
Where Eurus' blast holds sway; whence springs the rain
That ever fills the clouds; whether some day
The citadels of the world will pass away.
Propertius

Inquire, you who the laboring world survey.
Lucan

In this universe of things I ignorantly and negligently let myself be guided by the general law of the world. I shall know it well enough when I feel it. My knowledge could not make it change its path; it will not modify itself for me. It is folly to hope it, and greater folly to be troubled about it, since it is necessarily uniform, public, and common. The goodness and capacity of the governor should free us absolutely and fully from worrying about his government.

Philosophical inquiries and meditations serve only as food for our curiosity. The philosophers with much reason refer us to the rules of Nature; but these have no concern with such sublime knowledge. The philosophers falsify them and show us the face of Nature painted in too high a color, and too sophisticated, whence spring so many varied portraits of so uniform a subject. As she has furnished us with feet to walk with, so she has given us wisdom to guide us in life: a wisdom not so ingenious, robust, and pompous as that of their invention, but correspondingly easy and salutary, performing very well what the other talks about, in a man who has the good fortune to know how to occupy himself simply and in an orderly way, that is to say naturally. The more simply we trust to Nature, the more wisely we trust to her. Oh, what a sweet and soft and healthy pillow is ignorance and incuriosity, to rest a well-made head!

I would rather be an authority on myself than on Cicero. In the experience I have of myself I find enough to make me wise, if I were a good scholar. He who calls back to mind the excess of his past anger, and how far this fever carried him away, sees the ugliness of this passion better than in Aristotle, and conceives a more justified hatred for it. He who remembers the evils he has undergone, and those that have threatened him, and the slight causes that have changed him from one state to another, prepares himself in that way for future changes and for recognizing his condition. The life of Caesar has no more to show us than our own; an emperor's or an ordinary man's, it is still a life subject to all human accidents. Let us only listen: we tell ourselves all we most need.

He who remembers having been mistaken so many, many times in his own judgment, is he not a fool if he does not distrust it forever after? When I find myself convicted of a false opinion by another man's reasoning, I do not so much learn what new thing he has told me and this particular bit of ignorance—that would be small gain—as I learn my weakness in general, and the treachery of my understanding; whence I derive the reformation of the whole mass. With all my other errors I do the same, and I feel that this rule is very useful for my life. I do not regard the species and the individual, like a stone I have stumbled on; I learn to mistrust my gait throughout, and I strive to regulate it. To learn that we have said or done a foolish thing, that is nothing; we must learn that we are nothing but fools, a far broader and more important lesson.

The advice to everyone to know himself must have an important effect, since the god of learning and light had it planted on the front of his temple, as comprising all the counsel he had to give us. Plato also says that wisdom is nothing else but the execution of this command, and Socrates, in Xenophon, verifies it in detail.

The difficulties and obscurity in any science are perceived only by those who have access to it. For a man needs at least some degree of intelligence to be able to notice that he does not know; and we must push against a door to know that it is closed to us. Whence arises this Platonic subtlety, that neither those who know need inquire, since they know, nor those who do not know, since in order to inquire they must know what they are inquiring about. Thus in this matter of knowing oneself, the fact that everyone is seen to be so cocksure and self-satisfied, that everyone thinks he understands enough about himself, signifies that everyone understands nothing about it, as Socrates teaches Euthydemus in Xenophon.

I, who make no other profession, find in me such infinite depth and variety, that what I have learned bears no other fruit than to make me realize how much I still have to learn. To my weakness, so often recognized, I owe the inclination I have to modesty, obedience to the beliefs that are prescribed me, a constant coolness and moderation in my opinions, and my hatred for that aggressive and quarrelsome arrogance that believes and trusts wholly in itself, a mortal enemy of discipline and truth. Hear them laying down the law: the first stupidities that they advance are in the style in which men establish religions and laws. "Nothing is more discreditable than to have assertion and proof precede knowledge and perception" [Cicero].

This long attention that I devote to studying myself trains me also to judge passably of others, and there are few things of which I speak more felicitously and excusably. It often happens that I see and distinguish the characters of my friends more exactly than they do themselves. I have astonished at least one by the pertinence of my description, and have given him information about himself. By training myself from my youth to see my own life mirrored in that of others, I have acquired a studious bent in that subject, and when I am thinking about it, I let few things around me which are useful for that purpose escape my notice: countenances, humors, statements. I study everything: what I must flee, what I must follow. So I reveal to my friends, by their outward manifestations, their inward inclinations. I do not attempt to arrange this infinite variety of actions, so diverse and so disconnected, into certain types and categories, and distribute my lots and divisions distinctly into recognized classes and sections:

How many kinds there are, their titles manifold,
We are not told.

Virgil

The scholars distinguish and mark off their ideas more specifically and in detail. I, who cannot see beyond what I have learned from experience, without any system, present my ideas in a general way, and tentatively. As in this: I speak my meaning in disjointed parts, as something that cannot be said all at once and in a lump. Relatedness and conformity are not found in low and common minds such as ours. Wisdom is a solid and integral structure, each part of which holds its place and bears its mark. "Wisdom alone is wholly directed toward itself" [Cicero]. I leave it to artists, and I do not know if they will achieve it in a matter so complex, minute, and accidental, to arrange into bands this infinite diversity of aspects, to check our inconsistency and set it down in order. Not only do I find it hard to link our actions with one another, but each one separately I find hard to designate properly by some principal characteristic, so two-sided and motley do they seem in different lights.

We need very strong ears to hear ourselves judged frankly; and because there are few who can endure frank criticism without being stung by it, those who venture to criticize us perform a remarkable act of friendship; for to undertake to wound and offend a man for his own good is to have a healthy love for him. I find it a rough task to judge a man in whom the bad qualities exceed the good. Plato prescribes three qualities in a man who wants to examine another man's soul: knowledge, good will, boldness.

Sometimes people used to ask me what I would have thought myself good for, if anyone had thought of using me while I was young enough:

While better blood gave strength, before the snows
Of envious age were sprinkled on my brows.

Virgil

"For nothing" I said. And I readily excuse myself for not knowing how to do anything that would enslave me to others. But I would have told my master home truths, and watched over his conduct, if he had been willing. Not in general, by schoolmasterly lessons, which I do not know—and I see no true reform spring from them in those who know them—but by observing his conduct step by step, at every opportunity, judging it with my own eyes, piece by piece, simply and naturally, making him see how he stands in public opinion, and opposing his flatterers.

There is not one of us who would not be worse than the kings if he were as continually spoiled as they are by that rabble. How could it be otherwise, if Alexander, that great man both as king and as philosopher, could not defend himself against them?

I should have had enough fidelity, judgment, and independence for that. It would be a nameless office; otherwise it would lose its effect and its grace. And it is a part that cannot be played indiscriminately by all. For truth itself does not have the privilege to be employed at any time and in any way; its use, noble as it is, has its circumscriptions and limits. It often happens, as the world goes, that people blurt it out into a prince's ear not only fruitlessly, but harmfully, and even unjustly. And no one will make me believe that a righteous remonstrance cannot be applied wrongfully, and that the interest of the substance must not often yield to the interest of the form.

For this occupation I should want a man who is content with his fortune,

> Who would be what he is, and nothing else prefers,
> Martial

and born to a middle rank; because on the one hand he would not fear to touch his master's heart deeply and to the quick, at the risk of losing his preferment thereby; and on the other hand, being of middle station, he would have easier communication with all sorts of people. I would have this an office for one man alone, for to spread the privilege of this freedom and intimacy among several would engender a harmful irreverence. And certainly I should require of that man, above all, the fidelity of silence.

A king is not to be believed when he boasts of his constancy in awaiting the shock of the enemy for the sake of his glory, if, for his own good and improvement, he cannot endure the freedom of a friend's words, which have no other power than to sting his ears, the rest of their effect being in his own hands. Now, there is no class of men that has as great need as they of true and frank admonitions. They endure a public life, and have to suit the opinions of so many spectators, that, since people have formed the habit of concealing from them anything that disturbs their plans, they find themselves, without realizing it, the object of the hatred and detestation of their people, often for reasons that they could have avoided at no sacrifice, even of their pleasures, if they had been advised and set right in time. Ordinarily their favorites look out for themselves more than for their master; and this serves them well, since in truth most of the duties of true friendship are hard and dangerous to attempt toward a sovereign; so that there is need, not only of much affection and frankness, but of much courage as well.

In fine, all this fricassee that I am scribbling here is nothing but a record of the essays of my life, which, for spiritual health, is exemplary enough if you take its instruction in reverse. But as for bodily health, no one can furnish more useful experience than I, who present it pure, not at all corrupted or altered by art or theorizing. Experience is really on its own dunghill in the subject of medicine, where reason yields it the whole field. Tiberius used to say that whoever had lived twenty years should be responsible to himself for the things that were harmful or beneficial to him, and know how to take care of himself without medical aid. And he might have learned this from Socrates, who, advising his disciples, carefully and as a principal study, the study of their health, used to add that it was difficult for an intelligent man who was careful about his exercise, his drinking, and his eating not to know better than any doctor what was good or bad for him.

And indeed, medicine professes always to have experience as the touchstone for its workings. So Plato was right in saying that to become a true doctor, the candidate must have passed through all the illnesses that he wants to cure and all the accidents and circumstances that he is to diagnose. It is reasonable that he should catch the pox if he wants to know how to treat it. Truly I should trust such a man. For the others guide us like the man who paints seas, reefs, and ports while sitting at his table, and sails the model of a ship there in complete safety. Throw him into the real thing, and he does not know how to go at it. They make a description of our diseases like that of a town crier proclaiming a lost horse or dog: such-and-such a coat, such-and-such a height, such and-such ears; but present it to him, and he does not know it for all that.

For heaven's sake, let medicine some day give me some good and perceptible relief, and you will see how I shall cry out in good earnest:

> At last I yield to an efficient science.
> Horace

The arts that promise to keep our body in health and our soul in health promise us much; but at the same time there are none that keep their promise less. And in our time those who profess these arts among us show the results of them less than any other men. The most you can say for them is that they sell medicinal drugs; but that they are doctors you cannot say.

I have lived long enough to give an account of the practice that has guided me so far. For anyone who wants to try it I have tasted it like his cupbearer. Here are a few items, as memory supplies me with them. I have no habit that has not varied according to circumstances, but I record those that I have seen most frequently in action, which have had most hold on me up to this moment.

My way of life is the same in sickness as in health; the same bed, the same hours, the same food serve me, and the same drink. I make no adjustments at all, save for moderating the amount according to my strength and appetite. Health for me is maintaining my accustomed state without disturbance. Do I see that sickness dislodges me in one direction? If I trust the doctors, they will turn me aside in another. And both by fortune and by art, there I am off my road. I believe nothing with more certainty than this: that I cannot be hurt by the use of things that I have been so long accustomed to.

It is for habit to give form to our life, just as it pleases; it is all powerful in that; it is Circe's drink, which varies our nature as it sees fit. How many nations, and three steps from us, regard as ridiculous the fear of the night dew, which appears so hurtful to us; and our boatmen and peasants laugh at it. You make a German sick if you put him to bed on a mattress, like an Italian on a feather bed, and a Frenchman without curtains and a fire. A Spaniard's stomach cannot stand our way of eating, nor can ours stand to drink Swiss fashion.

A German pleased me at Augsburg by attacking the disadvantages of our fireplaces by the same argument we ordinarily use to condemn their stoves. For in truth, that stifling heat, and the smell of that material they are made of when it gets hot, give most of those who are not used to them a headache; not me. But after all, since this heat is even, constant, and general, without flame, without smoke, without the wind that the opening of our chimneys brings us, it has good grounds in other respects for comparison with ours.

This German, hearing me praise the comforts and beauties of his city, which certainly deserves it, began to sympathize with me because I had to leave it; and one of the first discomforts he mentioned to me was the heavy-headedness that the fireplaces elsewhere would cause me. He had heard someone make this complaint, and associated it with us, being disabled by habit from noticing it at home.

All heat that comes from fire makes me feel weak and heavy. Yet Evenus said that the best condiment of life was fire. I prefer any other way of escaping from the cold.

We are afraid of the wine at the bottom of the cask; in Portugal its flavor is considered delicious, and it is the drink of princes.

In short, each nation has many customs and usages that are not only unknown, but savage and miraculous, to some other nation.

What shall we do with this people that admits none but printed evidence, that does not believe men unless they are in a book, or truth unless it is of competent age? We dignify our stupidities when we put them in print. It carries very different weight with this people if you say "I have read it" than if you say "I have heard it." But I, who do not disbelieve men's mouths any more than their hands, and who know that people write just as injudiciously as they speak, and who esteem this age just as if it were another that is past, I quote a friend of mine as readily as Aulus Gellius or Macrobius, and what I have seen as what they have written. And, as they hold that virtue is no greater for being of longer standing, so I consider that truth is no wiser for being older. I often say that it is pure stupidity that makes us run after foreign and scholarly examples. There is as great an abundance of them in this age as in that of Homer and Plato. But is it not true that we seek rather the honor of quoting than the truth of the statement? As if it were greater to borrow our proofs from the shop of Vascosan or Plantin than from what may be seen in our own village. Or rather, indeed, that we have not the wit to pick out and put to use what happens before our eyes, and to judge it keenly enough to make it an example? For if we say we lack authority to gain credence for our testimony, we say so without reason. By the same token, in my opinion, from the most ordinary, commonplace, familiar things, if we could put them in their proper light, can be formed the greatest miracles of nature and the most wondrous examples, especially on the subject of human actions.

Now, on my subject, leaving aside the examples that I know from books, and what Aristotle says about Andro of Argos, that he crossed the arid sands of Libya without drinking, a gentleman who has acquitted himself worthily in several charges said in my presence that he had gone from Madrid to Lisbon in midsummer without drinking. He is in vigorous health for his age, and has nothing extraordinary in his way of living except this, that he will go two or three months, even a year, so he told me, without drinking. He feels some thirst, but he lets it pass, and maintains that it is an appetite that easily grows languid by itself; and he drinks more out of caprice than from need or for pleasure.

When I dance, I dance; when I sleep, I sleep; yes, and when I walk alone in a beautiful orchard, if my thoughts have been dwelling on extraneous incidents for some part of the time, for some other part I bring them back to the walk, to the orchard, to the sweetness of this solitude, and to me. Nature has observed this principle like a mother, that the actions she has enjoined on us for our need should also give us pleasure; and she invites us to them not only through reason, but also through appetite. It is unjust to infringe her laws.

When I see both Caesar and Alexander, in the thick of their great tasks, so fully enjoying natural and therefore necessary and just pleasures, I do not say that that is relaxing their souls, I say that it is toughening them, subordinating these violent occupations and laborious thoughts, by the vigor of their spirits, to the practice of everyday life: wise men, had they believed that this was their ordinary occupation, the other the extraordinary.

We are great fools. "He has spent his life in idleness," we say; "I have done nothing today." What, have you not lived? That is not only the fundamental but the most illustrious of your occupations. "If I had been placed in a position to manage great affairs, I would have shown what I could do." Have you been able to think out and manage your own life? You have done the greatest task of all. To show and exploit her resources Nature has no need of fortune; she shows herself equally on all levels and behind a curtain as well as without one. To compose our character is our duty, not to compose books, and to win, not battles and provinces but order and tranquillity in our conduct. Our great and glorious masterpiece is to live appropriately. All other things, ruling, hoarding, building, are only little appendages and props, at most.

The nice inscription in which the Athenians honored the entry of Pompey into their city is in accord with my meaning.

> You are as much a god as you will own
> That you are nothing but a man alone.
>
> Amyot's Plutarch

It is an absolute perfection and virtually divine to know how to enjoy our being rightfully. We seek other conditions because we do not understand the use of our own, and go outside of ourselves because we do not know what it is like inside. Yet there is no use our mounting on stilts, for on stilts we must still walk on our own legs. And on the loftiest throne in the world we are still sitting only on our own rump.

The most beautiful lives, to my mind, are those that conform to the common human pattern, with order, but without miracle and without eccentricity. Now old age needs to be treated a little more tenderly. Let us commend it to that god who is the protector of health and wisdom, but gay and sociable wisdom:

> Grant me but health, Latona's son,
> And to enjoy the wealth I've won,
> And honored age, with mind entire
> And not unsolaced by the lyre.
>
> Horace

NOTES

[1]Montaigne inserts numerous Latin quotations from classical authors in his writings. These quotations have been translated by the editor of the Stanford University Press edition, which we use here.

Religion, Politics, and the Supernatural

In sixteenth- and seventeenth-century England, a growing body of literature was gaining popularity. This literature is known as the "reportorial pamphlet," a version of news printed and sold in the stationers shops that proliferated in early modern London. While these pamphlets covered all sorts of topics, those which focused on women usually took the form of eulogies or condemnations.[1] The selection here is one of the latter. In relating how Joan Flower and her two daughters were convicted of torturing, through the use of witchcraft, an earl and his family, the women are portrayed not as freaks of society, but as representative of the depraved and frail nature of all women.

While the issue of witchcraft is of course central to this pamphlet, the implicit concern in publishing this particular story is to reveal and condemn the subversion of "natural" hierarchies: that of man over woman and of God over Satan. What connections can be made between the issues at stake in this reading and in those readings concerned with political philosophy, especially James's *True Law of Free Monarchy* and Mornay's *A Defense of Liberty against Tyrants*?

[1]Information for this introduction was taken from Katherine Usher Henderson and Barbara F. McManus, eds. *Half Humankind: Contexts and Texts of the Controversy about Women in England, 1540-1640.* (Urbana and Chicago: University of Illinois Press, 1985) 63-70.

THE
WONDERFVL
DISCOVERIE OF THE
Witchcrafts of *Margaret* and *Phillip Flower*, daughters of *Ioan Flower* neere *Beuer Caſtle*: Executed at Lincolne, *March* 11. 1618.
Who were ſpecially arraigned and condemned before Sir *Henry Hobart*, and Sir *Edward Bromley*, Iudges of Aſſiſe, for confeſſing themſelues actors in the deſtruction of *Henry* L. *Roſſe*, with their damnable practiſes againſt others the Children of the Right Honourable FRANCIS Earle of *Rutland*.
Together with the ſeuerall Examinations and Confeſſions of *Anne Baker*. *Ioan Willimot*, and *Ellen Greene*, Witches in *Leiceſterſhire*.

Printed at London by *G. Eld* for *I. Barnes*, dwelling in the long Walke neere Chriſt-Church. 1619.

Title page of The Wonderful Discovery of the Witchcrafts of Margaret and Phillipa Flower.

The Wonderful Discovery of the Witchcrafts of Margaret and Philippa Flower

daughters of Joan Flower, near Belvoir Castle; Executed at Lincoln March 11, 1618.

1619

My meaning is not to make any contentious arguments about the discourses, distinction, or definition of witchcraft, the power of devils, the nature of spirits, the force of charms, the secrets of incantation, and suchlike, because the Scriptures are full of prohibitions to this purpose and proclaims death to the presumptuous attempters of the same. Besides, both princes (yea, our own learned and most judicious King), philosophers, poets, chronologers, historiographers, and many worthy writers have concurred and concluded in this: that divers impious and facinorous mischiefs have been effectuated through the instruments of the devil, by permission of God, so that the actors of the same have carried away the opinion of the world to do that which they did by witchcraft, or at least to be esteemed witches for bringing such and such things to pass. For howsoever the learned have charactered delinquents in this kind by titles of sundry sorts and most significant attributes, as *pythoness* dealing with artificial Charms; *magi* anciently reputed so for extraordinary wisdom and knowledge in the secrets of simples and herbs; *chaldei* famous for astronomy and astrology; *necromancers* for practicing to raise dead bodies; *geomantici* for conversing with spirits and using incantations; *genethliaci* for presuming on the calculating of nativities or, if you will, assuming the credit of figure-casting; *ventriloqui* for speaking with hollow voices as if they were possessed with Devils; *venefici* for dealing with poison and either killing or curing that way (for you must understand however the professors aforesaid practice murder and mischief, yet many times they pretend cures and preservation, with many others carrying the show of great learning and admired knowledge): yet have they all but one familiar term with us in English called "witches." As for the conceit of wise men or wise women, they are all merely cozeners and deceivers; so that if they make you believe that by their means you shall hear of things lost or stolen, it is either done by Confederacy or put off by protraction to deceive you of your money.

[Certain people afflicted with "melancholy and atheism" and motivated by malicious envy or a desire for revenge study "exotic practices of loathsome arts and sciences." Others seek a reputation for godlike power and knowledge, "making you believe with Medea that they can raise tempests, turn the sun into blood, pull the moon out of her sphere, and sail over the sea in a cockle shell." The devil presents himself to these people, showing them how to achieve their desires and offering to attend them "in some familiar shape of rat, cat, toad, bird" or other animal. They enter into a contract with the devil, forfeiting their souls to be avenged on their neighbors' bodies or to enjoy a reputation for possessing supernatural power. However, God will not allow them indefinitely "to abuse his holy name nor deceive others by their profane lives"; sooner or later the law convicts and executes them.

[The author cites several recent works on witchcraft: "that learned discourse of demonology . . . by the high and mighty Prince James, by the grace of God King of England, Scotland, France, and Ireland"; a treatise by a Norfolk preacher, Alexander Roberts, on the witchcraft of Mary Smith; a work by John Cotta, a Northampton doctor who exposed women professing to help the sick; and a dialogue concerning witchcraft by a Maldon minister named George Gifford. He then notes further cases of English witches who were tried and executed, including Mother Sutton and her daughter Mary from Bedford, the infamous Lancashire witches, and Janet Preston from York, convicted of the murder by witchcraft of one Mr. Lister. These treatises on witchcraft and actual trials of witches serve to refute the erroneous opinions of some people "who suppose there be none at all, or at least that they do not personally or truly effect such things as are imputed unto them."]

But yet because the mind of man may be carried away with many idle conjectures—either that women confessed these things by extremity of torture, or that ancient examples are by this time forgotten (although the particulars are upon record for the benefit of all posterity), or that they were beside themselves or subject to some weak device or other—rather to bring in question the integrity of justice than to make odious the lives of such horrible offenders, I have presumed to present on the stage of verity for the good of my country and the love of truth the late woeful tragedy of the destruction of the Right Honorable the Earl of Rutland's children, who to his eternal praise proceeded yet both religiously and charitably against the offenders, leaving their prosecution to the law and submitting himself and deplorable case to the providence of God, who afflicteth his best servants with punishments and many times sendeth extraordinary vengeance as well on the innocent as the bad deserver to manifest his glory. Therefore by way of caution I advise thee, gentle Reader, whosoever thou art, to take heed how thou dost either despise the power of God in his creatures or vilipend the subtlety and fury of the Devil as God's instrument of vengeance, considering that truth in despite of gainsayers will prevail, according to that principle, *Magna est veritas et prevalebit*.

The story follows:

After the right honorable Sir Francis Manners succeeded his brother in the Earldom of Rutland, and so not only took possession of Belvoir Castle but of all other his domains, lordships, towns, manors, lands and revenues appropriate to the same earldom, he proceeded so honorably in the course of his life (as neither displacing tenants, discharging servants, denying the access of the poor, welcoming of strangers, and performing all the duties of a noble lord) that he fastened as it were unto himself the love and good opinion of the country: wherein he walked the more cheerfully and remarkably because his honorable Countess marched arm in arm with him in the same race, so that Belvoir Castle was a continual palace of entertainment and a daily receptacle for all sorts, both rich and poor, especially such ancient people as neighbored the same. Amongst whom one Joan Flower with her daughters Margaret and Philippa were not only relieved at the first from thence, but quickly entertained as charwomen, and Margaret admitted as a continual dweller in the castle, looking both to the poultry abroad and the washhouse within doors; in which life they continued with equal correspondency till something was discovered to the noble lady which concerned the misdemeanor of these women. And although such honorable persons shall not want of all sorts of people either to bring them news, tales, reports, or to serve their turn in all offices whatsoever (so that it may well be said of them, as it is of great kings and princes, that they have large hands, wide ears, and piercing sights to discover the unswept corners of their remotest confines, to reach even to their furthest borders and to understand the secrets of their meanest subjects), yet in this matter neither were they busybodies, flatterers, malicious politicians, underminers nor supplanters one of another's good fortune, but went simply to work as regarding the honor of the Earl and his Lady, and so by degrees gave light to their understanding to apprehend their complaints. First, that Joan Flower, the mother, was a monstrous malicious woman, full of oaths, curses, and imprecations irreligious and, for anything they saw by her, a plain atheist. Besides, of late days her very countenance was estranged; her eyes were fiery and hollow, her speech fell and envious, her demeanor strange and exotic, and her conversation sequestered, so that the whole course of her life gave great suspicion that she was a notorious witch. Yea, some of her neighbors dared to affirm that she dealt with familiar spirits and terrified them all with curses and threatening of revenge if there was never so little cause of displeasure and unkindness. Concerning Margaret, that she often resorted from the castle to her mother, bringing such provision as they thought was unbefitting for a servant to purloin, and coming at such unseasonable hours that they could not but conjecture some mischief between them; and that their extraordinary riot and expenses tended both to rob the lady and to maintain certain debauched and base company which frequented this Joan Flower's house (the mother) and especially her youngest daughter. Concerning Philippa, that she was lewdly transported with the love of one Thomas Simpson, who presumed to say that she had bewitched him, for he had no power to leave her and was, as he supposed, marvellously altered both in mind and body since her acquainted company. These complaints began many years before either their conviction or public apprehension. Notwithstanding, such was the honor of this Earl and his Lady; such was the cunning of this monstrous woman in observation towards them; such was the subtlety of the devil to bring his purposes to pass; such was the pleasure of God to make trial of his servants; and such was the effect of a damnable woman's wit and malicious envy that all things were carried away in the smooth Channel of liking and good entertainment on every side until the Earl by degrees conceived some mislike against her, and so peradventure estranged himself from that familiarity and accustomed conferences he was wont to have with her; until one Peak offered her some wrong, against whom she complained, but found that my Lord did not affect her clamors and malicious information; until one Mr. Vavasour abandoned her company, as either suspicious of her lewd life or distasted with his own misliking of such base and poor creatures, whom nobody loved but the Earl's household; until the Countess, misconceiving of her daughter Margaret, and discovering some indecencies both in her life and neglect of her business, discharged her from lying any more in the Castle, yet gave her forty shillings, a bolster, and a mattress of wool, commanding her to go home; until the slackness of her repairing to the Castle, as she was wont, did turn her love and liking toward this honorable Earl and his family into hate and rancor. Whereupon, despited to be so neglected, and exprobated by her neighbors for her daughter's casting out of doors and other conceived displeasures, she grew past all shame and womanhood and many times cursed them all that were the cause of this discontentment and made her so loathsome to her former familiar friends and beneficial acquaintance.

When the devil perceived the inficious disposition of this wretch, and that she and her daughters might easily be made instruments to enlarge his kingdom and be as it were the executioners of his vengeance, not caring whether it lighted upon innocents or no, he came more nearer unto them, and in plain terms (to come quickly to the purpose) offered them his service, and that in such a manner as they might easily command what they pleased; for he would attend you in such pretty forms of dog, cat, or rat, that they should neither be terrified nor anybody else suspicious of the matter. Upon this they agree and (as it should seem) give away their souls for the service of such spirits as he had promised them; which filthy conditions were ratified with abominable kisses and an odious sacrifice of blood, not leaving out certain charms and conjurations with which the devil deceived them, as though nothing could be done without ceremony and a solemnity of orderly ratification. By this time doth Satan triumph and goeth away satisfied to have caught such fish in the net of his illusions; by this time are these women devils incarnate and grow proud again in their cunning and artificial power to do what mischief they listed; by this time they have learned the manner of incantations, spells and charms; by this time they kill what cattle they list and under the cover of flattery and familiar entertainment keep hidden the stinging serpent of malice and a venomous inclination to mischief; by this time is the Earl and his family threatened and must feel the burden of a terrible tempest which from these women's devilish devices fell upon him, he neither suspecting nor understanding the same; by this time both himself and his honorable Countess are many times subject to sickness and extraordinary convulsions, which they, taking as gentle corrections from the hand of God, submit with quietness to His mercy and study nothing more than to glorify their Creator in heaven and bear his crosses on earth.

At last, as malice increased in these damnable women, so his family felt the smart of their revenge and inficious disposition, for his eldest son, Henry Lord Ros, sickened very strangely and after a while died. His next, named Francis, Lord Ros accordingly, was severely tormented by them and most barbarously and inhumanly tortured by a strange sickness. Not long after, the Lady Katherine was set upon by their dangerous and devilish practices and many times in great danger of life through extreme maladies and unusual fits; nay (as it should seem and they afterwards confessed) both the Earl and his Countess were brought into their snares as they imagined and indeed determined to keep them from having any more children. Oh unheard-of wickedness and mischievous damnation! Notwithstanding all this did the noble Earl attend his Majesty both at Newmarket before Christmas and at Christmas at Whitehall, bearing the loss of his children most nobly and little suspecting that they had miscarried by witchcraft or suchlike inventions of the devil, until it pleased God to discover the villainous practices of these women and to command the devil from executing any further vengeance on innocents but leave them to their shames and the hands of justice that they might not only be confounded for their villainous practices but remain as a notorious example to all ages of his judgment and fury. Thus were they apprehended about Christmas and carried to Lincoln Jail after due examination before sufficient justices of the peace and discreet magistrates, who wondered at their audacious wickedness. But Joan Flower, the mother, before conviction (as they say) called for bread and butter and wished it might never go through her if she were guilty of that whereupon she was examined; so mumbling it in her mouth, never spake more words after, but fell down and died as she was carried to Lincoln Jail with a horrible excruciation of soul and body, and was buried at Ancaster. When the Earl heard of their apprehension, he hastened down with his brother Sir George and, sometimes examining them himself and sometimes sending them to others, at last left them to the trial of law before the judges of Assize at Lincoln; and so they were convicted of murder and executed about the eleventh of March, to the terror of all the beholders and example of such dissolute and abominable creatures. And because you shall have both cause to glorify God for this discovery and occasion to apprehend the strangeness of their lives and truth of their proceedings, I thought it both meet and convenient to lay open their own examinations and evidences against one another, with such apparent circumstances as do not only show the cause of their misliking and distasting against the Earl and his family, but the manner of their proceedings and revenges, with other particulars belonging to the true and plain discovery of their villainy and witchcraft.

The examinations of Anne Baker, Joan Willimot, and Ellen Greene, as followeth, etc.

[This part of the pamphlet consists of the "confessions" of five women: Anne Baker, Joan Willimot, Ellen Greene, and Margaret and Philippa Flower. Although Anne Baker, a spinster from Bottesford, was examined by the earl of Rutland and his brother, the charges against her do not involve the earl's family. On the first day of her examination she testifies to seeing a vision and hearing voices in the air but pleads innocent to the charge of bewitching a child to death. On the second day of her examination she admits that about three years ago she heard from some members of the earl's household that "my young Lord Henry was dead, and that there was a glove of the said Lord buried in the ground and as that glove did rot and waste, so did the liver of the said Lord rot and waste." The examination of Anne Baker is followed by three examinations of Joan Willimot taken by various justices of the peace and a doctor of divinity. In the first she testifies that Joan Flower had confided in her that "she had spied my Lord's son and had stricken him to the heart." In the third she admits that at Joan Flower's house she saw "two spirits, one like a rat and the other like an owl, and one of them did suck under her right ear." Willimot swears that she used her own spirit only to help people "which were stricken or forspoken." Ellen Greene of Stathern contends in her examination that

Joan Willimot persuaded her to "forsake God and betake her to the devil." Greene does not mention the Flowers, but she admits to murdering by witchcraft a total of six persons who had offended her or her friends.]

The examination of Philippa Flower, sister of Margaret Flower and Daughter of Joan Flower, before Sir William Pelham and Mr. Butler, Justices of the Peace, February 4, 1618, which was brought in at the Assizes as evidence against her sister Margaret.

She saith that her mother and her sister maliced the Earl of Rutland, his Countess, and their Children, because her sister Margaret was put out of the Lady's service of laundry and exempted from other services about the house; whereupon her said sister, by the commandment of her mother, brought from the castle the right-hand glove of the Lord Henry Ros, which she delivered to her mother, who presently rubbed it on the back of her spirit Rutterkin and then put it into hot boiling water. Afterward she pricked it often and buried it in the yard, wishing the Lord Ros might never thrive; and so her sister Margaret continued with her mother, where she often saw the cat Rutterkin leap on her shoulder and suck her neck.

She further confessed that she heard her mother often curse the Earl and his Lady, and thereupon would boil feathers and blood together, using many devilish speeches and strange gestures.

The examination of Margaret Flower, Sister of Philippa Flower, etc., about the twenty-second of January, 1618.

[Several parts of Margaret's testimony echo that of her sister; she admits to bringing the glove of Henry, Lord Ros, to her mother and describes her mother's use of the glove in the bewitching of Lord Ros. She expands upon Philippa's confession, however, by recounting how her mother (with the help of her two daughters) bewitched other members of the earl's family. She reports that her mother also exercised her evil power against Francis, Lord Ros, again by using the boy's glove. She testifies that she and her mother and sister took wool from the mattress given her by the Countess, mixed it with blood, and rubbed it on Rutterkin's belly, hoping thereby to afflict the couple with sterility. Her mother also tried her devilish practices against Katherine, the Earl's daughter, but concluded that "Rutterkin had no power over the Lady Katherine to hurt her."]

The examination of Philippa Flower, the twenty-fifth of February, 1618, before Francis, the Earl of Rutland; Francis, Lord Willoughby of Eresby; Sir George Manners; and Sir William Pelham.

She confesseth and saith that she hath a spirit sucking on her in the form of a white rat, which keepeth her left breast and hath so done for three or four years; and concerning the agreement betwixt her spirit and herself, she confesseth and saith that when it came first unto her she gave her soul to it and it promised to do her good and cause Thomas Simpson to love her if she would suffer it to suck her, which she agreed unto; and so the last time it sucked was on Tuesday at night, the twenty-third of February.

The examination of Margaret Flower at the same time, etc.

She confesseth that she hath two familiar spirits sucking on her, the one white, the other black-spotted; the white sucked under her left breast and the black-spotted within the inward parts of her secrets. When she first entertained them she promised them her soul, and they covenanted to do all things which she commanded them, etc.

She further saith that about the thirtieth of January last past, being Saturday, four devils appeared unto her in Lincoln jail at eleven or twelve o'clock at midnight. The one stood at her bed's feet with a black head like an ape and spoke unto her, but what, she cannot well remember, at which she was very angry because he would speak no plainer or let her understand his meaning; the other three were Rutterkin, Little Robin, and Spirit, but she never mistrusted them nor suspected herself till then.

[In her final examination, taken February 4, 1618, Margaret concedes that she and her mother and sister sought revenge against the Earl's family "for turning her out of service"; she then rehearses again the steps taken by her mother that caused Lord Ros to sicken and die.]

These examinations and some others were taken and charily preserved for the contriving of sufficient evidences against them, and when the judges of assize came down to Lincoln about the first week of March (being Sir Henry Hobart, Lord Chief Justice of the Common Pleas, and Sir Edward Bromley, one of the Barons of the Exchequer) they were presented unto them; who not only wondered at the wickedness of these persons, but were amazed at their practices and horrible contracts with the devil to damn their own souls. And although the right honorable Earl had sufficient grief for the loss of his children, yet no doubt it was greater to consider the manner and how it pleased God to inflict on him such a fashion of visitation. Besides, as it amazed the hearers to understand the particulars and the circumstances of this devilish contract, so was it as wonderful to see their desperate impenitency and horrible distraction, according to the rest of that sort exclaiming against the devil for deluding them and now breaking promise with them when they stood in most need of his help.

Notwithstanding all these aggravations, such was the unparalleled magnanimity, wisdom, and patience of this generous nobleman that he urged nothing against them more than their own confessions, and so quietly left them to judicial trial, desiring of God mercy for their souls and of men charity to censure them in their condemnation. But God is not mocked and so gave them over to judgment, nor man so reformed but for the Earl's sake they cursed them to that place which they themselves long before had bargained for.

The author draws several religious and moral lessons from the history of these witches. God is omnipotent; even the devil is His "mere servant and agent." God chastises the godly as well as the wicked: "the very just shall be tried like gold and no man exempted from castigation whom God doth love." Man must submit patiently to His will, as the noble earl has done. The wicked will be punished, either in this life, the life to come, or both; furthermore, they are condemned by their own utterances, as these witches were. The law of England will not suffer anyone to converse with spirits or blaspheme God's name with spells and incantations. After a warning to the "sons of men" to be instructed by the terrible example of the witches, the author concludes by regretting that exposure of a lie is easier than discovery of the truth.]

Relations Between the Sexes

1620

Literary attacks on women have been prevalent in Western society since antiquity. Hesiod's mythical tale of Pandora (eighth century B.C.E.), Juvenal's Sixth Satire (first century), and the Bible are obvious early examples of misogynistic accounts of "the woman question." Like the medieval literary debate that prompted Christine de Pisan to rise up in defense of women, the "pamphlet wars" in Renaissance England reflected the cultural controversies surrounding the nature of woman.[1] While these debates inherited the conventions established in earlier periods, they departed from them in several important ways: the printing press naturally increased the number of attacks and the dissemination of them; the treatises began to reflect the interests of a growing middle-class culture; and more defenses of women were published in response to the attacks. Many of these pamphlets were written anonymously or the authors adopted pseudonyms.

The pamphlets included here illustrate one of the most hotly debated questions during the period and reflect the ways in which a culture's anxieties about social stability, personal identity and power can be articulated in popular literature. In sixteenth- and seventeenth-century England, women were vehemently attacked for dressing in masculine attire. These attacks can be found in sermons, satires and even in the proclamations of King James. *Hic Mulier* (the man-woman) berates women's desire to dress up in men's clothing as a sign of women's more troubling desire to usurp male power. *Haec Vir* (the womanish-man) ostensibly launches a counter-attack by pointing to the effeminate trends in male fashion and ultimately works to reinforce clear gender distinctions and traditional social roles for each sex.

Why would changes in one's style of dress be so threatening to this society? What does this debate reveal about the culture's world view? In what ways does the subject of fashion relate to the shifting notions of the self in early modern Europe? How might this debate reflect the tensions in the political philosophy of absolutism? In reading these pamphlets, also think about how popular literature from twentieth-century American culture has inherited and built upon this long tradition of the battle of the sexes.

[1] Information for this introduction was taken from Katherine Usher Henderson and Barbara F. McManus, eds. *Half Humankind: Contexts and texts of the Controversy about Women in England, 1540-1640*. (Urbana and Chicago: University of Illinois Press, 1985) 3-23, 52-53.

HIC MVLIER:

OR,

The Man-Woman:

Being a Medicine to cure the Coltiſh Diſeaſe of *the Staggers in the Maſculine-Feminines* of our Times.

Expreſt in a briefe Declamation.

Non omnes poſſumus omnes.

Miſtris, will you be trim'd or truſſ'd?

London printed for I.T. and are to be sold at Christ Church gate. 1620.

Title page of "Hic Mulier: or the Man-Woman."

HÆC-VIR:
OR
The Womanish-Man:

Being an Anſwere to a late Booke intituled *Hic-Mulier*.

Expreſt in a briefe Dialogue betweene *Hæc-Vir* the Womaniſh-Man, and *Hic-Mulier* the Man-Woman.

London printed for *I.T.* and are to be ſold at Chriſt Church gate. 1620.

Title page of "Haec-Vir: Or the Womanish-Man."

Hic Mulier; or, The Man Woman: Being a Medicine to cure the Coltish Disease of the Staggers in the Masculine-Feminines of our Times, Expressed in a brief Declamation: *Non omnes possumus omnes.*[1]

HIC MULIER: How now? Break Priscian's head at the first encounter? But two words, and they false Latin? Pardon me, good Signor Construction, for I will not answer thee as the Pope did, that I will do it in despite of the grammar. But I will maintain, if it be not the truest Latin in our kingdom, yet it is the commonest. For since the days of Adam women were never so masculine: masculine in their genders and whole generations, from the mother to the youngest daughter; masculine in number, from one to multitudes; masculine in case, even from the head to the foot; masculine in mood, from bold speech to impudent action; and masculine in tense, for without redress they were, are, and will be still most masculine, most mankind, and most monstrous. Are all women then turned masculine? No, God forbid, there are a world full of holy thoughts, modest carriage, and severe chastity. To these let me fall on my knees and say, "You, oh you women, you good women, you that are in the fullness of perfection you that are the crowns of nature's work, the complements of men's excellences, and the Seminaries of propagation; you that maintain the world, support mankind, and give life to society; you that, armed with the infinite power of virtue, are castles impregnable, rivers unsailable, seas immovable, infinite treasures, and invincible armies; that art helpers most trusty, sentinels most careful, signs deceitless, plain ways fail-less, true guides dangerless, balms that instantly cure, and honors that never perish. Oh do not look to find your names in this declamation, but with all honor and reverence do I speak to you. You are Seneca's graces, women, good women, modest women, true women—ever young because ever virtuous, ever chaste, ever glorious. When I write of you, I will write with a golden pen on leaves of golden paper; now I write with a rough quill and black ink on iron sheets the iron deeds of an iron generation.

Come, then, you masculine women, for you are my subject, you that have made admiration an ass and fooled him with a deformity never before dreamed of; that have made yourselves stranger things that ever Noah's Ark unloaded or Nile engendered; whom to name, he that named all things might study an age to give you a right attribute whose like are not found in any Antiquary's study, in any Seaman's travel, nor in any Painter's cunning. You that are stranger than strangeness itself; whom Wise men wonder at. Boys shout at, and Goblins themselves start at; you that are the gilt dirt which embroiders Playhouses, the painted Statues which adorn Caroches, and the perfumed Carrion that bad men feed on in Brothels: 'tis of you I entreat and of your monstrous deformity. You that have made your bodies like antic Boscadge or Crotesco work, not half man/half woman, half fish/half flesh, halt beast/half monster, but all odious, all devil; that have cast off the ornaments of your sexes to put on the garments of shame; that have laid by the bashfulness of your natures to gather the impudence of harlots; that have buried silence to revive slander; that are all things but that which you should be, and nothing less than friends to virtue and goodness; that have made the foundation of your highest detested work from the lowest despised creatures that record can give testimony of: the one cut from the commonwealth at the gallows; the other is well known. From the first you got the false armory of yellow starch (for to wear yellow on white or white upon yellow is by rules of heraldry baseness, bastardy, and indignity), the folly of imitation, the deceitfulness of flattery, and the grossest baseness of all baseness, to do whatever a greater power will command you. From other you have taken the monstrousness of your deformity in apparel, exchanging the modest attire of the comely hood, cowl, coif, handsome dress or kerchief, to the cloudy ruffianly broad-brimmed hat and wanton feather; the modest upper parts of a concealing straight gown, to the loose, lascivious civil embracement of a French doublet, being all unbuttoned to entice, all of one shape to hide deformity, extreme short waisted to give a most easy way to every luxurious action; the glory of a fair large hair, to the shame of most ruffianly short locks; the side, thick gathered, and close guarding safeguards to the short, weak, thin, loose, and every hand-entertaining short bases; for needles, swords, for prayerbooks, bawdy legs; for modest gestures, giantlike behaviors; and for women's modesty, all mimic and apish incivility. These are your founders, from these you took your copies, and, without amendment, with these you shall come to perdition.

Sophocles, being asked why he presented no women in his tragedies but good ones and Euripides none but bad ones, answered he presented women as they should be, but Euripides, women as they were.

[These "Mermaids or rather Mer-Monsters who dress bizarrely in men's fashions probably never practiced "comeliness or modesty." Although they may associate with or be related to persons of gentle birth, they themselves are "but rags of Gentry, torn from better pieces for their foul stains." Some are not even descended from gentry but are rather "the stinking vapors drawn from dunghills"; these people may exist on the fringes of good society for a time, but eventually they will fall back "to the place from whence they came, and there rot and consume unpitied and unremembered."]

And questionless it is true that such were the first beginners of these last deformities, for from any purer blood would have issued a purer birth; there would have been some spark of virtue, some excuse for imitation. But this deformity hath no agreement with goodness, nor no difference against the weakest reason. It is all base, all barbarous: base, in respect it offends man in the example and God in the most unnatural use; barbarous, in that it is exorbitant from nature and an antithesis to kind, going astray with ill-favored affectation both in attire, in speech, in manners, and, it is to be feared, in the whole courses and stories of their actions. What can be more barbarous than with the gloss of mumming art to disguise the beauty of their creations? To mould their bodies to every deformed fashion, their tongues to vile and horrible profanations, and their hands to ruffianly and uncivil actions? To have their gestures as piebald and as motley-various as their disguises, their souls fuller of infirmities than a horse or prostitute, and their minds languishing in those infirmities? If this be not barbarous, make the rude Scythian, the untamed Moor, the naked Indian, or the wild Irish, lords and rulers of well-governed cities.

But rests this deformity then only in the baser, in none but such as are the beggary of desert, that have in them nothing but skittishness and peevishness, that are living graves, unwholesome sinks, quartan fevers for intolerable cumber, and the extreme injury and wrong of nature? Are these and none else guilty of this high treason to God and nature?

Oh yes, a world of other—many known great, thought good, wished happy, much loved and most admired—are so foully branded with this infamy of disguise. And the marks stick so deep on their naked faces and more naked bodies that not all the painting in Rome or Fauna can conceal them, but every eye discovers them almost as low as their middles.

It is an infection that emulates the plague and throws itself among women of all degrees, all deserts, and all ages; from the capitol to the cottage are some spots or swellings of this disease. Yet evermore the greater the person is, the greater is the rage of this sickness; and the more they have to support the eminence of their fortunes, the more they bestow in the augmentation of their deformities. Not only such as will not work to get bread will find time to weave herself points to truss her loose breeches; and she that hath pawned her credit to get a hat will sell her smock to buy a feather; she that hath given kisses have her hair shorn will give her honesty to have her upper parts put into a French doublet. To conclude, she that will give her body to have her body deformed will not stick to give her soul to have her mind satisfied.

But such as are able to buy all at their own charges, they swim in the excess of these vanities and will be manlike not only from the head to the waist, but to the very foot and in every condition: man in body by attire, man in behavior by rude complement, man in nature by aptness to anger, man in action by pursuing revenge, man in wearing weapons, man in using weapons, and, in brief, so much man in all things that they are neither men nor women, but just good for nothing.

[Neither great birth nor great beauty nor great wealth can save these foolish women from "one particle of disgrace." To support this point, the author includes two stanzas by the poet S. T. O.; the speaker in the poem attests that he would love a virtuous woman above one of high birth, beauty, or wealth.]

Remember how your Maker made for our first parents coats—not one coat, but a coat for the man and a coat for the woman, coats of several fashions, several forms, and for several uses—the man's coat fit for his labor, the woman's fit for her modesty. And will you lose the model left by this great Workmaster of Heaven?

The long hair of a woman is the ornament of her sex, and bashful shamefastness her chief honor; the long hair of a man, the vizard for a thievish or murderous disposition. And will you cut off that beauty to wear the other's villainy? The vestals in Rome wore comely garments of one piece from the neck to the heel; and the swordplayers, motley doublets with gaudy points. The first begot reverence; the latter, laughter. And will you lose that honor for the other's scorn? The weapon of a virtuous woman was her tears, which every good man pitied and every valiant man honored; the weapon of a cruel man is his sword, which neither law allows nor reason defends. And will you leave the excellent shield of innocence for this deformed instrument of disgrace? Even for goodness' sake, that can ever pay her own with her own merits, look to your reputations, which are undermined with your own follies, and do not become the idle sisters of foolish Don Quixote, to believe every vain fable which you read or to think you may be attired like Bradamant, who was often taken for Ricardetto, her brother; that you may fight like Marfiza and win husbands with conquest; or ride astride like Claridiana and make giants fall at your stirrups. The morals will give you better meanings, which if you shun and take the gross imitations, the first will deprive you of all good society; the second, of noble affections; and the third, of all beloved modesty. You shall lose all the charms of women's natural perfections, have no presence to win respect, no beauty to enchant men's hearts, nor no bashfulness to excuse the vilest imputations.

The fairest face covered with a foul vizard begets nothing but affright or scorn, and the noblest person in an ignoble disguise attains to nothing but reproach and scandal. Away then with these disguises and foul vizards, these unnatural paintings and immodest discoveries! Keep those parts concealed from the eyes that may not be touched with the hands; let not a wandering and lascivious thought read in an enticing index the contents of an unchaste volume, imitate nature, and, as she hath placed on the surface and superficies of the earth all things needful for man's sustenance and necessary use (as herbs, plants, fruits, corn and suchlike) but locked up close in the hidden caverns of the earth all things which appertain to his delight and pleasure (as gold, silver, rich minerals, and precious stones), so do you discover unto men all things that are fit for them to understand from you (as bashfulness in your cheeks, chastity in your eyes, wisdom in your words, sweetness in your conversation, and severe modesty in the whole structure or frame of your universal composition). But for those things which belong to this wanton and lascivious delight and pleasure (as eyes wandering, lips billing, tongue enticing, bared breasts seducing, and naked arms embracing), oh, hide them, for shame hide them in the closest prisons of your strictest government! Shield them with modest and comely garments, such as are warm and wholesome, having every window closed with a strong casement and every loophole furnished with such strong ordinance that no unchaste eye may come near to assail them, no lascivious tongue woo a forbidden passage, nor no profane hand touch relics so pure and religious. Guard them about with counterscarps of innocence, trenches of humane reason, and impregnable walls of sacred divinity, not with antic disguise and mimic fantasticalness, where every window stands open like the Subura, and every window a courtesan with an instrument, like so many sirens, to enchant the weak passenger to shipwreck and destruction. Thus shall you be yourselves again and live the most excellent creatures upon earth, things past example, past all imitation.

Remember that God in your first creation did not form you of slime and earth like man, but of a more pure and refined metal, a substance much more worthy: you in whom are all the harmonies of life, the perfection of symmetry, the true and curious consent of the most fairest colors and the wealthy gardens which fill the world with living plants. Do but you receive virtuous inmates (as what palaces are more rich to receive heavenly messengers?) and you shall draw men's souls unto you with that severe, devout, and holy adoration, that you shall never want praise, never love, never reverence.

But now methinks I hear the witty offending great ones reply in excuse of their deformities: "What, is there no difference among women? No distinction of places, no respect of honors, nor no regard of blood or alliance? Must but a bare pair of shears pass between noble and ignoble, between the generous spirit and the base mechanic? Shall we be all coheirs of one honor, one estate, and one habit? Oh men, you are then too tyrannous and not only injure nature but also break the laws and customs of the wisest princes. Are not bishops known by their miters, princes by their crowns, judges by their robes, and knights by their spurs? But poor women have nothing, how great soever they be, to divide themselves from the enticing shows or moving images which do furnish most shops in the city. What is it that either the laws have allowed to the greatest ladies, custom found convenient, or their bloods or places challenged, which hath not been engrossed into the city with as great greediness and pretense of true title as if the surcease from the imitation were the utter breach of their charter everlastingly?

For this cause these apes of the city have enticed foreign nations to their cells and, there committing gross adultery with their gewgaws, have brought out such unnatural conceptions that the whole world is not able to make a Democritus big enough to laugh at their foolish ambitions. Nay, the very art of painting, which to the last age shall ever be held in detestation, they have so cunningly stolen and hidden amongst their husbands' hoards of treasure that the decayed stock of prostitution, having little other revenues, are hourly in bringing their action of detinue against them. Hence, being thus troubled with these popinjays and loath still to march in one rank with fools and zanies, have proceeded these disguised deformities, not to offend the eyes of goodness but to tire with ridiculous contempt the never-to-be-satisfied appetites of these gross and unmannerly intruders. Nay, look if this very last edition of disguise, this which is so full of faults, corruptions, and false quotations, this bait which the devil hath laid to catch the souls of wanton women, be not as frequent in the demi-palaces of burgers and citizens as it is either at masque, triumph, tiltyard, or playhouse. Call but to account the tailors that are contained within the circumference of the walls of the city and let but their hells and their hard reckonings be justly summed together, and it will be found they have raised more new foundations of this new disguise and metamorphosized more modest old garments to this new manner of short base and French doublet only for the use of freeman's wives and their children in one month than hath been worn in court, suburbs, or county since the unfortunate beginning of the first devilish invention.

"Let therefore the powerful statue of apparel but lift up his battleax and crush the offenders in pieces, so as everyone may be known by the true badge of their blood or Fortune. And then these chimeras of deformity will be sent back to hell and there burn to cinders in the flames of their own malice."

Thus, methinks, I hear the best of offenders argue, nor can I blame a high blood to swell when it is coupled and counterchecked with baseness and corruption. Yet this shows an anger passing near akin to envy and alludes much to the saying of an excellent poet:

> Women never
> Love beauty in their sex, but envy ever.

They have Caesar's ambition and desire to be one and alone, but yet to offend themselves to grieve others is a revenge dissonant to reason. And, as Euripides saith, a woman of that malicious nature is a fierce beast and most pernicious to the commonwealth, for she hath power by example to do it a world of injury.

[A woman's disposition should be gentle; her thoughts, according to a poet cited by the author, should be "attended with remorse." In contrast to the ideal woman, those who indulge in the new fashion have given "a shameless liberty to every loose passion." In their attempt to control the men who should rule them, they endanger their personal fortunes and reputations as well as those of their families and their sex. The author includes a stanza by Edmund Spenser from the Book of Justice of *The Faerie Queene*:

> Such is the cruelty of womenkind,
> When they have shaken off the shamefast band
> With which wise Nature did them strongly bind
> T'obey the hests of man's well ruling hand,
> That then all rule and reason they withstand
> To purchase a licentious liberty.
> But virtuous women wisely understand
> That they were born to base humility,
> Unless the heavens them lift to lawful sovereignty.]

To you therefore that are fathers, husbands, or sustainers of these new hermaphrodites belongs the cure of this impostume. It is you that give fuel to the flames of their wild indiscretion; you add the oil which makes their stinking lamps defile the whole house with filthy smoke, and your purses purchase these deformities at rates both dear and unreasonable. Do you but hold close your liberal hands or take strict account of the employment of the treasure you give to their necessary maintenance, and these excesses will either cease or else die smothered in the tailor's trunk for want of redemption.

Seneca, speaking of liberality, will by no means allow that any man should bestow either on friend, wife, or children any treasure to be spent upon ignoble uses, for it not only robs the party of the honor of bounty and takes from the deed the name of a benefit, but also makes him conscious and guilty of the crimes which are purchased by such gratuity. Be, therefore, the scholars of Seneca, and your wives, sisters and daughters will be the coheirs of modesty.

Lycurgus the law-giver made it death in one of his statutes to bring in any new custom into his Commonwealth. Do you make it the utter loss of your favor and bounty to have brought into your family an new fashion or disguise that might either deform Nature or be an injury to modesty? So shall shamefastness and comeliness ever live under your roof, and your wives and daughters, like vines and fair olives ever spread with beauty round about your tables.

The Lacedaemonians, seeing that their children were better taught by examples than precepts, had hanging in their houses in fair painted tablets all the virtues and vices that were in those days reigning with their rewards and punishments. Oh, have you but in your houses the fashions of all attires constantly and without change held and still followed through all the parts of Christendom! Let them but see the modest Dutch, the stately Italian, the rich Spaniard, and the courtly French with the rest according to their climates, and they will blush that in a full fourth part of the world there cannot be found one piece of a character to compare or liken with the absurdity of their masculine Invention. Nay, they shall see that their naked countryman, which had liberty with his shears to cut from every nation of the world one piece or patch to make up his garment, yet amongst them all could not find this miscellany or mixture of deformities which, only by those which whilst they retained any spark of womanhood were both loved and admired, is loosely, indiscreetly, wantonly, and most unchastely invented.

And therefore, to knit up this imperfect declamation, let every female-masculine that by her ill examples is guilty of lust or imitation cast off her deformities and clothe herself in the rich garments which the poet bestows upon her in these verses following:

> Those Virtues that in women merit praise
> Are sober shows without, chaste thoughts within,
> True Faith and due obedience to their mate,
> And of their children honest care to take.

NOTES

[1] "We cannot all be everybody."

Haec-Vir; or, The Womanish Man: Being an Answer to a late Book entitled *Hic Mulier*, Expressed in a brief Dialogue between Haec Vir, the Womanish Man, and Hic Mulier, the Man-Woman.

HAEC VIR: Most redoubted and worthy sir (for less than a knight I cannot take you), you are most happily given unto mine embrace.

HIC MULIER: Is she mad or doth she mock me? Most rare and excellent Lady, I am the servant of your virtues and desire to be employed in your service.

HAEC VIR: Pity of patience, what doth he behold in me, to take me for a woman? Valiant and magnanimous Sir, I shall desire to build the tower of my fortune upon no stronger foundation than the benefit of your grace and favor.

HIC MULIER: Oh, proud ever to be your servant.

HAEC VIR: No, the servant of your servant.

HIC MULIER: The tithe of your friendship, good Lady, is above my merit.

HAEC VIR: You make me rich beyond expression. But fair Knight, the truth is I am a man and desire but the obligation of your friendship.

HIC MULIER: It is ready to be sealed and delivered to your use. Yet I would have you understand I am a woman.

HAEC VIR: Are you a woman?

HIC MULIER: Are you a man? O Juno Lucina, help me!

HAEC VIR: Yes, I am.

HIC MULIER: Your name, most tender piece of masculine.

HAEC VIR: Haec Vir, no stranger either in court, city, or country. But what is yours, most courageous counterfeit of Hercules and his distaff?

HIC MULIER: Near akin to your goodness, and compounded of fully as false Latin. The world calls me Hic Mulier.

HAEC VIR: What, Hic Mulier, the Man-Woman? She that like an alarm bell at midnight hath raised the whole Kingdom in arms against her? Good, stand and let me take a full survey, both of thee and all thy dependents.

HIC MULIER: Do freely and, when thou hast daubed me over with the worst colors thy malice can grind, then give me leave to answer for myself, and I will say thou art an accuser just and indifferent. Which done, I must entreat you to sit as many minutes that I may likewise take your picture, and then refer to censure whether of our deformities is most injurious to nature or most effeminate to good men in the notoriousness of the example.

HAEC VIR: With like condition of freedom to answer, the articles are agreed on. Therefore, stand forth, half Birchenlane, half Saint Thomas Apostle's (the first lent thee a doublet, the latter a nether-skirt); half Bridewell, half Blackfriars (the one for a scurvy block, the other for a most profane feather); half Mulled Sack the Chimney Sweeper, half Garrat the Fool at a Tilting (the one for a yellow ruff, the other for a scarf able to put a soldier out of countenance); half Bedlam, half Brimendgham (the one for a base sale boot, the other for a beastly leaden gilt spur); and, to conclude, all Hell, all Damnation for a shorn, powdered, borrowed hair; a naked, lascivious, bawdy bosom; a leadenhall dagger; a highway pistol; and a mind and behavior suitable or exceeding every repeated deformity. To be brief, I can but in those few lines delineate your proportion for the paraphrase or compartment to set out your ugliness to the greatest extent of wonder. I can but refer you to your godchild that carries your own name—I mean the book of *Hic Mulier*. There you shall see your character and feel your shame with that palpable plainness, that no Egyptian darkness can be more gross and terrible,

HIC MULIER: My most tender piece of man's flesh, leave this lightning and thunder and come roundly to the matter; draw mine accusation into heads, and then let me answer.

HAEC VIR: Then thus. In that book you are arraigned and found guilty, first, of baseness, in making yourself a slave to novelty and the poor invention of every weak brain that hath but an embroidered outside; next, of unnaturalness, to forsake the creation of God and customs of the kingdom to be pieced and patched up by a French tailor, an Italian babymaker, and a Dutch soldier beat from the army for the ill example of ruffianly behavior; then of shamefulness, in casting off all modest softness and civility to run through every desert and wilderness of men's opinions like careless untamed heifers or wild savages; lastly, of foolishness, in having no moderation or temper either in passions or affections, but turning all into perturbations and sicknesses of the soul, laugh away the preciousness of your time and at last die with the flattering sweet malice of an incurable consumption. Thus baseness, unnaturalness, shamefulness, foolishness are the main hatchments or coat-armors which you have taken as rich spoils to adorn you in the deformity of your apparel; which, if you can execute, I can pity and thank Proserpina for thy wit, though no good man can allow of the reasons.

HIC MULIER: Well then, to the purpose. First, you say I am base, in being a slave to novelty. What slavery can there be in freedom of election, or what baseness to crown my delights with those pleasures which are most suitable to mine affections? Bondage or slavery is a restraint from those actions which the mind of its own accord doth most willingly desire, to perform the intents and purposes of another's disposition, and that not by mansuetude or sweetness of entreaty, but by the force of authority and strength of compulsion. Now for me to follow change according to the limitation of mine own will and pleasure, there cannot be a greater freedom. Nor do I in my delight of change otherwise than as the whole world doth, or as becometh a daughter of the world to do. For what is the world but a very shop or warehouse of change? Sometimes winter, sometimes summer; day and night; they hold sometimes riches, sometimes poverty; sometimes health, sometimes sickness; now pleasure, presently anguish; now honor, then contempt; and, to conclude, there is nothing but change, which doth surround and mix with all our fortunes. And will you have poor woman such a fixed star that she shall not so much as move or twinkle in her own sphere? That were true slavery indeed and a baseness beyond the chains of the worst servitude! Nature to everything she hath created hath given a singular delight in change: as to herbs, plants, and trees a time to wither and shed their leaves, a time to bud and bring forth their leaves, and a time for their fruits and flowers; to worms and creeping things a time to hide themselves in the pores and hollows of the earth, and a time to come abroad and suck the dew; to beasts liberty to choose their food, liberty to delight in their food, and liberty to feed and grow fat with their food; the birds have the air to fly in, the waters to bathe in, and the earth to feed on; but to man both these and all things else to alter, frame, and fashion, according as his will and delight shall rule him. Again, who will rob the eye of the variety of objects, the ear of the delight of sounds, the nose of smells, the tongue of tastes, and the hand of feeling? And shall only woman, excellent woman, so much better in that she is something purer, be only deprived of this benefit? Shall she be the bondslave of time, the handmaid of opinion, or the strict observer of every frosty or cold benumbed imagination? It were a cruelty beyond the rack or strappado.

But you will say it is not change, but novelty, from which you deter us, a thing that doth avert the good and erect the evil, prefer the faithless and confound desert, that with the change of opinions breeds the change of states, and with continual alterations thrusts headlong forward both ruin and subversion. Alas, soft Sir, what can you christen by that new imagined title, when the words of a wise man are, "That what was done, is but done again; all things do change, and under the cope of Heaven there is no new thing." So that whatsoever we do or imitate, it is neither slavish, base, nor a breeder of novelty.

Next, you condemn me of unnaturalness in forsaking my creation and contemning custom. How do I forsake my creation, that do all the rights and offices due to my creation? I was created free, born free, and live free; what lets me then so to spin out my time that I may die free?

To alter creation were to walk on my hands with my heels upward, to feed myself with my feet, or to forsake the sweet sound of sweet words for the hissing noise of the serpent. But I walk with a face erect, with a body clothed, with a mind busied, and with a heart full of reasonable and devout cogitations, only offensive in attire, inasmuch as it is a stranger to the curiosity of the present times and an enemy to custom. Are we then bound to be the flatterers of time or the dependents on custom? Oh miserable servitude, chained only to baseness and folly, for than custom, nothing is more absurd, nothing more foolish.

It was a custom amongst the Romans that, as we wash our hands before meals, so they with curious and sweet ointments anointed all their arms and legs quite over, and by succession of time grew from these unguents to baths of rich perfumed and compound waters in which they bathed their whole bodies, holding it the greatest disgrace that might be to use or touch any natural water, as appears by these verses:

> She shines with ointments to make hair to fall,
> Or with sour chalk she overcovers all.
>
> Martial

It was a custom amongst the ancients to lie upon stately and soft beds when either they delivered embassies or entered into any serious discourse or argument, as appears by these verses:

> Father Aeneas thus gan say,
> From stately couch whereon he lay.
>
> Virgil

Cato Junior held it for a custom never to eat meat but sitting on the ground; the Venetians kiss one another ever at the first meeting; and even at this day it is a general received custom amongst our English that when we meet or overtake any man in our travel or journeying, to examine him whither he rides, how far, to what purpose, and where he lodgeth. Nay, and with that unmannerly boldness of inquisition that it is a certain ground of a most insufficient quarrel not to receive a full satisfaction of those demands which go far astray from good manners or comely civility. And will you have us to marry ourselves to these mimic and most fantastic customs? It is a fashion or custom with us to mourn in black; yet the Aegean and Roman ladies ever mourned in white and, if we will tie the action upon the signification of colors, I see not but we may mourn in green, blue, red, or any simple color used in heraldry. For us to salute strangers with a kiss is counted but civility, but with foreign nations immodesty; for you to cut the hair of your upper lips, familiar here in England, everywhere else almost thought unmanly. To ride on Sidesaddles at first was counted here abominable pride, etc. I might instance in a thousand things that only custom and not reason hath approved. To conclude, custom is an Idiot, and whosoever dependeth wholly upon him without the discourse of reason will take from him his pied coat and become a slave indeed to contempt and censure.

But you say we are barbarous and shameless and cast off all softness to run wild through a wilderness of opinions. In this you express more cruelty than in all the rest. Because I stand not with my hands on my belly like a baby at Bartholomew Fair that move not my whole body when I should, but only stir my head like Jack of the Clockhouse which hath no joints; that am not dumb when wantons court me, as if, asslike, I were ready for all burdens; or because I weep not when injury grips me, like a worried deer in the fangs of many curs, am I therefore barbarous or shameless? He is much injurious that so baptized us. We are as freeborn as men, have as free election and as free spirits; we are compounded of like parts and may with like liberty make benefit of our creations. My countenance shall smile on the worthy and frown on the ignoble; I will hear the wise and be deaf to idiots; give counsel to my friend, but be dumb to flatterers. I have hands that shall be liberal to reward desert, feet that shall move swiftly to do good offices, and thoughts that shall ever accompany freedom and severity. If this be barbarous, let me leave the city and live with creatures of like simplicity.

To conclude, you say we are all guilty of most infinite folly and indiscretion. I confess that discretion is the true salt which seasoneth every excellence, either in man or woman, and without it nothing is well, nothing is worthy; that want disgraceth our actions, staineth our virtues, and indeed makes us most profane and irreligious. Yet it is ever found in excess, as in too much or too little. And of which of these are we guilty? Do we wear too many clothes or too few? If too many, we should oppress nature; if too few, we should bring sickness to nature; but neither of these we do, for what we do wear is warm, thrifty, and wholesome. Then no excess, and so no indiscretion—where is then the error? Only in the fashion, only in the custom. Oh, for mercy sake, bind us not to so hateful a companion, but remember what one of our famous English poets says:

> Round-headed custom th' apoplexy is
> Of bedrid nature, and lives led amiss,
> And takes away all feelings of offense.
>
> G. C.

Again, another as excellent in the same art saith:

> Custom the world's judgment doth blind so far,
> That virtue is oft arraigned at vice's bar.
>
> D'Bart.

And will you be so tyrannous then to compel poor woman to be a mistress to so unfaithful a Servant? Believe it, then we must call tip our champions against you, which are beauty and frailty, and what the one cannot compel you to forgive, the other shall enforce you to pity or excuse. And thus myself imagining myself free of these four Imputations, I rest to be confuted by some better and graver judgment.

[Haec Vir responds by claiming that the freedom that Hic Mulier has assumed is merely "a willful liberty to do evil." According to Divines of the Church, a woman may dress like a man only to avoid persecution, and Hic Mulier does not have this excuse. It would be better had "the first inventor of your disguise perished with all her complements about her," for her invention has caused infinite scandal and sin. To delight in sin is to yield to baseness, and to yield to baseness is foolish and barbarous. Thus, until Hic Mulier returns to traditional dress, she is base, unnatural, shameful, and foolish.]

HIC MULIER: Sir, I confess you have raised mine eyelids up, but you have not clean taken away the film that covers the sight. I feel, I confess, cause of belief and would willingly bend my heart to entertain belief, but when the accuser is guilty of as much or more than that he accuseth, or that I see you refuse the potion and are as grievously infected, blame me not then a little to stagger. And till you will be pleased to be cleansed of that leprosy which I see apparent in you, give me leave to doubt whether mine infection be so contagious as your blind severity would make it.

Therefore, to take your proportion in a few lines, my dear feminine-masculine, tell me what charter, prescription, or right of claim you have to those things you make our absolute inheritance? Why do you curl, frizzle, and powder your hairs, bestowing more hours and time in dividing lock from lock, and hair from hair, in giving every thread his posture, and every curl his true sense and circumference, than ever Caesar did in marshalling his army, either at Pharsalia, in Spain, or Britain? Why do you rob us of our ruffs, of our earrings, carcanets, and mamillions, of our fans and feathers, our busks, and French bodies, nay, of our masks, hoods, shadows, and shapinas? Not so much as the very art of painting, but you have so greedily engrossed it that were it not for that little fantastical sharp-pointed dagger that hangs at your chins, and the cross hilt which guards your upper lip, hardly would there be any difference between the fair mistress and the foolish servant. But is this theft the uttermost of our spoil? Fie, you have gone a world further and even ravished from us our speech, our actions, sports, and recreations. Goodness leave me, if I have not heard a man court his mistress with the same words that Venus did Adonis, or as near as the book could instruct him. Where are the tilts and tourneys and lofty galliards that were danced in the days of old, when men capered in the air like wanton kids on the tops of mountains and turned above ground as if they had been compact of fire or a purer element? Tut, all's forsaken, all's vanished.

[Hic Mulier claims that men have stolen women's pastimes, especially shuttlecock, which had been "a very Emblem of us and our lighter despised fortunes." Having relinquished the arms that "would shake all Christendom with the brandish," men now languish in "softness, dullness, and effeminate niceness."] To see one of your gender either show himself in the midst of his pride or riches at a playhouse or public assembly: how, before he dare enter, with the Jacob's Staff of his own eyes and his page's, he takes a full survey of himself from the highest sprig in his feather to the lowest spangle that shines in his shoestring; how he prunes and picks himself like a hawk set aweathering, calls every several garment to auricular confession, making them utter both their mortal great stains and their venial and lesser blemishes, though the mote be much less than an atom, then to see him pluck and tug everything into the form of the newest received fashion, and by Dürer's rules make his leg answerable to his neck, his thigh proportionable with his middle, his foot with his hand, and a world of such idle, disdained foppery. To see him thus patched up with symmetry, make himself complete and even as a circle and, lastly, cast himself amongst the eyes of the people as an object of wonder with more niceness than a virgin goes to the sheets of her first lover, would make patience herself mad with anger and cry with the poet:

> O Hominum mores, O gens, O Tempora dura,
> Quantus in urbe Dolor; Quantus in Orbe Dolus![1]

Now since according to your own inference, even by the laws of nature, by the rules of religion, and the customs of all civil nations, it is necessary there be a distinct and special difference between man and woman, both in their habit and behaviors, what could we poor weak women do less (being far too weak by force to fetch back those spoils you have unjustly taken from us), than to gather up those garments you have proudly cast away and therewith to clothe both our bodies and our minds?

[Hic Mulier asserts that women adopted masculine clothing and behavior reluctantly, only to preserve "those manly things which you have forsaken." To prove that men were dressing in an effeminate manner long before women assumed masculine dress, she recites two stanzas by the Italian poet Ariosto describing a bejeweled man who "was himself in nothing but in name." Because the "deformity" of the effeminate man has a longer history than that of the masculine woman, it will be more difficult to eradicate; men must return to traditional dress and behavior, however, before women can be expected to do so.]

Cast then from you our ornaments and put on your own armor; be men in shape, men in show, men in words, men in actions, men in counsel, men in example. Then will we love and serve you; then will we hear and obey you; then will we like rich jewels hang at your ears to take our Instructions, like true friends follow you through all dangers, and like careful leeches pour oil into your wounds. Then shall you find delight in our words, pleasure in our faces, faith in our hearts, chastity in our thoughts, and sweetness both in our inward and outward inclinations. Comeliness shall be then our study, fear our armor, and modesty our practice. Then shall we be all your most excellent thoughts can desire and having nothing in us less than impudence and deformity.

HAEC VIR: Enough. You have both raised mine eyelids, cleared my sight, and made my heart entertain both shame and delight in an instant—shame in my follies past, delight in our noble and worthy conversion. Away then from me these light vanities, the only ensigns of a weak and soft nature, and come you grave and solid pieces which arm a man with fortitude and resolution: you are too rough and stubborn for a woman's wearing. We will here change our attires, as we have changed our minds, and with our attires, our names. I will no more be Haec Vir, but Hic Vir; nor you Hic Mulier, but Haec Mulier. From henceforth deformity shall pack to Hell, and if at any time he hide himself upon the earth, yet it shall be with contempt and disgrace. He shall have no friend but poverty, no favorer but folly, nor no reward but shame. Henceforth we will live nobly like ourselves, ever sober, ever discreet, ever worthy: true men and true women. We will be henceforth like well-coupled doves, full of industry, full of love. I mean not of sensual and carnal love, but heavenly and divine love, which proceeds from God, whose inexpressable nature none is able to deliver in words, since it is like his dwelling, high and beyond the reach of human apprehension, according to the saying of the poet in these verses following:

Of love's perfection perfectly to speak,
Or of his nature rightly to define,
Indeed doth far surpass our reason's reach
And needs his Priest t'express his power divine.
For long before the world he was yborn
And bred above its highest celestial Sphere,
For by his power the world was made of yore,
And all that therein wondrous doth appear.

NOTES

[1] "O morals of men, O race, O harsh times! How much anguish in the city; how much treachery in the world!"

ANNE HUTCHINSON

1591-1643

Born in Lincolnshire, England in 1591, Anne Hutchinson was the daughter of a clergyman. She married in 1612 and bore fourteen children before emigrating with her family to Massachusetts Bay Colony in 1634. Like many of that first generation of emigrants to New England, Anne and her husband William desired a further reform in the Church of England. Their opponents derided these followers of Calvin with the label "Puritan".

Once in Boston, Anne began holding religious meetings at her house where she would normally discuss the sermon of the previous Sunday. Gradually she began to extend these discussions by claiming her own direct intuition of divine grace: what she opposed to the "covenant of works" represented by the laws of church and state. She was joined in these views by the Reverend John Cotton and the Reverend John Wheelwright. Critics of this lay religious leader—most of whom were university-trained ministers—called her an Antinomian, or one who claims freedom from the moral law by virtue of a purported indwelling of the Holy Spirit, a direct connection with God.

Hutchinson's concern with the need for an inward, personal experience of God's saving grace put her directly at odds with the majority of the clerical establishment supported by the Commonwealth and its indomitable governor, John Winthrop. Church leaders drew little comfort from the fact that their female opponent considered the bulk of them to be under a covenant of works and therefore unfit to preach God's word. In 1637 a synod of the churches was called and her views were officially condemned. John Cotton conformed but John Wheelwright was banished from the colony. Hutchinson was then brought to trial "for traducing the ministers and their ministry." After the court found against her, she was excommunicated and expelled from the colony, settling first in Rhode Island and later in New York.

Evaluate Hutchinson's defense in this account of her examination in 1637 before the Court at Newton. Does she hold her own against her accusers? Do her principles negate the role of churches and human authority in their entirety? How does Hutchinson answer the question: "How do we know"? How might she address our problem of the relationship between self and society, or between self and God? What role did gender play in the prosecution's case?

The Examination at the Court of Newtown

November 1637
THE EXAMINATION OF MRS. ANN HUTCHINSON AT THE COURT AT NEWTOWN

Mr. Winthrop, Governor
Mrs. Hutchinson
Mr. Endicot
Mr. Bradstreet
Mr. Dudley, Deputy Governor

Gov. Mrs. Hutchinson, you are called here as one of those that have troubled the peace of the commonwealth and the churches here; you are known to be a woman that hath had a great share in the promoting and divulging of those opinions that are causes of this trouble, and to be nearly joined not only in affinity and affection with some of those the court had taken notice of and passed censure upon, but you have spoken divers things as we have been informed very prejudicial to the honour of the churches and ministers thereof, and you have maintained a meeting and an assembly in your house that hath been condemned by the general assembly as a thing not tolerable nor comely in the sight of God nor fitting for your sex, and notwithstanding that was cried down you have continued the same, therefore we have thought good to send for you to understand how things are, that if you be in an erroneous way we may reduce you so that you may become a profitable member here among us, otherwise if you be obstinate in your course that then the court may take such course that you may trouble us no further, therefore I would intreat you to express whether you do not hold and assent in practice to those opinions and factions that have been handled in court already, that is to say, whether you do not justify Mr. Wheelwright's sermon and the petition.

Mrs. H. I am called here to answer before you but I hear no things laid to my charge.

Gov. I have told you some already and more I can tell you.

(Mrs. H.) Name one Sir.

Gov. Have I not named some already?

Mrs. H. What have I said or done?

Gov. Why for your doings, this you did harbour and countenance those that are parties in this faction that you have heard of.

(Mrs. H.) That's matter of conscience, Sir.

Gov. Your conscience you must keep or it must be kept for you.

Mrs. H. Must not I then entertain the saints because I must keep my conscience.

Gov. Say that one brother should commit felony or treason and come to his other brother's house, if he knows him guilty and conceals him he is guilty of the same. It is his conscience to entertain him, but if his conscience comes into act in giving countenance and entertainment to him that hath broken the law he is guilty too. So if you do countenance those that are transgressors of the law you are in the same fact.

Mrs. H. What law do they transgress?

Gov. The law of God and of the state.

Mrs. H. In what particular?

Gov. Why in this among the rest, whereas the Lord doth say honour thy father and thy mother.

Mrs. H. Ey Sir in the Lord.

(*Gov.*) This honour you have broke in giving countenance to them.

Mrs. H. In entertaining those did I entertain them against any act (for there is the thing) or what God hath appointed?

Gov. You knew that Mr. Wheelwright did preach this sermon and those that countenance him in this do break a law.

Mrs. H. What law have I broken?

Gov. Why the fifth commandment.

Mrs. H. I deny that for he saith in the Lord.

Gov. You have joined with them in the faction.

Mrs. H. In what faction have I joined with them?

Gov. In presenting the petition.

Mrs. H. Suppose I had set my hand to the petition what then?

(*Gov.*) You saw that case tried before.

Mrs. H. But I had not my hand to the petition.

Gov. You have councelled them.

(*Mrs. H.*) Wherein?

Gov. Why in entertaining them.

Mrs. H. What breach of law is that Sir?

Gov. Why dishonouring of parents.

Mrs. H. But put the case Sir that I do fear the Lord and my parents, may not I entertain them that fear the Lord because my parents will not give me leave?

Gov. If they be the fathers of the commonwealth, and they of another religion, if you entertain them then you dishonour your parents and are justly punishable.

Mrs. H. If I entertain them, as they have dishonoured their parents I do.

Gov. No but you by countenancing them above others put honour upon them.

Mrs. H. I may put honour upon them as the children of God and as they do honour the Lord.

Gov. We do not mean to discourse with those of your sex but only this; you do adhere unto them and do endeavour to set forward this faction and so you do dishonour us.

Mrs. H. I do acknowledge no such thing neither do I think that I ever put any dishonour upon you.

Gov. Why do you keep such a meeting at your house as you do every week upon a set day?

Mrs. H. It is lawful for me so to do, as it is all your practices and can you find a warrant for yourself and condemn me for the same thing? The ground of my taking it up was, when I first came to this land because I did not go to such meetings as those were, it was presently reported that I did not allow of such meetings but held them unlawful and therefore in that regard they said I was proud and did despise all ordinances, upon that a friend came unto me and told me of it and I to prevent such aspersions took it up, but it was in practice before I came therefore I was not the first.

Gov. For this, that you appeal to our practice you need no confutation. If your meeting had answered to the former it had not been offensive, but I will say that there was no meeting of women alone, but your meeting is of another sort for there are sometimes men among you.

Mrs. H. There was never any man with us.

Gov. Well, admit there was no man at your meeting and that you was sorry for it, there is no warrant for your doings, and by what warrant do you continue such a course?

Mrs. H. I conceive there lyes a clear rule in Titus, that the elder women should instruct the younger and then I must have a time wherein I must do it.

Gov. All this I grant you, I grant you a time for it, but what is this to the purpose that you Mrs. Hutchinson must call a company together from their callings to come to be taught of you?

Mrs. H. Will it please you to answer me this is and to give me a rule for then I will willingly submit to any truth. If any come to my house to be instructed in the ways of God what rule have I to put them away?

Gov. But suppose that a hundred men come unto you to be instructed will you forbear to instruct them?

Mrs. H. As far as I conceive I cross a rule in it.

Gov. Very well and do you not so here?

Mrs. H. No Sir for my ground is they are men.

Gov. Men and women all is one for that, but suppose that a man should come and say Mrs. Hutchinson I hear that you are a woman that God hath given his grace unto and you have knowledge in the word of God I pray instruct me a little, ought you not to instruct this man?

Mrs. H. I think I may.—Do you think it not lawful for me to teach women and why do you call me to teach the court?

Gov. We do not call you to teach the court but to lay open yourself.

Mrs. H. I desire you that you would then set me down a rule by which I may put them away that come unto me and so have peace in so doing.

Gov. You must shew your rule to receive them.

Mrs. H. I have done it.

Gov. I deny it because I have brought more arguments than you have.

Mrs. H. I say, to me it is a rule.

Mr. E. You say there are some rules unto you. I think there is a contradiction in your own words. What rule for your practice do you bring, only a custom in Boston.

Mrs. H. No Sir that was no rule to me but if you look upon the rule in Titus it is a rule to me. If you convince me that it is no rule I shall yield.

Gov. You know that there is no rule that crosses another, but this rule crosses that in the Corinthians. But you must take it in this sense that elder women must instruct the younger about their business, and to love their husbands and not to make them to clash.

Mrs. H. I do not conceive but that it is meant for some publick times.

Gov. Well, have you no more to say but this?

Mrs. H. I have said sufficient for my practice.

Gov. Your course is not to be suffered for, besides that we find such a course as this to be greatly prejudicial to the state, besides the occasion that it is to seduce many honest persons that are called to those meetings and your opinions being known to be different from the word of God may seduce many simple souls that resort unto you, besides that the occasion which hath come of late hath come from none but such as have frequented your meetings, so that now they are flown off from magistrates and ministers and this since they have come to you, and besides that it will not well stand with the commonwealth that families should be neglected for so many neighbours and dames and so much time spent, we see no rule of God for this, we see not that any should have authority to set up any other exercises besides what authority hath already set up and so what hurt comes of this you will be guilty of and we for suffering you.

Mrs. H. Sir I do not believe that to be so.

Gov. Well, we see how it is we must therefore put it away from you, or restrain you from maintaining this course.

Mrs. H. If you have a rule for it from God's word you may.

Gov. We are your judges, and not you ours and we must compel you to it.

Mrs. H. If it please you by authority to put it down I will freely let you for I am subject to your authority.

Mr. B. I would ask this question of Mrs. Hutchinson, whether you do think this is lawful? for then this will follow that all other women that do not are in a sin.

Mrs. H. I conceive this is a free will offering.

Bradst. If it be a free will offering you ought to forbear it because it gives offence.

Mrs. H. Sir, in regard of myself I could, but for others I do not yet see light but shall further consider of it.

Bradst. I am not against all women's meetings but do think them to be lawful.

Dep. Gov. Here hath been much spoken concerning Mrs. Hutchinson's meetings and among other answers she saith that men come not there, I would ask you this one question then, whether never any man was at your meeting?

Gov. There are two meetings kept at their house.

Dep. Gov. How; is there two meetings?

Mrs. H. Ey Sir, I shall not equivocate, there is a meeting of men and women and there is a meeting only for women.

Dep. Gov. Are they both constant?

Mrs. H. No, but upon occasions they are deferred.

Mr. E. Who teaches in the men's meetings none but men, do not women sometimes?

Mrs. H. Never as I heard, not one.

Dep. Gov. I would go a little higher with Mrs. Hutchinson. About three years ago we were all in peace. Mrs. Hutchinson from that time she came hath made a disturbance, and some that came over with her in the ship did inform me what she was as soon as she was landed. I being then in place dealt with the pastor and teacher of Boston and desired them to enquire of her, and then I was satisfied that she held nothing different from us, but within half a year after, she had vented divers of her strange opinions and had made parties in the country, and at length it comes that Mr. Cotton and Mr. Vane were of her judgment, but Mr. Cotton hath cleared himself that he was not of that mind, but now it appears by this woman's meeting that Mrs. Hutchinson hath so forestalled the minds of many by their resort to her meeting that now she hath a potent party in the country. Now if all these things have endangered us as from that foundation and if she in particular hath disparaged all our ministers in the land that they have preached a covenant of works, and only Mr. Cotton a covenant of grace why this is not to be suffered, and therefore being driven to the foundation and it being found that Mrs. Hutchinson is she that hath depraved all the ministers and hath been the cause of what is fallen out, why we must take away the foundation and the building will fall.

European Expansion

CHRISTOPHER COLUMBUS

1451-1506

Christopher Columbus, born Cristóbal Colón, achieved fame for sailing west across the Atlantic Ocean in search of a route to Asia but finding instead the islands of the Caribbean Sea. Based on his experiences as a mariner for both Portugal and Spain, Columbus hypothesized that since the earth was mostly land and smaller than conventionally thought, Asia could be reached quickly by sailing west. Initially rebuffed by the Portuguese, Columbus eventually won support from Spain's Isabella and Ferdinand. The first expedition of three ships sighted land on October 12, 1492. Columbus explored islands in the Bahamas, claimed them for Spain, and returned home in January, leaving behind a small fort. The widely published report of his voyage made Columbus famous throughout Europe and gained him the title of Admiral of the Ocean Sea and further royal patronage. Columbus, who never abandoned the belief that he had reached Asia, led three more expeditions to the Caribbean. Unfortunately, his education in theology, his excellent gifts as a navigator, and his zeal for his project did not make Columbus an able manager. Political intrigues against him and his own administrative failings brought disappointment and political frustration to his final years. Columbus left behind numerous writings including letters, *Diario* (the journal of his voyages), *Libro de los privilegio* (a petition for rewards from his exploits), and a surprising collection of religious prophecies, *Libro de las profecias*.

The selections below are from Columbus's *Diario*, or *Journal*. Through an accident of fate, Columbus's original journal of the first voyage disappeared. The only surviving version is a transcription by the priest Bartolomé de las Casas (1474–1566). De las Casas, the son of a merchant who accompanied Columbus on his second voyage, was a willing participant in the conquest of the Caribbean during his first twelve years there. Later, he became the first great advocate for the rights of the indigenous people in the Americas, freeing his own serfs and tirelessly petitioning the government in Spain for humane treatment of the natives. Because the content and tone of this transcription seem consistent with Columbus's other writings, most scholars believe this is an accurate version of what Columbus wrote on his first expedition.

What are Columbus's expressed objectives in exploring the New World? What strikes you about Columbus's attitudes toward the natural environment and these new peoples he meets? In the U.S., October 12 is designated as Columbus Day, commemorating Columbus's actions on that day in 1492. What are your feelings about the appropriateness of this holiday?

from *Journals*

THURSDAY 11 OCTOBER

He steered west-southwest. They took much water aboard, more than they had taken in the whole voyage. They saw petrels and a green bulrush near the ship. The men of the caravel *Pinta* saw a cane and a stick, and took on board another small stick that appeared to have been worked with iron, and a piece of cane, and other vegetation originating on land, and a small plank. The men of the caravel *Niña* also saw other signs of land and a small stick loaded with barnacles. With these signs everyone breathed more easily and cheered up. On this day, up to sunset, they made 27 leagues.

After sunset he steered on his former course to the west. They made about 12 miles each hour and, until two hours after midnight, made about 90 miles, which is twenty-two leagues and a half. And because the caravel *Pinta* was a better sailer and went ahead of the Admiral it found land and made the signals that the Admiral had ordered. A sailor named Rodrigo de Triana saw this land first, although the Admiral, at the tenth hour of the night, while he was on the sterncastle, saw a light, although it was something so faint that he did not wish to affirm that it was land. But he called Pero Gutiérrez, the steward of the king's dais, and told him that there seemed to be a light, and for him to look: and thus he did and saw it. He also told Rodrigo Sánchez de Segovia, whom the king and queen were sending as *veedor* of the fleet, who saw nothing because he was not in a place where he could see it. After the Admiral said it, it was seen once or twice; and it was like a small wax candle that rose and lifted up, which to few seemed to be an indication of land. But the Admiral was certain that they were near land, because of which when they recited the *Salve*, which sailors in their own way are accustomed to recite and sing, all being present, the Admiral entreated and admonished them to keep a good lookout on the forecastle and to watch carefully for land; and that to the man who first told him that he saw land he would later give a silk jacket in addition to the other rewards that the sovereigns had promised, which were ten thousand *maravedís* as an annuity to whoever should see it first. At two hours after midnight the land appeared, from which they were about two leagues distant. They hauled down all the sails and kept only the *treo*, which is the mainsail without bonnets, and jogged on and off, passing time until daylight Friday, when they reached an islet of the Lucayas, which was called *Guanahani* in the language of the Indians. Soon they saw naked people; and the Admiral went ashore in the armed launch, and Martín Alonso Pinzón and his brother Vicente Anes, who was captain of the *Niña*. The Admiral brought out the royal banner and the captains two flags with the green cross, which the Admiral carried on all the ships as a standard, with an F and a Y, and over each letter a crown, one on one side of the ✝ and the other on the other. Thus put ashore they saw very green trees and many ponds and fruits of various kinds. The Admiral called to the two captains and to the others who had jumped ashore and to Rodrigo Descobedo, the *escrivano* of the whole fleet, and to Rodrigo Sánchez de Segovia; and he said that they should be witnesses that, in the presence of all, he would take, as in fact he did take, possession of the said island for the king and for the queen his lords, making the declarations that were required, and which at more length are contained in the testimonials made there in writing. Soon many people of the island gathered there. What follows are the very words of the Admiral in his book about his first voyage to, and discovery of, these Indies. I, he says, in order that they would be friendly to us—because I recognized that they were people who would be better freed [from error] and converted to our Holy Faith by love than by force—to some of them I gave red caps, and glass beads which they put on their chests, and many other things of small value, in which they took so much pleasure and became so much our friends that it was a marvel. Later they came swimming to the ships' launches where we were and brought us parrots and cotton thread in balls and javelins and many other things, and they traded them to us for other things which we gave them, such as small glass beads and bells. In sum, they took everything and gave of what they had very willingly. But it seemed to me that they were a people very poor in everything. All of them go around as naked as their mothers bore them; and the women also, although I did not see more than one quite young girl. And all those that I saw were young people, for none did I see of more than 30 years of age. They are very well formed, with handsome bodies and good faces. Their hair [is] coarse—almost like the tail of a horse—and short. They wear their hair down over their eyebrows except for a little in the back which they wear long and never cut. Some of them paint themselves with black, and they are of the color of the Canarians, neither black nor white; and some of them paint themselves with white, and some of them with red, and some of them with whatever they find. And some of them paint their faces, and some of them the whole body, and some of them only the eyes, and some of them only the nose. They do not carry arms nor are they acquainted with them, because I showed them swords and they took them by the edge and through ignorance cut themselves. They have no iron. Their javelins are shafts without iron and some of them have at the end a fish tooth and others of other things. All of them alike are of good-sized stature and carry themselves well. I saw some who had marks of wounds on their bodies and I made signs to them asking what they were; and they showed me how people from other islands nearby came there and tried to take them, and how they defended themselves; and I believed and believe that they come here from *tierra firme* to take them captive. They should be good and intelligent servants, for I see that they say very quickly everything that is said to them; and I believe that they would become Christians very easily, for it seemed to me that they had no religion. Our Lord pleasing, at the time of my departure I will take six of them from here to Your Highnesses in order that they may learn to speak. No animal of any kind did I see on this island except parrots. All are the Admiral's words.

As soon as it dawned I ordered the ship's boat and the launches of the caravels made ready and went north-northeast along the island in order to see what there was in the other part, which was the eastern part. And also to see the villages, and I soon saw two or three, as well as people, who all came to the beach calling to us and giving thanks to God. Some of them brought us water; others, other things to eat;

others, when they saw that I did not care to go ashore, threw themselves into the sea swimming and came to us, and we understood that they were asking us if we had come from the heavens. And one old man got into the ship's boat, and others in loud voices called to all the men and women: Come see the men who came from the heavens. Bring them something to eat and drink. Many men came, and many women, each one with something, giving thanks to God, throwing themselves on the ground; and they raised their hands to heaven, and afterward they called to us in loud voices to come ashore. But I was afraid, seeing a big stone reef that encircled that island all around. And in between the reef and shore there was depth and harbor for as many ships as there are in the whole of Christendom, and the entrance to it is very narrow. It is true that inside of this belt of stone there are some shallows, but the sea is no more disturbed than inside a well. And I bestirred myself this morning to see all of this, so that I could give an account of everything to Your Highnesses, and also to see where a fort could be made. And I saw a piece of land formed like an island, although it was not one, on which there were six houses. This piece of land might in two days be cut off to make an island, although I do not see this to be necessary since these people are very naive about weapons, as Your Highnesses will see from seven that I caused to be taken in order to carry them away to you and to learn our language and to return them. Except that, whenever Your Highnesses may command, all of them can be taken to Castile or held captive in this same island; because with 50 men all of them could be held in subjection and can be made to do whatever one might wish. And later [I noticed], near the said islet, groves of trees, the most beautiful that I saw and with their leaves as green as those of Castile in the months of April and May, and lots of water. I looked over the whole of that harbor and afterward returned to the ship and set sail, and I saw so many islands that I did not know how to decide which one I would go to first. And those men whom I had taken told me by signs that they were so very many that they were numberless. And they named by their names more than a hundred. Finally I looked for the largest and to that one I decided to go and so I am doing. It is about five leagues distant from this island of San Salvador, and the others of them some more, some less. All are very flat without mountains and very fertile and all populated and they make war on one another, even though these men are very simple and very handsome in body.

MONDAY 15 OCTOBER

I had killed time this night for fear of reaching land to anchor before morning, because of not knowing whether the coast was clear of shoals, and as soon as it dawned I spread sail; and as the island was farther than five leagues, rather about seven, and the tide detained me, it was around noon when I reached the said island and I found that the face which is in the direction of San Salvador runs north-south and that there are in it five leagues; and the other, which I followed, runs east-west, and there are in it more than ten leagues. And since from this island I saw another larger one to the west, I spread sail to go forward all that day until night because [otherwise] I would not yet have been able to reach the western cape of the island, to which island I gave the name Santa María de la Concepción. And close to sundown I anchored near the said cape in order to find out if there was gold there, because these men that I have had taken on the island of San Salvador kept telling me that there they wear very large bracelets of gold on their legs and on their arms. I well believe that all they were saying was a ruse in order to flee. Nevertheless, my intention was not to pass by any island of which I did not take possession, although if it is taken of one, it may be said that it is taken of all. And I anchored and remained here until today, Tuesday, and at dawn went ashore with the armed launches. I got out, and the natives, who were numerous and naked and of the same character as those of the other island of San Salvador, let us go around on the island and gave us what was asked of them. And because the wind increased and blew toward shore from the southeast, I did not wish to stay and departed for the ship; and a large dugout was alongside the caravel *Niña*. And one of the men from the island of San Salvador who was in the *Niña* threw himself into the sea and went away in the dugout. And the night before at mid-.... thrown the other and went after the dugout, which fled [so speedily] that there was never ship's launch that could overtake it even if we had a big head start. However, the dugout made land, the natives left the dugout, and some of the men of my company went ashore after them; and they all fled like chickens. And the dugout that they had left we brought alongside the *Niña*, to which now from another cape came another small dugout with one man who came to trade a ball of cotton; and some sailors jumped into the sea because the man did not want to enter the caravel and they laid hold of him. And I, who was on the poop of the ship and saw all this, sent for him and gave him a red bonnet, and some small green glass beads which I put on his arm, and two bells which I put on his ears, and I ordered his dugout, which I also had in the ship's launch, returned to him and sent him to land. And then I set sail to go to the other large island that I had in view to the west. And I also ordered the other dugout, which the caravel *Niña* was bringing along at her stern, let loose. And later I saw, on land, at the time of arrival of the other man—[the man] to whom I had given the things aforesaid and whose ball of cotton I had not wanted to take from him, although he wanted to give it to me—that all the others went up to him. He considered it a great marvel, and indeed it seemed to him that we were good people and that the other man who had fled had done us some harm and that for this we were taking him with us. And the reason that I behaved in this way toward him, ordering him set free and giving him the things mentioned, was in order that they would hold us in this esteem so that, when Your Highnesses some other time again send people here, the natives will receive them well. And everything that I gave him was not worth four *maravedís*. And so I departed when it was about the tenth hour, with the wind southeast and shifting to the south, in order to pass to this other island, which is exceedingly large and where all these men that I am bringing from San Salvador make signs that there is very much gold and that they wear rings of it on their arms and on their legs and in their ears and on their noses and on their chests. And from this island of Santa María to this other island it is nine leagues east-west, and all this part of the island runs northwest-southeast. And it appears that there may well be on this coast more than 28 leagues on this side. And it is very flat without any mountains, just like San Salvador and Santa María. And all the beaches are without rocks, except that at all of them there are some big rocks near land under the water, where it is necessary to keep your eyes open when you wish to anchor and not to anchor close to land, although the waters are always very clear and one sees the bottom. And two lombard shots [away] from land in all of these islands the bottom is so deep that you cannot reach it. These islands are very green and fertile and with sweet-smelling breezes; and there may be many things that I do not know about because I do not want to stop, so I can investigate and go to many islands in order to find gold. And since these people make signs that they wear it on their arms and on their legs—and it is gold because I showed them some pieces that I have of it—I cannot fail with the help of Our Lord to find out where it originates. And when we were mid-sea between these two islands, that is, Santa María and this big one to which I gave the name Fernandina, I found a man who was passing alone in a dugout from the island of Santa María to Fernandina and who was bringing a small amount of their bread, which was about the size of a fist, and a calabash of water and a piece of red earth made into dust and then kneaded and some dry leaves, which must be something highly esteemed among them, because earlier, in San Salvador, they brought some of them to me as a present. And he was bringing a little native basket in which he had a string of small glass beads and two *blancas*; because of which I recognized that he was coming from the island of San Salvador and had passed to that of Santa María and was passing to Fernandina. He came up to the ship and I had him enter, which was what he asked, and I had his dugout put in the ship and all that he brought watched over, and I ordered him given bread and honey and something to drink, and so I will transport him to Fernandina and I will give him all of his belongings in order that, through good reports of us—Our Lord pleasing—when Your Highnesses send [others] here, those who come will receive courteous treatment and the natives will give us of all that they may have.

Huamán Poma

1479-1569

The purpose of Huamán Poma's work, known as *Letter to a King*, is to argue the case of the Peruvian people before the King of Spain, Philip III. The people of the Andes, then under harsh Spanish rule, had previously been part of the Inca Empire. In the middle of the 15th century the Inca undertook a major imperialistic expansion which reached its greatest extent in 1493-1525 under Huayna Capac. Capac's indecision over his successor left the kingdom vulnerable to the Spanish adventurer and explorer Francisco Pizarro who arrived on the coast with firearms and a force of about 180 men in 1532. By 1542 Pizarro had eliminated the last of the Inca rulers and amassed amazing stores of treasure through abuse of the royal family and the natives. In 1569 the Spanish colonial administration of the Andes was fully established and, at the same time, ninety-year-old Huaman Poma was finishing his manuscript which told the story of his people from the beginning of the world to the present colonial rule. His letter is written in a mixture of Spanish and Quechua, the official language of the Inca, which is still widely spoken over a large area of South America. The completed work evidently arrived in Madrid, but Philip probably never saw it. This amazing manuscript was discovered in modern times in a Danish museum, perhaps carried there by the Danish ambassador to the Spanish court.

The full version is prefaced by an invocation to the Holy Trinity, a letter to the Pope, and two letters to the King of Spain, one purporting to be written by the author's father and one by himself. In trying to show himself of proper lineage to address a king, Poma claims descent from the pre-Inca rulers of the Andes and exaggerates his family's subsequent status under the Incas and the Spaniards. The numerous drawings in the manuscript are as valuable and intriguing as the text. From these illustrations (such as Adam farming with an Inca tool) we have a much fuller knowledge of the dress, customs, and religion of the Inca than from any other single source.

In addressing his foreign overlord, Poma evokes European history, literary conventions and concepts to present his argument. Which European authors can you see reflected in Poma's text? And why would he want to do this? What do you think of the soundness of Poma's instruction to the king?

from *Letter to a King*
A Peruvian Chief's Account of Life under the Incas and under Spanish Rule

AUTHOR'S LETTER

Don Felipe Huamán Poma de Ayala
to H.M. King Phillip III of Spain

Your Majesty, I hesitated for a long while before writing this letter. Even after beginning, I wanted to retract my words. I decided that my intention was a rash one and that, once started upon my story, I would never be able to complete it in the way in which a proper history ought to be written. For I lacked all written evidence and had to rely on the coloured and knotted cords, on which we Indians of Peru used to keep our records. Among our people I also sought out the oldest and most intelligent, on whom I could rely as witnesses of the truth.

In weighing, cataloguing and setting in order the various accounts I passed a great number of days, indeed many years, without coming to a decision. At last I overcame my timidity and began the task which I had aspired to for so long. I looked for illumination in the darkness of my understanding, in my very blindness and ignorance. For I am no doctor or Latin scholar, like some others in this country. But I make bold to think myself the first person of Indian race able to render such a service to Your Majesty.

In short I determined to write this history, which describes the lineage and the famous deeds of the Kings, lords and officers who were our grandparents; the life of our Indians and their descent over many generations; the idolatrous and heretical Incas with their Queens and concubines; and the great nobles who could be compared with the Dukes, Counts and Marquísses of Spain.

My story continues with the rivalry between Huascar, the legitimate Inca, and his bastard brother Atahuallpa and the generals Challcuchima, Quizquiz and others. It tells of Manco Inca's struggle to defend himself against the Spaniards after the conquest of our country, in the time of the Emperor Charles V; the revolts against the Crown of Don Francisco Pizarro, Don Diego de Almagro, Gonzalo Pizarro, Carbajal and Girón; and the succession of the Spanish Viceroys from Don Blasco Nuñez de Vela onwards.

It recounts the life of the officials, the notaries, the deputies, the proprietors of Indian labour, the priests, the miners and the Spaniards who travel from post to post along the roads and rivers of Peru; the visitors, the judges, the Indian chiefs and their subjects, including the very poor.

In my work I have always tried to obtain the most truthful accounts, accepting those which seemed to be substantial and which were confirmed from various sources. I have only reported those facts which several people agreed upon as being true.

I chose the Castilian tongue for the writing of my work, as our Indians of Peru are without letters or writing of any kind, and I had to translate into Spanish the phrases of the different languages and dialects which we speak, such as Aymará and Quechua.

My work as a historian has been inspired by the wish to present to Your Majesty this book called 'The First New Chronicle and Good Government'. It is for the benefit of all faithful Christians and is written and drawn by my own hand, with those talents which I possess. I have given greater clarity to the text by means of pictures and drawings, knowing Your Majesty to be greatly addicted to these. I have also wished to alleviate the dullness and annoyance likely to be caused by reading a work so lacking in ornament and polished style, such as more distinguished writers devote to the preservation of the Catholic faith, the correction of errors and the salvation of souls.

Your Majesty, for the benefit of both Indian and Spanish Christians in Peru I ask you to accept in your goodness of heart this trifling and humble service. Such acceptance will bring me happiness, relief and a reward for all my work.

On 1 January 1613 in the Province of Lucanas, from your humble servant

DON FELIPE DE AYALA, THE AUTHOR

The First Part of this Chronicle
THE INDIANS OF PERU

THE AUTHOR'S FAMILY

My history begins with the exemplary life which was led by my father Huaman Mallqui and my mother Curi Ocllo Coya, daughter of Tupac Inca Yupanqui, the Peruvian ruler.

My father interested himself in the education of his adopted son Martin de Ayala, a half-caste of mixed Spanish and Indian blood. He caused this boy to enter the service of God and take the habit of a Christian friar when only 12 years old. This was a happy chance for myself. For my half-brother Martin, once he had grown into a man, gave instruction to his brothers including myself. Thus I came to be able to write my 'First New Chronicle', having been taught my letters at an early age.

As one of the principal Indians of Peru, my father had duly presented himself to the envoy of the Emperor Charles V, Don Francisco Pizarro, and other Spaniards in order to kiss their hands and offer peace and friendship to the Emperor. He was received by them at the port of Tumbes before their march to Caxamarca. My father was on the side of Inca Huascar, the legitimate ruler, whom he served as Viceroy. After his reception by the Christians he returned to his province.

My father served in an important capacity during all the wars, battles and revolts against the Spanish Crown. In one of these wars he was in the service of a loyal Captain named Luis de Avalos de Ayala, the father of the half-caste Martin about whom I have written, and they both took part in the bloody battle of Huarina. The Captain was unhorsed by a lance-thrust while fighting against the partisans of Gonzalo Pizarro. He was defended and saved from certain death by my father, who knocked down and killed Martin de Olmos, one of the rebel side. The Captain, on rising from the ground, acknowledged his debt and declared that my father, even though an Indian, deserved a grant of land from the Crown. Thus my father, having gained some honour from this service, thenceforward took the name of Ayala and adopted the style of Don Martin de Ayala.

THE HISTORY OF THE WORLD

Our Lord and Saviour Jesus Christ was born in the time of Caesar. In kingdom of the Incas, in the same age, the first Inca Manco Capac began to reign over the city of Cuzco, which was called Aca Mama or 'mother of the fermented maize'. On his death Manco Capac left the government to his son Sinchi Roca, who extended his rule to Collao and Potosi by conquering the tribes.

The Roman Empire was founded and its rulers have succeeded another until the present day. During the reign of Robert the existence of our kingdom of the Indies became known, and how our land was rich in gold and silver, and how we possessed beasts of burden like small camels.

The discovery of the Indies and the discovery of Peru were events which transformed many of the ideas held at the time in Castile and Rome. The roundness of the world was proved. While the people of Castile, Rome and Turkey were hidden by night in the lower part of the world, the Indians of Peru were in broad daylight in the upper part. The name of India is derived from the Castilian words *'en día'*, in day.

Philosophers, astrologers and poets are aware of the relation between height and riches in the world and they know that everything is created by God, who is the Sun. So the greatest wealth is found in the part nearest to the Sun. It is important for astrologers to know that our King called himself the son of the Sun, and called the Sun his father. Our King, the Inca, was right in considering himself the richest of the rich.

There was excitement in the whole of Castile, caused by rumours about the gold and silver of the Indies. Don Diego de Almagro and Don Francisco Pizarro, with a schoolmaster named Fernando de Luque, succeeded in recruiting soldiers in Castile. Felipe, a Peruvian Indian, was engaged as an interpreter of the Quechua language. The Holy Father was represented by Friar Vicente.

The Spaniards first conquered Panama, Nombre de Dios and Santo Domingo. Then, during the Papacy of Marcellus II, they embarked their ships and landed at the port of Tumbes. The first person to greet them was my father in his capacity as envoy and second person in the State after Huascar Inca, the lawful ruler. As a sign of his peaceful mission my father kissed the hands of the newcomers and thus indirectly of the Emperor. Later, the Spaniards received the envoy of Huascar's brother, the bastard Atahuallpa Inca.

When they landed at Tumbes the Spanish captains only had it in mind to play the peaceful part of ambassadors, charged with the duty of kissing the hand of the Peruvian King. But when they saw with their own eyes a the riches of gold and silver which were to be had, greed awoke in them and they did not hesitate to seize and kill Atahuallpa.

LAWS AND STATUTES

Since the earliest times there were primitive laws in Peru, which were later amplified by the Incas. Their purpose was to regulate religious ritual, holidays and feast-days, fasts, initiation ceremonies, sacrifices, selection of virgins, stores of food and clothing and other matters.

The laws and statutes formulated during the reign of Tupac Inca Yupanqui are as follows:

Whatever is lawfully commanded must be carried out on pain of death. Those who resist an order of the Inca shall be scourged, condemned to death and executed. The whole of their families shall be exterminated. Their dwellings shall be destroyed and the ground sown with salt. Only wild beasts and birds of prey shall inhabit these places.

Such penalties are imposed for all time. Dispute and controversy can never occur, since the operation of justice is immediate and irrevocable.

Registrars shall travel through the country to count the population and record to the nearest month and year the birth of all children, and especially the descendants of chiefs. This and the other dispositions which have been made are for the purposes of good government and justice.

No person shall utter any slander against the Inca's father, the Sun, against his mother, the Moon, against the Day-Star and other stars, against the sacred idols and shrines, or against the Inca and the Coya. Any violation of this ordinance shall be punished with death. Slanders against the Council, the principal nobles and even against persons of humble position shall also be punished.

Women shall not be permitted to give evidence before the law because of their propensity for tale-bearing, lying and dissembling. People without property are similarly debarred as witnesses, because they are capable of being bribed or suborned.

All people are required to bury their dead in special vaults and not inside their houses, on pain of banishment. The burial shall be performed according to local custom. Vessels, food, drink and clothing shall be provided for the corpses.

Children and young people are required to obey their father and mother, their elders and those set in authority. They shall be flogged for a first act of disobedience and banished to the gold-and silver-mines for a second act.

Thieves and highwaymen shall not be permitted to live. For a first offence they shall be given 500 strokes of the lash. For a second offence they shall be stoned to death and their bodies left unburied, so that they are eaten by the foxes and condors.

A son shall inherit his father's property, including house, farm and orchard. If the only child is a daughter, she shall inherit half the property and the other half shall be divided between the close relations of the deceased person.

A father with one son shall be accepted as an honest man; the father of two shall be treated with favour; gardens, pasture and other land shall be given to the father of three; the father of four shall be considered as a person of consequence; the father with five sons shall have the standing of a foreman; ten children shall entitle a father to authority in the community; and in the case of even greater numbers the fathers shall have the right to choose estates for themselves, either in the village or in untilled land, and establish themselves there.

Nobody shall spill maize on the ground or peel or mutilate vegetables such as the potato, for if these foods were capable of understanding they would weep tears at being used in this manner. Those who commit such faults are to be punished.

There shall always be abundance of food throughout the country. Maize, potato, yacca and other crops shall be sown on a large scale. Root vegetables shall be preserved by drying and freezing, and maize by blanching. The crops, including green vegetables, shall be arranged in sequence so that the people have something to eat all the year round. The sowing of maize, potatoes, chilli and cotton shall be the responsibility of each community. Flowers and leaves of certain kinds shall be collected to make dye for woven fabrics. *Llipta* for chewing with coca leaves shall be prepared by the burning of grain.

The magistrates called *tocricoc* shall superintend the completion these measures and any backsliding shall be punished severely.

Twice a year an inspection shall be carried out of every house and property to control the volume of clothing, pots and pans, animal work in the orchards. Those found to have failed in their duty shall receive 100 strokes of the lash. The inspectors shall ask for an account a garden produce, taking care that there is abundance of everything and that the warehouses are full, for the service of the Inca or any other visiting notability. The posting-houses shall be properly looked after, the royal highways kept clear by the runners and the bridges repaired when necessary, so that journeys can be made at all times and the usual ceremonies can be observed.

FESTIVALS AND SONGS

The songs and dances of our people do not involve any element of magic or witchcraft. If it were not for the drunkenness associated with them, they would be a pure expression of relaxation and joy. The popular songs cal *aravi* and *taqui* are brimming with happiness. The *haylli aravi*, which celebrates victory in war or success in the harvest, is sung by girls to accompaniment of flutes played by young men. The shepherds have their own special song called *llamaya* and the farm-labourers have one called *pachaca harauayo*. There is also the *aimarana*, a dance on going out to fields; and the *huanca*, on the return, which is sung by the girls while boys play the instrument called the *quena quena*. There is no cause for any criticism or censure of these entertainments of the people. It is simply a case of the poor mitigating their hard work by singing and dancing among themselves.

The words of the *huanca*, translated from the Quechua language, are as follows: 'Queen, we are kept apart by misfortune. We are separated by an illusion of the senses. You are my darling *Cicllallay*, the flower of Chinchircoma. I shall always carry you with me in my thoughts and in my heart. You were a lie and an illusion, like everything which is reflected in the waters. You were a deception, like the images which disappear when the waters are stirred. Your mother is a false friend, who wants to separate and destroy us. Your evil father is the cause of our misfortune. Perhaps, if God approves, my Queen, we shall one day meet and be together for ever. Remembering your smiling eyes, I feel faint; remembering your playful eyes I am near to death. I have been seeking you everywhere with a heavy heart, looking among the rivers, mountains and villages. As a last hope, I shall wait for you in my despair on the edge of the flowery ravine, my beautiful *Ciclladay*.'

The version in the Aymará language runs: 'The two of us shall go together through snow and ice. For me there is nobody but you, you. Brimming with tenderness, you hold me in your power. Our cup is full of sweetness. Yet your mother and your wicked father have kept us apart. Come to me all alone. I am waiting with happiness in my heart. Presently we shall saddle a horse and a mule and ride together by day and night like two lost orphans, nourishing ourselves on grass and roots like the sheep which you used to tend. Whoever tries to deprive me of your songs shall die at my hands and be put to sleep for ever; and his life shall be like a broken thread. I implore you to listen to me in this icy cold of the night. Come in one movement into my arms, where I shall hold you for eternity; if you say "No", my heart will weep.'

ADMINISTRATION

Warehouses were maintained by the Inca in all the four provinces. Frozen dried potato, cooked potato, cooked cassava, dried meat and wool were usually stored in the Collao. Maize, sweet potato, yacca, chilli, cotton and dyestuff were kept at scattered points throughout the rest of the country. Each warehouse corresponded to a particular farming area. Some of them belonged to the local community, some to the Inca and some to the Sun and Moon. They were all under the control of the central farming administration.

In the same way in which he supervised the value of goods and stores, the Inca assessed the courage and endurance of his subjects, both male and female. He was specially interested in their aptitude for fighting in battle and he identified this in the Indians of Chinchaysuyu above all others. Although these people are small in stature, they have an amazing vitality which is derived from their diet of fresh mutton, maize and maize-spirit. By contrast, the Colla Indians are corpulent and greasy. They have no spirit in them and have a feeble physique, since they eat quantities of starch and drink bad liquor made from potatoes.

The most nimble of the Indians were trained under the Inca's orders become runners and to jump with the agility of young bucks. They were put through a difficult course of cross-country running, and those who excelled in these tests had the speed of sparrow-hawks. It was possible for one of these runners to cover the distance between Cuzco and the coast in four days, arriving at his destination before lunchtime.

No taxation or tribute in the form of money was payable by the people to the Inca or anyone else. The individual's obligation to the State was expressed in the form of work and service. The artisans and their families could count themselves free people; and domestic service was confined to those who waited upon the small class of the nobility.

Porters for short distances were drawn from the Indians of Callahuaya and for long distances from my own tribe of Lucanas. They were known as 'the feet of the Inca'.

OFFICIALS

The Viceroy, who was called *Incap rantin*, was second only to the Inca and his position at court was comparable to that of the Duke of Alba in Castile. He was never of humble birth and neither wealth nor wisdom had anything to do with his selection. His position derived solely from his descent from an ancient dynasty of Kings. Lesser chiefs, who were not even entitled to be carried in a litter, were never entrusted with such a high office.

All the messengers were under the authority of an official chosen from among the Inca's children. This person kept a keen eye open to detect any breakdowns in the system and remedy them when they occurred. Under the Inca's authority, he also regulated the issue of rations from the warehouses. The messengers were treated as a permanent force, the members which were never moved to other employment. Reliance was placed on their fidelity, devotion to duty and speed of travel. It was unheard-of for *chasqui* to let down his relief.

[H]ighways were all carefully measured and marked with the distances to their destinations. They followed a straight course some eleven feet wide, the edges being contained by evenly placed kerb-stones. Their rectilinear form was so accurately carried through that no other authority on Earth could have matched the achievement.

Control-posts and inns were placed at intervals along the highways and administered by the province concerned. Travellers could find lodging, service and food there, important officials paused there on their journeys and the messengers were always in a state of readiness. The highways were kept in perfect order. Where they passed through marshes, stone causeway were laid down to make a firm footing.

Long bridges over the river-gorges existed at a number of places and there were many smaller bridges. The strength of the construction varied with the size of the rivers. Sometimes fibre ropes and timbers were used and sometimes floating rafts. These last were contrived by the ferrymen of the Collao.

Under the Incas, all the bridges came under the control of a single official. When the Spanish Viceroys took over, they ordered the construction of stone bridges, thus saving the lives of many poor Indians who used to be employed in mending our own hazardous contraptions. It would be a mercy for our people if all the bridges could be built of stone.

THE KING'S QUESTIONS

Your Majesty may wish to ask the author of this book some questions with the object of discovering the true state of affairs in Peru, so that the country can be properly and justly governed and the lot of the poor improved. I, the author, will listen attentively to Your Majesty's questions and do my best to answer them for the edification of my readers and Your Majesty's greater glory. This is an important service which I am able to render, for Your Majesty hears many lies as well as truths, and much of what is reported is simply a means of obtaining preferment for the writer in Church or State.

In my capacity as a grandson of the Inca of Peru I would like to speak to Your Majesty face to face, but I cannot achieve this because I am now 80 years old and in frail health. I cannot take the risk of the long journey to Spain. However, I am ready to pass on the observations which I have made in the last 30 years, since I left my home and family to live the life of a poor traveller on the roads of my country. We can communicate with one another by letter, with Your Majesty asking for information and myself replying, as follows:

'Tell me, author, how is it that the Indians were able to prosper and increase in numbers before the coming of the Incas?'

'Your Majesty, in those days there was only one King. He was well served by his nobles, who superintended the mining of gold and silver, the work on the farms and the herding of the Peruvian sheep. Although the population was considerable, enough was produced to provision the fortresses as well as feed the women and children at home. The smallest settlement possessed 1,000 soldiers and some could put an army into the field.'

'Tell me then, Don Felipe de Ayala, how was the population maintained after the Incas came?'

'Your Majesty, the Inca himself was a supreme ruler although there were nobles of different ranks, similar to your Dukes, Marquesses and Counts, under his sovereignty. But all these nobles were tireless in their obedience to the Inca's laws and commands. So the people as a whole remained prosperous and never went short of food.'

'Tell me, author, what is wrong nowadays? Why is the population declining and why are the Indians getting poorer and poorer?'

'I'll explain to Your Majesty. The best of our girls and women are all carried off by your priests and the other Spanish officials. Hence the large number of half-castes in the country. Usually the priests give the excuse that they want to stop our women living in sin, but their next step is to appropriate them for themselves. As a result, many of our people give up hope and want to hang themselves, following the example of a group of Chanca Indians who collected on a hill-top at Andaguaylas and decided to finish with their miserable lives for once and all.'

'Tell me, author, how can the population be made to increase again?'

'I have already written, Your Majesty, that priests and others ought to try living a decent Christian life for a change. Indians ought to be allowed to enjoy their married lives and bring up their daughters in peace. Above all, the number of would-be Kings ruling over us ought to be reduced to one, namely Your Majesty.'

'And how can the prosperity of the ordinary Indian be raised?'

'Well, Your Majesty, a lot depends on the community, the *sapci*, which is responsible for growing maize, wheat, potatoes, chillies, coca, fruit and cotton. There are also the mines to be worked. Young girls and widows can be put to spinning and weaving, with ten of them engaged on a single garment. Castilian cattle and Peruvian sheep are another source of wealth to the community, but individuals need to have their own livestock as well. Usually the *sapci* keeps one third of all produce. Another seventh can go to the local administrator and of course Your Majesty is entitled to one fifth at any time. Within these arrangements the community ought to prosper.'

'And tell me, author, how can the Indians who have fled from their homes be persuaded to return?'

'The young ones can be tempted back to the abandoned villages if they are provided with fields and pastures with clearly marked boundaries. They should pay taxes, but the collection should be the responsibility of one salaried official only, and any money left over should go to the Crown. This official could well be the Indian chief. For it is a fact that we chiefs have never joined in rebellions and have proved ourselves to be remarkably loyal subjects. We handed over ourselves and our vassals to Your Majesty, together with the silver-mines of Potosi, the gold-mines of Carabaya and the mercury-mines of Huancavelica. For all this Your Majesty ought to show us some mark of gratitude. It ought to be recalled, too, that twelve learned men and four clerks of your own Council, as well as issuing a pronouncement against slavery, forbade the payment of taxes to the clergy. Thus the parish priests are no longer entitled to earn money as tax-collectors. They must live on the contributions which are left at the foot of their altars. These usually amount to between 1,000 and 2,000 pesos a year. They are made up of payments for Masses, voluntary offerings, responsories for the dead, presents, Christmas-boxes and alms. The quantity is adequate to provide them with enough to live on, dress and feed themselves decently. To go beyond this and arrogate to themselves the rights of landowners and employers is an offence against their calling. They ought to be content with our people's offerings and what they get from the Spaniards.'

'But tell me, author, why are you so much opposed to parish priests getting proper salaries?'

'Your Majesty, the first priest of our religion was Jesus Christ, who lived on earth as a poor man, and his Apostles did the same. None of those holy men asked for salaries, but they were content to live by the charity of others. By the same token parish priests can manage quite well without collecting taxes or setting themselves up as men of property. If they do not care for such a way of life, Your Majesty should consult with the Pope in order to admit Indians to the priesthood. Being good Christians our people will not require any salary and the savings which Your Majesty will make can be used for the general good of the Church.'

'Tell me this, author. What can be done to prevent so much death, suffocation and hardship in the mines?'

'The first point, Your Majesty, is that a stop should be put to the practice of hanging miners up by the feet and whipping them with their private parts openly displayed. Also the miners are forced to work day and night and paid only half of what is owed to them. Finally they are sent off to the high plateau where they die of exposure. The remedy would be to be more selective in the choice of labour and to allow any particular locality a six months' rest in between recruiting visits. It would also help if experts could be appointed and paid, who know how to cure the condition caused by poisonous fumes. That would alleviate much of the present hardship. Your Majesty should give orders that a store of provisions and water should be kept on the premises at every mine. In the case of miners being trapped by a collapse of the roof it would be a godsend to have food and drink available whilst day-and-night operations were in progress to free the trapped men.'

'And tell me, author, how can we discover all the hidden mines in Peru?'

'Very well, I'll tell Your Majesty. In these times, whenever an Indian reports the discovery of gold, silver, mercury, lead, copper, tin or even pigment, the Spaniards at once take over and the Indian is maltreated. So naturally enough no Indian is keen to make any such report to the authorities. But if Your Majesty were to enter into personal relations with the discoverer in each case, and treat him well, all the best mines would soon be brought to light. The result would be that Your Majesty would indeed be the richest and most important King in the world, and this would benefit Peru. As matters stand at present, the Indians are in the process of dying out. In twenty years' time there will be none of them left to defend the Crown and the

Catholic Faith. The Emperor, who is now in glory, was great because of his possession of the Indies and the same was true of Your Majesty's father. I dare to say that it is also true of Your Majesty, and yet it is possible that Peru will lose all its value and. your Indian subjects will no longer exist. Where once there were 1,000 souls, now there are hardly 100 left. Those who remain are many of them old and incapable of having children. The young men cannot find young brides to bear them sons. The girls and women, whether single or married, are all removed into the Spaniards' homes. It is impossible to remedy this state of affairs because the Spaniards support one another in all circumstances. They not only treat the Indians as slaves or servants, but dispossess them of their land and property. Even to set these facts down on paper is enough to make me weep tears. And the worst of it is that nobody dares to tell Your Majesty what is going on. If I were asked to put a price on the Peruvian Indian, I would put the figure very high and I would draw the conclusion that he or she ought to be treated with care and kindness, in the interests of the country. If by any chance one of our girls bears a child to an Indian man, the parish priest and the other authorities treat her like a criminal. Then the priest takes her into his kitchen so that he can sleep with her whenever he likes. She starts to bear him children and finds this style of life much to her taste. Other Indian girls, too, notice the privileges which she enjoys and want share them. As I say, the real indignation is aroused when an Indian woman bears children to an Indian man. It is as if the sky had fallen on the earth. The father is tied to a pillar and flogged, and the mother has her hair cut off. If I ever started telling the story of such cases in any detail, I would never stop.'

'Tell me, author Ayala, now that you have recounted all these sad things tell me how it is that the Indians are being exterminated, their women taken from them and their property stolen, when I never intended my judges and officials to do any wrong or damage. On the contrary, I expected them to treat the Indian chiefs with honour and allow the common people to lead useful and productive lives. Tell me, my good Ayala, what can done to put things right?'

'All I can say, Your Majesty, is that the Spaniards ought to live like Christians. They should marry and be content with ladies of their own race and class, and allow the Indians to keep their own women and property. Anyone who has used his power to steal property from others should be made to give it back, and should also pay for what he has enjoyed. These penalties should be imposed summarily, without room for delay.'

AUTHOR'S DECLARATION

I, Huamán Poma, chief of Lucanas, have opened the secrets of the quipu *to my readers. I have recounted what has been told me by descendants of the Incas and the other dynasties of rulers. I have traced our history from the arrival of the first Indian sent by God to these shores through the various ages which followed. Everything has been conscientiously set down in this book and now I am able to proceed further and tell what I have personally observed and experienced from my years of service with the Christians.*

Your Majesty, in your great goodness you have always charged your Viceroys and prelates, when they came to Peru, to look after our Indians and show favour to them, but once they disembark from their ships and set foot on land they forget your commands and turn against us.

Our ancient idolatry and heresy was due only to ignorance of the true path. Our Indians, who may have been barbarous but were still good creatures, wept for their idols when these were broken up at the time of the Conquest. But it is the Christians who still adore property, gold and silver as their idols.

Hernando De Soto

1500?-1542

Hernando De Soto was a Spanish adventurer and explorer who began his career in the New World in Central America and Peru serving under the famous conqueror of Peru, Francisco Pizarro. With the fortune he gained as his share of the spoils of Peru, De Soto organized an expedition to explore the Spanish-owned region of Florida. His company of nearly 1,000 men landed on the west coast of Florida in 1539 and prepared to search for a rich empire, believed to exist somewhere in the wilderness. The search for the nonexistent region lasted three years, during which time De Soto and his company ranged over present-day Florida, South Carolina, North Carolina, Alabama, and Mississippi. In 1541 he was the first European to cross the Mississippi River and explore territory now part of Arkansas, Oklahoma, and northern Texas. Finding no gold or treasure, the expedition turned back in the spring of 1542, and De Soto died of fever after they returned to the Mississippi River. His men sank his heavily weighted body in the river to keep the Native Americans from learning of his death and desecrating the body. A few members of the expedition survived to reach Spanish settlements on the Gulf of Mexico.

There are several contemporary versions of De Soto's travels, which agree in general but differ somewhat in their particulars. Two chroniclers of De Soto, Luis Hernandez de Biedma and the Knight of Elvas, had first hand knowledge of the expeditions, while another version was produced by El Inca (Garcilaso de la Vega), the son of a conquistador and an Inca Princess. The following text is a composite of various versions.

The exact locations of many parts of De Soto's explorations are hotly contested, but in the following excerpt, De Soto travels through familiar landscape. The modern names of the places mentioned in De Soto's account appear in parentheses. He had begun his travels in Apalache, now Panama City, Florida. "Cofachiqui" home of the "la Senora" is Columbia, South Carolina; "Xuala" is Tryon, North Carolina; and "Guaxule" is Asheville, North Carolina. "Jua Gaux-u-le" in Cherokee meant "The place where they race" because, as the Spaniards noted, the city was surrounded by a public walk along which six men could pass abreast. Cherokee legend holds that its tribes met in Asheville in order to compete from time to time; the "walk" described by the Spaniards was probably a Cherokee racetrack.

In what ways do De Soto's motives recall Christopher Columbus's? Are they different? What attitudes do we see expressed here concerning Native Americans?

Appalachian Travels

De Soto in the Carolinas
Columbia, South Carolina

"[Cofitachique, or "Eupaha" according to the Indian boy, Perico] was on the bank of a river that we believed was the river of Santa Elena (the Congaree-Santee River, which had been discovered years earlier by the lawyer Ayllon, whose colony had failed and his people scattered. Some of them made it back to Spain with wild stories of gold in this land before De Soto's people had departed Spain) . . . some Indians brought (the Lady) on a litter with much prestige. And she sent a message to us that she was delighted that we had come to her land, and that she would give us whatever she could, and she sent a string of pearls of five or six strands to the Governor. She gave us canoes in which we crossed that river (the Saluda) and divided with us half of the town . . ." (The Broad River splits today's Columbia: the Spaniards got the west side, which they called "the point," between the Saluda and Broad Rivers which join at Columbia to become the Congaree River, which the Spaniards had followed to Columbia.)"

"She was young and of fine appearance, and she removed a string of pearls that she wore about her neck and put it on the Governor's neck, in order to ingratiate herself and win his good will . . . And the Indians walked covered down to the feet with very excellent hides, very well tanned, and blankets of sable and mountain lions which smelled; and the people are very clean and very polite and naturally well developed. Monday the third of May, all the rest of the army arrived, and all could not cross (the Saluda River just below Columbia's Zoo) until the next day, Tuesday, and not without cost and loss of seven horses which drowned. These were among the fattest horses, which fought against the current, but the thin ones, which let themselves go (survived)."

"As soon as he was lodged in the town (Boozer Mall is built there today), another gift of many hens was made to him. The land was very pleasing and fertile, and had excellent fields along the rivers (the Saluda, Broad and Congaree Rivers), the forests being clear and having many walnuts and mulberries. They said that the sea (the Atlantic Ocean) was two days' journey away ("According to the Indians, the sea was up to thirty leagues (eighty miles) from there." It's actually ninety miles to Charleston, on the Atlantic Ocean, two days below Columbia). Around the town within the compass of a league and a half (four miles) were large uninhabited towns, choked with vegetation, which looked as though no people had inhabited them for some time (the Lady probably resided in today's downtown Columbia, on the east bank of the Broad River). The Indians said that two years ago there had been a plague in that land and they had moved to other towns (the lawyer Ayllon, or other wayward Spaniard, probably introduced the foreign virus which caused this plague). In the *barbacoas* (storage bins) of the towns there was considerable amount of clothing and blankets made of thread from the bark of trees and feather mantles (white, gray, vermilion, and yellow) made according to their custom, elegant and suitable for winter. There were also many deerskins, well tanned and colored, with designs drawn on them and made into pantaloons, hose and shoes. The chief, observing that the Christians esteemed pearls, told the Governor that he might order certain graves in that town to be examined, for he would find many, and that if he wished to send to the inhabited towns (up the east bank of the Saluda River), they could load all their horses. The graves of that town were examined and fourteen *arrobas* (175 pounds) of pearls were found, babies and birds being made of them."

". . . although they were not good because they were damaged through being below the ground and placed amidst the adipose tissue of the Indians. Here we found buried two Castilian axes for cutting wood, and a rosary of beads of jet and some (trinkets) of the kind that they carry from Spain to barter with the Indians. All this we believed they had obtained from barter with those who went with the (lawyer) Ayllon."

"On the seventh of May . . . Gallegos (one of De Soto's Captains) went with most of the people (the foot soldiers) of the army to Ilapi . . . (thence to Talimeco, today's Camden) to eat seven *barbacoas* of corn that they (the Indians) said was there, which were a deposit of the Chieftainess . . . This Talimeco was a town of great importance, with its very authoritative oratory on a high mound; the house of the chief (was) very large and very tall and broad, all covered, high and low, with very excellent and beautiful mats, and placed with such fine skill that it appeared that all the mats were only one mat. Only rarely (in that village) was there a hut which might not be covered with matting. This town has very good savannas and a fine river (the Wateree River), and forests of walnuts and oak, pines, evergreen oaks and groves of sweetgum, and many cedars. In this river was . . . found a bit of gold; and such a rumor became public in the army among the Spaniards, and for this it was believed that this is a land of gold, and that good mines would be found there (which happened in 1799, just upstream of Camden in Cabarrus County, setting off America's first goldrush)."

"In the villages under the jurisdiction and overlordship of Cofachiqui through which our Spaniards passed they found many Indians native to other provinces who were held in slavery. As a safeguard against their running away, they (Cofachiqui's people) disabled them (their neighbors) in one foot, cutting the nerves above the instep where the foot joins the leg, or just above the heel. They held them in this perpetual and inhuman bondage in the interior of the country away from the frontiers, making use of them to cultivate the soil and in other servile employments. These were the prisoners they captured in the ambushes that they set against one another at their fisheries and hunting grounds, and not in open war of one power against another with organized armies (as was the European habit at that time)."

"The people were dark, well set up and proportioned, and more civilized than any who had been seen in all the land of Florida (North America); and all were shod and clothed. The youth (Perico) told the governor that he was now beginning to enter that land of which he had spoken to him. And since it was such a land and he understood the language of the Indians, some credence was given him. He requested that he be Baptized, for he wished to become a Christian. He was made a

Christian and was called Pedro. The governor ordered him to be loosed from the chain in which he had gone until then ("The Castilins did not offer the lady Baptism . . ."). That land, according to the statement of the Indian (now named Pedro), had been very populous and was reputed to be a good land. According to appearances, the youth (Pedro), whom the governor had taken as guide, had heard of it, and what he had learned from hearsay he asserted to have seen, and enlarged at will what he saw. In that town were found a dagger and some beads of Christians, whom the Indians said had been in the port (of Charleston), two days journey thence; and that it was now many years since Ayllon had arrived there in order to make a conquest of that land; that on arriving at the port he died; and there ensued a division, quarrels, and deaths among several of the principle persons who had accompanied him as to who should have the command; and without learning anything of the land they returned to Spain from that port. All the men (with De Soto) were of the opinion that they should settle in that land as it was an excellent region; that if it were settled, all the ships from New Spain, and those from Peru, Santa Marta, and Tierra Firme, on their way to Spain, would come to take advantage of the stop there, for their route passes by there; and as it is a good land and suitable for making profits."

"Since the governor's purpose was to seek another treasure like that of Peru, he had no wish to content himself with good land or with pearls, even though many of them were worth their weight in gold and, if the land were to be allotted in repartimiento, those pearls which the Indians would get afterward would be worth more; for those they have, inasmuch as they are bored by fire, lose their color thereby. The governor replied to those who urged him to settle that there was not food in that whole land for the support of his men for a single month; that it was necessary to hasten to the port of Ochus (Mobile, Alabama) where (Captain) Maldonado was to wait; that if another richer land were not found they could always return to that one whenever they wished; that meanwhile the Indians would plant their fields (with seeds the Spaniards gave them) and it would be better provided with corn. He asked the Indians whether they had heard of any great lord farther on. They said that twelve days' journey thence was a province called Chiaha which was subject to the lord of Coosa (Lord of the Cherokee). Thereupon the governor determined to go in search of that land; and as he was a man hard and dry of word, and although he was glad to listen to and learn from the opinion of all, after he had voiced his own opinion he did not like to be contradicted and always did what seemed best to him. Accordingly, all conformed to his will, and although it seemed a mistake to leave that land for another land that might have been found round about where the men might maintain themselves until the planting might be done there and the corn harvested, no one had anything to say to him after his determination was learned."

". . . because the Indians had already risen and that it was learned that the Lady was minded to go away if she could without giving guides or *tamemes* for carrying because of offenses committed against the Indians by the Christians—for among many men there is never lacking some person of little quality for who for very little advantage to himself places the others in danger of losing their lives—the governor ordered a guard to be placed over her and took her along with him, not giving her such good treatment as she deserved for the good will she had shown him and the welcome she had given him."

"We (stayed) in the town of this lady for about ten or eleven days, and then it was advisable for us to leave from there in search of food, because here there was none . . . the horses and people had used it up very quickly) . . . We (with De Soto and the Lady) turned again north and traveled (up the west bank of the Broad River)."

"Wednesday, the (twelfth) of May, the Governor (with the horsemen) left Cofitachequi (the rest of the army had gone east, over the Broad River and to Camden, with Captain Gallegos), and in two days (De Soto having camped at Newberry) he arrived at the province of Chalaque (Cherokee in English, near today's Union) but he could not find the town of the lord, nor was there an Indian who would disclose it (it is possible that these Cherokee were recent arrivals, given that their village was difficult to locate following the conspicuous, well traveled roads). And they (with De Soto) slept in a pine forest, where many (Cherokee) Indian men and women began to come in peace with presents . . ."

"The Indians live on roots of herbs which they seek in the open field and on game killed with their arrows. The (Cherokee) people are very domestic, go quite naked and (are) very fatigued (perhaps due to constant food gathering given their recent move to this land). There was a lord who brought the governor two deerskins as a great act of service. In that land are many wild hens (turkeys). In one town they performed a service for him, presenting him seven hundred of them, and likewise in others they brought those they had and could get."

". . . the soldiers (with Captain Gallegos, in the meantime) were marching along at midday when suddenly a great tempest of strong contrary winds blew up, with much lightning and thunder, and quantities of large hailstones that fell upon them, so that if there had not happened to be some large walnut trees near the road and some other dense trees under which they took shelter, they would have perished, for the largest of the hailstones were the size of a hen egg and the smallest were the size of a nut. The rodeleros held their shields over their heads, but even so when the stones struck an unprotected part of their bodies they hurt them badly. It was God's will that the storm last only a short time; if it had been longer the shelter they had taken would not have been enough to save their lives, and short as it had been they were so battered that they could not march that day or the next."

". . . on Monday, the seventeenth of that month, they (with De Soto) departed from there (near Union) and spent the night in a forest; and on Tuesday they went to Guaquili (Spartinburg), and the Indians came forth in peace and gave them corn, although little, and many hens roasted on *barbacao*, and a few little dogs, which are good food. These are little dogs that do not bark (opossum perhaps), and they rear them in the houses in order to eat them. They also gave them *tamemes*, which are Indians who carry burdens. And on the following Wednesday they went to a canebrake (Inman), and on Thursday to a small savannah (Landrum) where a horse died; and some foot soldiers of (Captain) Gallegos arrived, making known to the Governor that he was approaching."

NORTH CAROLINA

[Captain Gallegos, who had led most of the army's foot soldiers from Columbia, South Carolina, to Camden for food, had come up the east bank of the Broad River, recrossing that river just east of Spartanburg. De Soto waited for Gallegos at Landrum in order to make a dawn raid on the first village of today's North Carolina.]

"The next day, Friday (the 21st of May, on the morning of the full moon), they went to Xuala (Tryon, North Carolina) which is a town on plain between some rivers (the Pacolet Rivers); its chief was so well provisioned that he gave to the Christians however much they asked for: *tamemes*, corn, little dogs, *petacas*, and however much he had . . . In that Xuala it seemed to them that there was better disposition to look for gold mines than in all that they had passed through and seen in that northern part."

[The view of the Appalachian Mountains is spectacular from Tryon; the Cherokee place name Xuala, spelled "Saluda" by the English, means "the bushy place." When viewed from the mountains above Tryon, the plains and foothills below appear to be bushy; they are covered with very bushy scrub oak, unlike the tall, colorful trees of the mountains.]

". . . the village and province of Xuala, which, although it was a separate province from that of Cofachiqui, belonged (at least hereditarily) to the same lady (alliances may have been changing at that time, given the Cherokee intrusion, noted above, caused, perhaps, by the pestilence which had depopulated some of her land) . . . This village was situated in the foothills of a mountain range (the Appalachians) on the bank of a river (North Pacolet) that, though not very large, had a very strong current. The territory of Cofachiqui extended to that river (which flows from the mountains and to Columbia, her home town; that river was, most likely, the western border of her province). In the village of Xuala they served and entertained the governor and all his army most attentively, for as it was a part of the Lady's kingdom, and as she had sent orders to that effect, the Indians did everything in their power both to obey their lady and to please the Spaniards."

"They found little corn, and for that reason, although the men were tired and the horses very weak, the governor did not stop over two days."

"Gauxule (Asheville) . . . was situated among many small streams that flowed through various parts of the village. Their sources were in these mountains where the Spaniards had passed through and in others beyond (the rivers converge at Asheville) . . . All around it was a public walk along which six men could pass abreast (Cherokee legend holds that its tribes met in today's Asheville in order to compete from time to time; the "walk," described by the Spaniards, was probably a Cherokee race track. "Jua Gaux-u-le," in Cherokee, means "The Place where they Race"). The governor was in this village four days . . . from there he went in six daily journeys of five leagues each (thirteen miles each day) . . ."

". . . and went with his army (first) to an oak grove alongside a river (the Pigeon River at Canton), and the next day we passed through Canasoga (in Cherokee that means "against the slopes;" it's at Bethel Church) and spent the night in the open (in Hazelwood's broad, flat valley, just west of Waynesville). And on Wednesday we (crossed the Blue Ridge and) spent the night alongside a swamp (just above Sylva, there's a Budweiser warehouse there today), and the next day we ate a very great number of mulberries (just below today's Cherokee Reservation, across the Tuckasegee River from the Oconaluftee River). The next day we went alongside a creek . . . and now it was large (the Tuckasegee River fed by the Oconaluftee River; they camped opposite Bryson City) . . . the next day, Friday, we went to a pine forest and a creek (they had followed the course of today's railroad, for the most part, from Asheville to Alarka Creek).. And the next day, Saturday, in the morning, we crossed a very broad river, across a branch of it (the Little Tennessee River where it intersects with the Tuckasegee River; the railroad has a trestle where De Soto crossed the Little Tennessee River) . . . and entered Chiaha, which is on an island of the same river . . . (located at the base of today's "Chiaha" Mountain; the entire region is called Chiaha by the Cherokee people. The village was on Sawyer Creek. The horses were pastured on Tuskeegee Creek.) . . ."

Permissions Acknowledgements

St. Benedict of Nursia. From *The Rule of Saint Benedict*, edited and translated by Abbot Justin McCann. Copyright © 1952. Reprinted by permission of the publisher, Burns Oates.

Procopius. Materials from *History of the Wars* and *The Secret History* are reprinted here in two sections. *History of the Wars* and second selection of *The Secret History* reprinted by the permission of the publishers and the Loeb Classical Library, from *Procopius: History of the Wars, Vol. I* and *The Anecdota or Secret History, Vol. VI*, translated by H. B. Dewing, Cambridge, Mass.: Harvard University Press, 1914, 1935. The first selection reprinted from *The Secret History* by Procopius, translated by G. A. Williamson (Penguin Classics, 1966), pp. 37-39, 192-194. Copyright © G.A. Williamson, 1966. Reproduced by permission of Penguin Books, Ltd.

Einhard. Reprinted from *The Life of Charlemagne* by Einhard, translated by Samuel Epes Turner, copyright © 1960 by the University of Michigan Press. Used by permission of the University of Michigan Press.

"The Dream of the Rood." Translated by R. F. Yeager. Copyright © 1998 by R. F. Yeager.

Hildegard of Bingen. *Scivias*, from *Hildegard of Bingen,* translated by Mother Columba Hart and Jane Bishop. Copyright ©1990 by the Abbey of Regina Laudis: Benedictine Congregation Regina Laudis of the Strict Observance, Inc. Used by permission of Paulist Press.
Letters reprinted with permission from, *Hildegard of Bingen's Book of Divine Works* edited by Matthew Fox, copyright © 1987, Bear & Co., Santa Fe, NM.

Marie de France. From *The Lais of Marie de France*, translated and with introduction and notes by Robert W. Hanning and Joan M. Ferrante. Copyright © 1978. Reprinted by permission of Labyrinth Press, an imprint of Baker Book House.

St. Francis of Assisi. *Later Rule* and "Canticle of Brother Sun" from *Francis and Clare* translation and introduction by Regis J. Armstrong, O.F.M. CAP, and Ignatius C. Brady, O.F.M. Copyright © 1982 by the Missionary Society of St. Paul in the State of New York. Used by permission of Paulist Press.

St. Clare of Assisi. From *Clare of Assisi: Early Documents*, ed. and trans. by Regis J. Armstrong, O.F.M. CAP. Copyright © 1993. Reprinted with the permission of The Franciscan Institute Publications, St. Bonaventure, NY.

Maimonides. From *The Wisdom of Israel*, ed. Lewis Browne. Copyright © 1945 by Lewis Browne, renewed. Reprinted by permission of Curtis Brown, Ltd.

St. Thomas Aquinas. From *The Basic Writings of Saint Thomas Aquinas*, ed. Anton C. Pegis (pp. 21-23, 686-693, 879-882). Reprinted by permission of Hackett Publishing Company, Indianapolis and Cambridge. All rights reserved.

The Rise of European Universities. From *University Records and Life in the Middle Ages*, ed. Lynn Thorndike. Copyright © 1944, Columbia University Press. Reprinted with the permission of the publisher.

Peter Abelard and John Peckham. From *Great Issues in Western Civilization, Vol. I, Third edition*, eds. Brian Tierney, Donald Kagan, and L. Pearce Williams. Copyright © 1992 by the McGraw-Hill Companies. Reprinted with the permission of the McGraw-Hill Companies.

Marsilius of Padua. From *Marsilius of Padua, the Defender of Peace*, tr. Alan Gewirth. Copyright © 1986, Columbia University Press. Reprinted with the permission of the publisher.

Christine de Pizan. Selections from *The Book of the City of Ladies* by Christine de Pizan, translated by Earl Jeffrey Richards. Copyright 1982 © by Persea Books, Inc. Reprinted by permission of Persea Books, Inc.

Margery Kempe. Ca. 2,200 words (pp. 41-43, 46-48, 196-198) from *The Book of Margery Kempe*, translated by Barry Windeatt (Penguin Classics, 1985). Copyright © B. A. Windeatt, 1985. Reproduced by permission of Penguin Books, Ltd.

Sirat 'Antar. From *Antar and Abla: A Bedouin Romance, The Fourth Story*, ed. Diana Richmond. Reprinted with the permission of Quartet Books.

Ibn Khaldun. Khaldun, Ibn; *The Muqaddimah*. Translated by Franz Rosenthal. Edited by N. J. Dawood. Copyright © 1958, renewed 1967 by Princeton University Press. Reprinted by permission of Princeton University Press.

Zahiruddin Muhammad Babur. From *The Baburnama: Memoirs of Babur, Prince and Emperor*, edited by Wheeler M. Thackston, translated by Wheeler M. Thackston. Translation copyright © 1996 by Smithsonian Institution. Used by permission of Oxford University Press, Inc.

Al 'Omari, Duarte Pires, and **Affonso of Congo.** From *African Civilization Revisited: From Antiquity to Modern Times*, ed. Basil Davidson. Copyright © 1991. Reprinted with the permission of Africa World Press.

Shu Yueh-Hsian, Wen T'ung, and **Ch'eng I.** Selections from *Inner Quarters: Marriage and the Lives of Chinese Women in the Sung Period* by Patricia Buckley Ebrey. Copyright © 1993, The Regents of the University of California. Reprinted with permission of University of California Press.

THE ASHEVILLE READER
THE MEDIEVAL AND RENAISSANCE WORLD
Designed by Leda Neale and Julie Kowal
for the University of North Carolina at Asheville
Composed by Sans Serif, Inc.
in Garamond Book with titles in Herculanum
Printed and bound by Quinn-Woodbine, Inc.